JUMPING THE COLOR LINE

JUMPING THE COLOR LINE:
VERNACULAR JAZZ DANCE IN AMERICAN FILM, 1929–1945

SUSIE TRENKA

British Library Cataloguing in Publication Data

Jumping the Color Line:
Vernacular Jazz Dance in American Film, 1929–1945

Trenka, Susie

A catalogue entry for this book is available from the British Library

Paperback ISBN: 0 86196 743 8
Ebooks:
EPUB: 0 86196 975 3
EPDF: 0 86196 978 4

Cover image: Jeni LeGon and Bill Robinson, publicity still for *Hooray for Love* (1935). Credit: Everett Collection.

Published by
John Libbey Publishing Ltd, 205 Crescent Road, New Barnet, Herts EN4 8SB, United Kingdom   e-mail: john.libbey@orange.fr; web site: www.johnlibbey.com

Distributed Worldwide by
Indiana University Press, Herman B Wells Library—350, 1320 E. 10th St., Bloomington, IN 47405, USA. www.iupress.indiana.edu

© 2021 Copyright John Libbey Publishing Ltd. All rights reserved.
Unauthorised duplication contravenes applicable laws.

Printed and bound in the USA.

Contents

	Acknowledgments	vii
	A Note on "Black" and "White"	ix
Introduction	**Jazz Dance on the Silver Screen: Race, Gender, Genre**	1
	The Conspicuous Absence of the Black Dancing Woman	8
	The Film Musical and Resistance on the Margins	12
	Summary	18
Chapter 1	**Doomed Divas: Black Dancing Women in Early Sound Film**	25
	Hallelujah and the Denial of Agency and Mobility to Black Women	29
	Ambiguous Images of Black Modernity	39
	One of a Kind: Non-Narrative Dance Performances by Black Women	45
Chapter 2	**Kids and Class Acts: Male Dancers in Black-Cast Music Shorts**	53
	Fantasies of Achievement and Abundance	62
	Creative Composer and Exuberant Entertainer: The Short Films of Duke Ellington and Cab Calloway	78
	Hot and Classy: Black-Cast Shorts in the Trade Press	89
Chapter 3	**Potential Pioneer: The Film Career of Black Tap Dancer Jeni LeGon**	93
	A Promising Start: Mid-1930s	95
	Broken Promises: Late 1930s	108
	Uncredited: 1940s	117
	Offscreen Successes and Struggles: 1950s and Beyond	122
	"A Footnote in Hollywood History": Late but Still Limited Recognition	123

Chapter 4	**Jumpin' at the Jukebox, Dancin' in the Street: Dance, Race, and Space in 1940s Soundies**	**129**
	Integrating Film Viewing in the Public Sphere	132
	Jukebox Swing	135
	Block Parties and Living Room Dances: Vernacular Aesthetics in Mundane Settings	140
	"You Do It Any Way You Will": Soundies' Black Women	147
	Black Stardom in a Liminal Medium	153
Chapter 5	**Harlem to Hollywood: Whitey's Lindy Hoppers and the Crossover Success of a Black Dance**	**157**
	Rewriting Rules, Shifting Perceptions	158
	From the Savoy to the Screen	162
	Star Turns in *A Day at the Races*	165
	Sidelined: The Forgotten Films	175
	Hellzapoppin'	179
	Jitterbug Dancing in Mock-Educational Short Films	186
Chapter 6	**"A Savage Exhibition"? Swing and White Youth Culture in B Movies**	**199**
	Swing, Youth Culture, and Racial (De)Segregation	201
	Swing Kids Go to Hollywood	204
	Hep to the Jive: The Jivin' Jacks and Jills at Universal	206
	The Alternative Embodiments of Peggy Ryan and Donald O'Connor	217
	World War II and Traces of Racial Integration	225
	Youth Culture, the Vaudeville Aesthetic, and the Adolescent Audience	228
	Hollywood Swing as Marginal Mainstream	239
Conclusion	**Dance History, the Swing Dance Revival, and Vintage Movies in the Digital Age**	**243**
	Filmography	255
	Bibliography	261
	Index of Names and Titles	269

Acknowledgments

The classic musicals from Hollywood's golden age and the swing music of the 1930s provided the soundtrack of my childhood, and I am immensely grateful to my parents for introducing me to what they simply called "old films" and "old jazz". At the time, none of us could have predicted that I would one day aspire to be a swing dancer as well as a film historian.

Years later, as an amateur Lindy hopper, I still had no intention of turning my newfound passion into a research endeavor. It simply didn't occur to me that I might try to personally meet and interview the "old-timers" – that is, the swing and tap dancers who had been active as far back as the 1930s and who were still teaching and lecturing around the world. Nevertheless, I have fond memories of their presence at Herräng Dance Camp in Sweden and other events I attended in the late 1990s and early 2000s, and I am especially grateful to Lindy hoppers Frankie Manning and Norma Miller for sharing their stories. Much gratitude is also due to those dancers of the "revival" generation who did the work of researching the history, and who generously shared their extensive knowledge, as well as their film collections. Peter Loggins and Lennart Westerlund deserve a special mention here.

It was several more years and many film studies courses later that my various interests finally converged in my dissertation project, which the present book is based on. A very big thank you goes to my advisor, Margrit Tröhler, for supporting me in so many ways over the years (not least by helping to keep me employed in a variety of functions). The Department of Film Studies at the University of Zurich was much more than just an office, and it would not have felt like a second home without all my wonderful coworkers there – thank you to Adrian, Alice, Andrea, Daniel, Geesa, Henriette, Jan, Julia, Kristina, Marian, Mattia, Philipp, Seraina, Silvia, Simon, Tereza, Wolfgang, and everyone else at the department for sharing ideas, offices, and lunch hours, and for being the best team.

Bernd Hoffmann kindly agreed – more or less at the last minute – to act as coadvisor and to travel to Zurich for my dissertation's defense, for which I am extremely grateful. Wolfgang Fuhrmann offered to take on the role of coexaminer, which made the experience considerably less stressful. And to Jörg Schweinitz I owe the contact to John Libbey, and thus, ultimately, the publication of this book.

The opportunity to spend a year in New Orleans (and to travel for conferences and archival research elsewhere in the States) was crucial to this project – and in unforeseen ways to my life overall. Joel Dinerstein at Tulane University and Bruce Raeburn, then the curator of the Hogan Jazz Archive at Tulane, were so kind as to provide me with an invitation, as well as access to Tulane's facilities and archival holdings, and I will forever be grateful for their support. Huge thanks are also due to the Swiss National Science Foundation for their generous grant, which made this year away from my regular duties in Zurich possible.

I am indebted to a number of scholars who were willing to meet with me and who offered much-needed inspiration and encouragement along the way. I particularly thank Richard Dyer for our meeting in Weimar and Krin Gabbard for responding to my out-of-the-blue email and inviting me to lunch in New York. I also thank Andrea Kelley for sharing her excellent research on Soundies with me, including some material that remains unpublished to this day. Additional helpful feedback and ideas came from the conferences where I had an opportunity to present some of my work; thank you to all the participants and organizers – namely, Karen McNally and the European Association of Dance Historians in London, the Society of Cinema and Media Studies, and Mary Simonson at Colgate University.

Whether during in-person visits or remotely, I have encountered nothing but the best service at archives and libraries; my gratitude for their friendly and competent help goes to the staff of the Hogan Jazz Archive and the Amistad Research Center at Tulane University in New Orleans, the Jerome Robbins Dance Division and the Schomburg Center for Research in Black Culture at the New York Public Library, the Moving Image Research Center at the Library of Congress and the Smithsonian Institution in Washington, DC, and the HistoryMakers in Chicago. Big thanks also to the folks at Photofest and at the Everett Collection for their prompt and professional assistance with my image search.

A very special thank you goes to my publisher, John Libbey, for taking on this project and for being almost endlessly patient with me.

And to Adrian – for always pointing out when something didn't make sense, for proofreading (again and again), and for everything.

A Note on "Black" and "White"

In the United States, the recent wave of protests against police violence and racial injustice has rekindled a longstanding debate about the spelling of adjectives denoting race and skin color. Major style guides and news outlets recently moved to capitalize "Black" in reference to people of African descent,[1] which has long been a common practice in Black publications and within social justice organizations. Apart from concerns of empowerment and respect, the main argument for capitalization is that the word is not used to refer to skin color in a literal sense but to a socially constructed identity, and it should therefore be treated as a proper noun, not as a natural category. Since the capital "Black" is quickly becoming the new standard, and because every text inevitably reflects the historical context of its own creation, I have adopted it for this book.

"White", by contrast, still remains lowercased in a lot of writing (though that is also beginning to change). Two reasons are typically given for this: one, that the capitalization of the word is common in White supremacist circles, and two, that there is less of a sense of a shared identity with respect to people of European descent. I have chosen to also capitalize "White" here, not just for the sake of orthographic symmetry, but also because I disagree with the second claim. Instead, I concur with those who argue that White identity, too, must be seen as a social construct – with its own complex history – rather than simply as a neutral, objective fact. As for the White supremacists (who I obviously do not support in any way), normalizing the capital letter in antiracist circles would strip the convention of its racist implications.[2]

1 See, for instance, Dean Baquet and Phil Corbett, "Uppercasing 'Black'", June 20, 2020, The New York Times Company, https://www.nytco.com/press/uppercasing-black/; and David Bauder, "AP Says It Will Capitalize Black but Not White", *AP News*, July 20, 2020, The Associated Press, https://apnews.com/7e36c00c5af0436abc09e051261fff1f.

2 See also Kwame Anthony Appiah, "The Case for Capitalizing the B in Black", *The Atlantic*, June 18, 2020, The Atlantic Monthly Group,
https://www.theatlantic.com/ideas/archive/2020/06/time-to-capitalize-blackand-white/613159/.
Appiah offers an excellent and nuanced summary of the debate on "Black" and "White", making a convincing case that "whatever rule applies to one should apply to the other".

INTRODUCTION Jazz Dance on the Silver Screen: Race, Gender, Genre

> At this point, even though Whitey's Lindy Hoppers had made several movies, *Day at the Races*, *Everybody Sing*, and *Manhattan Merry-Go-Round*, we still didn't have a sense of that being a bigger deal than appearing in a nightclub. We certainly didn't have any ideas about becoming stars. We were just following the money. It was only after the Nicholas Brothers started being in films that we saw the power in them.
>
> – Frankie Manning

In the musical comedy *Vogues of 1938* (1937), a White couple (Joan Bennett and Warner Baxter) visit the Cotton Club on their night out in Manhattan.[3] The African American stage show that they attend begins with the entrance of chorus girls wrapped in long, shiny, fur-trimmed cloaks, wearing tall, feathery headpieces, and holding lorgnettes (fig. 1). During their dignified strut, a brief passage from Duke Ellington's composition "Sophisticated Lady" is heard before the women start singing about how "blasé" they are, with their taste for classical music and ballet, and how they "only go for the elegant touch". But when a brief jazzy phrase by blaring horns interrupts this self-mocking display, they ask, "what's that music they're playing so hot", and soloist Dorothy Saulters responds that "it's that new heat". The tempo picks up, the music becomes jazzier and so does the singing style and the women's movement, as they give in to the "hot" music and start to bounce and sway rhythmically. They drop their cloaks to reveal more typical chorus girl attire – that is, they wear almost nothing – and as they go into a dance routine, they sing, "turn on the red hot heat and burn the blues away" (fig. 2). After the song, the chorus leaves the stage to Saulters, who performs a brief tap solo, flinging her legs sideways and expansively waving her arms, with her mouth wide open. Four male dancers in gleaming white suits (the Four Hot Shots) join her from the wings and dance with her briefly before she exits. The male group's synchronized tap dancing then transitions into an acrobatic routine

---

3 By this time, the legendary Black nightclub had already moved from its original Harlem location to Midtown Manhattan, where it continued to provide African American entertainment to an almost exclusively White clientele, until it closed for good in 1940. See, for instance, Haskins, *The Cotton Club*.

Figures 1 and 2. In the Cotton Club scene from *Vogues of 1938* (1937), sophisticated ladies give in to the rhythms of "red hot" jazz.

of floor moves that anticipate break dancing. Next, pianist and singer Maurice Rocco delivers his version of "Red Hot Heat", singing and scatting, partly standing at the piano, flinging his head, rolling his eyes, grinning at the camera, wiggling his hips, and banging violently on the piano.[4] After a brief cutaway to the audience, the chorus girls return for the show's climax, the lights are dimmed and eventually turned to red, and the music and singing become more dramatic. The women get down on the floor, wriggling and undulating their bodies, throwing arms and legs up in the air. The Four Hot Shots reappear and mingle with the women before they all get up and exit, still singing. The film's main plot then resumes, with the White couple politely applauding the performance before they are seen back in the street in pursuit of the next nocturnal diversion.

As a Black "specialty act", this musical interlude is in many ways typical of 1930s Hollywood films, yet it is also somewhat unusual, which makes it an excellent example to outline some of the issues at stake here. This book looks at vernacular jazz dance in American films from the late 1920s to the mid-1940s – and at the *power* of dance in film when it comes to negotiating the color line. In film history, the period discussed here roughly corresponds with the most successful years of the so-called studio system, when a handful of large film studios dominated film production, distribution, and exhibition.[5] In music and dance history, it encompasses the end of the Jazz Age of the 1920s, when jazz music and dance styles entered the mainstream, as well as the swing era of the 1930s and early 1940s, when big band swing was America's most popular (dance) music.[6]

While music and dance styles of African American origin have been influential throughout American history, this influence takes on new dimensions in the early twentieth century, enhanced by technological innovations, such as sound recording and film. During the Harlem Renaissance of the 1920s, the nightlife of New York's major Black neighborhood attracted substantial crowds of upper- and

---

4   The film's opening credits list the number's soloists as "Rocco and Saulter". Spelling variants of the dancer's name included Dorothy, Dotty, and Dottie for her first name, and Salter, Salters, Saulter, and Saulters for her last name. At the time of *Vogues*, she had been appearing successfully with Maurice Rocco at New York's Kit Kat Club. Later, she teamed with her dancer husband Charles "Cholly" Atkins, and the couple performed with bandleader-singer Cab Calloway, among others. See Atkins and Malone, *Class Act*, 47–58; Frank, *Tap!*, 267; and Pitet, "Dotty Saulters".

5   The studio era, often called the golden age of Hollywood, lasted well into the 1950s, but the studios' power was significantly weakened by a 1948 Supreme Court decision, which ended the industry's "vertical integration" by mandating the separation of production from distribution and exhibition. For a comprehensive history of the studio era, see Schatz, *The Genius of the System*.

6   The terms "Jazz Age" (usually capitalized) and "swing era" are often used as generalized designations for America's cultural history during these periods. 1935 is commonly considered the beginning of the swing era due to Benny Goodman's enormous success that year, which helped propel the music to mainstream popularity. Arguably, the swing era started around 1930, with the development of the big band swing style by (mostly Black) bandleaders, such as Fletcher Henderson, Chick Webb, and Cab Calloway. See, for instance, Erenberg, *Swingin' the Dream*, 3–31.

middle-class Whites, who were fascinated by the perceived exoticism and eroticism of Black music and dance.[7] With the onset of the Great Depression in the late 1920s, the Harlem Renaissance dwindled, but Black entertainment remained hugely popular with White audiences. As the mass media of radio, records, and film increasingly supplemented and supplanted live entertainment, these media became a key factor in disseminating the sounds and images of Black popular culture. Throughout the 1920s, 1930s, and 1940s, American popular music and dance were dominated by styles originating in African American culture. At the same time, Black styles were adopted, adapted, and commercialized by White performers, often without acknowledgment of their origins.

Films of the period testify to this colonization of Black popular culture by Whites – encapsulated in the phrase "love and theft"[8] – through a number of phenomena: the White Charleston-dancing heroines of 1920s silent flapper comedy; the invisible (and usually uncredited) presence of Black musicians on movie soundtracks; the often unacknowledged Black influences on the performance styles of White tap dancers, jazz/swing musicians, and singers; and, of course, the continuation of minstrelsy's complex and contradictory blackface tradition in film musicals from *The Jazz Singer* (1927) onward. But even though the film industry remained overwhelmingly White-dominated while profiting from Black popular culture, the period also brought an increased visibility of African American performers. With the arrival of synchronized sound film in the late 1920s, Hollywood discovered Black musical talent and exploited it as a novelty to promote the new medium. African American musicians, vocalists, and dancers appeared in a few all-Black-cast feature films and, more numerously, in jazz-themed musical short films. From the mid-1930s on, Black specialty acts were a common ingredient in otherwise White-cast feature-length films of all genres. As in *Vogues of 1938*, these musical interludes often had little or no bearing on the movies' plots, and they could easily be cut from the films (as was routinely done in the South). In the early 1940s, Soundies – three-minute music shorts played on a jukebox – introduced an additional mainstream outlet for Black musical talent onscreen.[9]

7   For a history of the Harlem Renaissance, see Lewis, *When Harlem Was in Vogue*.

8   The expression "love and theft" comes from the title of Eric Lott's 1993 study of nineteenth-century minstrelsy, in which the author examines the ambiguous fascination Black culture held for White working-class audiences; see Lott, *Love and Theft*. The phrase has become shorthand for the dialectic of envy and repulsion that has characterized White attitudes towards Black culture in many contexts, and for the pattern of Whites stealing and profiting from Black culture.

9   While Black musical screen performance was especially common during the period examined here, music and dance have played a central role throughout African American film history, from the earliest pseudo-ethnographic (White-produced) films with telling titles like *The Pickaninny Dance* (1894) or *Dancing Darkies* (1896) to the utopian depictions of a multiracial American society in Hollywood's twenty-first-century hip-hop teen films, such as *Step Up* (2006).

As the cultural practices of a socially and economically marginalized group became central in American (and consequently global) popular culture, they also developed into a crucial force in the Black struggle for integration and equality, for more visibility and respect. During the period discussed here, when jazz and jazz-inflected music were the prevalent popular dance music in America, vernacular jazz dance was an especially powerful tool in this struggle, constantly pushing the boundaries of how African Americans were represented and perceived.[10]

Vernacular jazz dance is an umbrella term referring to the large variety of popular dances of African American origin that were fashionable in the first half of the twentieth century. This encompasses styles that were danced solo, in pairs, or in groups, both improvised and choreographed. Examples include the Charleston of the 1920s, the Lindy hop and other partnered swing dances of the 1930s, and the whole range of tap dancing. Vernacular jazz dance was practiced by amateurs and professionals, as social dance, as performance, and in competitions. It is important to note that in the African American tradition, these categories of social, performative, and competitive dance are not always clearly separate from each other, nor is there necessarily a strict boundary between dancer and audience. In African American culture, performers and spectators typically bond and interact with each other, and one can take the place of the other. Further, music and movement are regarded as a whole, with the fusion of body and music a key feature of jazz expressivity, in contrast to the traditional mind/body dualism of European culture.

A number of aesthetic and social principles characterize Black vernacular dance. Rhythm has always been a defining element of the tradition, which features rhythmic repetition and drive as well as polyrhythms. At the physical level, there is an emphasis on polycentrism and isolation – that is, body parts can be moved in isolation, and each body part can become the center. Instead of linearity, the focus is on angularity (flexed joints), flexibility, asymmetry, and a grounded posture. An "aesthetic of the cool", which gives an impression of control as well as effortlessness, dominates the expressive level. Innovation (while staying *within* the tradition), improvisation, and individual self-expression are hallmarks, even in the context of choreographed performance. The interactive component involves call-and-response patterns, competitive interaction between dancers, and interaction between dancers, musicians, and audience. In sum, the vitality of the

---

10 This is neither to deny the White influences on jazz dance nor to discount the achievements of White dancers. Like jazz music, vernacular jazz dance evolved from a fusion of different styles, including various European roots, such as Irish step dancing, which played an important role in the development of tap dance, to name but one example. Nevertheless, it is important to note that the vernacular jazz dance of the early twentieth century largely developed within Black communities and in White contexts where Black styles were imitated (whether consciously or not).

process is valued over the static product; dynamic individuality and originality – rather than rigid uniformity – are admired and expected. All of these principles generally stand in contrast to European traditions and aesthetics, and they have been termed "Africanist" because they can be traced back to African cultures.[11]

From the 1920s to the 1940s, vernacular jazz dance was ubiquitous in ballrooms, nightclubs, and speakeasies, on the stages of Broadway, Harlem, and the vaudeville circuits, at house parties, and on street corners. It was also virtually omnipresent in films of all kinds. By looking at cinematic images of vernacular jazz dance from the period when these images were most common, I consider questions of identity construction through dance, with a focus on race and gender: How does the racialized and gendered body in film perform, challenge, and negotiate identities and stereotypes through jazz dance? How do these identity constructions relate to the films' narratives, settings, and costumes? In other words, what is the function of the dancers and dance performances within the films? How do they confirm or subvert stereotypes and power hierarchies defined by racial, gender, and class categories, and how do these categories intersect with each other? How do the dancers articulate the tension between agency and objectification that is inherent in any dance performance? In trying to answer these and other questions, I variously focus on the film careers and images of specific dancers, on certain dance styles, and on groups of similar films. My discussion encompasses fictional feature films, short films that were screened in cinemas, and the Soundies jukebox films of the 1940s. While jazz dance from the early twentieth century is sometimes called authentic jazz dance,[12] I avoid this term because of its implication that there is such a thing as inauthentic jazz dance. Questions of authenticity or purity are not at issue here. As jazz and film scholar Krin Gabbard notes, "there is no such thing as a pure, uncorrupted, uncommercialized black music that is somehow knowable without the apparatus of the culture industry".[13] Instead of a futile quest to identify what is or isn't authentic, my aim is to explore how and to what end vernacular jazz dance was used by the film industry and to illuminate why these uses make it a focal point of Black/White race relations in America.

---

11 These Africanist elements remain relevant to this day, manifest in newer forms of African American dance, such as the numerous styles found in hip-hop culture. For more detailed discussions of the general principles of African American dance, see, for instance, Gottschild, *Digging the Africanist Presence*, 11–19; Malone, *Steppin' on the Blues*, 1–36; and Stearns and Stearns, *Jazz Dance*, 14–16.

12 See, for instance, Guarino and Oliver, *Jazz Dance*, 24–31. This glossary of jazz dance styles is an attempt at defining and distinguishing the terms used for the myriad forms of jazz/jazz-influenced dance that have emerged over the past century. As the authors point out, this is a difficult undertaking, because the categories have no strict boundaries, terminology is always shifting, and many labels have more than one definition.

13 Gabbard, *Jammin' at the Margins*, 17.

The number in *Vogues of 1938* encapsulates the complex role of Black music and dance in mainstream film (and American culture at large) in unusually explicit ways. Ironically, during the Harlem Renaissance, the White practice of "slumming" in the Black neighborhood was considered a sign of elite sophistication, in line with a more general modernist fascination with the "primitive". By the mid-1930s, the idea of "Harlem" had become shorthand for Black entertainment, and its use in film was conventionalized to such a degree that it had lost some of its exoticism as well as its upper-class pretensions. Black music and dance had become commonplace, something to be enjoyed by everybody rather than only by the urban elites. Sophistication was no longer seen as a trait of the audience; instead, the performances themselves were increasingly considered classy.

The scene in *Vogues* is quite ambiguous and self-reflexive in its treatment of class issues. The film is set in New York's haute couture fashion scene, and its main romantic plot intersects with economic concerns, having an impoverished heiress jilt her rich fiancé in order to pursue a career in fashion modeling, which inevitably leads to her falling in love with the clothing designer. The song lyrics and costuming in the Cotton Club show allude to issues of class and highlight elegant fashion, thus providing a sort of oblique commentary on the film's central plotline. The number's introductory segment, with the women slowly gliding and posing in their elegant robes, could even be read as an ironic comment on the *Ziegfeld Follies*, the successful theatrical revues whose idealized White showgirls also functioned as high-end fashion models.[14] As the Black chorus girls give in to the sounds of jazz, the dropping of their elegant cloaks signifies the dropping of the mask of sophistication. This seems to suggest that they are unable to uphold the "elegant touch" in the face of hot jazz, which makes them reveal their true nature instead. The women's sexy appearance and dancing, as well as pianist Maurice Rocco's excessive performance style, certainly cater to White preconceptions about the primitive nature of Black people, and the song title "Red Hot Heat" refers to the excitement supposedly inherent in hot Black jazz, which is contrasted with the restrained refinement of White classical music and dance. This struggle between "civilized" (White) sophistication and "wild" (Black) jazz, between self-control and abandon, between the classy and the primitive, is emblematic of the period's cinematic representations of Black music and dance, but the explicitness with which it is presented here makes "Red Hot Heat" unusual. With its excessive artifice, the scene self-consciously presents the performers *as* performers who are well aware of their role, rather than as natural entertainers. African American music and dance is explicitly and self-reflexively

---

14 See Mizejewski, *Ziegfeld Girl*, especially 89–108.

presented as a commodity for White consumption, its primitivism exposed as a performance, staged to please the White audience – both *in* and *of* the film. And with their "blasé" behavior during the number's opening segment, the chorus girls make fun of the upper-class pretensions of the Cotton Club's White clientele, mockingly holding up the mirror to their own audience.

By showing how hot jazz triumphs over classical music, the number also condenses a narrative pattern commonly found in Hollywood musicals: the victory of (American) popular culture over (European) elite culture. This formula structures many studio-era musicals, in which White appropriations and adaptations of Black culture come to stand for the Americanness of popular culture – often without acknowledgment of the Black roots.[15] It is relatively rare, however, that a Black specialty number celebrates Black popular culture as something better than White elite culture as explicitly and emphatically as in *Vogues of 1938*.

Finally, the Cotton Club scene is also somewhat exceptional in its depiction of sexualized Black women. As the nearly naked chorus girls are literally crawling on the floor at the end, with undulating legs, arms, and torsos, throwing bare legs in the air, mingling with the men and singing about red-hot heat, the scene's climax is nothing less than orgiastic. Dance scenes of such an explicitly erotic kind were generally quite unusual at that time. In 1934, under growing outside pressure for stricter film censorship, Hollywood studios finally began enforcing the 1930 Production Code, the industry's attempt at self-censorship.[16] While Black female performers onscreen were commonly sexualized in the first few years of sound film, they were rarely featured as individual musical performers after the early 1930s. But even the handful of performances by Black women from the pre-Code era don't quite compare with this decidedly erotic scene in *Vogues of 1938*. And what's especially remarkable here is that the women in "Red Hot Heat" seem to be enjoying *themselves* as much as they are entertaining and titillating their audiences. Such a display of Black female pleasure is, in fact, quite sensational in a 1930s Hollywood film.

The Conspicuous Absence of the Black Dancing Woman

At a conference dedicated to the Hollywood musical, I heard an excellent talk that presented the results of research about censorship and dance during the studio era. Not too surprisingly, the study of numerous production files had revealed (among other things) that censorship was directed almost exclusively at the female body, while there seems to have been very little interest in censoring

---

15 See, for instance, Feuer, *The Hollywood Musical*, 54–65.
16 See Belton, introduction to "The Production Code".

displays of the male body. Since nothing was said about race during this talk, I asked if there were any known cases of censorship concerning Black dancing women. The answer – which did not invite further discussion – was simply that there were no Black female dancers in studio-era Hollywood, that the Black dancers onscreen were all men.

At the time, I had mostly finished the research for chapter 3 of the present book, which concerns the film career of African American tap dancer Jeni LeGon. LeGon performed in a few Hollywood films, among them the RKO musical *Hooray for Love* (1935), where she was partnered with the legendary Black tap dancer Bill "Bojangles" Robinson. Apart from LeGon, I also knew about the groups of male and female Black Lindy hoppers who performed impressive acrobatic dance routines in several Hollywood films of the late 1930s and early 1940s, at the height of the swing era and the jitterbug dance craze. Today, these dancers are little known outside of the modern swing dance community, and back in the day, their film scenes probably didn't cause much concern over sexualized display. Nevertheless, these scenes unmistakably show Black dancing women in studio-era Hollywood films. Singer-dancer Dorothy Saulters in *Vogues of 1938* is, of course, another example, and one certainly wonders what the Production Code Administration had to say about the "Red Hot Heat" number.

My aim in listing these examples is not so much to prove anyone wrong. Looking at any random sample of films from the studio era, one could easily reach the conclusion that there were no Black female dancers in classical Hollywood cinema. It would, in fact, be fair to say that there were almost none, whereas there *were* a good number of Black male dancers familiar to mainstream audiences. But instead of dismissing the few exceptions as irrelevant oddities, I would suggest that the very rarity of Black female dancers on the silver screen makes them worthy of study. In other words, their absence – or near absence – is significant. After all, history is told through what is missing or invisible as much as through what is obviously present. Thus, one of the aims of this project has been to look at when and how Black dancing women *did* appear in films, and to ask – though perhaps not to fully answer – why they didn't appear more frequently. If we ask why women are so dramatically underrepresented in a specific field, then the answer must have something to do with men's dominance in that field – just like the underrepresentation of Black people obviously has a lot to do with White dominance.

Dance has, of course, always been a somewhat "feminized" realm, in which the erotic display of women's bodies is often a key component. During the Jazz Age and the swing era, stage and screen certainly tended to objectify performing women as sexualized showgirls or, by contrast, to contain them within a domesticated Victorian femininity (especially in the case of White women). But women's dance (and music) performances also resisted simple objectification and containment, and it is important to note that the moving body on display always simultaneously expresses agency and objectification. In other words, dance scenes don't fit within the traditional feminist view, according to which screen performance is divided along gendered lines, with active, male subjects, who are mainly involved in doing, and passive, female objects, whose purpose it is to be looked at. As dance critic Sally Banes points out, in dance "the distinction between *doing* versus *being looked at* is a category error. ... When characters (male or female) in any dance-fiction are 'being looked at', they are seldom passive objects of the gaze – male or female; instead, it is precisely their *doing* that is the active subject of the gaze".[17]

In a similar vein, film scholar Adrienne L. McLean offers a view of women dancers as active and competent performers displaying creativity, skill, and agency through dance, noting that "surprisingly little attention has been paid to how dancing women, in particular, contributed to a destabilization of the presumed gender divisions of classical Hollywood cinema".[18] Likewise, Kristin A. McGee speaks of "tensions between feminine subjectivity and objectivity" in her wide-ranging study of jazz women – bandleaders, vocalists, and instrumentalists – who appeared in films from 1928 to 1959, and who often danced as well.[19] Tracing women's struggles for more respect in the male-dominated music world, McGee also shows how dance – both as an erotic spectacle *and* as a spectacle of competence – played an important role in some cases, and how race and gender intersect in the representation and reception of these female performers. As gender historian Joan W. Scott summed up in her influential essay from 1986, "inequalities of power are organized along at least three axes", namely those of class, race, and gender;[20] these categories intersect both with each other and variously with other categories in determining individual experience. This kind of intersectional approach has since become something of a commonplace across academic disciplines, and it is also crucial for examining vernacular jazz dance in film.

The White/Black power imbalance provides the first, most obvious axis of analysis for the study of Black and Black-derived dance in a White-dominated film

---

17 Banes, "TV-Dancing Women", 216 (italics in the original). Banes specifically critiques the psychoanalytical approaches that follow Laura Mulvey's influential essay on the male gaze in classical Hollywood cinema; see Mulvey, "Visual Pleasure".
18 McLean, *Being Rita Hayworth*, 116.
19 McGee, *Some Liked It Hot*, 31.
20 Scott, "Gender", 1054.

industry.²¹ The Hollywood industry during the studio era was essentially controlled by White people, who were in charge of producing, writing, directing, marketing, and distributing films. Behind-the-scenes involvement of African Americans was largely limited to jobs in technical trades and to some contributions in the fields of music and dance, with Blacks employed as musicians or dance teachers, for instance. Despite a margin of creative control in these fields, decision-making at almost every level was ultimately in White hands, and Black contributions usually remained unacknowledged. The only Black participants in the Hollywood studio system to regularly receive official recognition were the performers onscreen. That even the most successful of these performers never gained the respect, fame, and salary of the White stars of the period is well known. With the arrival of synchronized sound in film, the increasing popularity of Black screen performers evidenced their struggle over representation; at the same time, it confirmed the continuing inequality of power between Whites and Blacks.

Second, the male/female gender hierarchy exists both within and across the White/Black racial hierarchy. Of the Black performers to achieve relative prominence in studio-era Hollywood, the majority were men. And of the women who were somewhat successful, few had the opportunity to develop their talents in the same way as the most successful Black men (say, for instance, bandleader-composer-pianist Duke Ellington or the tap-dancing Nicholas Brothers). While a substantial number of Black men managed to establish screen images of competent and creative performers, women were mostly depicted as eroticized showgirls or submissive servants, at least until singer Lena Horne came along in the 1940s and embodied a more sophisticated African American femininity. Race and gender inequality thus intersect and discriminate against Black women more than against Black men (and more than against White women).

Third, there is also an intraracial hierarchy between light-skinned and dark-skinned African Americans, which affected women much more strongly than men. For darker-skinned Black women, only the roles of maids and mammies were commonly available. With very rare exceptions, the most successful female musical performers in Hollywood were light-skinned "dusky belles". This preference for light-skinned African American women, who were generally judged by White beauty standards, continues to this day, as exemplified by contemporary

---

21 For the purposes of this project, I am limiting the discussion to the White/Black dichotomy, which has disproportionately shaped racial discourses in America. I am well aware, of course, that African Americans are not the only minority to be marginalized and othered in American culture (or around the world, for that matter). Other groups of people (Asians, Latinos, Indians, Jews, etc.) have variously been framed as non-White and discriminated against on racial or ethnic grounds, and films have always both reflected and contributed to these power dynamics. See Shohat and Stam, *Unthinking Eurocentrism*, for a thorough discussion of multiculturalism and the media.

Black stars like actress Halle Berry or pop star Beyoncé. Finally, issues of class – defined in economic as well as in cultural terms – intersect with these racial and gender divisions.

The Film Musical and Resistance on the Margins

For all the obviousness of these intersecting hierarchies and power structures, there has always been room for negotiation and resistance. To argue in the tradition of postcolonial studies, the power hierarchy between Whites and Blacks (like any power relationship) should not be conceived of as a strict binary and fixed authority but as uneven negotiation and reciprocal dependencies. Since "ideology is a process or relation" that is "constantly negotiated", as Ed Guerrero explains, "Hollywood has increasingly attempted to maintain its contested hegemony by co-opting and incorporating emergent and dissonant styles, oppositional images, and resistant films".[22] The field of cultural studies has long held the view that social and cultural change comes from the margins. Subcultures introduce new trends and fashions, which are then incorporated into the commodified mainstream. As the subculture is transformed into a consumer product, it is robbed of much of its subversive potential. Nevertheless, in the process, the mainstream itself is transformed by what Stuart Hall has called "the voicing of the margins", in the course of which "what replaces invisibility is a kind of carefully regulated, segregated visibility".[23] From the late 1920s to the mid-1940s, the segregated visibility of African American musicians and dancers onscreen simultaneously confirmed and contested the racial hierarchy: while nonmusical Black actors in Hollywood were limited to servant roles, musical artists appeared in so-called specialty acts, in theatrical short films and Soundies, and in a handful of all-Black-cast feature-length musicals. In the words of Richard Dyer, they were used "nearly always in one kind of ghetto or another".[24] Yet this ghettoized presence was at times transformed into a privileged position, from which Black musicians and dancers exerted some control over their self-presentation. Their roles as servants and/or entertainers simultaneously – and paradoxically – highlight and suppress White America's debt to and dependence on Black culture, which can inadvertently lend Black performance a touch of the subversive and illicit.

To examine this negotiation with and resistance to White dominance requires dismantling uniform views of classical Hollywood, and especially of the musical genre, in favor of a more diverse picture that includes marginal film forms. The

22 Guerrero, *Framing Blackness*, 6.
23 Hall, "Black Popular Culture", 125–126.
24 Dyer, *Only Entertainment*, 39.

relationship between narrative and musical numbers has always been at the center of discussions concerning the film musical, with a tendency to conceive of the narratives as ideologically conservative and of the numbers as subversive. Some now-classic texts have postulated the dominance of narrative, arguing that whatever is momentarily subverted or questioned is ultimately reintegrated into the film's overall ideological agenda, which is the reaffirmation of the genre's "myth of entertainment".[25] However, more recent analyses have shifted the focus to the contradictory aspects and tensions that are not so easily resolved but instead remain visible *as* tensions and contradictions. The narratively integrated musical only became dominant after World War II, whereas many earlier films had a much more "aggregate" structure, where most numbers – not just those with Black performers – were disconnected from the narrative.[26] The principle of variety entertainment, inherited from the vaudeville stage, structured many musical films. In the popular revue musicals, but also in numerous B movies with flimsy storylines, narrative logic and coherence were secondary to the spectacle of musical performance. It is also worth noting that the musical specialty act as a non-narrative attraction was not limited to the musical genre but common across *all* film genres. In addition, variety was a guiding principle in film programming of the 1930s, with a diversity of short forms – newsreels, cartoons, short fiction, educational shorts – screened before feature films. The popular musical short films of the late 1920s and 1930s were often non- or only minimally narrative, and in the 1940s, the Soundies jukebox films took the idea of the largely non-narrative musical short to new extremes. Further, film exhibition was often combined with live performance, with unrelated variety acts (singing, dancing, acrobatics, comedy) supplementing the entertainment onscreen.[27] In short, the vaudeville tradition left its mark on cinema, where the conventions of variety and spectacle remained manifest well into the age of so-called classical narrative cinema.[28]

The movies' general continuance of the vaudeville tradition intersects with the segregated treatment of African Americans. To argue against the uncontested dominance of narrative in studio-era musicals also entails arguing against generalizations according to which every Black performance is necessarily subordinate to a White narrative. As Sean Griffin points out, "a critique arguing that minority performers are relegated to the musical portions of the film overlooks the fact that

---

25 See Feuer, "The Self-Reflective Musical"; and Altman, *The American Film Musical*, 127.
26 For a brief overview of the emergence of the integrated musical, see Griffin, "The Gang's All Here", 23–25.
27 See McGee, *Some Liked It Hot*, 19, 34, 49–51; and Staiger, *Perverse Spectators*, 20.
28 See Jenkins, *What Made Pistachio Nuts?*

those portions are the raison d'être of the genre".[29] In their nonintegrated musicals for 20th Century-Fox, for instance, the tap-dancing Nicholas Brothers did the same as everyone else at the studio, performing specialty numbers onstage. In these numbers, they articulated identities that deviated considerably from common Black stereotypes. Sometimes they even stole the show from Whites, as in the case reported by tap historian Constance Valis Hill: the duo's spectacular number in *Down Argentine Way* (1940) was such a hit with audiences that numerous theaters billed them as the movie's stars, even though they only appeared for three minutes and had no part in the film's narrative.[30] The Nicholas Brothers' crossover success probably represents the apex of the transformative potential of Black dance performance in White film. But while their case might have been unique in degree, others were similar in kind. It was not uncommon for a Black specialty act to be considered a film's highlight, and film historians have found that the same Black musical scenes that were excised in the South would sometimes be advertised as a special attraction in the North.[31] Such rupturing of White dominance, however singular and temporary, is what makes Black dance performance in classical Hollywood cinema significant. In addition, the numerous musical short films and Soundies where Blacks *were* the stars constituted simultaneously another ghetto *and* a relatively privileged forum for Black performance.

It should also be noted that Black artists, partly *because* of their secondary status, sometimes had a lot of artistic freedom within their segregated performances. African Americans were often recruited from Harlem nightclubs, Broadway shows, vaudeville, or radio because they were already somewhat successful and familiar from these contexts. To varying degrees, this enabled them to use their extracinematic cultural capital in Hollywood and thus to retain a comparatively high degree of creative control over the material they performed. Dancers were often partly or entirely in charge of their own choreography, with minimal intervention by (White) directors or choreographers. Dance numbers thus provided them with an opportunity for creative expression, a sphere of influence and agency outside of – or competing with – narrative limitations and stereotypes. Black dance acts, even more than purely musical numbers, functioned as sites of

---

29 Griffin, "The Gang's All Here", 22.

30 See Hill, *Brotherhood in Rhythm*, chapter 7. Hill reports that the scene was also shown in the South, and she even found a case of a local newspaper informing readers how many minutes into the film the Nicholas Brothers appeared, which led to people showing up in time for the scene and leaving afterwards. The brothers' dance in their next feature film, *Sun Valley Serenade* (1941), was also shown in some Southern theaters.

31 See Crease, "Divine Frivolity", 226n3.

freedom, with dance representing – quite literally – the freedom of movement otherwise denied to African Americans.

As Stuart Hall, among others, has pointed out, oppressed cultures "have used the body – as if it was, and it often was, the only cultural capital we had. We have worked on ourselves as the canvases of representation".[32] Nowhere could this be truer than in the case of Black vernacular dance in film. Film history is replete with Black dancers employing their body as cultural capital in the service of racial struggle, pushing the boundaries of the time. None of this is to deny the racial hierarchy and segregation that undeniably existed across all entertainment industries (and in society at large). But by looking at the ruptures, deviations, and tensions – as much as the continuities – in the history of Black vernacular dance onscreen, my aim is to highlight examples that don't entirely fit the dominant and well-known patterns (without denying the existence of such patterns).

The process of canonization is always also a process of exclusion: On the one hand, what is excluded is often the unusual; it is excluded because it doesn't fit the general pattern and because it is therefore not useful in supporting a historical narrative that aims to describe dominant patterns. On the other hand, what is excluded is sometimes also the everyday, the unremarkable, the mediocre. In writing about film history, unremarkable films are often excluded because they don't seem to warrant the same kind of detailed attention as the so-called masterpieces. Many of the films that I discuss would probably be deemed average or below average in terms of what is commonly considered quality filmmaking. But most moviegoers likely saw more such average movies than masterpieces. Many of the short films, Soundies, and B movies I discuss – and which have been excluded from analysis by the canonizing forces of scholarship – are interesting and relevant precisely because of their ordinariness. While musical shorts might not have represented the highlight of most people's filmgoing experience, it was an everyday experience, an integral part of the consumption of popular culture. The low-budget teen musicals of the 1940s rarely garnered critical praise, yet they are significant simply because many (mostly young) people saw them and likely saw something in them that spoke to their lives more directly or differently than a glamorous A feature.

Many of the films and performers I discuss have to date received little or no attention in academia. While the past two decades have produced a substantial body of scholarship on hitherto neglected topics, evidencing a growing tendency to concentrate on the marginalized, the noncanonical, the all-but-forgotten,

---

32 Hall, "Black Popular Culture", 128–129.

much work remains to be done.[33] Film studies has paid increasing attention to early pioneers of African American film history, and the White appropriation of African American music and dance styles in classical Hollywood is now widely acknowledged. And yet, despite a high degree of consensus that "the Hollywood musical's barely repressed ghosts [are] the bodies, sounds, and steps of African American vernacular dance",[34] the topic remains underexamined. The majority of literature on the film musical is still concerned with the same handful of stars and the same canonical films. The recent attention to female musical performers is mostly limited to White women. Studies of Black performance during the studio era still focus on men more often than on women. And until very recently, both theatrical music shorts and Soundies have been all but ignored in film history. Jazz scholarship also continues to marginalize dance, despite the fact that jazz was primarily dance music for roughly the first thirty years of its existence. What's more, the field of jazz studies is still overwhelmingly male-dominated, both with regard to the scholars and to their objects of study. Regarding Black dance history, a good number of scholars have added their diverse perspectives since Marshall and Jean Stearns's seminal 1968 book *Jazz Dance: The Story of American Vernacular Dance* (which remains a fundamental work of reference).[35]

---

33 Arthur Knight's *Disintegrating the Musical* can be considered a foundational text, perhaps providing the first in-depth study of Black performance in American musical film. Ryan Jay Friedman's more recent *Hollywood's African American Films* offers a thorough analysis of the early sound film period, looking at both canonical and barely known features and short films while also highlighting a number of Black female performers. Sherrie Tucker's *Swing Shift* on female swing bands of the 1940s and Kristin A. McGee's *Some Liked It Hot* on jazz women in film are among the few works examining the era's phenomenon of girl bands in detail. Constance Valis Hill's comprehensive *Tap Dancing America* emphasizes the numerous female dancers who have been all but forgotten. Joel Dinerstein's outstanding account of swing culture, *Swinging the Machine*, gives equal weight to music and dance – which is rare in jazz studies. German jazz historian Bernd Hoffmann is one of the few scholars to dedicate himself to the musical short films from Hollywood's golden age, criticizing jazz scholarship's one-sided focus on audio recordings and advocating for an increased use of visual source materials; see Hoffmann, "Alltag im Jazz-Himmel"; Hoffmann, "Lindy Hop und Cotton Club"; Hoffmann, "Ruß im Gesicht"; Hoffmann, "Suwannee River"; and Hoffmann, "'Und der Duke weinte'" (to date, none of Hoffmann's essays on musical short films have been translated into English). Andrea Kelley's recent *Soundies Jukebox Films* is probably the first book-length study of the jukebox music shorts, with the exception of the earlier filmographies, which also contain historical overviews; see Hose, *Soundies*; and MacGillivray and Okuda, *The Soundies Book*.

34 Brooks, "Ghosting the Machine", 359.

35 The key works that provide a historical overview are, in order of their first publication: Stearns and Stearns, *Jazz Dance*; Emery, *Black Dance*; Hazzard-Gordon, *Jookin'*; and Malone, *Steppin' on the Blues*. A more recent addition is the collected volume by Guarino and Oliver, *Jazz Dance*, which has a stronger focus on theatrical forms of jazz dance. With regard to tap dance, Rusty Frank's *Tap!*, a compilation of interviews with surviving dancers from tap's golden age, is a milestone; and Constance Valis Hill's *Tap Dancing America* offers an important historical reference work of unprecedented scope. Among the numerous other publications focusing on specific aspects, periods, or practitioners of African American dance, Brenda Dixon Gottschild's three volumes deserve special mention; see Gottschild, *The Black Dancing Body*; Gottschild, *Digging the Africanist Presence*; and Gottschild, *Waltzing in the Dark*. For a general history of social dance practices, see Giordano, *Social Dancing in America*; while this history is not limited to African American styles, Black dances conspicuously dominate the second volume, which is dedicated to the twentieth century.

Nevertheless, Black vernacular dance has long been marginal in dance studies as well as African American studies (which are both themselves relatively marginal fields in academia).[36]

With the present volume, my aim is to move the marginal to the center and to throw some light on a few blind spots of film and dance history. Films with all-Black, all-White, and racially mixed casts are included in my discussion, and I consider Black as well as White dancers, men as well as women. Nevertheless, the study is lopsided in several respects, in line with my desire to highlight that which has been marginalized historically and/or in writing about history: above all, African American performers are emphasized over Whites here; women are discussed somewhat more frequently than men; lesser-known films receive more attention than canonical works; and lesser-known dancers more than those who were relatively big stars.

In order to go beyond a purely textual analysis of films, I include nonfilmic materials, such as press reports, promotional materials, and interviews, to varying degrees throughout the book. My sources include film reviews from the mainstream "quality" press (namely the *New York Times*), from Black newspapers (the major weeklies *Chicago Defender* and *Pittsburgh Courier*), and from the trade press (magazines like *Variety*, *Film Daily*, and others). These materials provide an additional interpretive framework that helps to dismantle normative notions of a uniform classical cinema. They suggest some of the possible meanings and uses the films possessed for their audiences, and they offer insight into marketing strategies and intended audience address, thus giving some clues to what the industry thought and expected of its audience. While this is not primarily a study of reception, these issues enter my discussion because they suggest the possibility of what Janet Staiger has called "perverse spectators"[37] – that is, spectators whose interpretive strategies deviate from the presumed norm. Be it African Americans' celebration of a Black specialty performer as a star or White teenagers' enthusiasm for swing teen films, evidence of "deviant" spectatorship questions the idea of the uniformly manipulative powers of the entertainment industry. Last but not least, interviews and autobiographies can give voice to those who often remained unheard during their most active years; this is especially pertinent in the case of African Americans, who were unable to contribute to their own image-making in the same way as White stars. It is not by accident that Black dance history – as a history of the marginalized – has largely relied on the recording of oral testimony. Late-in-life accounts have offered performers an opportunity to

---

36 See DeFrantz, *Dancing Many Drums*, ix. DeFrantz gives an excellent critical overview of the field in the book's introduction (3–35).

37 See Staiger, *Perverse Spectators*, especially 28–42.

reclaim some discursive agency, allowing them to retrospectively shape their public persona and reception and to finally write their own history, so to speak. Though materials such as interviews or the entertainment sections of historic newspapers often provide anecdotal evidence rather than "hard" facts, they are instructive and valuable. While we will never have complete or direct access to historical "truth", examining a variety of sources can help us reconstruct some of the *possible* historical intentions behind, uses for, and interpretations of cultural products.

Summary

Before giving a summary of the following six chapters, a word on omissions is in order. There can be no question of providing a complete history of vernacular jazz dance in American film. I gave up a long time ago on seeing every dance performance from studio-era Hollywood. Even to see every dance scene featuring African American dancers seems impossible, as there are probably several thousand such scenes, many of them in hard-to-find or lost films. The scope of this project is by necessity exemplary rather than encyclopedic. In line with my aim to emphasize some of mainstream film culture's most marginalized phenomena, I am bypassing some of the more obvious choices of subject matter. This means, for instance, that I don't discuss Fred Astaire and his appropriation of the Black dance vocabulary. Some of the most iconic Black female dancers, such as Josephine Baker or Katherine Dunham, are also sidestepped, both because a sizable body of scholarship on them already exists and because film was not central to their careers.[38]

Further, the so-called race films of the 1920s to 1940s are marginal to my discussion. Produced independently from Hollywood for a segregated Black market, these films featured Black actors and were generally made by Black filmmakers (though sometimes with support from Whites). They offered Black audiences a wider variety of Black screen images than Hollywood films, and in their treatment of Black migration, urban life, and social mobility, they presented visions of Black life that resonated with audiences' real-life experiences of modernity. By largely excluding Whites, race films also provided utopian visions of a world free of racial prejudice. At the same time, race films were also strongly influenced by the White mainstream, partly through financial backing from liberal Whites, partly through imitation of Hollywood standards. Produced for the Black mainstream, they have also been criticized – both contemporaneously and retrospectively – for "aping" Hollywood with nothing but inferior imitations

---

38 Josephine Baker actually never appeared in an American film. On Baker's French films, see, for instance, Kalinak, "Disciplining Josephine Baker". On Katherine Dunham, see Clark and Johnson, *Kaiso!*

of mainstream genres like the Western or the gangster film. Race films also tend to follow Hollywood's patterns in their musical numbers, showcasing performers who conform to the happy-go-lucky natural entertainer stereotype. Nevertheless, the all-Black context makes a difference. As Alan Jay Friedman points out, race films showed the Harlem cabaret as exclusively Black, coded as a space of luxury and pleasure, and "neither as a threat to the racial-social order nor as an exotic territory to be colonized by white pleasure seekers".[39] A comparative analysis of musical numbers in Hollywood films and race films would doubtless be a worthwhile undertaking. For the purposes of this project, however, I focus on cinematic images that circulated in the White-dominated mainstream.

Cartoons are also excluded from my analysis. The era's popular animated short films offer a plethora of material for studying cinematic uses of jazz music, dance, and racial caricature – an extensive subject in its own right that lies outside the scope of this project.[40] Finally, I don't discuss blackface performance in any detail, since this is a subject on which a good deal of first-rate scholarship already exists, to which I have little to add at this point.[41]

The year 1929 offers itself as the starting point for discussing the uses and representations of vernacular jazz dance in American films because it was the year when sound film became established and when African American musicians and dancers first appeared as featured attractions onscreen in substantial numbers (although silent films had sometimes included Black dancers too). In the following decade and a half, Black musical performers were a frequent presence in a variety of films. During the same period, Black-originated music and dance styles, especially big band swing music and tap dancing, also dominated the stylistic repertoire of White performers. By the end of World War II, the swing era was coming to an end, as was the golden age of tap dancing. With the advent of bebop, the status of jazz was elevated from entertainment to art, as the music evolved from accessible dance music for the masses into an intellectualized art form for the discerning listener. Tap dance was increasingly replaced by jazz-inflected styles of ballet, which became dominant on the Broadway stage and consequently in Hollywood films. Meanwhile, the Hollywood musical also became more integrated narratively, offering less space for segregated specialty numbers.[42] There were also more directly political reasons for the changes occurring in the

39 Friedman, *African American Films*, 189.
40 See, for instance, Grant, "Animated Cartoon"; and Lehman, *The Colored Cartoon*.
41 On blackface in nineteenth-century minstrelsy, see especially Lott, *Love and Theft*; on blackface in film, see, for instance, Gubar, *Racechanges*; Knight, *Disintegrating the Musical*; Rogin, *Blackface, White Noise*; Stanfield, *Body and Soul*; and Willis, "Blackface Minstrelsy".
42 See also Knight, *Disintegrating the Musical*, 13–17.

early to mid-1940s. During the war, lobbying by civil rights organizations started to yield results with Hollywood's studio executives: demands by the NAACP (National Association for the Advancement of Colored People) for more dignified roles finally led to an agreement in 1942, changing the industry's hiring practices for Black performers.[43] The agreement did not take full effect immediately, but the end of World War II more or less spelled the end of what pioneering Black film historian Donald Bogle called Hollywood's "Negro Entertainer Syndrome" (even if its repercussions are felt to this day).[44] 20th Century-Fox's all-Black revue musical *Stormy Weather* (1943), which explicitly pays tribute to African American culture while subliminally advocating Black enlistment in the army, marks this transitional moment in African American film history. After the war, the struggle over Black cinematic representation moved to the so-called social problem film of the late 1940s and 1950s.[45]

What follows here is not a strictly chronological account, although the order is roughly chronological within each chapter as well as across the book overall; but the chapters also overlap with each other in terms of the time periods discussed. The first two chapters are dedicated to early sound films from the late 1920s to the mid-1930s. The conversion from silent to sound film brought a substantial increase in Black employment in Hollywood, with African Americans suddenly sought after as musicians and dancers. However, there is a striking imbalance between male and female performers, especially among dancers.

In chapter 1, I argue that this gender gap is linked to the narratives of mobility and self-determination often associated with dance. The role famously played by Nina Mae McKinney in the all-Black musical *Hallelujah* (1929) is reexamined in light of two popular dancing icons of the time – namely, the flapper and the chorus girl. While these dancing women were endowed with a new degree of freedom in their screen incarnations if they were White, Black women were denied the same possibilities in cinematic narratives. Many early Black-cast films betrayed an ambiguous fascination with Black culture, which was portrayed as simultaneously primitive and modern. In this contradictory framework, highly sexualized dancing women embodied the sinful pleasures of modern urban life, as *Hallelujah* and a handful of other examples show. At the same time, Black women were largely excluded from the associations of competence and professionalism often implicit in *non*-narrative dance performances, especially in the

---

43   See Bogle, *Bright Boulevards*, 211–212; and Cripps, *Slow Fade to Black*, 3, 373–378.
44   Bogle, *Toms, Coons*, 118.
45   See Bogle, *Toms, Coons*, 143–158. For more detailed accounts of African American film history during and after World War II, see Cripps, *Slow Fade to Black*, 349–389; and Cripps, *Making Movies Black*.

male-dominated realm of tap dance. A few rare exceptions to this general tendency are highlighted at the end of the chapter.

Chapter 2 focuses on Black male dancers in early sound film, namely in the underexamined popular music shorts. In the late 1920s and early 1930s, these short films were instrumental in increasing African American screen presence. Presenting their performers as stars and often framing them as skilled professionals rather than primitive "savages" or dimwitted "coons", Black-cast shorts pushed the racial boundaries of the time, frequently offering fantasies of African American achievement and affluence. Some films showed young Black boys dancing, thus framing their skill within the harmlessness and innocence of youth. But increasingly, adult tap dancers contributed to more dignified African American screen images. So-called class acts, teams of two or more male tap dancers who executed synchronized steps together, performed with elegance, precision, control, and composure, as much as with energy and exuberance. Challenging stereotypes of naturally rhythmic Black bodies, they embodied images of sophisticated professionalism, especially in their collaborations with the similarly elegant swing bands that often headlined Black-cast music shorts. Bandleaders Duke Ellington and Cab Calloway were probably the era's most successful Black performers. Both starred in several short films, which I discuss here with regard to the musicians' (screen) images and how they relate to dance. As I show in the last part of the chapter, the perception of Black (male) screen performance as increasingly classy is often confirmed by discourses in the trade press of the time.

Chapter 3 is a case study tracing the film career of a single dancer, Black female tap soloist Jeni LeGon. LeGon's short-lived and modest success in Hollywood underlines the way in which race and gender intersected in the film industry. Source materials ranging from press reports to interviews with the dancer herself also throw light on the creation of star images and the commodification of Black entertainment. LeGon presented an alternative to sexualized showgirls, a femininity based on agency, competence, and creativity, thus exemplifying the potential for a wider range of images for Black women in classical Hollywood. However, her obstructed career path also shows the limits of the time, and she ultimately remained a pioneer of unrealized potential. Highlighting LeGon's exceptional career *as* an exception thus also means to highlight the significance of absences and exclusions, in this case the virtual exclusion of Black dancing women from filmmaking and consequently from film history/historiography.

Chapter 4 is an excursion into a film-historical phenomenon that lies outside of the Hollywood industry. From 1940 to 1946, over 1,800 three-minute musical films were produced for exhibition on the Panoram, a film jukebox located in public spaces, such as restaurants, train stations, and department stores. Like the musical shorts of the early 1930s, these Soundies, as they were called, became a relatively privileged forum for African American performance. Instead of presenting escapist fantasies of entertainment, as the big-screen musical did, Soundies in a much more direct sense suffused spaces of everyday life with musical entertainment. Soundies featuring Black dancers offer particularly fitting examples to illustrate the unique space-screen-audience dynamics of the jukebox shorts. Many Black Soundies depict everyday scenes, with people just dancing at home or in the street. This everyday ordinariness of the onscreen representations is mirrored in the function of the Panoram as ambient, atmospheric entertainment – rather than spectacular cinematic attraction – in mundane, everyday spaces. It also resonates with the performer-audience interaction in African American culture. In addition, Black-cast Soundies showcased women as "stars" more often than Hollywood feature films.

The last two chapters are dedicated to the huge popularity of swing culture in the late 1930s and early 1940s. Chapter 5 discusses the crossover success of the Lindy hop, focusing on the film appearances of Whitey's Lindy Hoppers, a professional Black dance group from Harlem. Partnered swing dancing brought a new level of gender equality to dance floors and contributed to a shift in representations and perceptions of race. Cinematic instances of swing/jitterbug dancing, and specifically of the Lindy hop, offered interesting variations on and subversions of racialized and gendered screen images of dancers. Whitey's Lindy Hoppers modernized Black cinematic identities in the context of a swing culture that was increasingly perceived as all-American rather than African American. In a few cases, swing dancing in film also hinted at the interaction and exchange between Black and White cultures in ways that were unusual for mainstream films. Tellingly, this concerns short films more than feature films, again highlighting the relevance of various short film formats for Black film and dance history. I thus conclude the chapter with a discussion of two racially mixed comic short films.

Finally, in chapter 6, I shift the focus to White dancers, examining a series of largely forgotten low- and medium-budget productions made by Universal Studios in the early 1940s. Featuring the Jivin' Jacks and Jills, a group of teenage White dancers who mixed tap dancing and jitterbug styles, these B movies were produced during the peak of swing culture's mainstream popularity. Their depictions of a "hep" youth culture, epitomized by swing music and dancing, prefigure the film industry's later developments towards a separate teen market. Celebrating (White) youth culture, the films present swing as a rejuvenating force in American culture, at the price of largely excluding Blacks. Yet the dancers' embodiments of racial and gender identities also deviate from Hollywood's dominant representations, obliquely reflecting the democratic and pluralist tendencies of the larger swing culture in the context of World War II. Peggy Ryan, in particular, defies normative notions of femininity and Whiteness. As the main female soloist of the Jivin' Jacks and Jills, she embodies an African American dance aesthetic – free of primitivist connotations – in ways that are unique for a White screen dancer of the era. Last but not least, these films are another case in point against the inevitable dominance of narrative, as their strong focus on physical performance through dance and comedy offers an example of a vaudevillian aesthetic that often resists integration into a conservative ideology.

In exploring the phenomenon of vernacular jazz dance in film from a variety of perspectives, I hope to show that these dance representations are simultaneously symptomatic *and* constitutive of the period's race relations (as well as of gender and class issues). By looking at how vernacular jazz dance and dancers contributed to shifts in racial representations, I contest or complement one-dimensional views of White/Black hierarchies within the White-dominated film industry. Instead, I argue for the transformative and subversive potential of jazz dance performance in film by looking at how it negotiated the color line. It should be clear by now that I don't mean to make any naïve, simplistic claims about the positive influence of the dancers and films I discuss. The aim can only be to give examples that testify to the struggles over Black screen representation (as well as to the White appropriations of Black culture). In doing so, I hope to draw a picture of the cinematic dance floor as a dynamic and productive space where boundaries are constantly contested.

CHAPTER 1 Doomed Divas: Black Dancing Women in Early Sound Film

When inventor and radio pioneer Lee DeForest introduced his Phonofilm, an early synchronized sound film technology, to the New York public in 1923, the program included a short film featuring the Black vaudeville team of Noble Sissle and Eubie Blake. Whether or not *Noble Sissle and Eubie Blake Sing Snappy Songs* (1923) is the first sound film footage of African Americans, it is likely the first case of such footage being presented to a White audience.[46] At any rate, the introduction of sound film would play an important role in Black film history, and conversely, African American sounds and images would play an important role in the transition from silent to sound cinema.

This transitional period from silent to sound film coincided with the Harlem Renaissance, when African American intellectual and artistic activity reached unprecedented heights. Earlier in the decade, the Black musical revue *Shuffle Along* (1921) had been a big hit on Broadway, launching the careers of Josephine Baker and Paul Robeson, among others. That revue, with songs by Sissle and Blake, initiated a new trend for Black musical theater, which in turn kindled White interest in what was happening in Uptown Manhattan. Harlem became the capital of entertainment, with its theaters, nightclubs, and cafés attracting large numbers of White customers fascinated by the perceived exoticism and sensuality of Black music and dance. White "slumming" in the burgeoning Black neighborhood became a popular leisure activity of the urban middle and upper classes.[47] The Black Broadway shows and Harlem's live entertainment provided the raw material, so to speak, from which the film industry drew in the early years of sound film. The White fascination with Harlem as an exotic, thrilling place might at first have been limited to New York and a few other cities that had

46 See Bradley, *Hollywood Sound Shorts*, 14–17.

47 For a detailed history of the Harlem Renaissance, see Lewis, *When Harlem Was in Vogue*. On *Shuffle Along* and Black Broadway in the 1920s, see, for instance, Malone, *Steppin' on the Blues*, 75–79; Mizejewski, *Ziegfeld Girl*, 124–130; and Stearns and Stearns, *Jazz Dance*, 132–159. On White "slumming" in Harlem as a middle- and upper-class activity, see also Friedman, *African American Films*, 35–37.

growing and culturally vibrant African American neighborhoods, but sound film introduced a wider public to images of Black life. More often than not, these were *musical* images that featured singers, dancers, and musicians. In many ways, Black performance in sound film continued earlier traditions and reproduced stereotypes from minstrelsy and vaudeville, presenting images steeped in the nostalgic mythology of the rural South, with plantation settings and stereotyped mammy and coon figures. Yet sound film also challenged and modified these clichés, and under the influence of Harlem and Black Broadway, a more modern, urban image of African Americans emerged onscreen.

Film historians Alice Maurice and Ryan Jay Friedman, in their respective studies, have examined the significance of race in the period of transition from silent to sound cinema and found that for a short time around 1929, there was a lot of hype concerning the new "vogue" or "fad" for "Negro talking pictures".[48] In 1929, MGM released the first (White-cast) "all talking all dancing all singing" feature film, *The Broadway Melody*. This was also the year when Hollywood produced the first two of its all-Black-cast feature-length musicals: 20th Century-Fox's *Hearts in Dixie*, directed by Paul Sloane, and MGM's *Hallelujah*, directed by King Vidor.[49] A good number of musical short films also presented images of Black city life and Harlem entertainment that were probably new to many moviegoers. According to Alice Maurice, "selling the sound cinema via black performers and selling black performers (primarily to white audiences) via the sound cinema" was a common strategy during the early sound era.[50] Fetishizing the Black voice, filmmakers and critics considered African Americans the ideal protagonists of sound film, claiming that their voices were inherently more suited to the new technology and would thus make up for its deficiencies. Similarly, the assumed natural vitality of Black dancing bodies was thought to compensate for the limitations of early sound film, with its often stationary camera. As Maurice resumes, "African American performers 'cured' the ills of the sound cinema in many critics' eyes because the fetishization of racial characteristics made up for what the new technology lacked".[51]

48 See Friedman, *African American Films*; and Maurice, "Synchronizing Race".

49 During the studio era, major Hollywood studios made several Black-cast feature musicals, produced at irregular intervals over the course of thirty years. The term "all-Black-cast musical" is usually considered to include the following eight films: *Hearts in Dixie* (1929), *Hallelujah* (1929), *The Green Pastures* (1936), *Cabin in the Sky* (1943), *Stormy Weather* (1943), *Carmen Jones* (1954), *St. Louis Blues* (1958), and *Porgy and Bess* (1959). A case could be made to include Dudley Murphy's *The Emperor Jones* (1933), which starred singer Paul Robeson. Though the film is rarely mentioned in discussions of musicals, it does contain several musical numbers. For a detailed comparative discussion of the eight above-mentioned films, see Knight, *Disintegrating the Musical*, 123–168. For an analysis of *The Emperor Jones*, see Friedman, *African American Films*, 19–27.

50 Maurice, "Synchronizing Race", 31.

51 Maurice, 43. See also Friedman, *African American Films*, 30–35.

During the first years of sound film, employment of African Americans in Hollywood increased substantially, as the industry recruited Black performers from Broadway, vaudeville, and Harlem clubs.[52] However, as with many of Harlem's live entertainment venues, the new Black-cast films catered primarily to White audiences. Rather than aiming to satisfy Black spectators' desire for more and better cinematic representation, Hollywood produced and marketed the Black sound films as a fashionable novelty for White consumption. Thus, while all-Black-cast films presented an exclusively African American world, they generally implied a White audience. More specifically, Black-cast films were initially thought to appeal to a sophisticated, urban "class" audience rather than rural and small-town "mass" markets.[53] Although many African Americans received the films favorably too, they were clearly not the industry's primary target audience.[54] In this context, it is important to note the inherently problematic nature of White-produced, Black-cast films with regard to the world they depict: in one sense, all-Black-cast films can be seen as presenting a utopian Black world, a diegetic universe free of White-imposed constraints. But as Friedman and others have pointed out, such segregated narrative spaces also erase the signs of real-world segregation and discrimination and thus fail to challenge the social-racial hierarchies of the status quo.[55]

While Whites celebrated the "natural" talents of the "Negro", Black-cast "talkies" also elicited enthusiastic reactions from some African Americans who had high hopes about sound cinema's potential for racial uplift – although there were many critical voices too.[56] In the vein of Black discourses about the Great Migration, which saw the mass movement of African Americans from the rural South to the urban North as an expression of historical agency and self-determination, sound film was seen as "a crucial venue for aesthetic and social self-articulation".[57]

52 See Bogle, *Toms, Coons*, 26–27; Massood, "African American Stardom", 247; and Maurice, "Synchronizing Race", 35. Meanwhile, the transition to sound led to the demise of many independent Black film companies that lacked the financial means to keep up with the technological changes, and the early 1930s were a time of crisis for race film production; see Massood, *Making a Promised Land*, 8.

53 See Friedman, *African American Films*, 28–56. On the film industry's perception of its audience during this period, see also Maltby, "Sticks, Hicks and Flaps". Maltby examines the industry's discourse about its audience from 1929 to 1933 and finds that Hollywood conceived of its audience mainly through the overlapping binary distinctions of class/mass, sophisticated/unsophisticated, and Broadway/Main Street.

54 Friedman notes that "trade magazines tend to treat African American audiences with undisguised contempt, implying that exhibitors will (and ought to) discourage black patronage" (*African American Films*, 54). According to film historian Anna Everett, "Hollywood virtually ignored this large segment of its filmgoing public" until the premiere of *Imitation of Life* in 1934 (*Returning the Gaze*, 193).

55 See Friedman, *African American Films*, 99.

56 See Dismond, "The Negro Actor"; Everett, *Returning the Gaze*, 172–173, 181–182; Friedman, *African American Films*, 2–6, 29–31; Massood, "African American Stardom", 246–247; Maurice, "Synchronizing Race", 49; and Potamkin, "The Aframerican Cinema".

57 Friedman, *African American Films*, 63.

However, as Friedman observes, after a period of initial enthusiasm, talk of the "Negro film fad" subsided quickly in the Black press and virtually disappeared from White discourses. The "veritable deluge of Negro pictures" that a writer in the Black weekly *Pittsburgh Courier* expected never materialized.[58]

Seven years would pass before another Black-cast feature-length Hollywood musical, *The Green Pastures* (1936), followed *Hearts in Dixie* and *Hallelujah*. Some films inserted a Black musical number into an otherwise White-cast film, often with no connection to the narrative. But this practice was more of an occasional occurrence at first and wasn't established as a common convention until the mid-1930s. Meanwhile, submissive servant roles made up the bulk of Black screen presences in Hollywood feature films.[59] Instead of feature-length productions, the thriving short film industry was the prime site of African American screen performance from 1929 throughout the first half of the 1930s. So-called one- and two-reelers – that is, movies consisting of one or two film reels equaling a running time of about ten to twenty minutes – were produced abundantly by every Hollywood studio as well as by some specialized companies. This branch of the mainstream film industry brought forth dozens of Black-cast films that presented African American performers as the stars.

Looking specifically at Black dancers in early sound film, one finds a striking imbalance between male and female performers, both in terms of how they are depicted and in terms of how frequently they appear onscreen. This gender gap, as I argue, is linked to the narratives of mobility and self-determination often implied in dance. By and large, Black women were excluded from such narratives and even from the associations of competence and professionalism that are implicit in non-narrative dance performances framed as the products of a professional entertainment industry.

This is not to say that *White* female dancing stars were a dime a dozen. Tap dance onscreen – the prevalent dance form in film during the 1930s – was certainly dominated by men. But the 1930s did see a degree of emancipation of women dancers, who were no longer limited to the ornamental function of the objectified, anonymous chorus girl. From Ruby Keeler's backstage musicals and Ginger Rogers's rise to stardom in her films with Fred Astaire to tap soloist Eleanor Powell, the decade brought forth a number of White dancing women in film who were acknowledged as accomplished performers in their own right. Frequently,

---

58 "Race Films Making Hit", *Pittsburgh Courier*, September 7, 1929, quoted in Friedman, *African American Films*, 30; see also Friedman, 5–6.

59 Probably the most successful Black actor in Hollywood during the early 1930s was Lincoln Perry, better known under his stage name Stepin Fetchit. Perry's screen persona is a prime example of a Black actor adopting but also subverting the offensive Black stereotypes of the period. See Bogle, *Toms, Coons*, 38–44.

these women also portrayed professional dancers in their films, and their diegetic careers negotiated issues of self-determination, economic independence, and upward social mobility. Cinematic narratives focusing on the careers of dancing women – for instance, *Dancing Lady* (1933), *42nd Street* (1933), or *Gold Diggers of 1933* (1933) – generally ended by domesticating their protagonists through marriage, thus restoring their dependence on men. But White dancing women also frequently appeared in supporting roles, in non-narrative specialty acts, or in short films, where they had the opportunity to demonstrate their professionalism and competence unencumbered by narrative limitations, even if their appearance was still often strongly eroticized, as in the case of bandleader-singer-dancer Ina Rae Hutton, to name but one example.[60]

By contrast, Black female dancers apparently could not be depicted as simultaneously sexy, competent, *and* successful. For the most part, if Black women in film employed their dancing bodies in the service of agency and autonomy, their characters were morally condemned. In some cases, they were even doomed to death in their cinematic narratives. The best-known doomed dancing diva in early sound film is Nina Mae McKinney, who was hailed as the silver screen's first full-fledged Black star when she appeared in King Vidor's widely publicized all-Black-cast musical *Hallelujah* in 1929.[61] Her role as a Black *dancing* woman in this film offers a number of insights regarding the representation of African American women in Hollywood during this period.

Hallelujah and the Denial of Agency and Mobility to Black Women

Hallelujah has probably received more academic attention than any other Black-cast production made before the end of World War II. Over the years, scholars have offered interesting analyses of this intriguing and somewhat disturbing film's narrative dichotomies and its problematic representation of Blacks. Film historians have also examined its reception as well as Nina Mae McKinney's role, star image, and subsequent career.[62] My discussion of the film focuses on the relevance of dance to McKinney's performance as the film's female protagonist. In the role of Chick, McKinney sings and dances her way through *Hallelujah* as a fickle seductress torn between financial motivation, religious fervor, and sexual desire

---

60 On Ina Rae Hutton's film appearances, see McGee, *Some Liked It Hot*, 86–110.

61 The other early Black-cast Hollywood musical, *Hearts in Dixie*, is not commercially available and only survives in the shape of a few hard-to-find archival prints. Unfortunately, I have not been able to view a copy of the film, but from the literature on it, I gather that it centers on male characters.

62 For analyses of the film, see, for instance, Friedman, *African American Films*, 127–152; Knight, *Disintegrating the Musical*, 133–147; and Maurice, "Synchronizing Race". On the reception of *Hallelujah*, see also Bourne, *Nina Mae McKinney*, chapter 2; Cripps, *Slow Fade to Black*, 243–253; and Everett, *Returning the Gaze*, 175–177, 185, 189–192. On McKinney's career, see also Bogle, *Brown Sugar*, 56–57; and Regester, *African American Actresses*, 40–71.

– all of which are expressed in a highly physical manner through her moving body. I read McKinney's performance in light of two popular types of dancing women, two iconic figures of the era, whose images circulated in a variety of media and discourses at the time: the flapper and the chorus girl. In the case of White women, these dancing figures were endowed with a new degree of freedom in their screen incarnations. By contrast, Black women were denied the same possibilities in cinematic narratives.

The plot of *Hallelujah* ostensibly centers on cotton picker Zeke (Daniel L. Haynes), who is torn between two worlds: the unspoiled rural life, which revolves around honest work, family, and religion, versus the sinful pleasures of the city, where money, jazz, gambling, and illegitimate sex are on offer. This dichotomy is paralleled by a musical opposition of religious music versus jazz and blues, an opposition that structures most of Hollywood's Black-cast musicals.[63] At the level of character, the dichotomy is embodied by the two women vying for Zeke's affection: although Zeke's heart belongs to his virtuous adopted sister and fiancée Missy Rose (Victoria Spivey), he cannot resist the physical allure of the wanton, seductive city girl Chick (Nina Mae McKinney). Chick leads Zeke astray – twice – but eventually pays for her sins with her own life. For Zeke, by contrast, salvation is possible by returning to the rural idyll and to his family at the very end. Although this ending gives us the film's unmistakable moral message, *Hallelujah* clearly betrays a fascination with the urban, modern, and supposedly sinful lifestyle personified by Chick. While Zeke is supposedly the film's sympathetic protagonist, McKinney's Chick steals the show, as film historian Donald Bogle notes admiringly:

> Redemption and salvation are what we're supposed to think this film's about. But actually it's about mood, rhythm, energy, and sex. … Nina Mae McKinney plays talking pictures' first tragic mulatto character. … a footloose fancy-free kewpie doll of a star whose fearlessly kinetic Swanee Shuffle is a predecessor to the break dance maneuvres of the 1980s.[64]

While Bogle exaggerates a good deal here (McKinney's dancing is a far cry from 1980s break dancing), he is right in pointing to Chick's physical expressivity as a key feature of *Hallelujah*. McKinney's performance perfectly epitomizes the ambiguous status of any dancer: both objects of desire to be looked at and active

---

63 Arthur Knight has analyzed the dualistic syntax of Hollywood's Black folk musicals, with their good/evil dichotomies based on the opposition of country versus city and religious music versus jazz. With regard to *Hallelujah*, Knight points out that two of the songs representing the contrast between religious and secular music – namely, "At the End of the Road" and "Swanee Shuffle" – were in fact penned by Jewish composer Irving Berlin and "masqueraded as authentic Negro 'folk' productions" (*Disintegrating the Musical*, 141). Knight's detailed analysis of the film's music (138–144) deconstructs the superficial spirituals/jazz dichotomy and the film's supposedly authentic representation of Black "folk" culture.

64 Bogle, *Blacks in American Films*, 102–103.

performers, female dancers, in particular, simultaneously and paradoxically embody objectification and agency. McKinney's ambiguous role comes into sharper relief when considered in the context of and through comparison with popular figures of White female dancers of the period. The two prevalent types of dancing women – both on- and offscreen – were the Jazz Age flapper and the chorus girl/aspiring Broadway star. While the former preceded the transition from silent to sound film, the latter became especially popular in the numerous backstage musicals that followed the conversion to sound. Nina Mae McKinney's dancing Chick, appearing right at the junction of this transitional moment, incorporates the characteristics and connotations of both types. Yet she also deviates from them by virtue of her race.

Regarding the 1920s flapper, cultural scholar Lori Landay's essay on comedy and dance in the Jazz Age flapper film offers an instructive template for a comparative discussion.[65] Landay discusses the figure of the flapper in 1920s silent film comedy from a feminist perspective. The smoking, drinking, dancing (White) flapper girl became the symbol of the Jazz Age and the quintessence of a modern, emancipated femininity, shocking the public with her short skirts and bobbed hair and enjoying a lifestyle of leisure and consumption. Dance played an important part in the flapper's radical break with traditional role models. Landay talks about "a new kinaesthetic" emerging during the period – that is, a new aesthetic focus on corporeality and movement, expressed in popular dances of African American origin, such as the Charleston and the black bottom, but also in modern theatrical dance, which broke with the aesthetics of classical ballet.[66] The mass medium of film helped to disseminate both the flapper image and the new dance fads, and White movie stars like Joan Crawford, Louise Brooks, and Clara Bow embodied a comic version of this new type of woman in a series of flapper films. Landay accordingly links "moving pictures, moving women, and modernist acceleration" with the new social mobility of women who strove to liberate themselves from the corset of Victorian modesty and restraint.[67]

In the flapper films Landay discusses, the new image of women also manifests itself in "the power of the flapper's gaze".[68] This results from a partial reversal of the conventional model in which the active male gaze looks at the passive female object of desire. In the flapper film, the power of the active female gaze serves to express "modern female agency", and Landay notes that the female movie stars of the time were praised as much for their beautiful eyes as for their dancing

65 See Landay, "Flapper Film".
66 Landay, 224.
67 Landay, 231.
68 Landay, 226.

abilities.[69] However, this emancipation is a double-edged sword, narratively contained, since the flapper heroines employ their newfound powers and freedom mainly to find suitable husbands. In other words, the flapper's cinematic incarnations pushed the boundaries of acceptability without entirely crossing the line. As Sara Ross points out in another essay on the topic, the flapper was made acceptable through a "successful blending of sexual and social rebellion with girl-next-door innocence", and the transgressiveness of her behavior was further contained by the films' comic nature, often presenting the characters as laughable rather than truly threatening.[70]

As a Black-cast musical from the period of transition from silent to sound film, *Hallelujah* does not appear to have much in common with the silent flapper comedies that preceded it. For one thing, *Hallelujah* is not a comedy, and in some ways, Chick's character and tragic fate are more in the tradition of a femme fatale than of the comic heroines of silent cinema that Landay and Ross describe. The punishment for her provocative behavior – death – is of a different order than the gentle moral correctives to bad behavior employed in the flapper comedy. But while the setting, tone, and narrative structure of *Hallelujah* have little to do with silent-era flapper comedy, the character of Chick nevertheless inherits the flapper comedienne's traits and behavior. In fact, the Black press compared Nina Mae McKinney with Clara Bow, one of the most popular White flapper actresses of the 1920s.[71] Chick's dress, dancing, and gaze unmistakably associate her with the figure of the flapper right from the beginning.

Chick is first introduced dancing, as she entertains a predominantly male crowd in the streets of an unnamed Mississippi port town (fig. 3). Her dance is energetic and sexy but also somewhat comical. She stands broad-legged at first, stamping her feet. Emphatic arm movements underline the vigor of the performance, as do high knee-lifts and slaps. Her wiggling hips and shoulders are markedly sexy. It quickly becomes clear that she doesn't just dance for her own amusement but in order to attract the attention of men, with the performance and mise-en-scène connoting promiscuity and provocative playfulness. The short scene consists of long shots showing the dancer and her audience, close-ups of her bare legs (she wears a short dress in typical flapper fashion), and reverse shots of Zeke, who is immediately taken with her performance. Having just sold his family's cotton crop, Zeke is in the mood to party and flirtingly approaches the dancing girl. She mocks him at first but immediately changes her mind when he proudly shows

69 Landay, 226.
70 Ross, "Flapper Comedienne", 409, 414–415.
71 See Bourne, *Nina Mae McKinney*, introduction; and Regester, *African American Actresses*, 52.

Figure 3. In her first scene as Chick in *Hallelujah* (1929), Nina Mae McKinney entertains a crowd with her playful dancing. Credit: MGM/Photofest.

her his money. A close-up of her face reacting to Zeke's bundle of dollars leaves no doubt about her motivation for the ensuing seduction.

Zeke then follows Chick into a smoky bar where people are drinking and gambling, and a band is playing hot jazz. Here, Chick is revealed to be a professional performer when she sings "Swanee Shuffle" with the band and hints at a few dance moves. Through alternating long shots and close-ups of the performance, the scene emphasizes her physical presence as well as the seductive glances she throws at Zeke, thus illustrating the power of her gaze (figs. 4 & 5). When she leaves the floor to the next performers, she remains visible in the background, dancing provocatively in front of Zeke and snuggling up against him. She then takes the spotlight again, this time dancing the "Swanee Shuffle" with a team of six male waiters. While the previous performances were staged to appear improvised, this number is obviously a rehearsed routine, clearly identifying Chick as a professional dancer. While not particularly virtuosic, her dance is again highly expressive, energetic, and sexy, with hard-hitting stomps, provocative hip movements, and widely waving and flapping arms. At the end of the number, she prompts the audience to join the dancing, goes back to Zeke,

Figures 4 and 5. With her dancing and powerful gaze, Chick easily seduces naïve country boy Zeke (Daniel L. Haynes) in *Hallelujah* (1929).

and throws herself at him. As they dance to a slow bluesy tune in close embrace, with an emphasis on undulating pelvic movement, the link between dancing and sex becomes quite obvious. It also becomes clear that Chick won't give her body for free. The association with prostitution, which was implicit in Chick's first appearance, is now made quite explicit. The dialogue between the dancing couple, filmed in close shot, reveals that Chick wants to squeeze money out of the naïve country boy. She coaxes him into playing a game of dice with her partner in crime, Hot Shot. When Zeke loses all his money and finally realizes that he's been tricked, a fight ensues, in which he accidentally kills his own brother Spunk. This fall from grace, so to speak, marks the end of the film's first part. In the narrative's blatant good/evil dichotomy, Zeke's downfall is blamed on temptress Chick, whose dancing embodiment of evil combines the motifs of the city, jazz, money, and sex into a highly symbolic cluster.

Apart from the obvious aspects – the film's genre and the actors' race – the main point distinguishing Chick from the White flapper figure of 1920s comedy is her status as a professional singer and dancer. While the flapper dances both for her own pleasure and in order to attract a romantic partner, Chick is a working woman, using her body for more explicitly economic purposes. Though her complicity with Hot Shot suggests a pimp-prostitute relationship, she doesn't seem to be entirely dependent on him. As a musical performer crossing the line towards prostitution, she is thus associated with the figure of the chorus girl, who had a similarly liminal social status.

In her study of the White Ziegfeld Girl as an icon of race, sexuality, class, and consumerist desire, Linda Mizejewski traces the emergence of the chorus girl in the late nineteenth and early twentieth centuries as an emblem of a newly visible female sexuality.[72] Before Florenz Ziegfeld "glorified" the showgirls of his *Follies* revues as upper-class consumer items and as the ideal of Anglo-American White womanhood, the chorus girl was an ambivalent, liminal figure: marginalized, lower class, and associated with prostitution, on the one hand, but also a symbol of liberation, independence, and mobility, a modern, professional working woman, on the other.[73] The White chorus girl, ubiquitous onstage and onscreen, also became a common character in popular fiction, including Hollywood movies. The narratives of early backstage musicals – for instance, *On with the Show!* (1929) or *Gold Diggers of 1933* – often focused on the careers of chorus girls with their economic struggles, romantic endeavors, and ambitions to stardom, as they hoped to emerge from the anonymity of the chorus line. With the

---

72 See Mizejewski, *Ziegfeld Girl*, 16.

73 See Mizejewski, 67–68.

lowly chorus girl developing into a more respectable figure in search of the American Dream, the associations between her dance performance and prostitution became subdued (although they remained implicit in storylines concerned with women's economic dependence on their prospective husbands).

However, the elevation of the chorus girl from prostitute to respectable figure was largely limited to White women. The upgraded chorus girl's most extreme incarnation, Ziegfeld's "Glorified American Girl" as a racialized White ideal,[74] was in part a reaction to immigration from southern and eastern Europe and to the successes of Black Broadway shows. According to Mizejewski, the Ziegfeld Girl established and confirmed her respectability and Whiteness through the contrast with ethnic and racial Others. The light-skinned African American chorus girls, in particular, "embodied the Otherness against which the white Ziegfeld Girl had meaning".[75] At the same time, the "dusky belles" of Black Broadway shows and Harlem's "Black and tan" cabarets represented the thrill and threat of illicit interracial desire. Mizejewski also argues that "despite the Ziegfeld enterprise's horrified distance from vamps and flappers, the Jazz Age and the Ziegfeld Girl have become conflated as early models of sexiness and conspicuous consumption".[76]

The character of Chick in *Hallelujah* draws upon all these iconic White figures of the 1920s: the seductive vamp, the fun-loving flapper, and the dancing chorus girl as a working woman/prostitute. But as a relatively light-skinned African American woman, she additionally fuses these models with the figure of the "dusky" mulatto and the corresponding implications of illicit (White male) desire and uncontrollable (Black female) sexuality. If the White flapper and the White chorus girl were mildly transgressive figures, associated with Blackness through their sexuality and through their adaptations of African American dance styles, then the Black female dancer was the pinnacle of sexual transgression.[77]

74 Mizejewski, 2.
75 Mizejewski, 120.
76 Mizejewski, 193–194.
77 It is also worth noting that sexually aggressive and/or morally dubious White women in films of the period were often symbolically "Blackened", for instance, through associations with the musical styles of jazz and blues; see Stanfield, *Body and Soul*. A prime example of this is found in Dudley Murphy's short film *He Was Her Man* (1931), one of many film versions of the popular ballad "Frankie and Johnny". The role of Frankie is played by White *Ziegfeld Follies* star Gilda Gray, who had popularized the Black shimmy, a dance move with fast-shaking shoulders that was often considered obscene. In the film, Gray performs this sexy dance to a slow, jazzy version of "Frankie and Johnny" before shooting her lover Johnny for cheating on her. The dancing and music, coded as Black, serve to associate the characters with the lower classes, low morals, and uncontrollable sexual desire. Black domestic workers also sing as Johnny dies. On Gilda Gray and the shimmy, see Stearns and Stearns, *Jazz Dance*, 104–105. On other cinematic uses of the song "Frankie and Johnny", see Stanfield, *Body and Soul*, 44–77.

Throughout the film, Chick's sexual and moral transgressiveness is expressed physically, through her moving, dancing body. Whereas her behavior is economically motivated in the first part of the narrative, she is increasingly driven by uncontrollable sexual desire throughout the second part, after Zeke's first downfall. To atone for his wrongdoing, Zeke has become an itinerant preacher. During one of his sermons, he accidentally encounters Chick again, when she happens to be in the audience. After initially mocking him for his moralizing preaching, Chick is suddenly and surprisingly inspired by Zeke's warning words, and she decides that she wants to be baptized on the spot. While this plot twist of Chick's instant conversion is highly implausible, it serves to underline the Black woman's impulsive, fickle nature. During the river baptism that follows, a wildly gesticulating Chick expresses her newfound faith in a remarkably physical manner. Here, religious and sexual ecstasy are intermingled to a point where even Chick herself seems unable to distinguish between the two.[78] In a later church scene, Chick once again appears as the duplicitous seductress, luring preacher Zeke away from his congregation and into the woods with a dance that only appears to be motivated by religious fervor. As in the earlier bar sequence, the scene's editing emphasizes the power of her gaze as an important tool employed deliberately in the seduction process. But this time, Chick does not act out of financial greed, as she did during their first encounter. The scheming professional dancer/prostitute has transformed into a temperamental temptress, who falls prey to her own sexual desires as much as her victim Zeke does. Throwing her arms in the air and screaming, she appears as if possessed, with a crazed quality replacing the controlled playfulness of her earlier performances. Her ecstatic convulsions in the river and her dance at the church, when she lures Zeke from his righteous path for the second time, function to reveal her own volatile temper as much as to entice the weak-minded hero.

Chick's dance performances in the first part of the film are in line with the acts of "self-commodification and self-objectification" that Lori Landay attributes to the dancing flappers of 1920s silent comedy.[79] Exposing herself to the gaze of men with her eroticized dancing, Chick is not simply a victim. Instead, she manipulates her male audience consciously with her body language, glances, and words in an attempt to – literally – sell herself. The film thus posits its heroine simultaneously as a classic object of desire and as a modern woman seeking autonomy. Landay argues that the female figure's playful physicality in the flapper

---

78 For a more detailed discussion of this strange blend of religious and sexual ecstasy, see Maurice, "Synchronizing Race", 53–59.
79 Landay, "Flapper Film", 221.

films contains an emancipatory element: "the comedy in the flapper film, the kinaesthetic power of the flapper performance … exceed the processes of commodification. In other words, there is a ludic embodiment of femininity that transcends the limited subjectivity of self-commodification".[80] This also holds true for the dancer as played by Nina Mae McKinney in the first part of *Hallelujah*. But again, *Hallelujah* is not a comedy, and Chick's game with men does not end in happy marriage but in death. After leading Zeke astray for the second time, they live together for a while, but she soon starts cheating on him with her previous lover and business partner, Hot Shot. Zeke, furiously jealous, chases her and Hot Shot through the swamps and ends up shooting her. When she dies in Zeke's arms at the end, she asks for his forgiveness with the words "I never knew what I wanted". While Chick initially controls the men who fall prey to her charms, she is later increasingly controlled by her fickle nature, corroborating common stereotypes about "bad" Black women – duplicitous and calculating but also uncontrollably consumed by sexual desire. Further, Chick's death stands in the tradition of tragic mulatto narratives, in which the death of a light-skinned African American woman serves as an implicit warning against miscegenation (among other things).[81]

But *Hallelujah* does more than just morally condemn the duplicitous dancing woman. In addition, the film's ending implies that Black women could not enjoy the same emancipation as the modern White women of the time. Silent-era flapper comedies and early sound-era backstage musicals generally treated their White dancing women sympathetically, allowing them a degree of modern independence, mobility, and self-determination, of which dance was symbolic – even if this freedom was eventually contained by marriage. But narratives of Black female emancipation could hardly be expected at a time when the mere screen presence of African Americans was a somewhat sensational novelty.

It is important to emphasize the intersection of racial and gender aspects here. Ryan Jay Friedman has pointed out the paradoxical constructions of immobility in many early Black-cast Hollywood films: "In films that show African American

---

80   Landay, 223.

81   The tragic mulatto stereotype originated in nineteenth-century literature. With early examples dating from the 1840s, the tragic mulatto became a stock character of abolitionist literature, partly aiming to portray enslaved people as "more human". In the twentieth century, it became a common Black stereotype of Hollywood cinema. Well-known tragic mulattoes from classic musicals include the title character in *Carmen Jones*, played by Dorothy Dandridge, and the character of Julie in the various film versions of *Show Boat* (1929, 1936, and 1951). See, for instance, Bogle, *Toms, Coons*, 9, 147–154, 166–175; and Smith, *The Musical*, 19–24. While this mixed-race character was fairly common in studio-era films, the depiction of amorous relationships between Blacks and Whites was prohibited under the Production Code; see Association of Motion Picture Producers and Motion Picture Producers and Distributors of America, "The Production Code", 140. For a general overview of the stereotype, see, for instance, Pilgrim, "The Tragic Mulatto Myth".

protagonists moving physically (within the frame and within fictional geographic space), willing things to happen, and acting on desires but that symbolize these gestures as instances of black social stasis and immobility, a deep structural contradiction is at work".[82] *Hallelujah* has a circular narrative in the sense that the male protagonist ends up back where he started, which suggests the "simultaneous recognition and disavowal of black mobility" during a time of historically unprecedented African American mobility (in both geographic and social terms).[83] But the film's narrative denial of mobility is much more radical in the case of the female protagonist. Chick's attempt at economic and sexual self-determination is first undermined by portraying her as a hypersexual savage and then radically punished by letting her die.

And yet, that Chick is punished for her sins doesn't change the fact that she is the film's main attraction. Not only is this obvious to the audience, it is also acknowledged diegetically, as when even Zeke's "good" sweetheart, Missy Rose, shows sympathy for the hero's weakness because Chick has such pretty eyes. Chick's unbridled sexuality represents a threat to the central couple and the rural community. As is often the case in folk musicals, the threat needs to be removed so that the hero can return to the nostalgic idyll and his innocent love at the end.[84] Yet Chick is also the most attractive and interesting character, and the film devotes considerably more attention to her than to Missy Rose, who is thus deprived of her status as the central female character and depicted as rather plain and uninteresting.[85] On the surface, *Hallelujah* delivers its moral message from a backward-looking perspective that condemns modern and mundane pleasures. At the same time, the film acknowledges the appeal of modern urban life as well as betraying a fascination with its principal female character, who "symbolizes a world caught between the primitive and the modern", as Peter Stanfield notes.[86]

Ambiguous Images of Black Modernity

The same ambivalence towards Black urban modernity can be found in many other Black-cast films from the early sound era. Much like in *Hallelujah*, the dangers and immorality of contemporary city life are embodied by a dancing woman in the Vitaphone short *Yamekraw* (1930). This one-reeler also has a circular and "morally educational" narrative with respect to the male protagonist,

---

82 Friedman, *African American Films*, 19.
83 Friedman, 60–61.
84 See Altman, *The American Film Musical*, 312–315.
85 Ironically, the offscreen image of blues singer Victoria Spivey, who played Missy Rose, was anything but innocent, and she frequently performed songs with sexually suggestive lyrics.
86 Stanfield, *Body and Soul*, 93.

though it is much simpler than *Hallelujah*. *Yamekraw* deploys a seductive dancer (Louise Cook) in an urban jazz club, where she two-times the protagonist (Jimmy Mordecai), a naïve country boy unfamiliar with modern ways. The nameless protagonist, who set out to make good in the city, learns his lesson quickly. In the end, he returns to his rural home and true sweetheart, whereas the fate of the deceitful dancer remains unknown. Cook, during her few seconds of solo dancing, moves in a fashion similar to Nina Mae McKinney in *Hallelujah*: she stomps her feet, swings her legs, and energetically moves her bent arms. Narratively, she serves merely as a catalyst for the simple plot's turning point and resolution. But the short dance scene – and the entire sequence set in the city – betrays an ambiguous fascination with the pleasures of an urban jazz life, even if the story focuses on dissuading the male hero from leading such a life rather than on punishing the dancing woman who embodies it.

The tempo, rhythm, and disorienting frenzy of city life are underlined by a modernist-expressionist aesthetic with slanted camera angles, superimposition, spinning images, and fast cuts, all of which add up to what film scholar Noël Carroll has called a "moving-picture dance construction",[87] where the cinematography is as much part of the dance as the motion of the human beings in front of the camera. These stylistic elements are common in representations of Black music and dance in early sound film. At the same time, they were generally associated with modernism and considered "artistic". The resulting implications are ambiguous and contradictory. On the one hand, the highly stylized mise-en-scène and cinematography point to the artifice and technology of filmmaking, highlighting cinema's role in recreating and contributing to the experience of the modern, technologized world. At the same time, film – as the epitome of modern media – is used to convey a primitivist view of African Americans, emphasizing their supposedly natural musical talents and excessive sexuality. *Yamekraw*, subtitled a "negro rhapsody which expresses the moods and the emotional side of negro life", takes this principle to an extreme. Despite being a Vitaphone production using the eponymous synchronized sound film technology, the short has intertitles like a silent film instead of spoken dialogue, and it contains no identifiably diegetic music. The "settlement on the outskirts of Savannah, Georgia", which gives the film its title, is a markedly artificial movie set, with painted cardboard houses and the shadows of moving people projected against the "sky". In sum, the film employs an extremely antirealist, expressionist style to express the "moods" and "emotional side" of Black life. While no other film of the period goes as far as *Yamekraw* in this respect, there are nevertheless numerous scenes

---

87 Carroll, *Engaging the Moving Image*, 245.

using a similar modernist aesthetic to present a spectacle of Black bodies essentialized as primitive and exotic, in line with the general "modernist tendency to romanticize the primitive in art and to associate primitive expression with the clear expression of race".[88]

The same ambivalence towards African American culture is also evident at the level of content in most early White-produced sound films featuring Black performers. Implicitly or explicitly, the films exhibit a tension between the primitive and the modern, with one or the other dominating to varying degrees. But while the primitivist aspect appears mostly in the form of a harmless simple-mindedness in the case of Black men, it is in the representation of African American women that their supposed primitive sexuality is conflated with the sins and pleasures of modern life. If men are portrayed as sexual beings, it is as victims of these hypersexualized, seductive women. In the short scene in *Yamekraw* where the protagonist first watches the dancing woman before he dances with her, the cinematic effects – superimpositions, tilted and spinning images – also seem to indicate his mental state of being overwhelmed and bewitched by his surroundings and by the woman.

Dudley Murphy's short film *Black and Tan* (1929) also employs an expressionist aesthetic in some of the musical numbers, with high-contrast lighting, shadows, superimpositions, and kaleidoscope effects. And just like for Chick in *Hallelujah*, a tragic ending is in store for the film's female dancer, Fredi Washington. Washington appears under her own name as the dancing star of Duke Ellington's show. *Black and Tan* is among the most elaborately produced Black-cast shorts. The two-reeler has also been noted as perhaps the first White-produced film to portray a Black musician as a serious artist rather than just an entertainer, and the choice of Duke Ellington for this role is certainly no accident.[89] Fredi Washington's role in the narrative is also remarkably dignified, especially in comparison with Nina Mae McKinney's Chick in *Hallelujah*. As a professional dancer suffering from a heart condition, Washington appears as a modern, urban working woman and a loyal companion to Ellington (a romantic relationship is suggested but not emphasized). At the same time, she is framed as an eroticized object of desire in her dance scene, in which she wears a minimal costume consisting of a sequined bikini and a sort of skirt made of beaded strings (fig. 6). She comes onstage waving her arms widely, then wiggles her hips, kicks her long legs up high, and as she spins across the floor at the end, the bead skirt is lifted, swirling around. In addition, the camerawork in Washington's dance number

---

88 Maurice, "Synchronizing Race", 53.

89 See also chapter 2 in this book.

Figures 6 and 7. In her role as the ill-fated dancer in *Black and Tan* (1929), light-skinned Fredi Washington is staged as an object of desire for the (White) male gaze.

Chapter 1 Doomed Divas: Black Dancing Women in Early Sound Film

briefly gives the viewer "a kind of impossible visual access to the lower half of her body",[90] voyeuristically fetishizing her as an erotic spectacle (fig. 7). However, unlike with McKinney in *Hallelujah*, Washington's sexuality is not presented as uncontrollable but more self-consciously packaged as a spectacle for consumption by a (White) audience. The cabaret location is obviously meant to evoke Harlem's Cotton Club, where Ellington was appearing at the time of the film's production. Washington's solo dance is followed by light-skinned chorus girls in equally sexy (and very feathery) costumes, performing a routine with much butt-wiggling and leg-shimmying. With their expressionist cinematography, the film's cabaret scenes clearly cater to the White "slumming" audience's predilection for erotic, exotic Black entertainment, with all its contradictory modernist-primitivist associations and upper-class pretensions.

As with all of the era's Black-cast films produced by Whites, the ideological implications of *Black and Tan* are ambiguous. When the light-skinned dancer with the weak heart collapses onstage at the end of her performance and dies soon after, there are several possible interpretations. In the tradition of tragic mulatto narratives, Fredi's death can be read as a cautionary tale against interracial desire. Ironically, the film speaks to this same illicit desire by virtue of its own implied White audience. At the more direct level of character and narrative, the tragic ending is again a denial of agency and self-determination to the modern working woman, much like in *Hallelujah*.

The brief "vogue for Negro films" in early sound film gave African Americans unprecedented access to roles in Hollywood films, marking a significant shift not just in terms of their numbers but also by introducing individuated Black characters "with greater autonomy, agency, potential for change, and mobility"[91] than had been seen onscreen before. Despite stereotyped stories and characters, the new Black protagonists express "consumer desire and desire for upward mobility in social status".[92] While this is true of both male and female protagonists, there is a gender gap in how African American desires are fulfilled or denied fulfillment. Black female desire is rarely satisfied in early sound films. Blues singer Bessie Smith's character in *St. Louis Blues* (1929), for example, is victimized by her unfaithful and financially exploitative lover. The ill-fated women played by Nina Mae McKinney and Fredi Washington in *Hallelujah* and *Black and Tan*, respectively, are punished for their partial (economic) autonomy, which is epitomized by their status as professional dancers. As Black dancing women

---

90 Friedman offers a compelling analysis of the film's aesthetic and its possible interpretations with regard to "the traumatic subjection of African American bodies to (white) erotic gazes" (*African American Films*, 106).

91 Friedman, 69.

92 Friedman, 69.

whose livelihood depends on their profession as dancers, both Nina Mae McKinney and Fredi Washington embody an ambivalent, limited agency – highly sexualized objects of desire but also women engaged in willful self-commodification for the sake of economic independence, self-determination, and upward mobility. Given that such representations of femininity were a relatively new phenomenon even in the case of White women, it is perhaps not surprising that their African American counterparts were not destined for success in Hollywood's narratives. After 1929, individualized Black female performers all but disappeared from the silver screen. Only a handful of films presented Black women fairly prominently, and hardly any of them were dancers.

Fredi Washington would appear in very small nonmusical speaking roles in a few more Black-cast shorts – namely, *Mills Blue Rhythm Band* (1934) and *Cab Calloway's Hi-De-Ho* (1934). She soon moved on to purely dramatic roles in feature films and became one of the first African American women to play major supporting roles in Hollywood productions, most notably that of the mulatto passing for White in *Imitation of Life* (1934). Ironically, Washington's exceptional crossover success in films was based in part on her very light skin, which would have allowed her to pass for White in real life – an option she vehemently rejected. Despite her relative success, Washington saw little hope for African Americans in Hollywood. In the late 1930s, she turned her back on cinema, instead dedicating herself to her stage career in New York and to political activism in pursuit of racial equality.[93]

Nina Mae McKinney, though celebrated as the first true Black movie star, was never able to repeat the success of *Hallelujah*. In the 1930s, Hollywood studios cast her in a few minor roles and shorts, where she repeatedly appeared as a singer but not as a dancer again. Perhaps her sexualized image as a dancer in *Hallelujah* was henceforth considered too threatening? In any case, her small roles in the 1930s presented her in a less denigrating manner than *Hallelujah*, yet they were simultaneously more restrictive, denying her the freedom symbolized by dance. Meanwhile, McKinney also appeared in independently produced race films and in stage productions both at home and overseas (notably in London and Paris). When she was cast opposite Paul Robeson in the British feature film *Sanders of the River* (1935), a rather bizarre imperialist drama, the *New York Times* remarked wryly that the "talented Nina Mae McKinney is likely to impress you more as a Harlem night-club entertainer than a savage jungle beauty".[94] This

---

93 For a career overview see Regester, *African American Actresses*, 107–130.

94 Andre Sennwald, "'Sanders of the River', a British Film Based on the Edgar Wallace Stories, at the Rivoli", review of *Sanders of the River*, The Screen, *New York Times*, June 27, 1935, TimesMachine. This assessment is representative of the overall reception of McKinney's role in this film. See also Bourne, *Nina Mae McKinney*, chapter 4; and Regester, *African American Actresses*, 62.

acknowledgment of McKinney's talent and professionalism ridicules the idea of Black "savages" and indicates some awareness of the constructedness and absurdity of such stereotypes. However, even the role of a Harlem entertainer, less degrading but a stereotype nonetheless, was not easily accessible to Black women in American films. While Black men increasingly cultivated the figure of the professional musical entertainer in numerous films, the prime screen image available to Black women in 1930s Hollywood was the servile mammy type embodied by actresses like Louise Beavers and Hattie McDaniel. McKinney's attempted Hollywood comeback in the 1940s resulted mostly in minor maid roles, and by the time she died in 1967, she was virtually forgotten.

One of a Kind: Non-Narrative Dance Performances by Black Women

The portrayal of Black dancing women as sexy seductresses – but ultimately victims – severely limited the narrative agency of Black female characters. The non-narrative specialty act offered one possible alternative to these more or less moralistic narratives, and in 1929, it briefly seemed as if the sound film era might bring comparable numbers of male and female African American performers to the screen. In addition to the morally suspect dancing women discussed above, a handful of films presented women in song and dance numbers that were not narrativized but framed as "only" entertainment and performed for diegetic audiences.

Hallelujah, for instance, also included a short partner dance in the bar scene early in the film. The number alternates bits of basic tap and close-embrace dancing, with hips expressively swaying from side to side. However, at barely thirty seconds, this dance by uncredited performers serves as atmospheric background more than as a featured number. The elaborate, mostly White-cast backstage musical *On with the Show!* featured the Black tap dance team the Four Covans dancing in two production numbers (in addition to two solo numbers by Black singer Ethel Waters). While the scenery and costumes here are anything but progressive, with their evocation of the Old South, two aspects of these dance scenes are nevertheless noteworthy. One, the male and female members of the four-person tap team wear identical costumes, and two, the first of the two numbers features their versatile tap dancing in front of a large *White* chorus. In the first scene, the dancers wear striped overalls and straw hats; in the second, they are dressed as male waiters in uniforms. As they execute synchronized steps in a highly controlled manner (much like the all-male "class acts" that were becoming prominent onstage and increasingly onscreen), their gender doesn't seem to matter. Both the gender equality within the dance group and the fact of a Black specialty act outshining the simultaneously present White performers are relatively unusual, and neither would be repeated very often in Hollywood productions of the 1930s.[95]

Hereafter, with the exception of chorus girls, Black dancing women virtually disappeared again from mainstream film production. Given the general popularity of Black musical entertainment, it is somewhat surprising that even roles for competent musical performers were a rarity after 1929. While female singers and anonymous chorus girls nevertheless appeared with some regularity, featured dancers were the rarest of all, and they can virtually be counted on one hand.

The Paramount short *A Bundle of Blues* (1933) is one such rare instance of a film showcasing Black female dancers, and they are even mentioned by name in the opening credits: Cotton Club dancers Bessie Dudley and Florence Hill perform an up-tempo erotic dance to Duke Ellington's rendition of "Bugle Call Rag". While Ellington appears as his usual dignified self, the scantily clad, sexualized, light-skinned female dancers again represent the supposedly primitive aspect of modern Black entertainment in this one-reel revue, which has no plot. The women's dance includes shimmies, high kicks, thrusts of the pelvis and chest, and Florence Hill slowly gliding down into a split. Although they do some tap time steps and other obviously rhythmic footwork, there are no audible sounds from their steps. In their skimpy costumes, the emphasis is clearly on the women's eroticism rather than on the creativity and virtuosity generally associated with tap dancing (fig. 8).

Interestingly, these dancing women in *A Bundle of Blues* occasioned the only scathingly racist remark about a Black-cast short film that I have found in a trade magazine: "This would be a good novelty musical reel had the producer not put the She Negroes into it for a vulgar dance, which ruins it for the South".[96] Apparently, the exhibitor contributing this entry to the *Motion Picture Herald*'s recommendations would not have found the presence of African American performers objectionable per se – it is only the "vulgar" sexy dancing women who are demonized, whereas the other musical performers seem to be considered harmless. Despite the concern about Southern business as a seemingly rational reason not to book the film, the remark betrays the author's own racism. It is worth noting, however, that exhibitors' reports in various other editions of the

---

95 The Four Covans were also among the few Black performers to become prominent in White vaudeville in the 1920s. In the 1930s, the group's lead dancer, Willie Covan, moved to Hollywood, where he worked as a choreographer and instructor for many White stars, including Shirley Temple and Eleanor Powell. See Frank, *Tap!*, 23–29.

96 Exhibitor's report on *A Bundle of Blues*, *Motion Picture Herald*, June 9, 1934, 73, Media History Digital Library.

Chapter 1 Doomed Divas: Black Dancing Women in Early Sound Film

Figure 8. Bessie Dudley and Florence Hill as sexy jungle dancers in *A Bundle of Blues* (1933).

Herald recommend the film simply as a fine specimen of a musical one-reeler, which should appeal to "general patronage".⁹⁷

One remarkable deviation from the general pattern of representing Black female dancers appears in the Vitaphone short *That's the Spirit* (1933) by Roy Mack, the most prolific White director of Black-cast music shorts. A central attraction in this virtually plotless one-reeler is the solo number by singer and tap dancer Cora LaRedd, one of the very few Black female tap soloists to appear in a studio-era Hollywood production. Tap historian Constance Valis Hill writes of LaRedd: "The rhythmic brilliance, athleticism, and open sexuality of LaRedd's dancing made her not only the most noted female soloist at the Cotton Club in the 1920s and 1930s, but also the most extraordinary jazz tap dancer in those decades".⁹⁸ In addition to being regularly featured as a soloist at the Cotton Club, LaRedd

---

97 See, for instance, exhibitor's report on *A Bundle of Blues*, *Motion Picture Herald*, January 27, 1934, 62, Media History Digital Library.
98 Hill, *Tap Dancing America*, 92–93.

47

became a notable presence on Broadway, appearing in both Black-cast and racially mixed musicals. Yet *That's the Spirit* seems to be her only fiction film credit.[99] In an interview with author Hill, veteran tap dancer Bunny Briggs, who remembered LaRedd, pointed out that "she was really black",[100] thus giving one possible indication as to why she didn't appear in films more often: when it came to African American women, Hollywood has always preferred light-skinned beauties over those who were "really" Black. Briggs also reminds us of the general gender bias in the male-dominated world of tap dancing:

> But of course, the men wouldn't talk about her much because she was a woman. They were talking, like the women were trying to take over the business. Yeah. Because the chorus girls used to watch the men dance, so they stopped doing anything in front of them, the men, because they would be doing their act the next day – and they were good![101]

In *That's the Spirit*, LaRedd is first seen singing in a close-up that indeed reveals her to be really Black: her round face, wide nose, and untamed curly hair signify a Blackness that extends beyond literal skin color (fig. 9). The following full shot reveals her exceptionally muscular legs, liberally displayed by the tight-fitting shorts she wears (fig. 10). Simultaneously strong, athletic, and sexy, her appearance is certainly at odds with dominant beauty standards and not easily assimilated with those fantasies of forbidden interracial desire represented by light-skinned divas, such as Fredi Washington. Cora LaRedd's "open sexuality" could hardly be further removed from that of the glamorously seductive "dusky belles" known from African American chorus lines. Linda Mizejewski observes that the "light-skinned black women in the African American Broadway chorus suggest the predominance of White standards of beauty for women, as evidenced by the growing cosmetics industry, which pitched bleaching creams for whiter skin to white and black women alike".[102] Nevertheless, while Harlem nightclubs and Black Broadway favored light-skinned women who were judged by prevailing White standards of beauty, exceptionally skilled women would sometimes be given exceptional opportunities in contexts of live performance. However, this was much less the case in the film industry. Cora LaRedd's hard-hitting rhythm tap, performed to up-tempo hot jazz by Noble Sissle's band, is a one-of-a-kind performance as far as studio-era Hollywood cinema goes. Though her dance is anything but restrained, the performance is clearly presented as professional and

---

99   According to some sources, LaRedd was also featured in *Broadway Highlights No. 4* (1935), in which she is seen performing at the Cotton Club. This short was part of the Paramount Headliner series, which showcased entertainers headlining on Broadway. See Frank, *Tap!*, 303; and Meeker, *Jazz on the Screen*, 282. Unfortunately, I have not been able to locate a surviving copy of this film.

100 Bunny Briggs, quoted in Hill, *Tap Dancing America*, 93.

101 Bunny Briggs, quoted in Hill, *Tap Dancing America*, 109.

102 Mizejewski, *Ziegfeld Girl*, 123.

Chapter 1 Doomed Divas: Black Dancing Women in Early Sound Film

Figures 9 and 10. An exceptional performance by the "really Black" tap dancer Cora LaRedd in *That's the Spirit* (1933).

disciplined. She moves across the whole floor, then stays in place again to execute rhythmically intricate steps with clear force and precision, using her arms for expression and balance. While the performance is doubtless energetic and expressive, as well as sexy, the sexiness is of a different order than that of Nina Mae McKinney's wanton Chick or the lascivious exoticism of the objectified female dancers in *Black and Tan* or *A Bundle of Blues*. In contrast to these women, who are more objectified and presented as somewhat animalistic, Cora LaRedd appears fully in control and cool throughout. Accordingly, there is no negative verdict in the press similar to the one quoted above with regard to *A Bundle of Blues*. The trade paper *Film Daily* praises *That's the Spirit* in general and Cora LaRedd's performance in particular: "This colored gal Cora can certainly step. She is positively sensational. … Red hot rhythms done with plenty of class and pep".[103]

As White dancing women negotiated social and sexual boundaries in cinematic narratives, a growing number of female dancers made names for themselves as competent performers. This emergence of female dancing stars is also an acknowledgment of their individuality, in contrast to the – coexistent – anonymous uniformity of the chorus line, where women appear as dehumanized and abstracted images, as mass-produced consumer goods.[104] In contexts of live performance, Black female performers similarly carved out new spaces of public visibility, staging struggles for more agency, independence, and recognition of individuality. The chorus girls and headlining performers of the successful Black Broadway shows and Harlem cabarets became important emblems of a new Black female mobility and modernity, as historian Kristin McGee points out:

> Chorus girls' mediations of Jazz Age cultural, sexual, and racial prescriptions redefined postmigration urban modernity through their financial success, independence, transnational mobility, and the up-tempo physicality of their urban lifestyles and theatrical performances. …
>
> During the Jazz Age, chorus girls' increased financial security, urban modernity, and transnational mobility symbolized increased self-reliance, cultural freedom, and creativity.[105]

Constance Valis Hill's comprehensive history of tap dancing also shows the degree to which skilled Black women were actually very much a part of the world of tap dancing – despite the fact that tap was generally considered "a man's world". At Harlem's famous Apollo Theater, for instance, there were "a number of black female rhythm-tap teams and soloists. … And they played the Apollo to great

---

103 "Hot Musical", review of *That's the Spirit*, *Film Daily*, June 10, 1933, 4, Media History Digital Library.

104 According to Kristin A. McGee, a similar collaborative uniformity was also common in cinematic representations of female musicians, so that "women's individual voices were musically disavowed" (*Some Liked It Hot*, 84).

105 McGee, *Some Liked It Hot*, 57–58.

acclaim".[106] As Hill gives numerous examples of the careers and skills of female dancers during the heyday of tap, it becomes clear that Broadway, Harlem, and the various vaudeville circuits offered ample performance opportunities to capable women dancers, even if they did not have status equal to men. But the Hollywood industry was less amenable to these new representations of self-reliant, creative women than the stage, and throughout the 1930s, Black women dancers remained virtually absent from mainstream film production.[107] The few exceptions to this rule are all the more remarkable, and the fact that no Black female dancer from Hollywood's studio era managed to sustain a film career is indicative of the film industry's intersecting racial and gender biases. Meanwhile, Black male dancers were at the forefront of changing African American screen representation, as I suggest in the next chapter.

---

106 Hill, *Tap Dancing America*, 104–105.

107 It is worth noting that Josephine Baker, the most provocative and complex of all Black female dancers, played lead roles in several French films but never appeared in an American movie. See, for instance, Kalinak, "Disciplining Josephine Baker".

CHAPTER 2 Kids and Class Acts: Male Dancers in Black-Cast Music Shorts

As the brief Black film fad of 1929 subsided and Black dancing women mostly disappeared again from Hollywood films, African American men sustained a steadier screen presence in musical short films up until the mid-1930s. Along with prominent bandleaders, male dancers, especially tap dancers, contributed to significant shifts in Black cinematic images, both in number and in kind. Adrienne L. McLean, a prominent scholar of the Hollywood musical, has examined the changing views of dance as a skill during the 1930s. She observes that early in the decade, dancing was generally considered "a patchwork set of skills, acquired by whatever means and however quickly, not … an avocation that involved lengthy training, or even unusual or virtuosic talent".[108] Over the course of the decade, however, technical requirements for dancers would increase, as "idiosyncrasy and individuality [were] replaced by versatility".[109] There was a shift toward seeing dance as a specialized skill rather than just a bag of tricks, and "the dancer's body as an instrument of choreographic art, not only of entertainment".[110] According to McLean, the films of Fred Astaire and Ginger Rogers had a crucial influence on this change of attitude, and the author argues that the "effect of motion pictures on the popularity and meaning of dance in American culture during the 1930s is almost impossible to overestimate".[111] In conclusion, McLean sums up the transformations in the film musical that occurred in the 1930s as follows:

> of dance from something idiosyncratic, energetic, but at times a bit amateurish to a codified assortment of difficult techniques that were expensive and time-consuming to acquire and even more expensive and time-consuming to maintain; of jazz and swing from black dance (and music) forms to white; of dance as the province of powerful,

---

108 McLean, "Flirting with Terpsichore", 70.
109 McLean, 78.
110 McLean, 77.
111 McLean, 77.

competent and joyous women to dance as an expression of heterosexual romance, with male performers and choreographers leading in every sense of the term.[112]

McLean also points out the denial of the non-White origins of jazz dance in films like *King of Jazz* (1930) as well as in contemporaneous writings about dance. Yet her discussion of Black dancers doesn't go beyond this general observation. While she briefly refers to the enormous popularity of the tap-dancing child star Shirley Temple, for instance, there is no mention of Black tap dancer Bill "Bojangles" Robinson, who played major supporting roles in no less than four of Temple's feature films and often danced with her onscreen.[113] According to Black film historian Donald Bogle, Robinson was at least partly responsible for little Shirley's tap dance training, teaching her many of his routines.[114] Of course, Hollywood's dancing superstars of the 1930s and beyond were all White, and the denial of the Black origins of tap dance – the era's most popular performative dance style – was part and parcel of these White dancers' rise to stardom. That many White movie stars were influenced and sometimes directly taught by Black dancers was not a publicly acknowledged fact, and White stardom often came at the expense of rendering Black contributions invisible. Nevertheless, cinematic images of Black dancers were numerous, and we should not underestimate the effect that *they* had on "the popularity and meaning of dance". While Black forms of jazz and swing did become White in the Hollywood musical, I would suggest that the appearances of Black dancers *themselves* were also part of the process by which dance became increasingly seen as a "specialized skill".

Black-cast short films and specialty numbers in feature films certainly segregated and ghettoized African American performance as "only" entertainment. Yet most Black dance acts were anything but amateurish, merging the idiosyncratic and energetic with sophistication and a high level of technical skill and demonstrating extraordinary proficiency. Even if they never escaped the entertainment label, the film appearances of Black male tap dancers suggest that they also contributed something to the more general reevaluation of dance during the 1930s. In any case, there is no doubt that Black male dancers' often elegant appearance, professional comportment, and virtuosic dancing gave a significant boost to more dignified screen images of African Americans.

By the standards of the time, Bill Robinson achieved considerable star power in his feature films with Shirley Temple, although it came at the price of an "Uncle Tom" image. Around the same time, the much younger Nicholas Brothers began

---

112 McLean, 78–79.

113 The four films are *The Littlest Rebel* (1935), *The Little Colonel* (1935), *Rebecca of Sunnybrook Farm* (1938), and *Just Around the Corner* (1938).

114 See Bogle, *Bright Boulevards*, 158, 160.

leaving such submissive stereotypes behind, increasingly transcending the limitations of the period with the outstanding artistry of their rhythm tap dancing. Eventually moving on from musical shorts to feature films, they would take African American film fame to unprecedented heights in the early 1940s, showcasing unmatched versatility and virtuosity in their specialty numbers. A decade earlier, however, the boundaries of Black screen representation were primarily negotiated in the musical short film, and Black dancing men and boys were instrumental in this process.

While feature films were much more prestigious than shorts, short films were generally popular and profitable. All the major Hollywood studios had their own autonomous units producing "short subjects", as they were also called, at a high speed and in large numbers. Jazz historian Bernd Hoffmann estimates that during the 1930s, the American film industry produced about one thousand short films for exhibition in cinemas per year, with musical shorts accounting for about 25 percent of the total output.[115] In light of such numbers, a few dozen Black-cast musical shorts might seem a negligible quantity. Yet they are significant for several reasons. As the all-Black feature-length musical failed to establish itself as a durable genre, it was the Black-cast short films that afforded Blacks increased performance opportunities in the early 1930s, keeping the cinematic "Harlemania" of 1929 alive until the Black specialty act became a standard ingredient in feature films around the middle of the decade. Musical shorts provided a comparatively privileged forum for African Americans not only in number but also in kind. They allowed for performances that were at least partly at odds with the usually degrading servant roles seen in many feature-length Hollywood productions. The shorts showcased African Americans in the framework of an all-Black world, where they were the stars of the show rather than a supplementary, segregated attraction within an otherwise White narrative.

This is not to claim any sort of strict binary division between feature films and shorts in terms of the themes, aesthetics, and ideologies of Black screen images. Overall, the commonalities are greater than the differences. Like the early Black feature musicals, many Black-cast short films display a tension between old and new images, simultaneously referencing nostalgic clichés of Black rural life and the promises of the new urban lifestyle, which emerged as a result of the Great Migration. Most Hollywood representations show jazz culture "simultaneously as a product of an overcultivated metropolitan sensibility and the natural primitive instinctual urge of a rural premodern sensibility", as Peter Stanfield ob-

---

115 See Hoffmann, "Alltag im Jazz-Himmel", 103. Hoffmann's estimates are largely based on the filmographies in Bradley, *Hollywood Sound Shorts*, and Liebman, *Vitaphone Films*.

serves.[116] In other words, a somewhat contradictory urban primitivism pervades many early films with Black performers, conveying ambiguous images of Black urban life and entertainment as simultaneously titillating and threatening. Black-cast shorts like *Yamekraw* (1930) and *Ol' King Cotton* (1930), for instance, contain all the stereotypes of the idyllic Deep South while also evidencing their creators' fascination with city life. Both films tell the story of a naïve country boy leaving his Southern home for the promises of the Northern city, only to return at the end. Others, such as *Deep South* with Clarence Muse (1930), stay entirely within a romanticized, supposedly timeless rural South, presenting stereotypes of contented Black cotton-pickers that were perceived as outdated even at the time. By contrast, *A Rhapsody in Black and Blue* (1932), for example, tends more toward the primitivist jungle stereotypes of Harlem's urban entertainment catering to White audiences. Here, trumpet player Louis Armstrong performs in a leopard skin costume in a bizarre dream sequence, which makes it difficult to focus on the redeeming quality of the swinging music. Even though negative representations of Black male performers more commonly involved simpleminded rural types, this example shows that men were not entirely immune to the sometimes grotesque exoticism used predominantly for depicting sexy Black women. In sum, short films often contain Hollywood's racial ideologies in condensed and thus especially explicit form, operating with the same stereotypes as many feature-length productions. And, of course, the fundamentally problematic and ambiguous status of Black-cast but White-produced films also pertains to these shorts. It would thus be misleading to consider Black-cast shorts as inherently progressive simply because they showcase African Americans relatively prominently.

Nevertheless, the way in which Hollywood's early sound shorts treated African Americans as "stars" is significant. These films gave exposure to musicians, singers, and dancers, many of whom were already known from other contexts, whether Broadway stages, Harlem nightclubs, or radio. While most of these – often male – Black screen performers were not movie stars in the conventional sense, Black-cast shorts gave them a level of star treatment that was unheard of in mainstream feature films during the early 1930s. Additionally and crucially, the shorts often placed African Americans in contexts of cultural refinement, presenting them as skilled professional performers rather than primitive savages or dimwitted coons. Stereotypical notions of excessive and primitive Black energy certainly remain present. And while many Black-cast shorts have hardly any narrative interest to speak of, the little bits of perfunctory plot and dialogue are often filled with cringeworthy clichés and exaggerated dialect that serve to

116 Stanfield, *Body and Soul*, 95.

undermine the performers' displays of competence. At the same time, cinematography, elegant scenery and costumes, and narratives of class mobility often function to underline the sophistication demonstrated in performances of disciplined professionalism and technical virtuosity.

Frequently, representations of sophistication at the level of content are matched at the visual level, and many early Black-cast shorts are comparatively sophisticated in aesthetic terms. Bernd Hoffmann observes an evolution in the visual aesthetics of musical shorts. In general, early sound shorts often present their musical acts in a few static shots, lending the films a quasi-documentary quality, as if they simply recorded a live performance in a theater or nightclub. In these cases, dancers and some physically expressive musicians are employed to compensate for the static effect of a stationary camera centering on a stage performance. In the course of the 1930s, however, there is a development toward a more dynamic cinematic style, with faster-paced editing and more variety in shot sizes and angles – stylistic devices that prefigure the aesthetics of later music video.[117] The Black-cast shorts anticipate this trend, as even early examples often employ a more experimental visual style and a larger variety of formal means and settings than the average (White-cast) music short. As described in chapter 1, the expressionistic cinematic style commonly used in jazz-themed film scenes of the early sound years simultaneously points to the artifice of filmmaking and serves to express the "wild" rhythms of Black music and dance and the "primitive" nature of African Americans. There is, however, no one formula that applies to all Black-cast shorts. In fact, these films are remarkable for their variety, both in terms of the performance idioms they showcase and with regard to their visual styles and narrative strategies. Frequently, experimental cinematography is combined with elegant modernistic sets that connote contemporary urban sophistication and material abundance. In other cases, relatively simple visuals favor a focus on the performances themselves, which are in turn often coded as professional and respectable, especially when the performers are men. While Black women were generally sexualized and often victimized, for Black male dancers the visuals and settings of Black-cast shorts provided an arena for the emergence of so-called class acts onscreen.

The term "class act", which became common in the 1920s, was used to describe teams of male tap dancers whose elegant and sophisticated performance style expressed African Americans' "drive toward equality and respectability",[118] as Marshall and Jean Stearns put it:

---

117 See Hoffmann, "Alltag im Jazz-Himmel", 106; and Hoffmann, "'Und der Duke weinte'", 123–124.
118 Stearns and Stearns, *Jazz Dance*, 285.

The class acts came to constitute the cream of tap dancing. Unlike flash or acrobatic, Russian or legomania, comedy or Buck dancing – although elements from all these styles were sometimes incorporated – the class act added a specific quality: grace and elegance.

The true class act consists of two or more dancers – very often three – who perform *precision* dancing (among other things), that is, they execute identical steps together.[119]

In other words, class acts are prime manifestations of the aesthetic of the cool, which dancer-scholar Brenda Dixon Gottschild calls an "all-embracing" characteristic of African American dance that "combines composure with vitality" and "shows an attitude of carelessness cultivated with a calculated aesthetic clarity".[120] Or, as Jacqui Malone puts it, the aesthetic of the cool "functions to help create an appearance of control and idiomatic effortlessness".[121] The execution of rhythmically complex identical steps in the tap class act demonstrates a high level of control, evidencing disciplined and methodical training. Class acts thus belie the notion that Blacks are simply expressing their feelings spontaneously and uncontrollably with their innately rhythmic bodies. At the same time, the cool of African American dance is different from the "aloofness" and "detachment" of traditional European aesthetics, instead expressing vitality by focusing on elements like "asymmetricality (that plays with falling off center), looseness (implying flexibility and vitality), and indirectness of approach".[122] In live performance, class acts, which "consciously refuted the stereotype of the shiftless comedian", flourished from the late 1920s to the late 1940s.[123] They also began appearing onscreen as part of the "Black film fad" in the wake of the conversion to synchronized sound film, and with the rise of swing in the 1930s, tap class acts became an integral part of big band performances both on- and offscreen.

One of the first cinematic incarnations of the African American class act is the tap duo in the early Vitaphone short *Harlem-Mania* (1929). In this plotless one-reeler, dancers Stanley Brown and Alphonse Kennedy appear as part of the Norman Thomas Quintette, a vaudeville team with vocals, drums, and piano (fig. 11). The film's title obviously hints at the era's craze for Black entertainment, using "Harlem" as a selling point, even though the usual exotic, erotic Harlem stereotypes are missing here. Instead, the musicians and dancers are presented in an unusually sumptuous drawing room setting, and they all wear tuxedos. Although the singer and dancers briefly bow to the camera after the opening vocals, which suggests a context of live performance, the implied audience

---

119 Stearns and Stearns, 291 (italics in the original).
120 Gottschild, *Digging the Africanist Presence*, 16.
121 Malone, *Steppin' on the Blues*, 34.
122 Gottschild, *Digging the Africanist Presence*, 17.
123 Stearns and Stearns, *Jazz Dance*, 300. For an overview of the history of class acts, see 285–311.

Chapter 2 Kids and Class Acts: Male Dancers in Black-Cast Music Shorts

Figure 11. One of the first cinematic class acts: elegant tap dancers Stanley Brown and Alphonse Kennedy in *Harlem-Mania* (1929).

remains invisible and inaudible. The quasi-documentary effect of a filmed stage performance is thus undermined by the complete absence of an audience, visually as well as aurally. While this kind of static and rather uncinematic presentation of musical performance was common in early sound shorts, it is rather unusual for Black-cast films, which tended to be more elaborately staged and filmed.[124] But in this early example (the film was copyrighted in July 1929), the expressionist visuals that would soon become commonplace for illustrating the "moods and rhythm" of Black performance and Harlem nightlife were not yet conventionalized. Instead, the mise-en-scène and the self-effacing cinematography in *Harlem-Mania*, with its largely static camera, evoke a formal ambience that borders on the stiff.

Tap dancers Brown and Kennedy perform a soft shoe routine accompanied by drums and piano, executing synchronized steps in an elegant, controlled manner. The term "soft shoe" refers to tap dancing without special tap shoes – that is, without wood or metal plates on the soles – resulting in a softer, quieter sound of the rhythms. According to the Stearnses, the "standard class act generally

---

[124] It is worth noting that the film's director, Murray Roth, was also responsible for the Black-cast short *Yamekraw*, which has a very different, much more experimental aesthetic (see also chapter 1 in this book).

included a soft-shoe in slow tempo with light taps".[125] Onscreen, however, this element was not featured nearly as often as the hard-hitting, up-tempo rhythm tap often seen in connection with big band performances in the 1930s. In *Harlem-Mania*, the first slow part of the soft shoe dance is followed by a faster segment, which contains more expressive whole-body motion and some jumps, though the dancers still maintain an air of cool discipline. Their composure stands in stark contrast to drummer Freddy Crump, who laughs and shouts out loud, throws his drumsticks in the air, jumps around, and tumbles on the floor. During the film's only moments that explicitly draw attention to its cinematography, Crump is also briefly shown from above, filmed at a diagonal angle. At first, screen time is evenly divided between the dancers and Crump; but when Brown and Kennedy return towards the film's end (after a virtuosic piano solo), the focus shifts to the increasingly boisterous drummer, whereas the dancers are reduced to a background function. While showcasing remarkable dexterity, drummer Crump's performance feeds into stereotypes of Blacks as buffoonish entertainers as well as attesting to the legacy of vaudeville, with its "bag of tricks" formula. His circus-like antics provide a curious counterpoint not just to the dancers' tasteful performance style but also to the upper-class connotations of dress and setting. While the somewhat stiff atmosphere in *Harlem-Mania* is strangely dissonant with Crump's shenanigans, the fancy locale offers a suitable backdrop for the elegant tap class act of Brown and Kennedy, whose aesthetic of the cool undeniably combines composure with vitality. With their graceful yet lively performance, they quite literally "animate" the film's static, rather clumsy presentation without diminishing the overall impression of sophistication.

Compare, for contrast, the three young boys in the first dance scene from *Hallelujah* (1929), the feature-length all-Black-cast musical that seemed to herald a new trend in Hollywood. Within the film's narrative, the scene provides the innocent counterpart to female protagonist Chick's dancing, which is coded as both economically motivated and erotically sinful. The scene is set in the country, and it precedes cotton picker Zeke's trip to town, where he will meet Chick for the first time. After the day's work is done, Zeke's three younger brothers entertain the whole family with some spontaneous tap dancing to the sounds of neighbor Henry's banjo and the singing of other family members. In their tattered clothes, the boys dance around the outdoor wooden table, on stairs, chairs, the back of a cart, and eventually on top of the table, interrupting high-speed repetitive tap steps with some comic vernacular moves like the "itch", which consists of squirming body movement with arm and hand gestures suggesting frantic scratch-

---

125 Stearns and Stearns, *Jazz Dance*, 285.

ing. There is no ulterior motive for the music and dancing here, financial or otherwise. In fact, there is no narrative motivation of any kind. The kids dance without specific occasion, for the pure joy of it and in order to delight their loved ones. In the scene's timeless pastoral idyll setting, the "spontaneous" music and dancing are naturalized as an integral part of Black Southern country life. Like the work songs in the field at the film's beginning, this after-work scene suggests the contentment of these simple country folk, who are happy despite a life of poverty and hard work. In addition to buttressing common clichés about innate Black musicality, the scene exemplifies the American folk musical's more general myth of musical entertainment as a natural part of everyday life.[126] That it is also entertainment for the film's largely White audience is not acknowledged within the film itself, although this factor certainly resonates with the extradiegetic context of the fad for Black-cast films in the early sound film era. But diegetically, the dance is connoted as innocent, spontaneous, natural, and purposeless. In contrast to this harmless dancing by children, the professional and economically motivated dancing of the Black woman, Chick, is coded as transgressive and sinful. Both the "good" and the "bad", however, are ultimately framed as rooted in African American nature, thus representing the two sides of the same coin – the film's essentialist-primitivist depiction of Blacks as inherently musical people, who express their feelings as well as their very nature through music and dancing.

In a sense, the innocent, spontaneous country boys in *Hallelujah*, on the one hand, and the disciplined, cultured urban professionals in *Harlem-Mania*, on the other, represent the two prototypes for Black male dance acts in early Hollywood sound film. When Black-cast shorts increasingly framed African American performance as professional rather than natural in the early 1930s, young dancing boys remained a fairly common screen presence – albeit not so much as an antithesis to the adult class acts but rather as their antecedents. Instead of innocuous children with an innate dancing ability, even the youngest boys are presented as performers who deliberately engage in a cultural practice, and the films – sometimes implicitly, sometimes explicitly – frame them as future professionals. In addition, elegant settings and narratives of upward social mobility and professional achievement often help to elevate the status of sophisticated, accomplished musicians and dancers – at least within the utopian all-Black worlds of the Black-cast shorts.

---

126 See Altman, *The American Film Musical*, 272–327; and Dyer, *Only Entertainment*, 30–31.

Fantasies of Achievement and Abundance

The early Black-cast musical shorts were often directed and produced by White filmmakers who repeatedly worked with African American performers, among them Dudley Murphy, Joseph Henabery, and Fred Waller. A crucial figure for Black-cast shorts was Roy Mack, an enormously prolific director of short films with several hundred titles to his credit, who was responsible for a substantial proportion of the Black-cast shorts produced by Warner Bros. under the popular Vitaphone label in the early 1930s. Mack's films gave visibility to many African American performers otherwise rarely – or never – seen onscreen, and they contain some of the most remarkable Black dance performances captured on film.[127] While showcasing a wide variety of performance idioms in diverse settings, virtually all Black-cast shorts in one way or another offer fantasies of African American achievement and often of material abundance. Some of them feature young dancing boys prominently.

In *Rufus Jones for President* (1933), seven-year-old Sammy Davis Jr. plays the eponymous protagonist, who becomes president in a dream sequence. While this dream part takes up most of the two-reeler (at twenty-one minutes, it is among the longest of the Black-cast musical shorts), it is significant that the frame story shows Rufus and his "mammy", played by Ethel Waters, in an unspecified locale that evokes associations of rural poverty. The dream sequence remains highly ambiguous, with numerous cringeworthy jokes delivered in exaggerated dialect, and several of the musical performances employ old-fashioned minstrel show clichés that are anything but progressive. But the eclectic mix of numbers also includes the modern world of Harlem's urban entertainment, represented by chorus girls doing the Charleston and two couples briefly dancing the Lindy hop, the groundbreaking partner dance emerging from Harlem's increasingly popular Savoy Ballroom. The side-by-side of diverse performance idioms and contradictory racial imagery is fairly typical of Black-cast shorts. Despite the film's numerous racist caricatures, some of the musical performances momentarily surpass these narrative limitations, above all Ethel Waters's song "Underneath a Harlem Moon", in which she comments critically on racial stereotypes and celebrates Black migration and urban life. Her mammy character from the frame story has metamorphosed into an elegantly attired diva, who nominates herself "to the office of Presidentess". In stark contrast to her accommodationist stance in the first scene, where she cautioned little Rufus to "stay on your own side of

---

127 Roy Mack's short *That's the Spirit* (1933), for example, contains what is possibly the only film footage of tap dancer Cora LaRedd (see also chapter 1 in this book).

Chapter 2 Kids and Class Acts: Male Dancers in Black-Cast Music Shorts

the fence", Waters now embodies a degree of Black female autonomy as well as geographic and social mobility that is rarely seen in mainstream films.[128]

Young Sammy Davis's musical numbers offer a less explicit but nevertheless telling illustration of an upward career trajectory. When newly elected Rufus is asked to address his constituency, he does so quite incoherently by singing "I'll Be Glad When You're Dead, You Rascal You" (fig. 12). He then performs a brief and relatively simple tap dance while the crowd is bouncing around in the background. Pulling funny faces and holding a piece of fried chicken in his hand, young Davis remains firmly contained by demeaning clichés in this first rather nonsensical number. But later, he is called on to prove his qualification for the presidency, which he does by performing in front of the "senate", a rather minstrel-like assortment of Black stereotypes. In tailcoat and a top hat twice the size of his head, Davis dances for over a minute in a nearly unedited sequence, mostly filmed in full shot (fig. 13). Of course, the notion of a child president belittles Black political ambition. Nevertheless, there is an element of empowerment here: after all, the dance is Rufus's response to the senate's demands that he "do something" as president rather than just sitting around doing nothing. His dance is not a spontaneous expression of emotion but a willful act, and the scene suggests that it is through deliberate demonstrations of competence that African Americans are able to "do something" – that is, achieve some measure of success and bring about change. At its most self-reflexive, then, the film frames music and dance as the only weapons available to African Americans in their struggle for social, economic, and political advancement (in the White-dominated world, which is always implied even when it remains absent from the narrative). Black people are employing their disciplined, rhythmically skilled bodies as their "only cultural capital" and as "canvases of representation", in the words of Stuart Hall,[129] and this is what enables them to indirectly work towards political representation. Although becoming president is only a dream, this unique Vitaphone short presents a fantasy of Black achievement by explicitly addressing issues of social mobility, urbanization, and modernization. As Alan Jay Friedman notes, the "film's brief return to its original setting and discourse does little to offset its extensive endorsement of African American migration and self-assertion".[130]

Like *Rufus Jones*, many – though by no means all – Black-cast shorts frame their musical numbers as fantasy/dream sequences. At one level, this is simply a conventional cinematic device providing a feeble excuse for musical performance

---

128 For a more detailed reading of the film, especially of Ethel Waters's performance and the theme of migration, see Friedman, *African American Films*, 74–82.
129 Hall, "Black Popular Culture", 129.
130 Friedman, *African American Films*, 82.

Figures 12 and 13. Seven-year-old Sammy Davis Jr. sings and dances in the title role of *Rufus Jones for President* (1933).

while also enhancing a film's entertainment value, often with the help of some trick photography. At another level, the fantasy/dream gimmick lets African Americans achieve their dreams, but it simultaneously undermines their achievements by explicitly marking them as unreal. An adult Black president may have been too much for 1930s Hollywood, even in the framework of a dream sequence in a musical, which is itself already a fantastical, unrealistic genre by definition. Unlike *Rufus Jones*, most Black-cast shorts don't tackle politics, instead limiting their tales of Black ambition and accomplishment to the world of entertainment, which is arguably a sort of dream world too – but also a professional venture.

The young Nicholas Brothers showed that disciplined bodies showcasing rhythmic skill were indeed a powerful tool for African American advancement in the entertainment industry (and by extension, in society at large). While the brothers would eventually give a new distinction to the Black class act in their feature film appearances, Roy Mack's Vitaphone shorts paved the way for the team's remarkable screen career. In their very first film, *Pie, Pie, Blackbird* (1932), Harold and Fayard Nicholas were only eleven and sixteen years old, respectively. But neither their youth nor the conventional limitations imposed by narrative and mise-en-scène curtail the power of their dance number as displays of virtuosity and competence. When the Nicholases first appeared onscreen, Black musical performance in film was already more often represented as professional rather than simply natural, as the product of a cultural and commercial practice rather than an innate trait of Black people, even though most films oscillate between these two tendencies. In *Pie, Pie, Blackbird*, Nina Mae McKinney appears as a pie-baking mammy type in the first scene, set in a kitchen. The framing device, a nonstory about baking a pie, provides a down-home atmosphere and a weak pretext for the film's fantasy sequence, which presents Eubie Blake's band inside a giant pie, wearing chef's hats. McKinney is transformed into a glamorous diva in a shiny evening gown, sitting on a grand piano. While her song delivery, with a growl in her voice, is seductive and sexy in a calculated way, she simultaneously presents an image of cultured sophistication. No longer the wild and uncontrollable seductress from *Hallelujah*, her eroticism is much more contained in this elegant performance, and in her static pose on the piano, she is also contained in her freedom of movement. The dancing is left entirely to the Nicholas Brothers.

Appearing as regular kids in the framing scene, the brothers also change costume for the fantasy part, performing in chef's hats that appear too big for them (like Davis's top hat in *Rufus Jones*). But this detail does little to diminish the impact of their dance as the unmistakable climax of the short film, which doesn't return to the kitchen scene at the end – unlike *Rufus Jones*, where Rufus and his mother wake up from their presidential dream at the end. Like many other tap class acts, the Nicholas Brothers often combined their routines of synchronized precision dancing with challenge dance displays, in which dancers take turns demonstrating their skill individually, as if they were competing with each other. The competitive tradition of the challenge dance had always been a driving force in Black vernacular dance history, and choreographed challenges often entered (male) tap dance performances onstage and onscreen.[131]

Already at this early stage of their career, the brothers showcase a remarkably versatile movement vocabulary, with little Harold virtually a match for his older brother. Both perform a wide variety of steps with expansive whole-body motion, often leaning over heavily. They never lose their balance or miss a beat while sliding, jumping with one leg over the other, or going up on their toes. Fayard, in particular, fully exploits the asymmetrical dynamism of African American dance, playing with losing his balance. He also briefly drops down into splits, giving a preview of what would later become one of the team's trademark moves. The brothers take multiple challenge turns, during which the band in the background plays quietly at a moderate tempo and adds some breaks. They then finish their number together as the whole band joins back in for a swinging up-tempo finish (fig. 14). Synchronized time steps in upright position – basic rhythm steps that were a staple of the swing-era tap repertoire – are followed by more complex footwork and more expansive body movement. Finally, the dancers' "hot" rhythms set the floor on fire, transforming them and the band into skeletons for the film's last few shots. This kind of visual gag was common for short films lacking in story content. The skilled performances of musicians and dancers, trick photography, and a threadbare trace of a plot are combined into a fantasy of pure entertainment, in which music and dancing don't emanate from Black bodies spontaneously and uncontrollably but rather result from professional practice and performance. Though the dancers' performance is anything but reserved, it nevertheless remains dignified and disciplined throughout. Already at this young age, the Nicholases have fully absorbed the African American aesthetic of the cool, demonstrating a controlled effortlessness in their complex and precise rhythms and their play with asymmetry and falling off-center. The Nicholas Brothers' youth might work against their image as professionals, but their extraordinary versatility and virtuosity as tap dancers transcends both their representation as nothing more than cute kids and the silliness of the scenery and costumes.

Perhaps the casting of the Nicholas Brothers and Sammy Davis Jr. as the youthful dancing stars of these musical shorts was a coincidence. But in the retrospective

---

131 See, for instance, Hill, *Tap Dancing America*, 2–3, 87; and Malone, *Steppin' on the Blues*, 5.

light of the emergence of Black class acts, the screen performances of these underage tap dancers appear like an intermediary step: an attempt at containing the display of classy competence within the nonthreatening cuteness of the dancers' youth. The fantasy/dream device additionally downplays Black ambition, framing successful careers – whether in politics or "only" in entertainment – as imaginary. Throughout the early 1930s, there is an increasing tendency in Black-cast shorts toward more explicit representations of entertainment as a professional enterprise, sometimes in combination with a fantasy/dream sequence as a pretext for this same entertainment. At the same time, it should be noted that the shorts that set their musical numbers in more realistic environments still present fantasies implicitly, in the sense that they depict an all-Black utopian world where African Americans can control every aspect of life and occupy any role and status in society, which would have been impossible in the real world.

Sometimes, the shift towards depicting Black music and dance as professional performance, rather than something African Americans just can't help doing, also helps to more firmly segregate or ghettoize them, relegating them to the role of "only" entertainment. Roy Mack directed two more shorts featuring the Nicholas Brothers, and they lack both the dream element and the rural connotations of a corresponding frame story. However, the films and performers are othered – that is, explicitly marked as Black – by the titles, *An All-Colored Vaudeville Show* (1935) and *The Black Network* (1936). In the first of these, there is no story at all; instead the film delivers no more and no less than what its title promises. The four numbers, introduced by a girl holding a sign, are an acrobatic tumbling act called the Three Whippets, Adelaide Hall singing a ballad, the Nicholas Brothers' tap dancing, and a song and dance number with the Five Racketeers and Eunice Wilson. But as if the filmmakers couldn't quite decide to let these performances speak for themselves, some of the stage sets contain blackface minstrel caricatures and watermelons. This creates a strange tension with the performances, to which the décor seems entirely unrelated. The Nicholas Brothers, however, are not minstrelized like the other acts. Now fourteen and twenty-one years old, they wear elegant modern suits and there is none of the other numbers' minstrel scenery onstage. The background décor, representing the exterior of a brick building, is painted in a somewhat expressionist style. Dancing together for the most part, the brothers execute perfectly synchronized steps, refraining from acrobatics, with the exception of a few splits at the end. Taller Harold is more sweeping in his arm and upper-body motions, whereas young Fayard – by now just as skilled as his older brother – appears extraordinarily relaxed throughout. The routine incorporates a remarkable range of complex rhythms and moves, including the forward-and-back motion and leg swings of Charleston steps.

Figures 14 and 15. The young Nicholas Brothers in their first short film, *Pie, Pie, Blackbird* (1932), wearing chef's costumes. A few years later, in *An All-Colored Vaudeville Show* (1935), they perform in classy suits.

Filmed in frontal full shots, with a stationary camera and only a few (barely noticeable) cuts, there is little to distract from their performance as anything but a display of highly skilled rhythm dancing (fig. 15).

While the impressive acrobatics they later included in their numbers have led to the Nicholas Brothers sometimes being categorized as a "flash act", their roots are clearly in the class act tradition, to which they remained faithful even as their routines became more and more flashy in the late 1930s and early 1940s. Tap historian Constance Valis Hill, who has analyzed the evolution of their dance style in great detail, repeatedly points out how much the Nicholas Brothers "epitomized the most sophisticated jazz performance style in the Swing Era, known as the 'class act'",[132] describing their versatile style at the height of their career as follows:

> The smooth-flowing and open-partnered synchronization of adagio ballroom dance, the Africanist-inflected stage and social dance styles of the teens and twenties, the flash and acrobatics of turn-of-the-century black comedy dance, the formal elegance and fastidious movement rhythms of the class act, and the rhythmic drive of the challenge dance – all were absorbed by the Nicholases and then distilled into their own distinctive style of American jazz dancing.[133]

Film scholar Karen McNally has similarly pointed out how the brothers fused classiness with a specifically American style of dancing, presenting "an image of class that asserted its Americanness and provided an alternative to the European-based aesthetic of Fred Astaire".[134] Whereas the brothers would gain exceptional star power in their feature films of the early 1940s, their distinctively African American dance style is already on display in their earlier short films. Arguably, the minimal use of acrobatics even underlines an image of class that does not *need* the spectacle of more flashy elements.

The two-reeler *The Black Network* reunites the Nicholas Brothers with Nina Mae McKinney. This would be McKinney's last musical role in a Hollywood production, and like in *Pie, Pie, Blackbird*, she does some singing but no dancing. Here, a backstage story concerning a Black radio station in Harlem serves as the framework for a musical variety show. Highlights are the frantic up-tempo jazz of the Washboard Serenaders and another tap number by the Nicholas Brothers,

---

132 Hill, *Brotherhood in Rhythm*, chapter 6. Hill's book offers a thorough study of the Nicholas Brothers' dance style and career. For shorter career overviews, see also Frank, *Tap!*, 64–74; Hill, *Tap Dancing America*, 110–112, 132–138; and Stearns and Stearns, *Jazz Dance*, 276–282.

133 Hill, *Brotherhood in Rhythm*, chapter 8.

134 McNally, "The Nicholas Brothers". For a comparison between Astaire's dancing and that of the Nicholas Brothers, see Hill, *Brotherhood in Rhythm*, chapter 8.

who appear as eager participants in an amateur contest, as always using their real names. Filmed in medium shot and medium close-up as they take turns singing "Lucky Numbers", the first part of their scene still has a strong "cuteness factor", especially since younger Harold's voice hasn't broken yet. But with Fayard grown up and Harold a teenager, there is less and less emphasis on the brothers' youth with each film appearance, as they quite literally grow into their roles as the foremost standard-bearers of African American dance. Once again impeccably dressed in tasteful "adult" suits, they deliver yet another impressive class act routine. In a brief challenge sequence, Harold counters his older brother's spectacular legwork with a series of smooth turns and rapid-fire tapping during a break in the music. As in their previous short films, the brothers' number again consists of rhythmically complex tap without acrobatics. And again, unobtrusive cinematography is fully in the service of the dance, which is filmed in full shots and only minimally edited.

The basic plot of *The Black Network* frames the entertainment industry as a professional, commercial enterprise. Presenting a Black class system where African Americans can move up and down the social ladder, the film also alludes to the depression-era reality of unemployment, which affected the Black minority disproportionately. This is another common narrative strategy in Black-cast shorts: the diegetic world is presented as an all-Black utopia free from White intrusion while nevertheless hinting at extradiegetic realities where African Americans are socially and economically subordinate to Whites. Notably, many of these all-Black short films explicitly address money.

Smash Your Baggage (1932), for example, is set in a gigantic train station, and the occasion for the musical numbers is a benefit performance, organized by a union of porters to help one of their colleagues, who is in the hospital. This is another narratively weak pretext for a musical variety show – as well as for demeaning portrayals of uneducated African Americans telling bad jokes in ridiculous dialect. However, as a fairly obvious allusion to the Pullman porters, who formed the first all-Black union in 1925, it also points to social realities outside of the film's segregated diegetic fantasy. The show culminates in a big production number without ever having resumed the perfunctory plot. Featuring performers from Small's Paradise, one of Harlem's premier nightclubs, the variety show includes a large chorus of male and female dancers, acrobatic tap dancers, and a female blues singer, who sits on a suitcase and laments that her man is gone, underlining her plight with very dramatic hand gestures and facial expressions.

Chapter 2 Kids and Class Acts: Male Dancers in Black-Cast Music Shorts

All of the featured dance acts are men, and their numbers are relatively short.[135] The first is a tap duo alternating solid rhythm work with a range of acrobatics, including cartwheels, somersaults, and leaps over trunks. The leaps are accentuated with high-pitched whistling sound effects in the manner of slapstick comedy. Next, rope-skipping tap dancer Danny Alexander gets a remarkable solo number showcasing rapid-fire rhythmic precision, in between jumps and knee drops. In the finale, Henry "Rubberlegs" Williams gives a brief sample of his characteristic high-kicking legomania before the whole ensemble joins in the dancing. The term "legomania" referred to a dance style involving fast-moving legs and often high kicks, and it was considered a type of "eccentric" dancing.[136] Like the other dancing men in the film, Williams wears a porter's uniform here, and while his dance is doubtless entertaining and energetic, it is not exaggeratedly eccentric. In its short nine minutes, *Smash Your Baggage* contains a remarkable variety of dance styles, as would have been seen in live performances at Harlem cabarets at the time. The ensemble routines also offer brief glimpses of female dancers who are obviously highly skilled and not as eroticized as in many other films of the period. As usual, however, they only appear as members of the chorus.

The slapstick elements and snippets of "comic" dialogue in stereotypical dialect are conventional Hollywood devices feeding into demeaning clichés of African Americans, intended to belittle them and undermine the professionalism on display. Similarly, the musicians partly conform to stereotypes of a wild and excessive Black physicality in the way they jump, bounce, and wiggle their heads on the bandstand, as if they were unable contain their excitement for the hot rhythms. At the same time, the film also clearly draws on the legacy of vaudeville, with its emphasis on variety and spectacle, stringing its diverse acts together at an almost frantic tempo. With their focus on acrobatics and comic elements, some of the dance numbers partly rely on the vaudevillian principle of a "bag of tricks". Yet for all this emphasis on comedy, variety, speed, and spectacle, there is nothing amateurish about any of the performances in *Smash Your Baggage*. Rather, the short film offers a rare glimpse of the diversity and exceptionally high skill level of the era's Black live entertainment, making viewers wish that more of it had been captured and preserved on film.

King for a Day (1934), starring Bill "Bojangles" Robinson, is a rare case of a Black-cast short headlined by a single dancer, evidencing Robinson's exceptional

---

135 The film's opening credits simply announce "Small's Paradise Entertainers", without giving names of individual performers or teams. Roy Liebman (*Vitaphone Films*, 81) lists the following cast members: Doris Rubbottom, Lew Payton, Carrie Marrier, Gibson and Thompson, Henry "Rubberlegs" Williams, and Babe Wallace. Rusty Frank's filmography (*Tap!*, 302) attributes the film's first tap act to a team that performed under the name Ace and Eddie.

136 See Stearns and Stearns, *Jazz Dance*, 234.

status.[137] He dances in a rehearsal scene with chorus girls and in a solo stage number to a medley of mostly minstrel-era tunes, including "Swanee River" and "Poor Old Joe". This solo tap number is the centerpiece of the film, prominently showcasing Robinson's restrained, understated dancing style, with several close-ups of his feet but also of his face as he rolls his eyes in minstrel show fashion. At over three minutes, it is an unusually long number for a short film, especially for a solo dance, which additionally emphasizes Robinson's star status. The scene follows a sketch by men in blackface, who remain seated behind Robinson on the giant stage during his dance, along with numerous chorus girls. This background of immobile figures creates a strangely static effect, and the men's blackface presence also underlines the number's minstrelsy content.

While Robinson's persona in the dance number evokes minstrel-era clichés, it is noteworthy that his role in the plot differs from the submissive servant type that the dancer would play in his feature films with child star Shirley Temple beginning in 1935. In these later films, Robinson combined the era's two dominant Black stereotypes of servant and entertainer into a well-behaved "Uncle Tom" figure, who appeared nonthreatening to White audiences. His apparently accommodationist stance with regard to White expectations was doubtless partly responsible for his success as the first Black dancer to achieve a certain star status in prestigious Hollywood productions. Though generally adored by the Black community, Robinson was therefore sometimes also criticized for conforming to and perpetuating old stereotypes.[138] In the all-Black short *King for a Day*, however, Robinson doesn't serve anyone; instead, he appears as a vaudeville entertainer seeking to gain control of a musical revue. The rudimentary backstage plot thus frames entertainment as a professional endeavor, and it allows for Black business to succeed without White help (although, as always, this utopian Black independence contradicts the film's own White-controlled circumstances of production and exhibition). Notably, there are no other tap dancers in *King for a Day*; Robinson's fame likely precluded any of the younger class act teams appearing in the same short film, where they would compete with the older dancer, whose style was beginning to look outdated vis-à-vis the more flamboyant performances of the newer class acts.

As if for maximum contrast, Robinson's old-fashioned minstrel act is followed by a modern, jazzy number with expressionist high-contrast lighting, performed on an artificial-looking set representing an urban street. After a somewhat threatening rendition of "Got the Jitters" by a female vocalist (Babe Matthews),

---

137 According to Roy Liebman (*Vitaphone Films*, 115), the cast includes Ernest Whitman, Dewey Brown, Hattie Noel, Muriel Rahn, and Dusty Fletcher.

138 See Bogle, *Bright Boulevards*, 162; and Everett, *Returning the Gaze*, 213–214.

chorus girls in long shiny gowns dance to an instrumental version of the song. As they jitter everything they've got and throw their hands high up in the air, their tall shadows add to the stylized urban setting and menacing atmosphere evoked by the song. Much as in *Rufus Jones for President*, the musical numbers in *King for a Day* run the whole gamut of Black entertainment clichés, presenting outdated minstrelsy stereotypes side-by-side with modernist jazz performance.

This principle of vaudevillian variety, with its diverse mix of performance idioms, was a fairly common strategy in Black-cast shorts, especially in those directed by Roy Mack. But towards the mid-1930s, with the growing popularity of big band swing, the so-called band feature became the prevalent formula in Black (as well as White) musical shorts. Constructed around the performance of a popular dance band, these shorts are often also titled accordingly, as in the case of *Mills Blue Rhythm Band* (1934) or *Jimmie Lunceford and His Dance Orchestra* (1936), for instance. The advent of the swing era also helped with the success of the Black class acts when tap dancers began working with big band arrangers, as the Stearnses point out:

> With the consolidation of earlier jazz into special arrangements for big bands, closer integration between music and dance became possible. …
>
> Dance routines were soon created that not only dovetailed with the melody but also included special accents reinforced in the accompaniment. … The integration of music and dance gave the class acts a new distinction.[139]

While the bandleaders were generally the headliners at live venues as well as in films, virtually every Black swing band included tap class acts as part of their show, both onstage and onscreen. Typically, the big band shorts are set in elegant performance venues connoting affluence, with only minimal – if any – narrative framing.

Mills Blue Rhythm Band, for instance, offers a fantasy of financial abundance for African Americans (unlike *Smash Your Baggage* and *King for a Day*, which have their characters scrambling for funds). Bits of inconsequential (if again heavily stereotyped) dialogue serve mainly to code the setting of this nearly plotless one-reeler as middle- and upper-class Harlem, with protagonists roaming the town from one upscale nightspot to another. An instrumental version of "Underneath a Harlem Moon" plays over the title credits and into the first scene, which shows guests entering the fashionable Blue Rhythm Club, where the eponymous band is playing for elegant couples dancing in a relaxed but restrained manner. Next, an up-tempo instrumental by the elegant band provides the background for a rope-skipping solo tap number by one of the Three Dukes. Dancing very

---

139 Stearns and Stearns, *Jazz Dance*, 299.

upright and moving his legs mostly from the knees down, the rope skipper lifts his feet just high enough to go over the rope. Executing highly complex rhythms at breakneck speed while never losing his cool, the dancer's tempo, precision, and control almost defy belief. The second tap number with all of the Three Dukes incorporates solo, duo, and trio parts in a dynamically interactive routine that is carefully coordinated with the music. Without resorting to excessively flashy acrobatic elements, the dancers demonstrate a large repertoire of body and leg movements, many of which require exceptional balance and body control, as when one of them stands on the side of his toes while flinging the other foot out sideways, rhythmically hitting the floor. As in many swing-era performances, the musicians and dancers reinforce each other's image of sophistication with their elegant appearance and the virtuosic yet seemingly effortless delivery of hot rhythms with cool composure. On a side note, *Mills Blue Rhythm Band* also once again exemplifies the common gender divisions among African American performers, featuring male instrumentalists and tap dancers, on the one hand, and a female vocalist (Sally Gooding), on the other, while Fredi Washington appears in a minimal speaking role.

Overall, *Mills Blue Rhythm Band* projects an image of Black Harlem *for* Black consumers rather than Black performance commodified for White consumption (although, as always, the latter still provides the extradiegetic rationale of the film's own production and exhibition context). However, even though the film presents a fantasy of luxury and sophistication, it also undermines its portrayal of Black people as cultured and civilized. The upright, close-embrace partner dancing in the first scene is coded as refined, elegant, and – by extension – White. But a club guest at a table (vocalist Sally Gooding) explains that she can't sit still because "this music just goes in my ears and out my feet", thus very subtly hinting at the supposedly uncontrollable nature of Black people. About halfway through the film, the band and guests leave the club because they have been invited to go to a penthouse rent party. While this bit of action references the social reality of rent parties, where broke tenants raise money to pay rent by hosting a party, it also evokes clichés of romanticized Black poverty. The following scene belies and fantastically transcends the implied financial distress with its luxurious penthouse party venue. As the party there continues, a heavy-handed visual gag at the end curbs the film's previous emancipatory tendencies by explicitly reverting to primitivist stereotypes. During the final number, the up-tempo instrumental "Blue Rhythm", excitement among the dancing customers is rising, yet they are mostly still dancing in a fairly restrained manner, in close embrace with their partners. The bartender-host then exclaims that the scene reminds him of the "old days in the jungle", and after a dissolve, everybody – including the band –

is suddenly wearing grass skirts and other "jungle" costumes before another dissolve returns us to modern-day Harlem. The implication is that the hot rhythms of the swinging music bring out the savage in Black people, giving away their true nature, which is hidden beneath a surface of sophistication. In other words, Black sophistication is coded in terms of an aspiration to be like White people, a disguise that masks the underlying primitive essence of African Americans.

Another one of Roy Mack's big band shorts, *By Request* (1935), employs a miniplot of upward social mobility, in which the musicians move from an unspecified rural location connoting poverty to an upscale California nightclub, exchanging their stereotypical country outfits for tuxedos. A band feature for the orchestra of stride pianist Claude Hopkins, the film contains numbers ranging from up-tempo swing to a ballad featuring the high-pitched vocals of Orlando Roberson. The trio Tip, Tap, and Toe is credited as a "dance specialty", a designation that was also starting to become common for Black numbers in feature-length films around that time. Constance Valis Hill, borrowing from the Stearnses, sums up this team's act at Harlem's famed Apollo Theater: "Tip, Tap, and Toe (Sammy Green, Raymond Frazier, and Raymond Winfield) wooed the audience by dancing on small oval platforms, sliding forward, backward, sideways, and in circles, as if they had buttered feet on a hot stove".[140] This description also applies to their two-minute dance in *By Request*, which is most likely a very condensed version of one of their stage numbers. Like many other tap teams, they combine a group precision part with challenge dance sections, all choreographed to match the music, with several shifts in tempo and dynamics. Although the Stearnses portray Tip, Tap, and Toe as an acrobatic act,[141] the acrobatics here are limited to a few splits by one of the dancers at the very end. For the rest of their dance, they demonstrate remarkable balance and elegance in smoothly elegant whole-body motions as their feet glide and tap on the platform. Their tightly controlled close-to-the-floor movements with feet sliding in all directions have a strong focus on asymmetrical body postures; these are contrasted with wing steps, symmetrical moves in which arms and legs are flung out sideways from the body's center – in either case, the dancers demonstrate their ability to play with falling off-center while retaining control in a seemingly effortless manner.

Numerous other Black-cast shorts follow the same formula, focusing on a prominent band in combination with a team of male tap dancers presented in luxurious nightclub settings that indicate material abundance. The convention is

---

140 Hill, *Tap Dancing America*, 103. According to Stearns and Stearns (*Jazz Dance*, 272), the slides were the innovation of group member Raymond Winfield; in this short film, all three dancers use them.
141 Stearns and Stearns, *Jazz Dance*, 272.

Figure 16. The Three Brown Jacks perform in a sumptuous nightclub setting in *Jimmie Lunceford and His Dance Orchestra* (1936).

not limited to films by any one director or studio. Joseph Henabery, for example, another White director who made several Black-cast films for Vitaphone in the 1930s, repeatedly showcased tap class acts with big bands in swanky club settings. Here, too, elegant tap teams – for example, the Four Step Brothers performing with Claude Hopkins's band in *Barber Shop Blues* (1933) or the Three Brown Jacks in *Jimmie Lunceford and His Dance Orchestra* – underscore the overall impression of sophistication and affluence, performing in sumptuous settings that sometimes transcend real-life models (fig. 16).

The listing of examples could be continued. As jazz scholar Bernd Hoffmann observes, the presentation of (big) bands in musical short films becomes more standardized in the second half of the 1930s – that is, in the course of the general mainstreaming and commercialization of swing culture.[142] However, when big band swing developed from a largely Black subculture into a White mainstream phenomenon beginning in the mid-1930s, African American performers were for the most part replaced with Whites in jazz-themed short films. Following a

---

142 See Hoffmann, "Alltag im Jazz-Himmel", 105–108.

Chapter 2 Kids and Class Acts: Male Dancers in Black-Cast Music Shorts

comparatively strong presence in the early years of sound cinema, Black performers all but disappeared from musical short films after 1936 (though they simultaneously began appearing as specialty acts in feature-length productions more often).[143] In addition, short film production in general began to decline in the mid-1930s, when the double feature, or double bill, became increasingly popular – that is, the screening of two feature films for the price of one. Yet even as studios reduced their overall output of short films,[144] White big band shorts endured well into the 1940s.

Much like the Black-cast shorts of the early 1930s, the White swing shorts of the late 1930s and early 1940s often centered on showcasing so-called name bands. Like their African American counterparts, the bandleaders in self-titled shorts like *Artie Shaw and His Orchestra* (1939) are usually presented as sophisticated performers in elegant clubs, with the sets often designed in a modernist art deco style. Stylized, expressionist imagery also remains present to some extent, especially through high-contrast lighting, but the occasional visual tricks and stylish locales are exclusively employed in the service of elegance rather than to exoticize the performers. As discussed above, virtually every Black-cast short includes elements that serve to undermine images of respectability and competence by exoticizing and/or ridiculing African Americans – whether through dialogue, song lyrics, setting, costume, or by having the performers act in an exaggeratedly buffoonish manner. By contrast, most White swing shorts lack the thin pretense of a plot – with the attendant stereotyping – as well as the fantasy/dream framework seen in many of the Black-cast shorts. Instead, the settings generally remain realistic. Bernd Hoffmann also notes a contrast between the cool discipline of White bandleaders, on the one hand, and the expressive and improvisatory gesticulations of Blacks, such as Cab Calloway, on the other – a contrast which finds its equivalent in the respective visual aesthetic of the films, with White-cast shorts tending towards a more "distanced" mise-en-scène.[145]

Emphasizing the skilled musicianship of their headliners, the majority of White swing/jazz shorts also manage without the added attraction of dance numbers – in contrast to Black-cast shorts, which virtually always feature dancers

---

143 Bernd Hoffmann suggests a periodization along musical rather than racial lines, with the year 1932 as a turning point: up to that year, Hoffmann observes, musical shorts are dominated by earlier styles of syncopated music, such as ragtime – that is, styles that were already outdated at the time. From 1932 on, there is a shift to current styles of jazz and swing, which remain prominent in short films throughout the decade and into the 1940s; see Hoffmann, "Suwannee River".
144 See Maltin, *The Great Movie Shorts*, 5, 213.
145 See Hoffmann, "Alltag im Jazz-Himmel", 108–109.

prominently.¹⁴⁶ This common presence of dancers in Black-cast shorts is doubtless rooted in clichés of naturally rhythmic Black bodies, and dancers may have been introduced in early sound cinema to "animate" the often static film image with their "lively" Black physicality. However, especially in the big band shorts, the dance scenes are rarely overly buffoonish or minstrel-like. Instead, the elegant male tap class acts often transcend these stereotypes, presenting their dancing bodies as instruments they have mastered through deliberate, disciplined training. Rather than detracting from the musicians' expertise, dancers and musicians mutually reinforce each other's image of competence and sophistication, embodying an aesthetic of the cool in productions that emphasize expert musicianship, rhythmic virtuosity, and disciplined professionalism just as much as entertainment value.

Creative Composer and Exuberant Entertainer: The Short Films of Duke Ellington and Cab Calloway

For all the undeniable prominence of "classy" dancers in Black-cast music shorts, the headliners of these films tended to be bandleaders, and it is worth taking a closer look at the two most popular – and very different – African American performers of the era: Duke Ellington and Cab Calloway. Among the Black jazz musicians to most successfully cross over into the White mainstream, Ellington and Calloway were also the ones to most frequently appear in White-produced films. Both appeared in credited specialty performances in feature films in the early 1930s, before this became a widespread practice in Hollywood.¹⁴⁷ Both also headlined several shorts, in which they basically played fictionalized versions of their offscreen selves, as was common for bandleaders in musical short films. Projecting two very different (screen) images of the dignified artist and the exuberant entertainer, respectively, Ellington and Calloway delimit the era's range of Black male screen presences, and it is instructive to look at how the role of dance in their films relates to their personalities as presented onscreen.

Duke Ellington may well have been the first African American musician to be considered a serious artist by (some) White audiences. His early films amplify this

---

146 There are doubtless exceptions to the image of the "cool" White bandleader as well as to the absence of dancers in White-cast music shorts. Roy Mack's *Swing Cat's Jamboree* (1938), for instance, features an expressively gesticulating Louis Prima, whose enormous mainstream success in later years was very much based on his high-energy, comic entertainer persona. This short film also contains a remarkable up-tempo tap routine by White dancers Ted Gary and Mitzi Dahl, evidencing filmmaker Mack's continuing predilection for tap dance even after he stopped directing Black-cast shorts.

147 Ellington's band appeared in and was credited for performances in the feature films *Check and Double Check* (1930), *Murder at the Vanities* (1934), and *Belle of the Nineties* (1934). Calloway received screen credit for appearances in *The Big Broadcast* (1932), where he performed two numbers, and *International House* (1933); both films are feature-length productions.

Chapter 2 Kids and Class Acts: Male Dancers in Black-Cast Music Shorts

aspect of his image by emphasizing his role as a creative composer. As Krin Gabbard notes in his survey of Ellington's film career, "for many Americans, however, a Negro composer was an oxymoron".[148] Nevertheless, in his films, "Ellington was regularly shown in the act of creating – he was not simply a performer in front of an orchestra".[149] At the same time, Ellington's music was generally being promoted as "jungle music", and his short films are among the Black-cast Hollywood productions most conspicuously balancing a primitivist exoticism, on the one hand, and an aesthetic of the cool, on the other. While presenting Ellington as a creative composer and dignified artist in a way that was highly unusual for African Americans, all of his shorts are also steeped in the mythology of Harlem as an exotic place, which stands simultaneously for urban modernism and exoticized primitivism. The films' dance scenes are revealing in terms of the various aspects of Ellington's music and image as well as of Black performance in general.

In his first film – Dudley Murhpy's short *Black and Tan* (1929) – Ellington is shown as being "in complete control of the music he produces" and "as a composer in the process of creation".[150] But at the same time, the film contrasts Ellington's exceptional role here with some minstrel-style comedy from other performers (among other things). Gabbard points out White filmmaker Murphy's ambivalent interest in Black culture:

> Dudley Murphy was fascinated by the combinations of sophistication, savagery, and buffoonery that Harlem nightspots such as the Cotton Club served up to white audiences in the 1920s. In this sense, Murphy resembled many Negrophiles of that decade who did not distinguish between what we now consider to be positive and negative images. ... There is, after all, a certain racist logic in Murphy's willingness to elevate Ellington only within a milieu that is repeatedly characterized as "primitive".[151]

Within the film's mixed imagery, the dance performances can be distinguished along gendered lines. A male tap group billed as the Five Hot Shots provides a counterpoint to the highly sexualized "dusky belle" Fredi Washington and the light-skinned chorus girls, who are on display for the male (White) gaze.[152] One of the earliest cinematic instances of an African American class act, the Five Hot Shots are dressed in white ties and tailcoats. Unlike the minimally clothed women, these elegantly attired men "dance in a style that emphasizes precise footwork

---

148 Gabbard, *Jammin' at the Margins*, 160.
149 Gabbard, 176.
150 Gabbard, 161–162.
151 Gabbard, 166. See also Gabbard, 161, for a brief comparison between *Black and Tan* and Dudley Murphy's other Black-cast short from the same year, *St. Louis Blues* (1929), which stars blues singer Bessie Smith in her only film.
152 See also chapter 1 in this book.

Figures 17 and 18. The Five Hot Shots do the "One Man Dance" in *Black and Tan* (1929).

Chapter 2 Kids and Class Acts: Male Dancers in Black-Cast Music Shorts

over dramatic movement (especially of the torso or pelvis)",[153] presenting a perfect antithesis to the shimmying, kicking, spinning motions of Washington and the chorus girls. In their first number, which has become known as the "One Man Dance", the five dancers remain extremely close together, moving as one person, as it were (fig. 17). Maintaining an erect posture with minimal upper-body motion, they emphasize the precision of their perfectly synchronized rhythmic footwork and the unity of their body movement, which includes a series of hops across the floor on one leg. Their second routine allows for more expansive movement, with the dancers further apart from each other, their legs and arms swinging in a relaxed but no less controlled manner. Dancing to Ellington's "The Duke Steps Out" and "Black Beauty", these male dancers exhibit a restrained yet relaxed elegance demonstrating ease and control at the same time, offering a perfect embodiment of the aesthetic of the cool. The elegant nightclub setting enhances their classy presentation while also adding visual interest, with a shiny mirrored floor that shows the dance team's reflection upside down. Parts of both dance routines are replayed later in the film using a rotating kaleidoscope effect (fig. 18).[154] This visual trick is narratively motivated to suggest ailing Fredi Washington's increasingly distorted vision while simultaneously highlighting cinematography's aesthetic potentials, but it doesn't undermine the dancing men's demonstration of competence. Together, bandleader Duke Ellington and the Five Hot Shots represent a new kind of dignified screen image of African American men that deviates considerably from clichés of shiftless comedians or simpleminded country types.

Duke Ellington was featured in two more short films in the 1930s, both directed by Fred Waller, who made a number of Black-cast shorts for Paramount (as well as several Black-cast Soundies in the early 1940s). Waller's ambivalent representational strategies resemble those seen in Dudley Murphy's work with Black performers. In the plotless one-reeler *A Bundle of Blues* (1933), sexy dancers Florence Hill and Bessie Dudley embody an exotic eroticism similar to Fredi Washington in *Black and Tan*. There are no male tap dancers here, and Hill and Dudley's rhythmic footwork remains inaudible, with the focus on their sexuality. Unlike most other Black-cast shorts, *A Bundle of Blues* has no narrative framing at all, simply presenting a series of musical numbers in an elegant club. Nevertheless, rural clichés enter through a visualization of Ivie Anderson's song "Stormy Weather", instead of through a frame story. As Gabbard notes wryly, the "urban

---

153 Friedman, *African American Films*, 110.

154 Dudley Murphy had also served as an uncredited codirector on French painter Fernand Léger's now-classic experimental short film *Ballet mécanique* (1924).

81

sophistication of the tuxedoed Ellington orchestra and its vocalist somehow seem to demand a reminder of rural poverty".[155]

Fred Waller's second Ellington short, *Symphony in Black: A Rhapsody of Negro Life* (1934), has a minimal framing plot – without dialogue. Here, Ellington is reminded in a letter that his "new symphony of Negro Moods" needs to be completed soon. The short film "is organized entirely around music by Ellington", with three of six pieces written specifically for the film, and the framing of the performances in fact "inflates Ellington's status as a composer".[156] After receiving the letter, Ellington sits at the piano writing down his composition on score paper. This activity – along with the terms "rhapsody" and "symphony", as well as the opening credits stating "composed by Duke Ellington" – aligns the musician with the intellectual and artistic tradition of Western classical music. The following performance of Ellington's "symphony" takes place in a setting resembling a concert hall more than a nightclub, where a White audience, seen only from behind, is seated in rows. For all this sophistication, which is connoted as White, the elaborately staged and photographed scenes intended to illustrate and dramatize the various "Negro Moods" once again contain a remarkable number of Black clichés, among them a victimized woman (Billie Holiday) in the second segment and "the folkloric myth of simple, African American piety" in the third.[157]

A short but notable dance from the last of the four parts of *Symphony in Black* deserves special mention here. Titled "Harlem Rhythm", the final sequence uses many of the conventional expressionist devices to indicate the "mood" and rhythm of Black music and dance and the excitement of Harlem nightlife: slanted camera angles, superimposition, multiplied and mirrored images, and high-contrast lighting with shadows and silhouettes. Images of the popular Harlem dancer Earl "Snakehips" Tucker (1905–1937), who was hired by Ellington to dance at the Cotton Club and elsewhere, are partly mirrored (so that he seems to face himself) and superimposed over silhouettes of chorus girls, drinking customers, and blinking marquee lights (fig. 19). Tucker, who only appeared in a couple of films,[158] demonstrates his characteristic hip torsions as well as "the Tremble,

---

155 Gabbard, *Jammin' at the Margins*, 168.
156 Gabbard, 175.
157 Gabbard, 173.
158 Earl Tucker's known film appearances include an uncredited role in the feature-length *Love in the Rough* (1930) and a dance number in a short titled *Crazy House* (1930). The latter is a rather badly aged MGM Colortone comedy set in a sanitarium, where Tucker (credited only as "Snake Hips") appears for no reason whatsoever. The two-minute dance number allows him to elegantly showcase his idiosyncratic style without subjecting him to the ridicule of the narrative's "loony bin" setting.

Chapter 2 Kids and Class Acts: Male Dancers in Black-Cast Music Shorts

Figure 19. The "Harlem Rhythm" segment from the Duke Ellington short *Symphony in Black: A Rhapsody of Negro Life* (1934) evokes the excitement of Harlem nightlife through expressionist cinematography, as in this mirror image of Earl "Snakehips" Tucker, which is superimposed with silhouettes of chorus girls.

which shook him savagely and rapidly from head to foot".[159] As a recent portrait of Tucker in the *New York Times* put it, "it was the hip rotations and the shaking that distinguished him from Black male dancers of his day, in part because the moves were associated with the sexually charged ones of female dancers; 'shake' dancers were known to shimmy and grind".[160] Marshall Stearns, referring to himself in the third person, describes his reaction to seeing Tucker at the Cotton Club in the late 1920s as "being unable to believe what he saw and spending most of his energy trying not to look shocked"[161]; additional evidence quoted by Stearns suggests that he was far from the only one to perceive the dancer as exceptional. While eroticized dancing women were generally expected by (White) spectators of Black stage shows, a male dancer performing "sexually charged" moves must have been quite unusual – and not just in films.[162]

---

159 Stearns and Stearns, *Jazz Dance*, 237.

160 Brian Seibert, "Overlooked No More: Earl Tucker, a Dancer Known as 'Snakehips'", Overlooked, *New York Times*, December 18, 2019, https://nyti.ms/2PxEymZ.

161 Stearns and Stearns, *Jazz Dance*, 237.

162 It is also worth noting that dance scholar Brenda Dixon Gottschild uses the Stearnses' description of Tucker's dance act as her introductory example to outline the various facets of the Africanist dance aesthetic and to distinguish it from the Europeanist aesthetic. See Gottschild, *Digging the Africanist Presence*, 12–17.

Earl Tucker was also known for his violent temper and had a reputation for being a lady's man, aspects that enter an earlier dance scene in *Symphony in Black*. In the film's second segment, Tucker and Bessie Dudley briefly dance together in a living room, dressed in elegant street attire. When they leave to go out, they are confronted by Billie Holiday in the role of the jealous lover, and Tucker tosses her into the street. For the audience, it is not necessarily obvious that it is the same dancer appearing in the two scenes, since Tucker's face is hard to recognize in the "Harlem Rhythm" scene, and both dance scenes are very short. In the final section, Tucker is not particularly highlighted as an exceptional performer. Rather, by superimposing him with images of sexy, feather-adorned chorus girls, the film essentially equates him with the female dancers in terms of what they signify, thus simply fetishizing *all* Black dancing bodies as exotic and erotic. Nevertheless, while Tucker's appearance in this short film might not have stood out particularly to viewers, it is noteworthy that he embodies an eroticized dance aesthetic that is quite unlike that of the tap-dancing class acts of the time.

As in Duke Ellington's live shows in venues such as the Cotton Club, the inclusion of eroticized jungle dancing in his short films satisfies the White public's desire for exotic Black performance while allowing the composer-bandleader himself to project an image of disciplined, cultured sophistication. Even though the cinematic visualizations of Ellington's music connect his work with all manner of African American stereotypes, the musician himself remains dissociated from anything that could be construed as uncivilized, maintaining his image of the elegant and respectable artist. No matter how "hot" the music and dancing may get, Ellington himself always remains cool throughout.

If Duke Ellington exemplifies "the ambiguous status of jazz as both art and popular entertainment",[163] as Krin Gabbard puts it, Cab Calloway is firmly situated at the entertainment end of the spectrum. In stark contrast to Ellington as the epitome of a coolly disciplined Black musician, Cab Calloway personified the Black entertainer stereotype for White audiences, and his remarkable crossover success rested largely on his exuberant persona. As with Ellington, Calloway's relatively successful film career was the result rather than the cause of his extracinematic image and career, and his shorts (like Ellington's) are obviously designed as miniature star vehicles, as is evidenced by their titles: both of Fred Waller's Calloway shorts for Paramount, *Cab Calloway's Hi-De-Ho* (1934) and *Cab Calloway's Jitterbug Party* (1935), as well as Roy Mack's *Hi De Ho* (1937) for Vitaphone clearly count on the drawing power of Calloway's name and his

---

163 Gabbard, *Jammin' at the Margins*, 167.

big hit "Minnie the Moocher", with the famous call-and-response phrase from that song providing two of the titles.[164]

Calloway is primarily known as a vocalist and charismatic showman, albeit one who led a first-rate swing band. What is often overlooked is that much of his exuberance was expressed through *dancing*. Though he is not usually discussed as a dancer, he actually dances a lot in his films, and his shorts, which are essentially designed as star vehicles, likely lack additional dance numbers precisely because Calloway himself is in charge of bandleading, singing, *and* dancing. In fact, Calloway's idiosyncratic movement style is integral to his image. Both Fred Waller shorts, for example, open with a three-quarter shot of Calloway in his signature white suit crossing his legs and doing a smooth double spin followed by some applejacks, a vernacular dance move that involves the knees, hips, and feet twisting inwards and out while pushing into the floor (figs. 20 & 21). Like many swing-era tap dancers, Calloway dynamically uses his arms and upper body for balance, and although his feet are not visible, some sliding footwork that is both smooth and rhythmically precise can be deduced from his body motion. This opening dance move is virtually the same in the two films and lasts only about three seconds. It's a trademark move that is as instantly recognizable as Calloway's "hi-de-ho" vocals.

In *Cab Calloway's Hi-De-Ho*, Calloway conducts an extremely fast instrumental number during an "impromptu" rehearsal on a train, whose speed and drive seem to serve as inspiration for the tune. In addition to vigorously waving his baton, Calloway bounces, struts, twists, turns, jumps, wiggles his head, and shakes his whole body. What might seem like uncontrollable gesticulation at first turns into very deliberate, practiced dance moves the next moment, when the bandleader repeats his signature move, now at a much faster tempo, then rhythmically steps and struts in a dance pose, with one arm held out and one hand on his hips, expressly calling attention to his steps. He continues to dance in the following two Cotton Club numbers, performing smooth sliding turns as well as some remarkable Charleston legwork during "Zaz-Zuh-Zaz" and "Lady with the Fan", both of which he also sings. At one point, he even drops to his knees after a triple turn, quickly rises again with perfect timing, and continues to dance-walk across the stage, lifting his knees up high and shimmying his upper body. These are clearly dance moves that have been practiced and mastered, not simply excessive outbursts of energy by someone who cannot contain their excitement. The "Lady with the Fan" number also has a burlesque-style fan dance performed by light-

---

164 The phrase is reused as a film title a third time for the race movie *Hi De Ho* (1947); see also chapter 3 in this book.

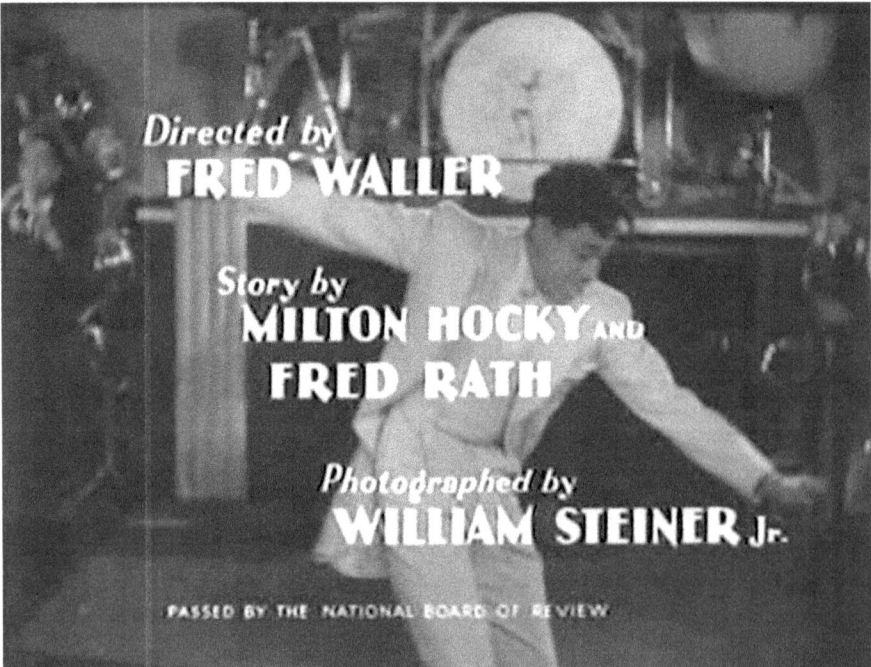

Figures 20 and 21. *Cab Calloway's Hi-De-Ho* (1934) begins with the bandleader performing his signature spinning move during the opening credits.

skinned women who enter the stage one by one. This is the only additional dance act in any of the Calloway shorts, and as a *dance* number, it is unremarkable, since the ladies with their fans do little more than walk around the stage and pose. Some half-shots and close-ups of the women are obviously intended to highlight their beauty, framing them as objects of desire. But Calloway, who never stops moving during his vocals, remains the scene's commanding presence throughout, dominating both the soundtrack and the image with his highly physical performance style.

The second Waller short, *Cab Calloway's Jitterbug Party*, reuses the Cotton Club setting, framing the band's performances as a live radio broadcast, announced by a White host. Again, Calloway's performance quickly progresses from what could be considered merely dramatic bandleading (bouncing, baton-waving, head-shaking) to "proper" dancing, this time with some distinctly rhythmic (if inaudible) tap dance footwork. After the second song, "Long about Midnight", which is introduced as "a musical description of darkest Harlem" by the White radio host, Calloway invites some of the Black club guests to go to a "jitterbug party". The final up-tempo number, "Jitterbug", is set in an apartment, where the musicians are jamming spontaneously, and guests are partner dancing. Finally, Calloway leads the party crowd in the shim sham, a popular swing-era line dance with rhythmic footwork rooted in tap.[165] The film then ends with a close-up of Calloway's grinning face as he draws out the final word of the song's vocals, "jitterbug".

Unlike Roy Mack's all-Black-cast music shorts, which offer visions of a Black utopia entirely free from White people, the Ellington and Calloway shorts directed by Fred Waller explicitly acknowledge their headliners' popularity with White audiences, who are shown (or at least implied) as consumers of Black popular culture. *Jitterbug Party* appears to be an attempt to have it both ways by including some African Americans as audience members at the Cotton Club (whereas the real-life Cotton Club usually only allowed White guests) and showing Black people entertaining themselves in the context of a private party. But due to the Cotton Club/radio broadcast framing, there is a stronger implication of a White audience voyeuristically intruding on the utopian Black world of Harlem.

Calloway's last cinematic short, the Vitaphone production *Hi De Ho* (1937),[166] was also Roy Mack's final Black-cast short (he continued to direct shorts featuring popular White bands into the 1940s). Combining the two popular strategies of

---

165 On the shim sham, see Manning and Millman, *Frankie Manning*, 70; and Stearns and Stearns, *Jazz Dance*, 195–196.

166 In the early 1940s, both Cab Calloway and Duke Ellington would be featured in several Soundies, three-minute musical films that were played on a jukebox rather than in cinemas.

a fantasy sequence, on the one hand, and a professional career plot, on the other, the film reverts to clichéd scenes of Black poverty, though this time in an urban rather than a rural setting: young Cab has big dreams of becoming a conductor, so that his poor mother no longer has to "take in that washing". The musical numbers following this introduction are framed as visions of the future that the fictionalized aspiring bandleader Calloway sees in a crystal ball. Scenes of Calloway singing in a dark courtyard and conducting his musicians positioned in the surrounding windows offer an opportunity for expressionist visuals with high-contrast lighting and shadows. The climactic up-tempo number shows his future success "on top of the world" – that is, in a fashionable club. Wearing a black tailcoat, he leads his elegant band of men in white suits, scatting frantically and again demonstrating his signature triple spin with legs locked. Though the dance component is less prominent here than in the earlier two short films, Cab Calloway is once again the commanding presence and uncontested star, and there are no other music or dance acts competing with him.

Duke Ellington and Cab Calloway represent two very different versions of the era's urban Black jazzman. As Krin Gabbard notes, "Ellington succeeded in combining 'high art' with 'low art', effectively undermining the hierarchies that separated the two".[167] Ellington's short films offer a diverse blend of various facets of Black vernacular culture and its reception by the White public, intermingling notions of urban jazz as both art and entertainment with references to minstrelsy, rural simplicity, and religiosity. But despite all the contradictory imagery in his films, Ellington undeniably came to represent a new level of respectability for Black performers. Calloway, by contrast, embodies the all-around urban entertainer, with no pretense to "art" nor recourse to old-fashioned minstrel buffoonery. For White audiences, Calloway's image as the epitome of the exuberantly energetic Black entertainer seems to have provided sufficient stereotyping, so that there was no need to additionally exoticize or minstrelize him through dialogue or scenery.

As discussed earlier, Hollywood's Black-cast musical shorts combine notions of excessive energy and elegant sophistication, natural Black musicality and musical expertise, hot rhythms and cool comportment, presenting these seemingly contradictory images side by side. In the case of Cab Calloway, these aspects are not so much juxtaposed as they are fully integrated in his entertainer persona: he is simultaneously elegant and excessive, flashy and classy, brash and controlled, exuberant and professional, hot and cool. As dance scholar Brenda Dixon Gottschild points out with regard to the aesthetic of the cool: "'Hot', its opposite,

---

167 Gabbard, *Jammin' at the Margins*, 175–176.

Chapter 2 Kids and Class Acts: Male Dancers in Black-Cast Music Shorts

is the indispensable complement of the Africanist cool. Hot illuminates cool; cool illuminates hot. It is in the embracing of these opposites, in being and playing the paradoxes … that the aesthetic of the cool exists".[168] What might seem like an irreconcilable contradiction between opposing principles is, in fact, inextricably linked in the African American dance aesthetic. In Duke Ellington's image, there is a separation between the cool musician and his hot music, and in his films, the hottest aspects of the music are "outsourced" to the dance numbers, so to speak. By contrast, Calloway's (screen) persona effortlessly combines the seeming opposites, and the combination is most distinctly expressed in his body language. The way Cab Calloway – who we usually think of as a singer and bandleader – moves his *dancing* body in his films perfectly embodies the simultaneously hot and cool African American dance aesthetic.

Hot and Classy: Black-Cast Shorts in the Trade Press

It seems that White filmmakers didn't see any problem with intermingling "what we now consider to be positive and negative images"[169] in their films featuring African Americans. Little is known about what White audiences thought of Black-cast musical shorts from the late 1920s and early 1930s. The general press paid virtually no attention to these short films (the *New York Times* all but ignored them), but the trade press discourse on these films suggests that they were considered popular mainstream movie fare. A cursory look at reviews and exhibitors' reports in trade magazines confirms the contradictions and tensions articulated in the films themselves. It also confirms that ideas of hot rhythm and excessive energy were not seen as a contradiction to the performer's expertise, professionalism, and sophistication.

The terms "class" and "classy" are frequently used in conjunction with the adjective "hot" to describe both the sophistication and the wild excitement supposedly inherent in Black jazz performance. A review of *Black and Tan*, for instance, says that "Duke Ellington and his all-colored orchestra put over the hot jazz, and how", and concludes by recommending the film as a "novelty done with class that should go big anywhere".[170] Another Ellington short, *A Bundle of Blues* is also said to be "quite artistically done".[171] Jimmie Lunceford and his orchestra in the self-titled short are called "a ritzy aggregation of hot-cha instrument

168 Gottschild, *Digging the Africanist Presence*, 17.
169 Gabbard, *Jammin' at the Margins*, 166.
170 "Hot Number", review of *Black and Tan*, *Film Daily*, November 17, 1929, 9, Media History Digital Library.
171 "Good Musical Novelty", review of *A Bundle of Blues*, *Film Daily*, September 13, 1933, 10, Media History Digital Library.

men".[172] In *Pie, Pie, Blackbird*, according to one reviewer, "Miss McKinney does several typical song numbers with a lot of class".[173] *By Request*, the Vitaphone short featuring Claude Hopkins's elegant orchestra, is also called a "classy presentation" by a reviewer fond of wordplay: "Plenty of color in this black-and-white short – but it is all swell Harlem tints. Directed with class by Roy Mack".[174] One brief review recommends the film because of the "smart modern music expertly played by Claude Hopkins" and the "clever tap dancing by Tip, Tap and Toe",[175] whereas an exhibitor considers it "first class entertainment".[176] Another short with Hopkins's band, Joseph Henabery's *Barber Shop Blues*, is also said to hit "the ultra-modern note in a lavish set of a dazzling barber shop", receiving praise for the "snappy songs in the up-to-date Cotton Club manner" and "the Four Step Brothers adding a lot of that colored class that is all the rage now".[177] Cab Calloway "conducts his present-day ork in the grand manner at a nite spot" in *Hi De Ho*.[178] As Black entertainment became more common and widely disseminated, not least through the medium of film, the classiness was increasingly associated with the performance itself rather than with the act of consumption by the Whites who could afford it.

Contrary to what the industry expected in the earliest days of sound – that Black-cast films would appeal only to sophisticated urban audiences – these musical shorts were apparently considered suitable for "general" and "small-town" patronage, as noted in many of the exhibitors' reports found in trade magazines. *Harlem-Mania* is recommended for a "family audience including young people".[179] Sometimes, Black-cast shorts are expected to be a special draw, as when the "peppy, amusing and vastly entertaining" *Rufus Jones for President* is considered "worth special billing".[180] Occasionally, a qualification accompanies a positive assessment, as in this review of *Pie, Pie, Blackbird*: "Fairly entertaining, moderately enjoyable if the patron likes the negro band, with its own peculiar

---

172 "Hot Jazz", review of *Jimmie Lunceford and His Dance Orchestra, Film Daily*, January 7, 1937, 30, Media History Digital Library.
173 "Novelty", review of *Pie, Pie, Blackbird, Film Daily*, June 11, 1932, 17, Media History Digital Library.
174 "Class Rhythm", review of *By Request, Film Daily*, October 18, 1935, 8, Media History Digital Library.
175 Review of *By Request, Motion Picture Daily*, October 17, 1935, 11, Media History Digital Library.
176 Exhibitor's report on *By Request, Motion Picture Herald*, October 17, 1936, 69, Media History Digital Library.
177 "Clicks", review of *Barber Shop Blues, Film Daily*, August 25, 1933, 9, Media History Digital Library.
178 "Autobiographical", review of *Hi De Ho, Film Daily*, February 20, 1937, 4, Media History Digital Library.
179 Listing for *Harlem-Mania, National Board of Review Magazine*, December 1929, 22, Media History Digital Library.
180 "Snappy Musical", review of *Rufus Jones for President, Motion Picture Herald*, September 2, 1933, 37, Media History Digital Library.

Chapter 2 Kids and Class Acts: Male Dancers in Black-Cast Music Shorts

type of melody, and the singing negress Nina Mae McKinney".[181] In a review titled "Colored Class", *Rufus Jones for President* is expected to be a sure hit "wherever they like the sepia atmosphere and hotcha music".[182] On the one hand, such "ifs" and "wherevers" presumably serve to avert any damage to exhibitors who have reason to believe that their patrons don't want to see African Americans onscreen. On the other hand, there are also some comments that completely refrain from mentioning the cast's race: *Mills Blue Rhythm Band* is simply recommended as a "good musical one-reeler that will please everybody",[183] and *Barber Shop Blues* as "good entertainment and just the type that every one likes".[184]

Despite occasional qualifications, the trade press discourse on Black-cast shorts suggests that these films would give exhibitors little cause for concern. The entertainment label and the segregation through all-Black casts were apparently sufficient to contain and ghettoize Black performance, so that it appeared nonthreatening to White audiences. Nevertheless, through their emphasis on elegance and virtuosity, cinematic images of African American performers contributed to a shift from viewing Black people as primitive savages or clueless clowns to seeing them as talented and sophisticated professional performers and occasionally even as creative artists – despite the fact that the more negative images also persisted, often within the same films. While the headliners were often bandleaders, dancers were a common and crucial presence in these early Black-cast films, and male tap dancers in particular were key to more dignified representations. Combining entertainment with elegant sophistication, the tap dance class acts in the musical shorts of the 1930s made a crucial contribution to improving cinematic images of Black performers, as their displays of rhythmic virtuosity, body control, and cool effortlessness often transcended the stereotypes imposed by settings, costumes, and narratives.

When both short film production overall and the relatively strong Black presence in shorts declined in the late 1930s, Hollywood feature films increasingly employed African Americans to appear in musical specialty acts. In other words, the segregated ghettoization of Black entertainment remained essentially the same, but its central location moved from musical shorts to feature films, where it was not limited to musicals but common in just about any genre. The racial segrega-

---

181 "Fair", review of *Pie, Pie, Blackbird*, *Motion Picture Herald*, June 25, 1932, 29, Media History Digital Library.
182 "Colored Class", review of *Rufus Jones for President*, *Film Daily*, August 25, 1933, 9, Media History Digital Library.
183 Exhibitor's report on *Mills Blue Rhythm Band*, *Motion Picture Herald*, April 21, 1934, 52, Media History Digital Library.
184 Exhibitor's report on *Barber Shop Blues*, *Motion Picture Herald*, January 20, 1934, 70, Media History Digital Library.

tion implicit in the all-Black utopia of the Black-cast musical short was thus replaced by the more explicit and visible segregation of the Black specialty number in the otherwise White-cast film. In this context, too, male tap dancers remained at the forefront of the fight for more and better screen representation for African Americans. The Nicholas Brothers epitomize this trend, representing a young generation of tap dancers who leave behind the servile images associated with older performers like Bill Robinson. Continuously enhancing their virtuosic and versatile dancing in non-narrative numbers in Hollywood feature films, the Nicholas Brothers would reach unprecedented success for Black dancers in the early 1940s.

Meanwhile, the gender gap among African American performers in Hollywood productions persisted. Featured Black female performers remained quite rare in mainstream films throughout the 1930s. For women who did not conform to the docile servant/mammy stereotype or content themselves with the role of the sexy jungle dancer/chorus girl, there were very few film roles available. Female vocalists appeared in White-produced films here and there – but not very often. Black female instrumentalists were also virtually unheard of in films of the 1930s.[185] Only in the 1940s did things slowly begin to change, when singer Lena Horne and pianist Hazel Scott started embodying new screen images of classy and cultured African American women in Hollywood films.[186] While Black dancing men were at a clear disadvantage compared with their White counterparts, and White dancing women were underrepresented compared with men, Black female dancers were the most marginalized, and there was hardly a place for them in Hollywood. But even in Hollywood, there is no rule without an exception, and I now turn to an exceptional case of a Black female dancer: chapter 3 is dedicated to the film career of Jeni LeGon, an African American tap soloist who did dance in several Hollywood feature films in the second half of the 1930s, even though she didn't manage to sustain a film career for very long.

---

185 Kristin McGee's wide-ranging study of jazz women shows that the situation described here for African American dancing women was not much different for musicians: Black female instrumentalists performed in a variety of settings ranging from vaudeville stages to hotels but rarely ever appeared in Hollywood films. White women musicians were also strongly underrated and underrepresented compared with their male counterparts, but they nevertheless had more opportunities for screen performances than Black female instrumentalists. See McGee, *Some Liked It Hot*.

186 On pianist Hazel Scott, see McGee, *Some Liked It Hot*, 113–133, 139–140. McGee notes that Scott's film appearances "dramatically transcended prior Hollywood depictions of Black female musicality, especially in contrast to the more frequently cast images of blues singers, chorus girls, and exoticized jungle dancers. In this respect, Scott was one of the first Black female jazz musicians featured as a serious jazz instrumentalist in a major Hollywood film" (113). On Lena Horne, see Dyer, *Space of a Song*, chapter 6; and McGee, *Some Liked It Hot*, 137–139.

CHAPTER 3 Potential Pioneer: The Film Career of Black Tap Dancer Jeni LeGon

The film career of African American tap dancer Jeni LeGon lends itself to an extended case study in the context of this book for a number of reasons. In Hollywood feature films, she was confined to specialty numbers and (often uncredited) maid roles. In addition, she played a handful of lead parts in independently produced Black films (known as race films at the time). Born in 1916, Jeni LeGon was the first African American woman to sign a long-term contract with a major Hollywood studio, after her 1935 screen debut *Hooray for Love*, in which she was partnered with famous tap dancer Bill "Bojangles" Robinson. The contract, however, was canceled after LeGon allegedly outperformed White queen of tap Eleanor Powell at a dinner party. While the ghettoization of Black performers was common industry practice, LeGon occupied an especially problematic position as a woman in the male-dominated realm of solo tap dance. Often dancing in pants and with a repertoire of moves matching that of many male tap acts, she mostly resisted the stereotyping and sexualization that other early Black female screen performers were subject to. The nonconformity of her appearance and dance style helped her to establish the persona of a competent, creative, and active performer as opposed to that of a more conventionally objectified, passive showgirl. While making her a potential pioneer in Black women's film history, this somewhat "impossible" place in what scholar Kristin McGee calls "Hollywood's Musical-Racial-Matrix"[187] also contributed to LeGon's relative failure in the mainstream film industry. The limited variety of possible screen images available to African American women in classical Hollywood cinema did not include that of the independent virtuoso dancer, a persona based on individuality and professional skill rather than female subordination and Black subservience.[188]

---

187 McGee, *Some Liked It Hot*, 113.

188 For brief overviews of LeGon's career, see Frank, *Tap!*, 120–123; Hill, *Tap Dancing America*, 124–126; and Bruce Weber, "Jeni LeGon, Singer and Solo Tap-Dancer, Dies at 96", *New York Times*, December 16, 2012, https://nyti.ms/V2ipua.

I trace Jeni LeGon's obstructed career path by examining her film appearances, as well as archival materials, especially press reports and interviews with the dancer herself. LeGon's career is both typical of its time and exceptional, and her image and problematic place in Black film history exemplify the marginalizing mechanisms of classical Hollywood's intersecting racial and gender politics. One of my aims is to add to recent reevaluations of female musical stars as competent performers, by focusing on an underexamined figure, that of the Black female dancer. Adrienne L. McLean, the leading scholar researching female dancers in classical Hollywood, has argued convincingly that dancing women destabilized the cinema's presumed gender roles and divisions.[189] Focusing on major stars like Rita Hayworth and Eleanor Powell, McLean pays little attention to Black female dancers; yet I would argue that her observations hold especially true for African American women. Jeni LeGon's film appearances provide an excellent case in point.

The realm of reception – especially the African American reception of Black performers in Hollywood – offers an additional illuminating framework for historical analysis. LeGon's star image as presented in the Black press illustrates some of the general tendencies and concerns of African American film criticism during the 1930s and 1940s. As Anna Everett shows in her history of early Black film criticism, the discourse on film in the mainstream Black press combined a generally accommodationist stance toward Hollywood with advocacy for better treatment of Black people. While some of the era's leftist Black magazines offered radical critiques of cinema as capitalist ideology, the Black "weekly newspapers, which appealed primarily to a popular and mass audience, often, but not exclusively, approached film news from a fan culture perspective".[190] They enthusiastically celebrated Black performers as stars, no matter how small their role in a Hollywood film was, and "the black press network's popular entertainment pages became an unacknowledged and unwitting extension of the white film industry's massive publicity machinery".[191] Nevertheless, the same papers were also ready to engage in journalistic "muckraking concerned with shaming Hollywood into doing fairly by its loyal black audience" when they felt the need to expose the industry's discriminatory practices.[192] Everett's general observations are confirmed by the star discourse on Jeni LeGon in two of the major Black weekly newspapers, the *Pittsburgh Courier* and the *Chicago Defender*, which I have

---

189 See McLean, *Being Rita Hayworth*, 116. On Eleanor Powell, see McLean, "Putting 'Em Down"; see also the chapter on Hollywood musicals in Brannigan, *Dancefilm*, 140–171, where the author analyzes the dance styles and general physical characteristics of Ginger Rogers, Rita Hayworth, and Marilyn Monroe.

190 Everett, *Returning the Gaze*, 177.

191 Everett, 188.

192 Everett, 217.

Chapter 3 Potential Pioneer: The Film Career of Black Tap Dancer Jeni LeGon

examined as representatives of the Black popular press. Like many other Black performers who only appeared in specialty numbers and bit parts, Jeni LeGon was celebrated as a full-fledged movie star by the Black press – at least for a short time.

By contrast, and rather unsurprisingly, the White press took relatively little note of her. But the very limited attention she did attract in mainstream publications is revealing with regard to the commodification of Black entertainment by the White film industry. LeGon's few musical specialty acts in Hollywood films illustrate how African Americans were sometimes simultaneously segregated and privileged as a special attraction by the films and their accompanying discourses.

Finally, LeGon's place in – or rather absence from – dance and film scholarship show how historians have, in a sense, replicated the industry's marginalizing processes by relegating individual Black performers to footnote status. As I have suggested before, this very absence from the historical narrative is significant, and thus, my goal here is to move the marginal to the center and upgrade the footnote to focal point.

A Promising Start: Mid-1930s

When Jeni LeGon came to Hollywood in 1935 and landed a role as the dance partner of the already legendary Bill "Bojangles" Robinson, followed by a contract with MGM, the Black press hailed her as the new "sepia sensation" of movieland.[193] Yet this highly promising start to her film career would come to look like a broken promise in retrospect.

Born in Chicago in 1916, Jeni LeGon grew up in a musical family. Her earliest childhood memories involve street shows with neighborhood kids as well as regular musical performances at her family's house. Later, she "started ditching school, going to the Oriental Theater", where she learned to dance by watching and copying tap dancers she saw onstage and in the movies.[194] She had her first encounter with professional show business as a chorus girl at age thirteen, briefly dancing in the chorus line with the Count Basie band. Soon after, she joined the Whitman Sisters' vaudeville troupe, where, in her own words, she "really got

---

193 See, for instance, Bernice Patton, "Jeni LeGon, Sepia Sensation, Stirs Hollywood", *Pittsburgh Courier*, January 12, 1935, ProQuest.

194 "I ... started ditching school, going to the Oriental Theater where they had all those wonderful – like Cab [Calloway] would come or Fletcher Henderson and Duke [Ellington] and all those, and they always had the dances, and that's how I really learned. I watched the dancers and I'd see the movie, watch the dancers, go over and practice what I saw, come back and see the next show to see if it had – I was doing the step correctly. And usually I would sort of change them because I didn't want to make – show that I was copying point blank". LeGon, interview, HistoryMakers, tape 2, story 4.

trained".[195] She toured with them for about six months before forming her own act with her foster sister Willa Mae Lane, working at nightclubs in Chicago. In 1935, the sisters were invited to perform in Los Angeles, only to find upon arrival that there would be no performance. But they heard about an audition held by Earl Dancer, Ethel Waters's former manager, and decided to try their luck. Dancer was so impressed with LeGon that he not only hired her for his stage show but also used his influence to get her the dancing role with Bill Robinson in RKO's *Hooray for Love*. Hollywood seemed the logical next step for an exceptionally talented dancer at a time when African American employment in the film industry was still on the rise, as musical performers were increasingly included in feature-length films (in addition to the Black actors who played small servant roles). Yet Jeni LeGon's promising screen debut would remain the highlight of her only briefly successful film career.

A mediocre (at best) musical comedy starring Ann Sothern and Gene Raymond as the leading romantic couple, *Hooray for Love* contains an eight-minute Black musical number featuring pianist Fats Waller along with Robinson and LeGon. Framed as the dress rehearsal for a stage show, directed by Whites and performed for a White (diegetic) audience, the number is typical of the era's Black specialty acts in at least two ways: first, in that its performers have no narrative function elsewhere in the movie, and second, in its positive yet patronizing depiction of Black musical culture. Somewhat less typical is the fact that the scene is not limited to "just" singing and dancing but tells a little story of its own. The setting is a stage set representing a Harlem street, and Jeni LeGon plays a resident evicted from her apartment because she can't pay her rent. Bill Robinson, in the role of the "mayor", tries to cheer her up by pointing out the neighborhood's attractions: electric light (from a street lantern) and running water (from a hydrant). He insists that with her smile, she's "the richest gal in Harlem", and he tries to bring the message home with the song "Living in a Great Big Way". She learns the lesson quickly, taking over the song after the first eight bars and finishing the chorus before they dance together for about a minute (fig. 22). After Robinson repeats the song with Fats Waller on the piano, LeGon picks it up one more time and then leaves the stage entirely to Robinson, whose two-minute solo dance concludes the sequence. As is often the case with Black specialty numbers in Hollywood films, the scene is ambiguous in ideological terms: its mere presence in the film celebrates African American culture, and its content praises the function of music and dance as a survival strategy, an important tool in dealing with everyday problems. Yet the subliminal message is that Black people need

---

195 LeGon, interview, HistoryMakers, tape 2, story 6. On the Whitman Sisters, see George-Graves, *Royalty of Negro Vaudeville*.

Chapter 3 Potential Pioneer: The Film Career of Black Tap Dancer Jeni LeGon

Figure 22. Jeni LeGon performs "Living in a Great Big Way" with Bill Robinson in her promising screen debut, *Hooray for Love* (1935). Credit: Everett Collection.

nothing but music and dancing to be perfectly happy, and thus, there is no need for social and economic equality. As the song lyrics claim, "a handful of nothing" is enough for them to live "in a great big way".

In terms of the number's mininarrative, Jeni LeGon is clearly under Robinson's wings, with him acting as a kind of father figure to the young girl, who appears somewhat helpless at first – though not for long. Robinson's final dance solo is longer than the preceding duet with LeGon, and it serves as the scene's climax, thus indicating his higher status and market value as a dancer and movie star. This is no surprise, given that Robinson, already fifty-seven at the time, was considered one of the world's best tap dancers. A legendary stage performer long before he ever appeared onscreen, he had become one of the first African Americans to achieve a certain – if limited – star status in Hollywood.[196] For the duration of their duet, however, Jeni LeGon is Robinson's equal partner, execut-

---

[196] On Robinson's career, see, for instance, Bogle, *Bright Boulevards*, 155–164; Bogle, *Toms, Coons*, 47–52; Hill, *Tap Dancing America,* 20–21, 62–67, 120–126, 165–168; and Stearns and Stearns, *Jazz Dance*, 180–188.

Figure 23. Publicity photos for *Hooray for Love* (1935) show Jeni LeGon as Bill Robinson's equal partner. Credit: Jeni LeGon Papers, Archives Center, National Museum of American History, Smithsonian Institution.

ing the exact same steps, thereby establishing her competence as a dancer. LeGon and Robinson dance side by side, starting with relatively simple footwork, additionally accenting rhythms and breaks with finger snaps and knee slaps. Throughout, LeGon matches Robinson's rhythmic precision and seemingly effortless elegance as well as his somewhat understated style: casual yet controlled, upright, with arms and legs not moving too far from the body's center. As their dancing becomes a little more expansive and the rhythms more complex, moving around the floor and with their limbs swinging further, Jeni LeGon actually appears as the more relaxed of the two. Arguably, she even subtly outshines her much older partner with her simultaneously loose and highly controlled quality of movement. In her simple outfit of pants and a turtleneck sweater, low-heeled tap shoes, and short hair, her boyish appearance differs considerably from that of other Black female stars, such as Nina Mae McKinney, Lena Horne, or Dorothy Dandridge, whose screen images were much more sexualized and glamorous.[197]

[197] For overviews of these three actresses' careers, see Regester, *African American Actresses*.

Chapter 3 Potential Pioneer: The Film Career of Black Tap Dancer Jeni LeGon

In his seminal book *Disintegrating the Musical*, Arthur Knight uses this scene as an introductory example to support one of his central arguments – namely, the significance of the Black specialty number as "a key mode of black reception".[198] He cites a press report on a screening of the film, according to which the Harlem scene was recognized as better than the rest of the film by the Black audience and provided them with a sense of identification based on Robinson's stardom.[199] While LeGon is not mentioned in the excerpt from the *Chicago Defender* quoted by Knight, the press report does, in fact, praise her towards the end: "That clever young lass, Jeni LeGon keeps up with Bill in no little fashion".[200] This kind of appraisal is representative of the film's reception in the Black press, as evidenced by various other articles that mention LeGon in the same breath with Robinson, without any indication of her being less important for the scene or a less excellent dancer. A photograph in the *Pittsburgh Courier* shows them in identical dress suits with top hats, and the caption reads: "Jeni LeGon and Bill Robinson, the dancing sensation of R.K.O.'s 'Hooray for Love', are pictured here stepping high, wide and handsome".[201] A series of studio publicity photographs for *Hooray for Love* supports this view of the two dancers' equality and their balanced partnership as well as giving further evidence of LeGon's often commented-on preference for pants (fig. 23).[202]

Both her role in *Hooray for Love* and her subsequent contract with MGM received ample coverage in the Black press, where she was variously hailed as the "Second Florence Mills" and "Girl With the Million Dollar Personality",[203] a "Sepia Sensation",[204] "Hollywood's Sepia Cinderella Girl",[205] and a "youthful genius of terpsichore".[206] The *Chicago Defender* and *Pittsburgh Courier* each mentioned her about twenty times in 1935. Each paper devoted several longer articles entirely to the dancer, whom they considered a rising star. According to film historian Donald Bogle, the favorable publicity was largely due to her manager Earl Dancer,

---

198 Knight, *Disintegrating the Musical*, 20.
199 See Knight, 20–21.
200 Tommye Berry, "Kansas City Likes the Film, 'Hooray for Love'", *Chicago Defender*, August 17, 1935, ProQuest.
201 "Jeni and Bill Step High, Wide, Handsome!", *Pittsburgh Courier*, April 27, 1935, Newspapers.com.
202 See also Bogle, *Bright Boulevards*, 161; and photos, box 1, folder 3, LeGon, Papers.
203 Bernice Patton, "RKO Signs Jeni LeGon, 'Second Florence Mills'", *Pittsburgh Courier*, December 22, 1934, ProQuest.
204 Bernice Patton, "Jeni LeGon, Sepia Sensation, Stirs Hollywood", *Pittsburgh Courier*, January 12, 1935, ProQuest.
205 Earl J. Morris, "Jeni LeGon, Hollywood's Sepia Cinderella Girl, Scoring in Chi[cago?]", *Pittsburgh Courier*, November 9, 1935, ProQuest.
206 C. Cecil Craigne, "Jeni LeGon", *Chicago Defender*, November 16, 1935, ProQuest.

who "made the right connections, which resulted in wide coverage for LeGon in the Negro press and also a movie contract".[207]

From a White mainstream perspective, it is easy to read Black press claims such as "she was signed to star with Bill Robinson" as a gross overstatement.[208] Yet as Anna Everett has pointed out, criticism of this tendency for journalistic hyperbole "fails to consider that to black film audiences, the bit actors *were* indeed the stars".[209] Further, while the journalists of the Black press were inevitably biased in treating "their" stars as if they were the film's stars, there is sufficient evidence to indicate that White audiences, too, were more excited about the Harlem number than about the rest of the film. The *New York Times* announced that "Mr. Robinson will appear in person tonight at the Roxy for the last stage show" on the occasion of the film's opening.[210] The next day, the paper published a fairly devastating review of the movie but conceded that some of the musical numbers were "passably performed by such entertainers as Bill Robinson, Jeni Le Gon".[211] Among the generally more favorable reviews in small provincial papers, it is common to find such statements as these: "A dance specialty with Bill Robinson, with the aid of Fats Waller and Jeni LeGon, is the highlight".[212] Another paper wrote, "Bill Robinson, who was Shirley Temple's partner in the Stair-case dance in 'Little Colonel', again dances; and this rapid fire tapping is matched by Jeni LeGon, with 'Fats' Waller joining".[213] Even Hollywood's influential gossip columnist Louella Parsons took note of the young dancer and mentioned her in her widely read, syndicated *Los Angeles Examiner* column months before *Hooray for Love* was released, claiming that "so far the screen has never had a colored actress who sings and dances".[214] Parsons was, of course, wrong about this, given that Nina Mae McKinney in *Hallelujah* (1929) preceded LeGon by six years in this respect. But the claim is nevertheless revealing of how marginal Black female singers and dancers were onscreen.

207 Bogle, *Bright Boulevards*, 176.
208 Billy Rowe, "Jeni LeGon Back in America from London Success", *Pittsburgh Courier*, October 17, 1936, ProQuest.
209 Everett, *Returning the Gaze*, 309 (italics in the original).
210 "Screen Notes", The Screen, *New York Times*, July 12, 1935, TimesMachine.
211 C. R. P., "At the Roxy", review of *Hooray for Love*, The Screen, *New York Times*, July 13, 1935, TimesMachine.
212 Hubbard Keavy, "Bill Robinson Dances", review of *Hooray for Love*, Screen Life in Hollywood, *Bluefield Daily Telegraph*, June 5, 1935, Newspapers.com.
213 "Movies", *Belleville Telescope*, June 13, 1935, Newspapers.com.
214 Louella O. Parsons, "Colored Actress to Head Revue! Jeni Legon Is Signed for RKO", *San Francisco Examiner*, December 12, 1934, Newspapers.com. Anecdote has it that it was also Parsons who inadvertently changed the dancer's name from Jennie Ligon to Jeni LeGon, the version that stuck (although the spelling of her last name was never consistent and included the variations Le Gon as well as Legon). See also LeGon, interview, Govenar, *Untold Glory*.

Chapter 3 Potential Pioneer: The Film Career of Black Tap Dancer Jeni LeGon

The other extended musical number in *Hooray for Love* is a five-minute ballet featuring Maria Gambarelli pirouetting in a sparkly costume.[215] These two numbers are the most substantial contributions to the film's series of rather randomly strung together variety acts, yet neither contributes anything to the nonmusical segments of the flimsy narrative. Of the two numbers, the Harlem sequence has more weight. Not only is it longer (eight minutes), it is also presented as the climax, occurring late in the film's total running time of only seventy-two minutes. There is also a small build-up to the number, when the producer of the show-within-the-film (Gene Raymond) refers to it during another rehearsal scene some twenty-five minutes earlier, calling it "the Bill Robinson number", thus clearly relying on name recognition. When he further suggests that the number be set in a Harlem street, because that way they could "get a lot more out of it", this self-reflexively points to the value of "Harlem" as a commodity, a marketable brand in the world of entertainment. Before the full number is shown as part of the dress rehearsal, it is announced one more time as "the Bill Robinson number", again promoting Robinson's name. Finally, as the plot resolves with the show turning out to be a hit, the Black performers are called to mind once more: a short montage sequence combines shots of the evening's playbill and clips from the numbers that were seen earlier. A program page announcing "Bill Robinson in A Night in Harlem with Jeni LeGon and Fats Waller" is followed by a few seconds of Robinson dancing, this time in slow motion.

Diegetically, the narrative framing of the Harlem number, especially with the repeated name-dropping, suggests that the Black specialty act in the White Hollywood movie was an asset from the perspective of the White mainstream. This view is confirmed extradiegetically, by the film's promotion and the press reports quoted above. Both within and outside of the film, Black entertainment is clearly marked as a desirable commodity for White audiences in ways that are typical of the era's "Harlemania". Whereas the film's opening credits list Fats Waller and Jeni LeGon next to last among the "Players", Bill Robinson is mentioned third, right after – and in the same frame as – the White starring couple. This moment of desegregation between Black specialty performer and White star performers clearly emphasizes Robinson's exceptional star power.

One additional detail sets the number in *Hooray for Love* apart from many (though not all) Black musical performances in otherwise White films: Bill Robinson and

---

215 Italian-born Maria Gambarelli Fenton appeared in a handful of Hollywood films in the mid-1930s and was prima ballerina of the Metropolitan Opera Ballet in New York from 1939 to 1941. See Jennifer Dunning, "Maria Gambarelli Fenton, 89, A Metropolitan Opera Ballerina", *New York Times*, February 9, 1990, TimesMachine.

Figure 24. Jeni LeGon and Bill Robinson reappear briefly in the finale of *Hooray for Love* (1935), dancing in top hats and tailcoats.

Jeni LeGon reappear during the film's final production number, a relatively modest two-minute affair, interrupted by several cutaways from the stage show to the backstage narrative. By prominently including Robinson and LeGon in this finale, the film implicitly acknowledges their contribution to the show's – and by extension the film's – success. Like the preceding diegetic references to the number, the ending functions as a self-reflexive commentary, inadvertently pointing to the film industry's mechanisms for exploiting Black talent. Wearing top hats and tailcoats and dancing in front of the White chorus, Robinson and LeGon become the number's commanding presence, framed as the stars, even if only briefly (fig. 24). Paradoxically, this appearance suggests the possibility – but denies the fulfillment – of racial equality and integration. What's more, it shows Bill Robinson in the elegant, upper-class attire most commonly associated with Fred Astaire; and it shows a Black *female* tap dancer in the exact same attire, a masculine-gendered costume that would soon also become one of the outfits donned by Hollywood's new White queen of tap – Eleanor Powell.[216]

---

[216] For a discussion of Eleanor Powell's star persona, including her appearances in male drag, see McLean, "Putting 'Em Down".

Judged by the standards of the time, *Hooray for Love* was certainly an exceptional screen debut for a young Black woman. After this success, Earl Dancer negotiated with both MGM and 20th Century-Fox and got MGM to sign Jeni LeGon to a long-term contract starting at $1,250 a week.[217] She was cast as a dancer in *Broadway Melody of 1936* (1935), which was to feature Eleanor Powell in her first leading part. But when both tap dancers performed at a cast dinner party to promote the film, LeGon – whose act preceded Powell's – stole the show. The next day, she was informed that they didn't need two tap dancers. As LeGon herself recalled, "because I was the brown one, they just let me go".[218] In addition to Powell, the film's cast also included the White tap dancing brother/sister duo Buddy and Vilma Ebsen, which also suggests that the decision had more to do with racism than with the number of tap dancers involved. Despite this abrupt reversal of fortune, the promise of a successful film career for Jeni LeGon was upheld for some time.

Having canceled the contract, the studio negotiated with Earl Dancer about a stage appearance, and Jeni LeGon was sent overseas to appear in the London stage revue *Follow the Sun* (1936), a renamed version of the successful Broadway production *At Home Abroad* (1935). Ironically, the original Broadway show had featured Eleanor Powell in two dance numbers, and one of them, "A Brand New Suit", was now performed by LeGon in London.[219] Her other solo number, "The Steamboat Whistle", had been performed by Ethel Waters in the original Broadway production. Inside the playbill, LeGon's photo was featured among "Mr. Cochran's Young Ladies", and she was in no way segregated or marked as different from the White women.[220] As LeGon herself recalled, "it was on my first trip to London that I experienced being a real person for the first time".[221]

The Black press in the US eagerly followed the overseas adventures of its newly crowned movie princess and again praised her to the skies: "Jeni LeGon, the sepia Cinderella girl, has set London agog with her clever dancing", wrote the *Pittsburgh Courier*, and it went on to quote a series of reviews from London papers that were no less enthusiastic.[222] A caption for a glamour shot clearly overstated that

217 See Hill, *Tap Dancing America*, 124; and LeGon, interview, Govenar, *Untold Glory*.
218 LeGon, quoted in Hill, *Tap Dancing America*, 125. See also LeGon, interview, Govenar, *Untold Glory*; LeGon, interview, HistoryMakers, tape 3, story 3; and LeGon and Smith, interview, Gray.
219 For cast and crew information on the original Broadway show, see "At Home Abroad", Internet Broadway Database, The Broadway League, https://www.ibdb.com/broadway-production/at-home-abroad-11985. For the London production, see "Follow the Sun", The Guide to Musical Theatre, http://www.guidetomusicaltheatre.com/shows_f/followsun.htm.
220 Playbill for *Follow the Sun*, directed by Charles B. Cochran (1936), box 1, folder 5, LeGon, Papers.
221 LeGon, quoted in event brochure, Black Filmmakers Hall of Fame annual event, 1987, box 1, folder 33, LeGon, Papers.
222 "Jeni LeGon, Sepia 'Cinderella Girl', Sets London Agog", *Pittsburgh Courier*, February 29, 1936, ProQuest.

LeGon's "pictures have graced the front pages of every major magazine and newspaper in Europe since the opening of the production".²²³ Later that year, the *Chicago Defender* mistakenly claimed that LeGon was working on the British production *King Solomon's Mines* (1937), which starred African American singer-actor Paul Robeson.²²⁴ While LeGon mentioned meeting Robeson in London,²²⁵ there is no evidence that she was ever involved in that project. She did, however, have a brief uncredited appearance as an exotic cabaret dancer in the British comedy *Dishonour Bright* (1936). The scene, set in a Paris cabaret, has her performing a jazz-influenced sensual dance in a knee-length, sexy dress, wide-brimmed hat, and high heels. She is accompanied by a male vocalist (billed simply as Bernardi in the opening credits), who sings in English with a French accent. LeGon doesn't tap in this number but mostly struts around the stage with undulating hip motion and upper-body shimmies. Towards the end, she shakes, swings, and crosses her legs, which are briefly shown in medium shot, followed by a close-up of her mugging face. While no less racist than the period's American screen images of Black people, this role constructs LeGon as a different kind of stereotype, a racially ambiguous but nevertheless exotic figure. Compared with the Black specialty acts in American films of the time, this heavily edited scene is not so much a featured attraction, instead serving more as atmospheric background (at times, the stage is literally in the image background while the audience sitting at their tables is foregrounded).

Some sources claim that LeGon actually appeared in two British films, and she herself mentioned the 1936 comedy *This'll Make You Whistle*.²²⁶ I have found no other evidence of LeGon's participation in that film, but various reviews and other accounts suggest that this adaptation of a popular West End stage musical had several of its musical numbers removed, and it is therefore possible that a number with LeGon was filmed but never used. During her one-year stay in London, she also appeared at the legendary Café de Paris.

After returning to the US, Jeni LeGon was cast in 20th Century-Fox's comedy *Ali Baba Goes to Town* (1937). The film's star was all-around entertainer Eddie Cantor, a household name at the time, familiar to millions, especially through his radio show. In the role of hobo Al, Cantor stumbles upon a film set where they are shooting the *Arabian Nights*, is hired as an extra, falls asleep, and dreams himself into a comic version of ancient Baghdad. The dream sequence makes up the bulk of the movie and has Al/Ali Baba lead the way to a revolution in a parody

---

223 Unidentified newspaper clipping, box 1, folder 5, LeGon, Papers.
224 See "London Wild over Petite Jeni LeGon", *Chicago Defender*, September 26, 1936, ProQuest.
225 See LeGon, interview, Govenar, *Untold Glory*.
226 LeGon, interview, HistoryMakers, tape 3, story 3.

Chapter 3 Potential Pioneer: The Film Career of Black Tap Dancer Jeni LeGon

of Roosevelt's New Deal. In such a narrative context, racial and ethnic stereotypes are hardly surprising, and the film's Black specialty act features a band of musicians in "tribal" costumes that signify "Africa". It also features Eddie Cantor in blackface. His song, "Swing Is Here to Sway", predicts that a thousand years from today, "there's gonna be a Harlem". After he briefly demonstrates the Harlem dances of the future – truckin', pecking, and the Suzie-Q – Jeni LeGon takes over, and this time she gets her own dance solo. The number then concludes with the song's reprise by the Peters Sisters, an African American vocal trio of overweight women, who also throw in a bit of tap dance footwork.

Film scholar Corin Willis references this scene in his article on the concept of copresence, a term he uses for scenes featuring Black performers together with White performers in blackface.[227] Typically, such scenes convey a subliminal ideological message of the White "elevating" of an essentialized, primitive Black rhythm. This idea is clearly present in Cantor's antics with the band of "savages", who wear little more than loincloths. After Cantor fails to communicate with them in any of several "civilized" Western languages, they finally respond when he addresses them with a "hi-de-ho" – thus providing the link between "primitive Africa" and contemporary Harlem. However, this demeaning caricature of the ancient African roots of modern American jazz is in tension with Jeni LeGon's performance. It is she who most fully embodies the youthful African American vernacular, challenging the scene's stereotypically primitivist slant and fulfilling the promise of the modern Harlem culture announced in Cantor's song.

Nowhere is the fusion of body and music, which is such a key feature of African American jazz expressivity, as apparent as in jazz *dance*. The percussive art of tap dance, with its synthesis of dance and musical rhythm, is the paramount example, and in this number, Jeni LeGon makes full use of the expressive potential of tap dance. This time, she wears a decidedly feminine and exotic costume, with a knee-length hula skirt, a tight-fitting top that leaves her belly exposed, big earrings, and feathers in her hair; yet she again dances in low-heeled tap shoes. Although she is exoticized and othered by the "tribal" costume, she looks considerably less ridiculous than any of the scene's half-naked Black male performers. There are no "minstrelizing shots" of her, such as Willis finds in many musical numbers from other films. The author uses this term, which he also calls a "racial cut", to describe "an edit specifically timed to frame and freeze the character in a stereotypical 'racial' pose or gesture".[228] The respective shots are often close-ups of wide-eyed and grinning faces, which are reminiscent of the

---

227 See Willis, "Blackface Minstrelsy".

228 Willis, 52.

denigrating caricatures of blackface minstrelsy. As Willis argues, minstrelizing shots are used to contain the (often small) degree of autonomy that Black performers sometimes attained in their screen performances, defusing the power of the African American vernacular. Given the widespread practice of this type of visual containment, it is arguably significant that there are no such "racial cuts" in Jeni LeGon's dance number here. Instead, she is shown in full shot the entire time, and her expansive but controlled movements across the floor at times cause Cantor and the musicians to retreat (figs. 25 & 26). There is, then, a brief threat to what Richard Dyer calls the "colonial structure" of musicals, in which "expansion into space, control over what's in that space" is generally reserved for White people, whereas "Black people doing the same thing would in the white imagination seem like a terrifying attempt to take over".[229] With her energetic moves, involving the whole body and loosely swinging arms, LeGon indeed takes over and controls the performance space, quite literally defying containment. Her obvious virtuosity as a dancer shows her as highly skilled and in control, willfully uncontrollable rather than savagely untamable. However obliquely and ambiguously, the scene – with its context of an affectionately spoofed New Deal – casts modern Harlem culture as a progressive force. And with Jeni LeGon's control over the performance and space, Eddie Cantor's character – as the intermediary promoting Black culture for White consumption – becomes temporarily redundant.

Moreover, control in this case – as well as in the earlier *Hooray for Love* – extends beyond what is visible onscreen. In both films, the Black specialty acts were staged by White dance director Sammy Lee, and the "Swing Is Here to Sway" number was nominated for an Academy Award for Dance Direction.[230] Lee, who had already staged dances for over a dozen films since coming to Hollywood in 1928 (after a successful Broadway career), was a competent dance director, but his strength lay in the arrangement of elaborate production numbers.[231] Unlike such spectacles, the dances in *Hooray for Love* and *Ali Baba Goes to Town* had little to offer in terms of chorus lines or fancy cinematography. Instead, they relied mostly on the skill of the dancers, who needed little more than a floor and a camera to create a great number. Generally, experienced tap soloists were in part – and often entirely – responsible for their own choreography, which was clearly the case with

---

229 Dyer, *Only Entertainment*, 41.

230 Lee had also been nominated for two dance numbers in *King of Burlesque* (1936). See Academy Awards Database, Academy of Motion Picture Arts and Sciences, http://awardsdatabase.oscars.org.

231 New York-born Sammy Lee started off as a self-taught vaudeville dancer. Over the course of his career, he became familiar with many dance styles, though not proficient in all of them. On his stage career, see Ries, "Sammy Lee: The Broadway Career". On his film career, see Ries, "Sammy Lee: The Hollywood Career". With regard to *Ali Baba Goes to Town*, Ries mistakenly claims that the swing number with LeGon features a solo by "the future Gypsy Rose Lee" (195).

Chapter 3 Potential Pioneer: The Film Career of Black Tap Dancer Jeni LeGon

Figures 25 and 26. Despite the bizarre "tribal" setting and costume, Jeni LeGon is fully in control for the duration of her dance solo in *Ali Baba Goes to Town* (1937), stealing the show from Eddie Cantor, who performs in blackface.

Robinson and LeGon's dances in these two films.²³² The dancers' commanding presence in these numbers is thus partly rooted in their command over the creative process.

The Black press's reaction to LeGon's performance in *Ali Baba* was similar in tone to *Hooray for Love*, but coverage was less extensive. The *Courier* titled a brief piece with "Critic Says LeGon Has Stolen Picture From Eddie Cantor!" and suggested that "the script writer might just have easily tagged the vehicle ... 'Jeni Goes to Town'".²³³ Positive mention of her appearance in the movie was made here and there, but overall, *Ali Baba* didn't attract nearly as much attention as LeGon's screen debut.²³⁴

Broken Promises: Late 1930s

With her next role in Warner Bros.' *Fools for Scandal* (1938), LeGon once again fell victim to the industry's racist bias. She appears in the number "There's a Boy in Harlem", singing the Rodgers and Hart song with Les Hite and his orchestra. As she runs offstage at the end of the song, she is obviously about to perform a dance, but the second part of the number was cut from the film.²³⁵ In an article lamenting Hollywood's treatment of Black artists, journalist Earl J. Morris mentions the scene as a typical instance of the industry's discriminatory practices. Morris was the *Pittsburgh Courier*'s film editor and one of the Hollywood industry's most vocal critics with regard to its treatment of African Americans. His article titled "Hollywood Ignores Black America" perfectly encapsulates the Black mainstream press's quandary in the 1930s. Courted by Hollywood's publicity departments, the popular weekly papers continually navigated between satisfying the industry's demands for promotion of its product and serving the Black community through advocacy for better treatment of African Americans. As documented by Anna Everett, film criticism and commentary in the popular

232 LeGon recalled working with Robinson and how much she learned from him, calling him a task master; see the documentary *Jeni LeGon: Living in a Great Big Way*, directed by Grant Greschuk, 1999.

233 Al Moses, "Critic Says LeGon Has Stolen Picture from Eddie Cantor!", *Pittsburgh Courier*, December 11, 1937, ProQuest.

234 It is worth noting that Black journalist Earl J. Morris praised Eddie Cantor for his continued support of entertainers regardless of their race: "Eddie Cantor ... gave us the Nicholas Kids, the Peters Sisters, and that adorable little dancing darling, Jeni LeGon". "The Earl of Morris' Paragraph Portraits", Grand Town Day and Night, *Pittsburgh Courier*, June 4, 1938, ProQuest. Such positive press coverage for White stars who appeared to support the African American quest for better treatment was typical of Black film journalism in the 1930s; see also Everett, *Returning the Gaze*, 216–217.

235 In an interview, LeGon claimed that the scene was reused in the British-American coproduction *This Was Paris* (1942), which she saw a long time ago but hadn't been able to find again; see LeGon and Smith, interview, Gray. IMDb lists her as an uncredited cabaret dancer in that film, but I have not been able to verify this; see "This Was Paris – Full Cast and Crew", IMDb, https://www.imdb.com/title/tt0035434/fullcredits?ref_=tt_cl_sm#cast.

Black press was mainly "concerned with effecting a progressive reform of Hollywood in matters of race and representation".[236] For this purpose, it combined a general rhetoric of uplift with occasional critique of the industry's injustices. With respect to LeGon in *Fools for Scandal*, Morris expressed his suspicion that the number was cut because it did not show the usual Black stereotypes:

> Jeni LeGon, that dancing darling, portrays a Harlem boy and is dressed as a smart Harlem lad would be. The three Brown Sisters wore lovely gowns that were designed by one of Hollywood's leading modiste [*sic*]. Les Hite and his bandsmen were dressed as any white or colored band would in a smart night club.
>
> There were no exaggerated plaids or pigtails on the chorus of lovely beautiful colored girls. No derbies, no calico or bandanas. They were depicted as sepias would be in real life under those same circumstances. ...
>
> But due to the length of the picture certain scenes had to be cut out. So studio heads said "here is a scene that we can cut out, it is not the type that white audiences want".[237]

In fact, the aesthetics of the "Boy in Harlem" scene recall cinematic images of Black jazz from the period following the transition to sound film, with its short-lived Black film fad. Apparently, these were images that White audiences *did* want to see, at least in terms of their music and visuals. Nevertheless, Morris might have been right in suggesting that the cut had something to do with how the Black performers were depicted. But it is not simply the absence of demeaning Black stereotypes that is relevant here. Rather, I would suggest that the root of the matter lies in how race, gender, and dance intersect in Jeni LeGon's performance.

The number starts with a Black man playing piano in an apartment – a stylized setting with an oversized window and a few artificial-looking props, lit in an expressionist high-contrast style. Filmed obliquely from behind, the man's face remains unrecognizable. With the mise-en-scène and lighting stylized and tending towards abstraction, the visual aesthetic corresponds to what Richard Dyer calls the "broadly modernist sensibility" of many early jazz films with their "visual evocation of modernist jazz making".[238] While this modernist-expressionist visual style was most common in the Black-cast short films of the early sound era, it remained tied to clichés of Black music and dance performance in later feature films. After the brief introductory segment, the image dissolves to Jeni LeGon as she begins the song: "There's a new dark music by a new dark man, and he writes his symphonies in Black and tan". As if to underline the lyrics, she appears out

---

236 Everett, *Returning the Gaze*, 180.
237 Earl J. Morris, "Hollywood Ignores Black America", *Pittsburgh Courier*, May 28, 1938, ProQuest.
238 Dyer, *Space of a Song*, chapter 6.

of the dark of a completely black screen. When a spotlight is turned on and Les Hite's band appears behind her, she is revealed to be on a nightclub stage.

Again, Jeni LeGon performs in low-heeled tap shoes. She also wears her most masculine film costume yet, a wide-cut white suit and top hat, which contrasts with the conventionally glamorous showgirl attire of the backing vocalists, the Three Brown Girls. The transition from the piano player – presumably the song's literal referent – to LeGon as "a Harlem boy" highlights the performative aspect of identities, specifically racial and gender identities. The fact that journalist Morris doesn't seem to find anything unusual in LeGon's gender masquerade and that he considers the scene to depict "sepias" as they would be "in real life" suggests the ordinariness of such performative identity transformations in Black show business – as well as in everyday life. At the same time, "Boy in Harlem" makes it clear that LeGon is presenting the spectacle of Black Harlem for White audiences (both in and of the film) in much the same way as she did in *Hooray for Love* and *Ali Baba Goes to Town*.[239]

But LeGon's outfit is more than just a gender masquerade. Her somewhat oversized costume is conspicuously similar to some of the suits worn by the popular Black singer-bandleader Cab Calloway. The "extreme drape style" suits that had become popular among African Americans and other minorities would culminate in the famous zoot suit of the 1940s, a fashion item with a multilayered history of cultural and political significations. As a subcultural fashion statement, the zoot suit became associated with the refusal to be subservient, with defiance rather than assimilation.[240] Retrospectively associating Jeni LeGon's 1938 costume with the subsequent subversive connotations of the zoot suit might be overinterpreting things. But it is surely no accident that her costume recalls that of Cab Calloway, who was himself a complex figure of nonconformity.[241] In fact, LeGon's wide-legged poses, her gestures – for example, when she slowly extends her arms sideways – and her sliding moves across the stage (without tap sounds) are so obviously inspired by Calloway that they can be considered quotations. Beyond simply concealing LeGon's feminine figure, the costume and performance thus add another layer to the scene's sense of role-play.

What Arthur Knight calls "a subversive cultural politics of style" with reference to the Nicholas Brothers and Cab Calloway in *Stormy Weather* (1943)[242] would

---

239 With the story set in London and Paris, the scene's setting is actually a fictional Paris nightclub called Le Petit Harlem. The number was staged by dance director Bobby Connolly.

240 For a comprehensive history of the zoot suit, see Peiss, *Zoot Suit*. For shorter discussions of some of the suit's cultural meanings, see, for instance, Cosgrove, "The Zoot-Suit", 77; and Kelley, "Riddle of the Zoot".

241 See, for instance, the documentary *Cab Calloway: Sketches*, directed by Gail Levin, 2012.

242 Knight, *Disintegrating the Musical*, 158.

Chapter 3 Potential Pioneer: The Film Career of Black Tap Dancer Jeni LeGon

find its way into Hollywood movies – and thus to mass audiences – mostly by way of Black male entertainers. There are, however, only very few scenes from the era's mainstream films in which Black women appear as anything other than servants or sexualized objects of desire. The sexy showgirl roles served to satisfy (White) male fantasy, and they were generally reserved for light-skinned African American women. The "Boy in Harlem" number is a rare exception to this practice, as it gestures towards the possibility of depicting Black women outside of Hollywood's usual racist and sexist framework. But at the same time, LeGon's number underlines the lack of variety in screen images available to Black women by having her appear in masculine garb.

Above all, of course, the scene's transformative potential is curtailed by the removal of LeGon's dance solo. And it is notable that only the dancing was excised, while the song was left intact. This is especially ironic in hindsight: LeGon comes to stand in for the faceless Harlem songwriter whose songs are all the rage, even though, as the last line of the verse explains, "the outside world has never heard his name". Through the song lyrics, her performance is thus associated with unacknowledged authorship and creativity – the very fate she and countless other Black artists suffered in White Hollywood. According to LeGon herself, the dance was cut because the film's leading lady, Carole Lombard, didn't like it.[243] While it is hardly surprising that tap star Eleanor Powell felt threatened by LeGon's dancing abilities, one does wonder about the nondancer comedienne's objection – after all, Lombard was among Hollywood's highest-earning stars in the late 1930s. The cut might very well have been a coincidence resulting from the film's generally unfortunate production history rather than from the star's personal influence or LeGon's performance in particular.[244] Nevertheless, from a historical distance, it is hard not to read this as an exemplary case, symptomatic of an industry regime that is both racist *and* sexist. While Black male dancers were allowed to "steal the picture" once in a while, a woman doing the same thing was more likely to be stopped. Perhaps whoever made the decision did not object to LeGon's presence per se nor even to her gender masquerade. Rather, the unsettling part might have been her demonstration of competence, which threatened to steal the show. A Black woman performing "as a smart Harlem lad" *and* demonstrating extraordinary skill and control in the male-dominated realm of solo tap – apparently, Hollywood was not quite ready for this.

---

243 As she recalled: "two of my movies that I dance in, the dance sections – I sing and dance – and two of the sections were disliked by the leading ladies, and so they cut out the dancing and left the singing". The other film she refers to here is *Start Cheering* (1938). LeGon, interview, Govenar, *Untold Glory*.

244 Rodgers and Hart were commissioned to write a score for the film, but several of their songs were discarded, while others only served as background music. "Boy in Harlem" was the only tune sung in the film's final version. For a brief production history, see Miller, "Fools for Scandal".

Figure 27. A still from the "Boy in Harlem" dance scene that was cut from *Fools for Scandal* (1938). LeGon's costume here is conspicuously similar to the suits typically worn by Cab Calloway. Credit: Everett Collection.

After the duet with Bill Robinson in *Hooray for Love* and the solo under Eddie Cantor's supervision in *Ali Baba Goes to Town*, *Fools for Scandal* was the first film to feature Jeni LeGon as the uncontested focus of a musical number. While most of the excised footage appears to be lost, evidence survives in the form of a publicity still and in a few seconds of footage in the film's trailer. In the trailer, not much detail is recognizable behind the big white letters announcing "New Hit Tunes by Richard Rodgers and Lorenz Hart", but LeGon in her white suit seems to dance in front of a large chorus of scantily clad girls.[245] The still confirms this, clearly indicating her role as the scene's conductor (fig. 27). That the "Boy in Harlem" scene only survives in such truncated form speaks volumes about how race and gender intersected in the Hollywood industry's ideological paradigm.

Interestingly, neither the *Pittsburgh Courier* nor the *Chicago Defender* reviewed the film or celebrated Jeni LeGon's appearance in it. The movie was a box office bomb as well as a critical failure, with the *New York Times* listing it as one of the "Worst Pictures of the Year", and LeGon's number seems to have gone unnoticed

---

245 See "Fools for Scandal – Original Trailer", video, TCM, Turner Classic Movies, https://www.tcm.com/video/91269/fools-for-scandal-original-trailer.

Chapter 3 Potential Pioneer: The Film Career of Black Tap Dancer Jeni LeGon

by Black and White critics alike.[246] The inevitable yet unanswerable question is: would the reaction have been any different if Jeni LeGon's dance solo had not been cut? Given the general popularity of tap dancing, it is very likely that the scene would have elicited a similar kind of praise as was bestowed on the Harlem sequence in *Hooray for Love*. And as with LeGon's screen debut, this might have been the case despite – or precisely because – the rest of the film was not received very favorably.

Jeni LeGon's three Hollywood films of the 1930s can be considered standard film fare of their time. Produced by three major studios,[247] featuring a few major and some minor stars, none of them ever entered the canon of classic musicals or comedies. All three films present African American performance in accordance with Hollywood's conventions – that is, as Black specialty acts performed for a White (diegetic) audience, but otherwise disconnected from the narrative. Even though each number explicitly celebrates Harlem's Black music and dance culture, White songwriting teams provided the music and lyrics in all three cases.[248] Apart from the generally limiting practice of the Black specialty act, Jeni LeGon is additionally restrained in various ways: in *Hooray for Love* by being in the shadow of Bill Robinson; in *Ali Baba Goes to Town* by her exoticized appearance and by the primitivist slant of the whole scene; and most radically in *Fools for Scandal*, where her solo dance was simply cut from the film. Yet LeGon also resists containment in these performances through her norm-defying appearance as well as through her extraordinary competence as a dancer.[249] Even in *Fools for Scandal*, which renders her dancing skills all but invisible, the remainder of the scene still allows her to display a movement quality and style – in part by physically "quoting" Cab Calloway – that is not seen in any other Black female screen performer of the time. One can only wonder about the full scope of her skill as a dancer. In later interviews, LeGon would talk about how she learned by watching male dancers and how she was able to do all the complex moves,

---

246 Bosley Crowther, "A Minority Report: In Which Will Be Found a List of the Ten Worst Pictures of the Year", *New York Times*, January 1, 1939, TimesMachine. In a generally tepid review of the film, the trade magazine *Variety* merely noted that "'Boy in Harlem', sung by a colored girl as part of a floor show routine in Paris, serves principally as background scenery". Review of *Fools for Scandal*, *Variety*, March 30, 1938, 15, Media History Digital Library.

247 RKO, 20th Century-Fox, and Warner Bros., respectively. Together with MGM and Paramount, these studios were known as the "Big Five" during Hollywood's studio era.

248 "Living in a Great Big Way" was written by Jimmy McHugh (music) and Dorothy Fields (lyrics), "Swing Is Here to Sway" by Harry Revel (music) and Mack Gordon (lyrics).

249 In all three films, Jeni LeGon's name appears in the title credits: in *Hooray for Love,* it is simply listed under the heading "The Players", in *Ali Baba,* she is credited together with the (Black) Peters Sisters and the (White) Raymond Scott Quintet. While it was fairly customary to credit Black performers in this way, it was by no means imperative, and African American specialties often remained uncredited.

including acrobatics, usually associated with tap-dancing men.[250] In at least one interview, Fayard Nicholas confirms this, claiming that she was capable of matching the male dancers.[251] If these accounts are even just partially accurate, then the surviving film footage gives us but a hint of what Jeni LeGon was really able to do. In any case, LeGon's musical numbers in Hollywood films suggest her potential to articulate alternative styles of Black femininity, thereby pushing the boundaries of the time. Yet they also show that those boundaries could only be pushed so far.

As promising as Jeni LeGon's start in the movies seemed, the promise was never realized, despite the efforts of manager Earl Dancer and of the Black press to make her a star. A 1935 article in the *Chicago Defender* simply titled "Jeni LeGon" – one of the most detailed press reports from her Hollywood years – speaks of her career as "one of those meteoric rises". In the first part, the author focuses on his impression of LeGon's personality: She is "unaffectedly curled up on the floor" and there "seems to be no studied effort on her part. ... Her twinkling toes and clicking heels seem to move involuntarily ... as if motivated by no effort from her". She is "not an artist nor an entertainer as we commonly know them", but "just a very ordinary girl distinguished by a captivating personality given an opportunity to do that which she loves above all else to do – dance". The author thus shifts the focus to the subject of dance: "her one ambition has ever been to dance. ... She had no formal training. ... But she had a girl friend ... who was taking dancing lessons. Her steps, she taught to Jeni, who practiced them assiduously". This leads to a discussion of LeGon's professional career, with the author recounting her trip to Los Angeles and her discovery by her future manager Earl Dancer: "Then came her break in pictures. Teamed with Bill Robinson, she scored so tremendously in 'Hooray for Love' that she was immediately signed up by MGM for several more. Offers began flying in from all directions at once".[252]

The image emerging from this portrait remains fairly consistent across different publications during this early period of LeGon's greatest media presence. Overall,

---

250 "I used to copy the boys so much that I danced more or less like the boys in a sense" (LeGon, interview, HistoryMakers, tape 2, story 6); "Well I did little steps like this that the Nicholas Brothers [Fayard and Harold] and the Berrys did. I did spins and drop on my knees and push-ups and things called over-the-tops and I did little kicks which was one of the steps that you hit on your hands and make your feet go over your back and you end up on them like this, you know. ... And then this wonderful step that Fayard does when he looks like he's going to do what we call the Chinese splits – he opens his legs real fast and slides forward. I did those too. Mostly all the boy steps. I tapped too. I mean I had real good footwork, yeah" (LeGon, interview, HistoryMakers, tape 3, story 4).

251 See the documentary *Jeni LeGon: Living in a Great Big Way*, directed by Grant Greschuk, 1999.

252 All quotations in this paragraph from C. Cecil Craigne, "Jeni LeGon", *Chicago Defender*, November 16, 1935, ProQuest.

coverage in the Black press of the mid-1930s reads very much like the beginning of a conventional star narrative, including a rags-to-riches rise and the typical star paradox, according to which a star is presented as simultaneously ordinary and uniquely talented.[253] Time and time again, she is described as natural, unaffected, charming, and just an ordinary girl. There is much emphasis on her youth and apparent innocence, and her name is often preceded by words like "cute", "little", or "petite". Her dancing is described as natural and effortless, yet she is also considered ambitious, hardworking, competent, and a creative dancer. Like some of her White contemporaries, Jeni LeGon thus complicates notions of the female dancer as a passive, objectified showgirl by appearing as a virtuosic, creative performer,[254] and her predilection for pants supports this image of an alternative femininity based on agency and competence.

Of course, reading LeGon's wardrobe choices as any sort of intended feminist statement would be far-fetched, to say the least, especially since, according to LeGon herself, this sartorial habit came about by accident.[255] Nevertheless, it is interesting to note how references to her wardrobe are often followed by a reaffirmation of her femininity. The abovementioned portrait in the *Chicago Defender* claims that "in spite of her youth, and her tendency toward masculine attire as evidenced by her choice of trousers for ordinary wearing apparel, she is quite the 'femme' possessing a love of children".[256] Another author surmises that she wears "tailor-made tight fitting slacks. ... to show off her lovely form".[257] By simultaneously highlighting and downplaying the nonconformity of LeGon's appearance, such statements have a reassuring effect. Similarly, monikers like "dancing darling" allowed journalists to belittle LeGon at the same time as they emphasized her exceptional skills. Thus, neither her dancing ability nor her masculine-gendered outfits were construed as threatening. Just as Adrienne McLean claims of White tap star Eleanor Powell,[258] LeGon's occasional masculine masquerade is fully integrated with her femininity. In fact, LeGon seems to

---

253 See, for instance, Dyer, *Stars*; and Ellis, *Visible Fictions*, 91–108.

254 See, for instance, McLean, "Putting 'Em Down", 89–90.

255 "I hadn't started to develop at all, and all the other girls had nice little figures with little bumpies and stuff like that. ... We all came out and posed, and my costume just hung off of me. It was ridiculous. The director said, 'Oh my God. What am I going to do with you!' I, with my big mouth, said, 'I don't dance in dresses in things like this, I dance ... in pants. I sing and dance in pants.' I really didn't do it, I just had a big mouth and said I did. But he said. 'Oh, well that's wonderful.' He said, 'Then you don't have to dance in the line. You can be the soubrette.' ... That's how I got into the pants, and I danced in the pants from then on". LeGon, quoted in Frank, *Tap!*, 120.

256 C. Cecil Craigne, "Jeni LeGon", *Chicago Defender*, November 16, 1935, ProQuest.

257 Jay Gould, "Race Track Gossip", *Chicago Defender*, October 31, 1936, ProQuest.

258 See McLean, "Putting 'Em Down", 93.

Figure 28. A publicity photo of Jeni LeGon (ca. 1936) showing her in a glamorous, conventionally feminine costume. Credit: Jeni LeGon Papers, Archives Center, National Museum of American History, Smithsonian Institution.

have been equally comfortable in more conventionally feminine attire, as evidenced by her numbers in *Ali Baba Goes to Town*, in the British production *Dishonour Bright*, and in the independently produced race film *Double Deal* (1939), as well as by various publicity photos (fig. 28).

As much as the African American press tried to promote LeGon as a star and figure of identification for Black audiences, excitement dwindled quickly. A 1939 feature in the *Chicago Defender* still calls her "a big favorite in filmdom", but proceeds with statements that range from exaggerated to speculative to downright false, claiming that she appeared in a film featuring Fred Astaire (which didn't happen until 1948) or that she was a popular casting choice for short films (she never appeared in a short).[259] By the end of the decade, no hyperbolic phrases could conceal or make up for her lack of success in the mainstream film industry.

[259] "Jeni Legon Weighs Hollywood's Offer", *Chicago Defender*, September 30, 1939, ProQuest.

Chapter 3 Potential Pioneer: The Film Career of Black Tap Dancer Jeni LeGon

Uncredited: 1940s

That Hollywood was not ready to support the solo career of a competent Black female dancer seems to be confirmed by the remainder of Jeni LeGon's film career. She was too dark-skinned for the role of the mulatto trying to pass for White, and with her somewhat boyish looks, she did not match the beauty standards of a conventionally glamorous showgirl. Nor did she fit the stereotype of the mammy played by actresses like Louise Beavers and Hattie McDaniel. Unlike Lena Horne or Dorothy Dandridge (who both came to prominence in the 1940s), LeGon could not so easily be presented as racially ambiguous. She was unambiguously African American, and despite her occasional gender masquerade, she was also unambiguously female. What Richard Dyer says of light-skinned singer Lena Horne is thus even truer of Jeni LeGon: "Hollywood didn't know what to do with her".[260] The unfortunate outcome of *Fools for Scandal* pretty much spelled the end for LeGon as a dancer in Hollywood films. That same year, her entire number (performed with the vocal group the Four Blackbirds) was cut from Columbia's college musical *Start Cheering* (1938). Reportedly, this was once again a White performer's doing, this time comedienne Gertrude Niesen's.[261] Unsurprisingly, the White press mostly ignored her after her initial successes as a dancer. Reviews of the films she appeared in occasionally listed her as a cast member but without further comment, thus implying both a degree of name recognition and a general lack of interest. That her potential star power started waning before it had the chance to fully unfold is confirmed by the media's almost complete indifference regarding her private life. Even the Black press showed little interest in it, and her marriage to prominent African American musician and songwriter Phil Moore, whom she had met on the set of the race film *Double Deal*, barely attracted any media attention.[262] By the mid-1940s, she seemed to be all but forgotten. One news article captioned two photos of LeGon and Moore rather condescendingly: "At home Phil Moore finds an able aide in ex-film starlet Jeni LeGon whom he married two years ago".[263]

Meanwhile, Lena Horne had caught Hollywood's attention. A pioneer in her own right, who became the first African American woman to sign and *keep* a long-term

---

260 Dyer, *Space of a Song*, chapter 6.

261 LeGon remembered that, like in *Fools for Scandal*, the dancing was cut, but the singing was left in the film. However, the only version I have had access to, on DVD, lacks any trace of the number. The DVD's running time of seventy-eight minutes corresponds to the entry in TCM's database, which lists Jeni LeGon with the Four Blackbirds among the film's cast; see "Start Cheering (1938)", TCM, Turner Classic Movies, http://www.tcm.com/tcmdb/title/3682/Start-Cheering/. See also LeGon, interview, HistoryMakers, tape 3, story 4; and LeGon and Smith, interview, Gray.

262 For an overview of Phil Moore's career, see Bogle, *Bright Boulevards*, 224–232.

263 Unidentified newspaper clipping (approximately 1945), box 1, folder 2, LeGon, Papers.

contract with a Hollywood studio,[264] Horne crossed professional paths with Jeni LeGon twice. In her first Hollywood feature film, *Panama Hattie* (1942), Lena Horne sang two songs, and the second number also featured a spectacular performance by the Berry Brothers, a Black male trio known for their acrobatic tap dancing.[265] The number's song, "The Sping", was written by LeGon's husband at the time, Phil Moore, who also worked as an arranger on the film's score. LeGon herself contributed the lyrics, with the title being an amalgam of the words "Spanish" and "swing". She later said that she had the idea after being introduced to Latin music and dancing in New York.[266] LeGon was also hired as a dance coach and stand-in for Lena Horne.[267] Neither the songwriters nor the performers received any onscreen credit. According to Richard Dyer, Lena Horne and the Berry Brothers were "inserted into *Hattie* after disastrous previews and their sequences shot by Vincente Minnelli (the rest of the film was directed by Norman Z. McLeod)".[268] We have, then, yet another White-produced film profiting from African American talent that was – quite literally – an added attraction.

The second film in which LeGon stood in Lena Horne's shadow was Fox's all-star Black revue musical *Stormy Weather*, which paired Horne with Bill Robinson.[269] *Stormy Weather* in many ways marked both the pinnacle and the beginning of the end of Hollywood's "Negro Entertainment Syndrome", as film historian Donald Bogle calls it.[270] It was the first Hollywood film explicitly dedicated to "celebrating the magnificent contribution of the colored race to the entertainment of the world during the past twenty-five years", as is announced in the first scene. That this patronizing yet celebratory tribute to Black entertainment didn't include a dance by a female tap soloist is symptomatic of the general marginalization of women tap artists. Relegating LeGon to the status of an uncredited chorus girl, even though the film would certainly have benefited from a solo tap number by

---

264 See Bogle, *Toms, Coons*, 125–128. According to Arthur Knight, Horne's two Hollywood star vehicles, *Stormy Weather* (1943) and *Cabin in the Sky* (1943), "worked in concert in an attempt to *make* the first black movie star, Lena Horne"; *Disintegrating the Musical*, 148 (italics in the original).

265 On the Berry Brothers, see Hill, *Tap Dancing America*, 91–92; and Stearns and Stearns, *Jazz Dance*, 272–279.

266 See LeGon, interview, HistoryMakers, tape 4, story 4.

267 See "Screenland's New Deal Gives Race Artists Pretty Shuffle", Theatricals, *Pittsburgh Courier*, June 20, 1942, Newspapers.com.

268 Dyer, *Space of a Song*, chapter 6.

269 In a brief passage on Jeni LeGon, tap dance historian Constance Valis Hill wonders why Bill Robinson did not choose to work with LeGon again after *Hooray for Love*, and she relates the story of Robinson's choice of White tap dancer Geneva Sawyer as his partner in *Café Metropole* (1937). See Hill, *Tap Dancing America*, 125.

270 Bogle, *Toms, Coons*, 118.

her, clearly shows how much Hollywood had lost interest in boosting the career of its Black "dancing darling".

LeGon's two encounters with Lena Horne might have been accidental, but they are telling in that they reveal how there was virtually no place in Hollywood for African American dancing women. Their creative authorship was made invisible in favor of – primarily – the White industry and – secondarily – male dancers and lighter-skinned female singers. This complicates the system of a simple binary racial segregation, adding layers of gender inequality as well as intraracial hierarchy. The resulting system favors lighter-skinned women over those with a darker complexion and male soloists over women performing with the same level of competence. In this system, Jeni LeGon's looks and skills didn't quite fit in anywhere.

Servant roles were clearly not what MGM had in mind in 1935, when the studio put LeGon under contract to appear in musical specialty numbers – the seemingly obvious career path for a talented Black dancer of the era. But when it turned out that her looks and skills lay outside the limited range of screen images available to Black female performers, there weren't many options left for her. During the 1940s, LeGon played a series of servant roles and other bit parts,[271] very much like her predecessor Nina Mae McKinney, whose attempted Hollywood comeback in the 1940s likewise stagnated with nothing but bit roles. In the gothic classic *I Walked with a Zombie* (1943), LeGon had a brief appearance as a dancer in a voodoo ceremony, for which she was credited on the list of major supporting players. But this tiny role gave her no real opportunity to display her dancing skills, and she is barely distinguishable from the other dancers in the scene, which is just one of many ingredients contributing to the exotic and mysterious atmosphere of the film's Caribbean locale. LeGon's minor, nonmusical roles seem particularly ironic in the case of musicals: she appears briefly as a nameless girl in jail in the Bing Crosby vehicle *Birth of the Blues* (1941), one of Hollywood's many "White man makes Black jazz respectable" narratives. But perhaps the most bitterly ironic casting choice was the one in *Easter Parade* (1948), which starred Fred Astaire, Judy Garland, and Ann Miller. Jeni LeGon had no dancing part in this film, instead playing the maid to Ann Miller – the tap dancer who had superseded Eleanor Powell as Hollywood's foremost White female tap soloist. In fact, LeGon's encounters with Fred Astaire are another poignant reminder of how the marginalization of Black people in studio-era Hollywood would be magnified in the case of women. In various interviews, LeGon recalled meeting Fred Astaire

---

271 "I've been an Arabian maid, I've been an African maid, I've been an American maid three or four times". LeGon, interview, Govenar, *Untold Glory*.

and Ginger Rogers on the RKO lot in 1935, when she was working on *Hooray for Love* with Bill Robinson. As Robinson and Astaire knew each other from New York, the two dance teams would visit each other in their respective rehearsal halls at RKO, where they "talked dance talk, traded steps and did things together".[272] Yet when LeGon was later assigned the servant role in Astaire's *Easter Parade*, he never acknowledged their earlier acquaintance and completely ignored her.[273] In the context of the times, it is hardly surprising that Blacks were ignored by Whites, but this anecdote suggests that gender intersected with and complicated simple racial binaries.[274]

Jeni LeGon's last musical appearance in a Hollywood feature film was in Paramount's biopic *Somebody Loves Me* (1952), which starred Betty Hutton as vaudeville star Blossom Seeley. It is once again bitterly ironic, as it self-reflexively sums up her fate in mainstream movies: in two consecutive numbers, LeGon accompanies Hutton as a singing onstage maid, serving the White star. The scenes give her no real opportunity to showcase her talent, as she only gets to do a few dance steps, which are little more than strutting. Perhaps Hutton or the studio was still worried that LeGon might steal the show with her tap dancing.

In between these sporadic and disappointing assignments in Hollywood productions, Jeni LeGon had a few bigger parts in Black independent films, beginning with *Double Deal* in 1939, where she played the female lead role of a nightclub dancer. The film starts with a medium shot of her practicing to piano music. The following scene, which alternates full shots of her with reverse shots of the club owner and several other men watching her, shows her in a short romper and low-heeled white tap shoes. In her only full-length number, in which she sings "Getting It Right with You" before dancing in front of the nightclub audience, she wears a short white dress and flowers in her hair (which is longer than in earlier films). Her appearance and performance in this dance number are in line with the cute, girly role she plays in the story. While she sings the song, her facial expressions and movements – small hip and shoulder wiggles – are playfully flirty and conventionally feminine. But during the two-minute solo dance that follows, this girlishness is overshadowed by her display of versatile rhythm tap. Much like in *Ali Baba*, LeGon's dancing is simultaneously dynamic and expressive – with wide arm and leg movements – as well as precise and controlled, as she alternately

---

272 LeGon, interview, HistoryMakers, tape 3, story 2.

273 See LeGon, interview, Govenar, *Untold Glory*; and LeGon and Smith, interview, Gray.

274 LeGon summed up Black/White relationships during the studio era concisely, saying "you didn't fraternize in Hollywood. You worked, and that was the end of it. And some of them spoke to you on the set and some of them didn't". LeGon, interview, HistoryMakers, tape 4, story 6. She also recalled that Al Jolson and Ruby Keeler were the only Whites in Hollywood socializing with her and other Black people (tape 4, story 7).

goes up on her toes, stamps her feet hard on the floor, and flings her legs. The short costumes that she wears for dancing display her thin legs and thus help to eroticize and objectify her for the pleasure of the male audience. At the same time, they also allow for the unrestrained exhibition of her dancing abilities. Much like the portrayals in the Black press, her image in the race movie *Double Deal* is simultaneously cute and innocent as well as competent and professional.

Curiously though, the producers of independent Black films didn't seem all that interested in LeGon's dancing skills, instead casting her in unrewarding dramatic roles like that of Cab Calloway's girlfriend Minnie in *Hi De Ho* (1947).[275] Just over an hour long, this melodramatic musical's plot is wrapped up halfway through, when Minnie dies after being accidentally shot. The second half consists of loosely connected musical numbers, including a sequence of three impressive tap routines by a trio known as Miller Brothers and Lois (George and Danny Miller and Lois Bright).[276] LeGon, however, has no dance numbers, and fares badly in the role of the sexy but neurotically jealous seductress.

Only two of Jeni LeGon's four race movies seem to have survived.[277] These are representative of the era's independently produced Black films in that they are cheaply made, and they appear somewhat clumsy in terms of plot, dialogue, and acting. But despite their many deficiencies, they also highlight the shortcomings of the White mainstream industry. By casting Jeni LeGon in lead roles, these films add an additional facet to her screen persona – not so much because she was a particularly talented or charismatic actress (by all appearances she wasn't), but simply because they suggest the possibility of a normalized Black femininity, for which there was no space in Hollywood's racial and sexual hierarchy.

One more question concerning the film career of Jeni LeGon remains: why did she never appear in a theatrical short film or a Soundie jukebox short? Again, the question is worth asking even if it ultimately remains unanswerable. Considering that these short forms have come to be regarded as a comparatively privileged forum for the showcasing of Black talent, LeGon's absence from them is noteworthy. As for theatrical shorts, the explanation might simply be timing: the Black-cast trend in short films was waning by the mid-1930s, right at the beginning of Jeni LeGon's film career, and henceforth, White big bands domi-

---

275   LeGon briefly talks about working with Cab Calloway on *Hi De Ho* in the documentary *In the Shadow of Hollywood: Race Movies & the Birth of Black Cinema*, directed by Brad Osborne, 2007.

276   According to tap historian Constance Valis Hill, the team had performed the same sequence of routines at the Apollo Theater in Harlem in 1939, accompanied by Jimmie Lunceford and his orchestra. See Hill, *Tap Dancing America*, 104.

277   The two other independent Black films in which she appeared were the crime dramas *While Thousands Cheer* (a.k.a. *Crooked Money*, 1940) and *Take My Life* (1942). I have not been able to locate any surviving copies of these films.

nated jazz-themed music shorts. The Soundies of the 1940s were perhaps the era's most democratic visual medium and tended to be more inclusive ethnically and racially than the standard Hollywood product, giving a lot of prominence to African Americans. Overall, Soundies retained Hollywood's intraracial hierarchy, employing mostly very light-skinned African American women as interchangeable objectified showgirls more often than as individualized, skilled performers. Nevertheless, there were notable exceptions to this, and several African American women who starred in Soundies presented images of competence, agency, and individuality. That Jeni LeGon was not one of these exceptions might have to do with the fact that audible tap dancing was extremely rare in Soundies, because the prerecording of the soundtracks made the synchronization of the tap sounds difficult. With respect to cinematic short forms, too, Jeni LeGon somehow fell through the cracks.

By the late 1940s, Hollywood was losing its penchant for Black specialty numbers. At the same time, as civil rights organizations began to successfully demand more substantial roles for Black actors, the era of race movies as an industry separate from Hollywood was also coming to an end. From 1951 to 1953, Jeni LeGon had a few appearances in the TV series *The Amos 'n' Andy Show*, and in 1953 she played her last Hollywood bit part as a teacher in MGM's *Bright Road*, after which she retired from film.

Offscreen Successes and Struggles: 1950s and Beyond

While Jeni LeGon is now primarily known for her film appearances, her career was in some ways more successful offscreen than onscreen. She had earned the male-dominated tap world's respect with her repertoire, which included knee drops, flips, slides, and flying splits, and she became one of the few women to be invited back to Harlem's famous Hoofer's Club, the informal stomping ground of the Black tap scene during its heyday.[278] In 1943/44, with her film career stagnating, she was cast in a major supporting role in the Broadway musical *Early to Bed*, appearing in four numbers with partner Bob Howard. The show, with music by Fats Waller, ran for 380 performances and was received favorably. Playbills and reviews evidence a lesser degree of discrimination against Black performers compared with the film industry. For example, the bios in two different playbills for the show contain neither direct nor indirect references to Jeni LeGon's race, instead simply listing her achievements.[279]

---

278 See Frank, *Tap!*, 126; and LeGon and Smith, interview, Gray (in this interview, LeGon mentions how nervous she was about dancing at the club).

279 Playbills for *Early to Bed*, produced by Richard Kollmar (1943), box 1, folder 8, LeGon, Papers. For opening night credits and songs, see also "Early to Bed," Internet Broadway Database, The Broadway League, https://www.ibdb.com/broadway-production/early-to-bed-1296.

Chapter 3 Potential Pioneer: The Film Career of Black Tap Dancer Jeni LeGon

After finally turning her back on Hollywood, LeGon went on to open a dance school in Los Angeles in 1953, where she taught jazz and tap. She also hired two other teachers, a Russian dancer for ballet, and Black dancer Archie Savage, who had danced with Katherine Dunham, for African and Caribbean dances.[280] But when LeGon formed a performance group of teenage dancers from the school, she soon ran into problems funding their shows and was repeatedly told that the world just wasn't ready for Black ballet dancers. Soon after, she shut the school down.[281] During her 1940s Broadway career, LeGon had met and taken lessons from Black modern dance pioneer Katherine Dunham, who was performing in New York at the same time. Having studied the dances of the Caribbean, LeGon founded her own music and dance group, Jazz Caribe, in the mid-1960s. Consisting of five dancers and a five-piece band, with LeGon herself on the conga drums (which she had also learned in the 1940s), the group toured nationally and internationally into the early 1970s. When performing in Vancouver, Canada, in 1969, LeGon met some former students who suggested that she stay there and teach – and she did.[282] She formed the youth dance group Troupe One in 1976, toured with another group named the Pelican Players in the 1980s, and from 1985 to 1988 performed with the Jazz Cinq Band, which included her second husband Frank Clavin, a White jazz drummer she had met in 1976.[283] In addition to teaching and performing live, she appeared in several Canadian TV productions. Her last film role was in the horror film *Bones* (2001), which featured rap star Snoop Dogg. Jeni LeGon eventually became a Canadian citizen and continued to live in Vancouver until her death in 2012, at age ninety-six. She summed up the contrast to life in the United States simply by saying, "we're people up here. They don't have any black and white problems".[284]

"A Footnote in Hollywood History": Late but Still Limited Recognition

A review of the 1989 stage show *Jazz Tap!* referred to Jeni LeGon as "the only black female tap dance star in film history, the forgotten Jeni LeGon".[285] The words "only" and "forgotten" are instructive here, both in terms of Black dance

280 See LeGon, interview, HistoryMakers, tape 4, story 5.
281 See *Jeni LeGon: Living in a Great Big Way*, directed by Grant Greschuk, 1999; and LeGon, interview, HistoryMakers, tape 5, story 6.
282 See LeGon, interview, Govenar, *Untold Glory*; and LeGon interview, HistoryMakers, tape 5, story 8.
283 See LeGon, interview, HistoryMakers, tape 6, story 2; and event programs, box 1, folders 15–25, LeGon, Papers.
284 LeGon, interview, Govenar, *Untold Glory*. See also LeGon, interview, HistoryMakers, tape 6, stories 3–4.
285 Gerald Nachman, "'Jazz Tap!' Show Is Sure-Footed", Cabaret, *San Francisco Chronicle*, September 8, 1989, box 1, folder 27, LeGon, Papers.

and film history *and* in terms of how this history has been transmitted. From the 1980s on, Jeni LeGon began receiving some of the recognition she was denied during much of her earlier career. Numerous tap festivals and shows paid tribute to her and invited her as a guest star. She was featured in newspapers and magazines in the US as well as in Canada. Californian dancer and preservationist Rusty Frank interviewed LeGon for her book *Tap!*, which is now a standard reference for the tap history of the first half of the twentieth century. Frank also featured LeGon in her all-star *Jazz Tap* revues of the late 1980s and early 1990s. In 1987, LeGon was inducted into the Black Filmmakers Hall of Fame, and in 1993, she was selected for the Los Angeles Tap Dance Hall of Fame. In 1999, Grant Greschuk's video documentary *Jeni LeGon: Living in a Great Big Way* premiered at the Cinéfestival in Montreal. Produced by the National Film Board of Canada, the documentary went on to win several prizes and created some interest in LeGon's career. In 2001, she received the Flo-Bert Award,[286] and in 2002, she was one of nine African American tap dancers – and the only woman – to receive an Honorary Degree of Doctor of Performing Arts from Oklahoma City University.[287] Two years later, the HistoryMakers, a Chicago-based project, recorded a four-hour interview with her for its digital video archive of African American oral histories; and in 2005, author Alan Govenar interviewed her for his book *Untold Glory: African Americans in Pursuit of Freedom, Opportunity, and Achievement*.

In other words, Jeni LeGon's career, especially her early career, has become something of a textbook example of undervalued and unacknowledged achievement in Black dance and film history. In many ways, these compensatory discourses are symptomatic of how African American achievement in general tends to receive late but still limited recognition – limited for several reasons. Popular discourses, especially in the context of awards and festivals, often rely on hyperbolic and sometimes simplistic positive accounts. Jeni LeGon's film appearances, in particular, have frequently been summed up in misleading celebratory ways. Tributes emphasizing that she appeared in such films as *Easter Parade* with Fred Astaire mainly serve to obscure the fact that these appearances were minor, unremarkable (servant) roles. To a degree then, some of these discourses replicate the rhetoric of uplift that was such a staple of the Black press in the 1930s and

---

[286] Named after African American vaudeville and Broadway legends Florence Mills and Bert Williams, the Flo-Bert Awards have been honoring tap dancers annually since 1991. See "The Flo-Bert Awards", Florence Mills, Bill Egan, http://www.florencemills.com/flobert.htm.

[287] The other eight recipients were Charles "Cholly" Atkins, Bunny Briggs, James "Buster" Brown, Henry LeTang, Fayard Nicholas, Leonard Reed, Jimmy Slyde, and Prince Spencer. See Hill, *Tap Dancing America*, 330.

1940s, rather than acknowledging and critiquing the injustice of reducing a talented performer to servant roles and other bit parts.

By contrast, more academically minded written accounts of LeGon's career (including those based on oral history projects or other interviews), as well as some journalistic portraits, highlight both her successes and her struggles. For example, various articles in Canadian publications occasioned by the release of Greschuk's documentary paid tribute to LeGon's pioneering achievements while also focusing on the obstacles she came up against. As in the film, the tone in these reviews is celebratory as well as critical, balancing respectful accolades with expressions of regret. This is important because, with regard to LeGon's career struggles, there is little publicly available evidence from the period in question. The occasional critique of Hollywood's hiring practices in the Black press is far outweighed by the often exaggerated praise for all Black people's screen performances. The relatively recent discourses thus serve an important function in filling in the gaps, to a large extent relying on LeGon's own testimony. Perhaps the best insight is gained by seeing and hearing Jeni LeGon herself talk in the Canadian documentary and in the HistoryMakers interview, where she seems to oscillate between satisfaction at finally receiving her due, on the one hand, and regret at the many missed chances of times gone by, on the other. Although she constantly reassures her audience how grateful she is for having lived in such a "great big way", she also displays a keen awareness of the injustices she suffered, relating stories of racial prejudice with an attitude of accepting resignation though never bitterness. Most importantly, perhaps, these interview opportunities give her back some of the discursive agency in constructing her own image that she was denied during most of her active years. While all stars "are involved in making themselves into commodities", as Richard Dyer points out,[288] not all stars have the same amount of control in the making of their star image. With limited role choices and the mainstream audience's refusal to see them as anything but entertainers, Black performers had few opportunities to contribute to their own public image outside of their screen roles in the way that White movie stars did.[289]

In film studies, Jeni LeGon has gone nearly unnoticed. As a Canadian paper put it, her talent "wasn't enough to make her more than a footnote in Hollywood history".[290] There is no mention of her in Donald Bogle's seminal *Toms, Coons,*

---

288 Dyer, *Heavenly Bodies*, 5.

289 This is not to suggest that movie stars are ever in full control of their image and public persona. As Dyer's examples of Paul Robeson, Marilyn Monroe, and Judy Garland show, the lack of control over one's image can in fact become an essential ingredient of that same image; see Dyer, *Heavenly Bodies*. On the general mechanisms of the star phenomenon, see also Dyer, *Stars*.

290 Tony Atherton, "Million-Dollar Personality Girl – Simply Priceless", *Ottawa Citizen*, March 6, 2000, Newspapers.com.

Mulattoes, Mammies, and Bucks (first published in 1973), for example, and Bogle's behind-the-scenes history of Black Hollywood, *Bright Boulevards, Bold Dreams*, only contains a few passing references, with the author suggesting that "the energetic, pixieish LeGon seemed out of step with those nurturing, full-figured women such as Beavers and McDaniel and never became a hot item in the movies".[291] Recent analyses of Black musical performance in classical Hollywood films generally focus on a few now-canonical performers, such as Bill Robinson, Lena Horne, or the Nicholas Brothers. Jeni LeGon's number from *Hooray for Love* is a frequently referenced example of the Black specialty act, but often only Bill Robinson and Fats Waller are mentioned, whereas LeGon's presence is overlooked. Dance history has been similarly neglectful: Marshall and Jean Stearns, for instance, ignore her in *Jazz Dance*, and her name only appears in the appendix, under the entry on *Hooray for Love* in the filmography compiled by film collector Ernie Smith.[292]

The only scholarly text that adequately balances LeGon's achievements with an account of the hindrances to her career is a very short section in Constance Valis Hill's comprehensive *Tap Dancing America*. In this extensively researched cultural history of tap dancing, the author points to women's important and often overlooked contributions to the art form, claiming that "twentieth-century women far outnumber men in tap".[293] Hill examines the complex intersections of race, class, and gender in the history of American tap dance and throws light on many female dancers' careers and performances. She shows how tap dance had been considered "a man's world" in which the biggest compliment for a woman was that she danced "like a man", and she chronicles the tap world's more recent attempts to set the record straight. Even more than as performers, women were marginalized by how they were – and weren't – talked about. Thus, their frequent absence from history – in the sense of recorded history – is a significant one.

It is precisely because Black women were even more marginalized in Hollywood than Black men that further light needs to be shed on their career paths and screen roles (as well as their behind-the-scenes involvement). Until a few years ago, scholars of African American film history tended to focus on male performers (mostly comedians, musicians, and dancers) or on directors. Black women from Hollywood's golden age, however, received little attention outside of Donald

---

291 Bogle, *Bright Boulevards*, 176. As I have suggested previously, the problems LeGon came up against likely had as much to do with her dance skills as with her looks.

292 Stearns and Stearns, *Jazz Dance*, 409.

293 Hill, *Tap Dancing America*, 4.

Bogle's work.[294] In recent years, there have been efforts to compensate for this deficiency, with authors dedicating articles and occasionally entire books to the most prominent performers, such as Nina Mae McKinney or Hattie McDaniel.[295] But much work remains to be done if we want to gain a fuller picture of the place of African American women in the White- and male-dominated industry of Hollywood's studio era. The Black female dancer's resistance to mere objectification through performances testifying to her competence, creativity, and agency offers one useful perspective on this area of study. There were others in the 1930s and 1940s who should and hopefully will receive more attention as occasional, marginalized presences onscreen. African American singer-dancer Marie Bryant, for instance, was widely recognized as a talented and charismatic performer from live contexts. Among other things, she was a featured attraction at Harlem's Apollo Theater and toured with Duke Ellington, but her film career was only modestly successful, comparable to Jeni LeGon's.[296] Juanita Pitts, an African American tap dancer from Philadelphia, was known as one of the best female hoofers, with her "close-to-the-floor rhythm tapping that was admired by men and women alike".[297] Like LeGon, she bent normative gender roles, performing in a white three-piece suit and low-heeled tap shoes. Pitts's only film appearance seems to be in the twenty-five-minute short film *It Happened in Harlem* (1945), an independently produced race movie. That Jeni LeGon is all but unique as a Black female tap soloist in studio-era Hollywood – despite the enormous popularity of tap dancing across all entertainment industries and the large number of female tap dancers in contexts of live performance – is revealing, to say the least.

In a sense, the lack of attention to Jeni LeGon is unsurprising, even justifiable, especially with regard to film history: apart from the servant roles and other bit parts, LeGon's noteworthy screen presence in Hollywood feature films totals about ten minutes running time. Further, two of the four independent Black films that featured her seem to be lost. With only three brief Hollywood appearances in the 1930s, the last of which went practically unnoticed, one can hardly speak of a star image that would lend itself to in-depth analysis. But

---

294 In addition to his now-classic *Toms, Coons, Mulattoes, Mammies, and Bucks*, which devotes considerable space to female performers, Bogle has published a biography of Dorothy Dandridge and a volume dedicated entirely to African American women; see Bogle, *Dorothy Dandridge*; and Bogle, *Brown Sugar*.

295 See Bourne, *Nina Mae McKinney*; and Watts, *Hattie McDaniel*. Charlene Regester's well-documented *African American Actresses* is another noteworthy work, with portraits of nine actresses: Madame Sul-Te-Wan, Nina Mae McKinney, Louise Beavers, Fredi Washington, Hattie McDaniel, Lena Horne, Hazel Scott, Ethel Waters, and Dorothy Dandridge. For a study of more recent Black female film stars, see Mask, *Divas on Screen*.

296 Among Bryant's early films were the Soundie *Bli-Blip* (1942), the theatrical jazz short *Jammin' the Blues* (1944), and the feature film *Carolina Blues* (1944), where she appeared in a Black specialty number with Harold Nicholas, the younger of the Nicholas Brothers.

297 Hill, *Tap Dancing America*, 255.

considered from a different angle, it is precisely their rarity and unusualness that make LeGon's screen appearances – and her whole film career and image – worthy of attention. With her individuality in a system of conformity, Jeni LeGon exemplifies the potential for a wider range of screen images for Black women in classical Hollywood. At the same time, her obstructed career path makes it clear that the time had not come for this potential to materialize. In her musical numbers, she pushed the boundaries of her time, but she was a pioneer whose full potential remained unrealized.

CHAPTER 4 Jumpin' at the Jukebox, Dancin' in the Street: Dance, Race, and Space in 1940s Soundies

In the Soundie *Rhythmania* (1943), a group of sleeping people in a living room is suddenly brought to life by the sounds of a small swing band. Mabel Lee enters and performs a solo dance facing the camera, exuberantly flinging and shaking her slim legs, twisting her hips, and lifting her knee-length skirt while the other women in the room, who are sitting on couches, clap, snap their fingers, and shimmy along to the rhythm. Lee's dance is followed first by a group of four stylishly dressed women (the Harlem Honeys) performing a brief choreographed routine with movements similar to Lee's, then by two male dancers (Harris and Hunt) in dark suits, who also present a choreographed sequence that focuses on wiggly leg movement. As they exit to slowing music at the end, the small audience sinks back into their slumber. Even though everybody is facing the camera and performing with unmistakable excitement, the suggestion is that these people are just having a good time at home, entertaining themselves. An outside audience is implied by the camera but not by the film's setting of a private living room.

The Soundies jukebox films of the 1940s introduced a new site – or rather, a wide variety of new sites – for musical screen performance and thus also for negotiating racial and gender identities. By the late 1930s, the huge popularity of the record jukebox had led various entrepreneurs to pursue the idea of a film jukebox that could show a movie at the same time that it played music. In 1940, the Mills Novelty Company of Chicago introduced the Mills Panoram, a coin-operated machine that was equipped with a 16-millimeter film projector and a looping film reel for the projection of Soundies, as the three-minute musical films produced for the new machine would be called. The Soundies venture got off to a promising start, but success didn't last long. The general restrictions of the wartime economy and the recording ban by the American Federation of Musicians (AFM), which affected Soundies production for fourteen months in 1942/43, soon limited the output and profits of Soundies, and the financially plagued enterprise discontinued production shortly after the war. Nevertheless, approximately 5,000 Panorams made it into circulation, and from 1940 to 1946, about 1,850 Soundies were produced for exhibition on the movie jukebox.[298]

Featuring a wide range of musical styles and employing over one thousand performers, including many who were otherwise rarely seen onscreen, Soundies are a treasure trove for the historical study of the era's popular music. Much like the theatrical music shorts discussed in chapters 1 and 2, Soundies form a substantial corpus of musical films that have long been overlooked in academia – whether in music, film, or dance studies. Some music scholars and jazz fans have valued the jukebox shorts as important historical documents preserving performances by famous (jazz) musicians, such as Fats Waller or Cab Calloway. In film history, Soundies tend to be reduced to the role of primitive precursors to present-day music videos, often mentioned only in passing. Recent years, however, have seen an increased academic interest in Soundies history and analysis. Andrea Kelley's 2018 book deserves special mention here as the most comprehensive study of Soundies to date, providing an in-depth look at the contents, aesthetics, and exhibition practices, as well as the discourses that accompanied the jukebox shorts.[299]

Since Soundies constituted their own industry and technology, with production and exhibition practices separate from the Hollywood industry, they warrant their own chapter in this discussion of vernacular jazz dance onscreen. Like the early sound shorts, but to an even greater extent, Soundies offered a comparatively privileged forum for African American performance. 287 Soundies – about 16 percent of the total output – were categorized as "Negro" in the Soundies catalogs for distributors.[300] These numbers are especially significant in light of the

---

298 For general historical overviews of the Soundies enterprise (and its various competitors), see Hose, *Soundies*; and MacGillivray and Okuda, *The Soundies Book*. Both books contain alphabetical listings of all Soundies titles as well as the known names of the performers who appeared in them. According to Wally Hose (*Soundies*, 3), the paper records of the Soundies Distributing Corporation of America were destroyed long ago, making it difficult to research the production history in greater detail.

299 Kelley, *Soundies Jukebox Films*. See also Kelley, "Dynamics of Site and Screen"; and Kelley, "From Attraction to Distraction". I am greatly indebted to Andrea Kelley's excellent work, and I would like to thank her for giving me early access to parts of her manuscript, including some sections that remain unpublished to date. Film collector, educator, and historian Mark Cantor is also working on a book about Soundies. His project is primarily dedicated to unearthing additional production information and identifying uncredited soundtrack musicians, onscreen performers, and production personnel. See Celluloid Improvisations, Mark Cantor and the Celluloid Improvisations Music Film Archive, https://www.jazz-on-film.com. Other noteworthy publications about Soundies include Herzog, "Discordant Visions"; and McGee, *Some Liked It Hot*, 145–167.

300 See Hose, *Soundies*, 15. This number does not include appearances of African Americans in racially mixed Soundies.

considerable reduction of African American employment in Hollywood during the war years.[301]

Perhaps unsurprisingly, Black-cast Soundies showcased dancers more prominently than Soundies in general. Black dancers also received screen credit more frequently than their White counterparts (sometimes instead of, sometimes in addition to the featured musicians). This comparatively strong presence and prominence of African American dancers was doubtless rooted in essentialist notions of naturally rhythmic Black bodies. The same clichés that pervaded Hollywood's imagery of African Americans persisted in Soundies, which often presented their Black performers in heavily stereotyped settings and costumes, sometimes exacerbated by equally clichéd film titles and song lyrics. At the same time, however, the relative simplicity of the quickly and cheaply produced Soundies sometimes defied or transcended these stereotypes.

In addition, the exhibition and viewing contexts of Soundies favored more racially integrated practices compared with the segregation of theatrical exhibition and spectatorship. In swing Soundies – both Black-cast and White-cast – dance performances suggest and encourage a type of screen-audience interaction that is different from feature films screened in theaters, thus underscoring the Panoram's function as a jukebox. Dance performances in swing-themed Soundies also evidence a strong focus on improvisation, which is rarely found in Hollywood films. Especially in Black-cast Soundies, this improvisational element combines with the films' often small-scale, mundane settings and the atmospheric, ambient function of the jukebox to lend representations of African American culture a quality of everyday ordinariness. All of this resonates with the general role and roots of Black vernacular culture as a ubiquitous, everyday resource that originated from and is practiced in informal contexts. To an extent, Soundies' depictions of this vernacular culture offer alternative visions that compete – or coexist – with the common Hollywood imagery. Further, Soundies gave above-average exposure to African American women, who were featured more frequently than in Hollywood productions, though mostly without reaching the same mainstream success as some of their male counterparts. Overall, Soundies enabled alternative modes of Black stardom and spectatorship, in part due to their liminal position as a medium that was marginal to – but nevertheless part of – the mainstream.

---

301 See, for instance, Everett, *Returning the Gaze*, 303–304.

Integrating Film Viewing in the Public Sphere

Soundies featured a diverse range of performers in musical as well as ethnic terms, and they are sometimes considered the period's most inclusive medium.[302] However, the content and performers are not the main aspects setting Soundies apart from other forms of audiovisual entertainment. Musically, thematically, and aesthetically, there was nothing *fundamentally* new or different about the jukebox shorts. Soundies were basically miniature musicals that differed from those made for the big screen in degree more than in kind, and this difference was partly due to the time and budget constraints of their mode of production.[303] The Soundies' true novelty lay in their mode of exhibition on the small screen of the Panoram jukebox in a variety of public spaces not primarily intended for film viewing: sites of leisure and consumption like restaurants, nightclubs, and department stores; spaces of transit, such as train and bus stations; work places, such as factories; and even institutional spaces, such as government buildings and military bases.[304] In her book, Andrea Kelley shows how Soundies "modeled emerging trends in film and media engagement, including the shift from large screens to small, from feature-length films to short formats, from collective to private viewing practices, and from site-specific film venues to ubiquitous screen encounters".[305] In other words, the Panoram film jukebox constitutes a transitional stage between the big screen in the cinema and the small television screen's everyday presence in the private home while also foreshadowing the ubiquity of the mobile, small-screen, short-form entertainment of the digital age.[306]

The Panoram film jukebox was designed for a reel of eight Soundies, which ran in a loop. Unlike with the music jukebox, there was no option to choose a specific film. Instead, a customer inserting a dime would simply get to see the next Soundie on the reel.[307] The catalogs for exhibitors published by the Soundies Distributing Corporation recommended a "balanced" program offering the widest possible variety of entertainment, in line with the vaudeville/variety

---

302 See, for instance, Kelley, *Soundies Jukebox Films*, 89–94; and McGee, *Some Liked It Hot*, 146–147.

303 Soundies were generally shot in just a few takes, with single-day sessions yielding up to four Soundies. The cost of production was typically around $5,000 in the first year (1941) but declined significantly in the following years. See Hose, *Soundies*, 12; and MacGillivray and Okuda, *The Soundies Book*, 385–387.

304 See Kelley, *Soundies Jukebox Films*, 4. On the military uses of Soundies, see also 54–67; and Kelley, "Dynamics of Site and Screen", 83–91.

305 Kelley, *Soundies Jukebox Films*, 4.

306 See Kelley, 15, 131–137.

307 In some contexts, the coin-operated mechanism was disabled in order to allow for the continuous screening of specifically curated programs – for example, in some military- and government-related settings, where the Panoram served an educational or propagandistic purpose. See especially Kelley, "Dynamics of Site and Screen", 87.

Chapter 4 Jumpin' at the Jukebox, Dancin' in the Street

tradition and its various cinematic descendants.[308] While exhibitors had the option to select their own assortment of Soundies for each reel, many chose to buy the films in preassembled reels, which typically contained one Black-cast Soundie (and sometimes more), most commonly in the sixth or eighth position.[309] Thus, even spectators who only watched a single Soundie had a fairly high chance of seeing a Black-cast film. As Kelley argues, the variety on the reel "inadvertently could promote an atmosphere of diversity and inclusion".[310] Unlike the non-narrative Black specialty numbers segregated from White narratives in many feature films, this side-by-side of mostly non-narrative White-cast and Black-cast films on the Soundies reels was inherently more integrated, even if by no means equal.

In this context, it is also worth noting how the discourses surrounding Soundies referenced – or didn't reference – the race of the performers. The Soundies catalogs for exhibitors generally listed Black-cast films in a separate "Negro" section, relegated to the back of the catalog. This points to the industry's awareness of segregationist markets *as well as* of the marketability of Black performance as a special attraction.[311] However, as Kelley has found, the segregation was not consistent: the annual catalogs also included Black Soundies within their general listings – sometimes without explicitly coding them as Black – in addition to the separate section.[312] A similar inconsistency is found in the reviews of Soundies programs regularly published in *Billboard*, which sometimes explicitly marked Black-cast Soundies with descriptive terms – for example, "colored", "negro", or "sepia" – or with mention of "Harlem". But just as often, there is no such indication of the performers' race in reviews of Black-cast Soundies. All of this suggests that the strict boundaries of racial segregation were becoming somewhat more fluid in the context of Soundies distribution and exhibition.

In addition – and just as crucially – the Panorams' locations in public spaces also enabled more integrated viewing practices in comparison with movie theaters. Segregation was still the norm in cinemas, by law in the South, by custom in the North.[313] By contrast, many of Soundies' exhibition sites, such as train stations or department stores, were accessible to everyone. With accidental viewers and passersby constituting much of Soundies' audience, the films were open to appropriation by diverse groups of spectators. Thus, with regard to their screening

---

308 See Hose, *Soundies*, 5. On the relationship between vaudeville and classical Hollywood cinema, see Jenkins, "Anarchistic Comedy"; and Jenkins, *What Made Pistachio Nuts?*
309 See Herzog, "Discordant Visions", 30; Hose, *Soundies*, 5; and Kelley, *Soundies Jukebox Films*, 9.
310 Kelley, *Soundies Jukebox Films*, 113.
311 See Kelley, *Soundies Jukebox Films*, 89; and MacGillivray and Okuda, *The Soundies Book*, 391.
312 Kelley, unpublished manuscript (outtakes from *Soundies Jukebox Films*, chapter 5).
313 On the history of racially segregated film exhibition, see Gomery, *Shared Pleasures*, 155–170.

133

practices, Black-cast Soundies don't imply and address a White gaze at Black culture to the same extent as many films produced for the big screen. The strong element of contingency involved in the exhibition and spectatorship of the jukebox shorts helped to blur the division between commodified Black performance, on the one hand, and its White consumption, on the other.[314] As with the musical shorts of the early sound film era, a handful of White directors and producers specialized in Black-cast Soundies, ensuring a steady output. But while White dominance in Soundies production remained unchallenged overall, Soundies also addressed African Americans as consumers more actively than most Hollywood productions of the time, and Panorams were placed in Black neighborhoods, where they were highly popular with audiences.[315]

The small-screen exhibition in public everyday spaces and the resulting dynamic between screen, space, and audience distinguish Soundies viewing from so-called classical cinema spectatorship. In the cinema, which is often regarded as an escape from everyday life, the Hollywood musical represents the pinnacle of escapist fantasy, offering utopian visions of ordinary life pervaded by music and dance. In comparison, Soundie minimusicals pervaded ordinary spaces of everyday life with musical entertainment in a much more direct sense. Unlike the immersive experience of a big-screen musical, the Panoram's presence in mundane spaces often blurred the line "between ambient media and cinematic attraction", as Kelley explains.[316] Accordingly, promotional and press discourses about Soundies didn't necessarily focus on the short films' visual appeal but just as often emphasized the Panoram's "more aural, atmospheric qualities" as an "'ambient' movie screen that does not need to be watched".[317] In addition, the relative spatial intimacy of many exhibition sites tended to be mirrored in the content of the films, which were often (though not always) staged to evoke "smaller-scale, more intimate venues",[318] especially after the first couple of years of Soundies production: "Rendering small-screen moving images into appropriate or often functional

---

314 It should be noted, however, that this division was never as strict as the industry might have intended it to be. There is evidence that White film distributors and exhibitors often shied away from attracting Black customers; see, for instance, Everett, *Returning the Gaze*, 175–176; and Friedman, *African American Films*, 54–55. Nevertheless, Black audiences did see – and often enjoy – Hollywood movies and were also targeted by the mainstream film industry to some extent.

315 Harlem was also home to the talent agency Sun Tan Studios, run by Black production manager and talent scout Fritz Pollard, a former football player and coach, who worked with William Forest Crouch, the most prolific White director-producer of Black-cast Soundies. Andrea Kelley has examined Pollard's Soundies career as an example of the comparatively strong Black presence in Soundies production but also of the limits to Black participation, concluding that he was little more than a middleman; Kelley, unpublished manuscript (outtakes from *Soundies Jukebox Films*, chapter 5).

316 Kelley, *Soundies Jukebox Films*, 27.

317 Kelley, 21.

318 Kelley, 38.

extensions of their exhibition sites, Soundies helped cultivate an atmosphere of screen-space connectivity, a patterning of moving image to its viewing context".[319]

This screen-space connectivity and Soundies' liminal status between ambient media and cinematic attraction also extend to the treatment of dance performances in the jukebox shorts. Although dancers appeared in hundreds of Soundies, they were not typically framed as a central attraction. Spectacular displays of virtuosic skill are relatively rare, and the large-scale production numbers common in Hollywood musicals remain absent from Soundies. With the soundtracks recorded before filming, the music generally constituted the foundation of Soundies, the source material to be accompanied by visuals rather than vice versa, as was the case with Hollywood films.[320] These circumstances of production are reflected in dance scenes, which often appear like an afterthought to the prerecorded soundtracks.[321] This secondary status of dance is especially evident in Soundies featuring tap dancers: with very rare exceptions, the rhythmic sounds of tap shoes remain inaudible in Soundies, even when the films feature performers known for their tap dancing.[322] In Hollywood productions, by contrast, tap sounds were generally recorded and synchronized with the image after shooting.

While more elaborately produced feature-length musicals often frame their thoroughly rehearsed and meticulously staged choreographies as improbably "spontaneous" expressions of feeling, there's an improvised quality to many dance scenes in Soundies, both at the level of the dancing itself and as regards the production. Even when Soundies feature highly skilled dancers in rehearsed routines, the dancing often appears more convincingly improvised than it does in high-end productions. This improvisational element is especially evident in Black-cast Soundies but also in many swing-themed Soundies featuring White performers. In both, it speaks to the participatory and interactive aspects of swing culture – and of African American culture more generally – in conjunction with Soundies' exhibition and viewing practices.

Jukebox Swing

Soundies showcased a wide variety of musical styles and performers, but swing was Soundies' most popular music genre, often played by big bands during the early years, whereas many later Soundies featured smaller ensembles playing in a

---

319 Kelley, 53.

320 See Herzog, "Discordant Visions"; and MacGillivray and Okuda, *The Soundies Book*, 385.

321 According to Wally Hose (*Soundies*, 15), only thirty-six Soundies (about 2 percent) were listed in the "Dance" category in the complete Soundies catalog from 1947.

322 Among the rare exceptions are the two Soundies that Bill "Bojangles" Robinson made toward the end of his career, *Let's Scuffle* (1942) and *By an Old Southern River* (1942).

swing style. Especially in its big band incarnation, swing was also the nation's most popular dance music during World War II. Serving as a symbol of American ideals during the war years, swing has often been described as a cultural force capable of bridging racial segregation and promoting diversity and equality in the context of "wartime conditions allowing for more fluidity within traditional racial, class, and gender roles".[323] While swing culture's comparatively progressive aspects will be discussed in more detail in chapters 5 and 6, it is important to note here how the prevalence of swing music and dance in Soundies resonates with the films' relatively integrated exhibition practices as well as with their function as ambient media.[324]

According to Andrea Kelley, the early promotional discourses of Soundies framed the Panoram as a music jukebox as much as a film screen.[325] In other words, it was promoted as a machine that played music for listening and potentially *for dancing* as much as for *watching* music and dance performances. Panorams could supplement or substitute for live performances, especially in the more intimate venues where they were most successful and "where people would dance in front of the screen, much like before a bandstand".[326] Since Soundies were primarily intended as a showcase for their musical performers, they often employed dance acts as a secondary feature, added for atmosphere, comedy, or sex appeal – or a combination thereof. This is also true of swing dancers. Only occasionally presented as a Soundie's central attraction, swing dance acts were typically added for a little bit of extra flavor, sometimes involving a comic element and often inviting audiences to join the dancers onscreen as much as to watch them, thus mirroring the films' possible exhibition contexts and underlining the Panoram's function as a (music) jukebox.

The early Black-cast bandstand Soundie *Air Mail Special* (1941), for example, features Count Basie's popular big band with the prominent dance group Whitey's Lindy Hoppers. A few long shots towards the beginning and end establish spatial unity by showing the band and the dance floor within the same image, but most of the Soundie cuts back and forth between the dancers and the band. Both are filmed from a variety of angles, with the editing timed rhythmically to match the dynamics of the song. There is no discernible choreography on the dance floor; instead, about a dozen couples are just dancing in what is framed as an amateur dance contest, even though the dancers' high skill level is quite evident. Basie's overweight vocalist Jimmy Rushing is among the dancers,

323 Kelley, *Soundies Jukebox Films*, 42.
324 See also Kelley, *Soundies Jukebox Films*, 42–43, 95–97.
325 See Kelley, 23–32.
326 Kelley, 37.

providing a comic element as he lazily bounces in place while his partner Winnie Johnson energetically dances around him.[327] Towards the end, couples start collapsing or just leaving the floor, apparently exhausted from dancing to the fast title tune, until only Rushing and Johnson remain, and Basie hands them the prize trophy. The punch line is that Rushing has been propped up by a stick chair the entire time while only pretending to be dancing.

Air Mail Special perfectly encapsulates the multiple, sometimes conflicting aims and functions of the Panoram as a music machine/jukebox for listening and dancing, on the one hand, and a movie machine/screen, on the other, where one can see a favorite musical performer in combination with the spectacle of a dance performance (and in this case also a comic miniature story). In addition, like many other swing Soundies, *Air Mail Special* evidences an improvisational element in the staging of the dance. The dancing couples here appear to be simply dancing, their moves not coordinated with each other. As a thoroughly rehearsed group of professional dancers, Whitey's Lindy Hoppers performed spectacular, often acrobatic routines at the Savoy Ballroom in Harlem, on nightclub and theater stages, and in several films. At the same time, they were also highly skilled social dancers, eminently capable of improvising on the dance floor. Their presence in *Air Mail Special* points to big band swing's function as music for largely improvised social dancing, thus mirroring the activities of Soundies' viewers, who might have chosen to watch the dancers onscreen *or* to dance themselves. In a comically exaggerated way, this Soundie also explicitly illustrates the kind of interaction between musicians and dancers that has often been described by eyewitnesses of the swing era.[328]

A similar emphasis on improvisation and interaction – at the expense of spectacular choreography and staging – can be observed in many swing-themed Soundies with White performers. *Basin Street Boogie* (1942) with Will Bradley's band, for example, presents the guests of a nightclub as listeners, dancers, *and* spectators of the dance: while two couples take turns dancing, their friends stand by, watching and encouraging them (fig. 29). One couple showcases an obviously rehearsed set of moves that culminates in a series of acrobatic feats. By contrast, the other couple seem to struggle to keep their act together – quite literally: after a move that separates the two dancers, they fail to catch each other's hands again in order to reconnect, and they generally seem somewhat disjointed and uncoordinated as a couple. While it is unclear here whether the small mishaps were added for

---

327 Winnie Johnson was not a member of Whitey's Lindy Hoppers but a celebrated Cotton Club dancer. She appeared in various Soundies but rarely danced much, generally being limited to the function of a sexy showgirl. See Watkins, *Stepin Fetchit*, 210–219.

328 See, for instance, Engelbrecht, "Swinging at the Savoy," 8; Erenberg, *Swingin' the Dream*, 56–58, 110–112; and singer Joe Williams quoted in Miller with Jensen, *Swingin' at the Savoy*, 215.

Figure 29. In the swing Soundie *Basin Street Boogie* (1942) with Will Bradley's band, White jitterbugging couples take turns dancing as others watch.

comic effect, for a semblance of realism, or if they were actual blunders, the latter is certainly a possibility.[329] Whether intended or not, this element of improvisation is typical of images of dance in Soundies, simultaneously evidencing the limitations of the fast and cheap mode of production (which doubtless required a good deal of improvisation) and emphasizing a fundamental aspect of the swing dance culture portrayed.

When the 1942/43 AFM recording ban prevented union musicians from recording, Soundies producers increasingly employed vocalists/vocal groups (who were excluded from the ban), minority performers who were not union members, and musicians from lesser-known, independent music markets and genres, such as western or rhythm and blues. In addition, they focused more on comedic acts and dancers.[330] These shifts – in conjunction with the growing restrictions of the wartime economy and the end of the big band era – would leave their mark on Soundies, affecting their contents and aesthetics well beyond the end of the recording ban. However, the increased use of dancers in Soundies didn't automatically lead to an elevation of their status. In *Juke Box Saturday Night* (1944), for example, four White swing dancers appear for a mere twenty seconds in total, adding just a hint of visual interest, whereas the focus is clearly on the vocal performance by the Glenn Miller Modernaires.[331] The café setting, where two couples get up from their tables to dance, reflects the Soundie's potential screening situation. The song lyrics reference the *music* jukebox as a provider of dance music, and the dancers serve as a mirror and inspiration for the consumers

---

329 MacGillivray and Okuda note that Soundies "were often photographed in two takes, and any mistakes the camera caught were either minimized by film editing or allowed to stand" (*The Soundies Book*, 386).

330 See Kelley, *Soundies Jukebox Films*, 6–7, 72–73, 77–84.

331 See Kelley, 111–112, on the White borrowing of Black cultural forms in this Soundie's vocal performance.

of the Soundie played on the *movie* jukebox, possibly motivating them to dance rather than to sit still and watch the short film. The brief, unremarkable display by the four dancers remains within an improvised social dance aesthetic, without any choreography. It offers an atmospheric element that is not so much presented as a performance in its own right but rather as a participatory reaction to the featured musical performance.

Some White-cast swing Soundies did feature more proficient dancers and give them more screen time. But even so, dancers still tended to model the possible activities of Soundies' viewer-listeners. *Juke Box Joe's* (1944), for instance, also lacks onscreen instrumentalists, and like *Juke Box Saturday Night*, it explicitly plays with the self-reflexive jukebox theme, with the title card telling the audience to "Keep the Nickel Slot Filled, That's All You Are Billed". The Soundie opens with vocals by Carol Adams, who sings while serving young customers in a diner. Then, three couples emerge from various corners of the locale and take over the dance floor in front of the bar. The music jukebox in the film, inconspicuously positioned in the background, stands in for the absent musicians.[332] Employing some of the era's most skilled White swing dancers, *Juke Box Joe's* dedicates more attention to the staging of its dance act than most other swing Soundies, featuring choreographed ensemble parts, carefully coordinated turn-taking between the couples, and well-timed editing.[333] But even though the diminished availability of recording artists led to Soundies including more dancers, the staging of dance performances is generally a long way from big screen musicals. The jitterbugging couples in *Juke Box Joe's* function simultaneously as a modest cinematic attraction and as a stand-in audience for the viewers of the Soundie, again mirroring its possible exhibition context in a diner or similar venue. While the women wear 1940s street fashion – knee-length skirts and low wedge shoes – the male dancers sport an assortment of uniforms, hinting at swing's popularity during the war, when it was an integral part of entertaining American troops as well as a cultural export that came to symbolize the American way of life around the globe.[334] Meanwhile, the Soundie's "star", Carol Adams, fulfils multiple functions as a vocalist, a dancer with a brief solo showcasing expansive leg movement, and a provider of sex appeal in her very short sexy outfit.

---

332 According to David Meeker (*Jazz on the Screen*, 1197), the soundtrack was recorded by Wingy Manone's band.

333 I have found no reliable information on the complete cast of *Juke Box Joe's*, but there appears to be some overlap with the cast of the 1944 theatrical short *Groovie Movie* (see chapter 5 in this book), with the dancers likely including Jeanne Phelps Veloz, Arthur Walsh, and Irene Thomas.

334 On swing during World War II, see, for instance, Erenberg, *Swingin' the Dream*, 181–210.

White swing dancers in Soundies typically remained uncredited, even when they played quite a prominent role. Overall, Black-cast Soundies tended to feature more proficient dancers, who were also billed by name more often and presented more prominently than their White counterparts. Across racial boundaries, however, swing Soundies very rarely relied *primarily* on skilled and expertly staged dancing to attract and hold the viewers' interest. Instead, they almost always combined dance as a cinematic attraction with comedy, sex appeal, and/or the showcasing of a musical act. For the most part, the dancers in these Soundies function simultaneously as modest visual attractions and as atmospheric elements, thus acting to blur the boundary between performers *in* and audiences *of* the films and more or less explicitly inviting viewers to actively participate in the swing culture presented onscreen. While the actual screening sites of these swing Soundies will likely remain lost to history, there is at least a strong possibility that they were shown in venues similar to those depicted onscreen.[335]

Block Parties and Living Room Dances: Vernacular Aesthetics in Mundane Settings

The interactive, participatory aspect of Soundies' exhibition and consumption practices, as well as the improvisational component of many dance scenes, resonate with elementary principles of African American vernacular culture – namely, improvisation, (audience) interaction, and individual expression. Many Black-cast Soundies offer striking examples of the aesthetics of Black vernacular dance as described, for example, by dance scholar Jacqui Malone: "It's hallmarks are improvisation and spontaneity, propulsive rhythm, call-and-response patterns, self-expression, elegance, and control".[336] Malone calls improvisation "an additive process" and considers it "Africa's most important contribution to the Western Hemisphere".[337] Rather than being in opposition to (professional) performance, improvisation is a key feature of the Black vernacular performance aesthetic, which generally values the process over the product.[338] A driving force of this dynamism in African American culture is the competitive interaction between performers as well as the dynamic exchange between spectators and performers.[339]

This is not to suggest that these elements are absent from Black performance in other films. Nor are they necessarily always foregrounded in Soundies. Overall, one might argue that the commonalities between Soundies and other films from

---

335 See, for instance, Kelley, *Soundies Jukebox Films*, 37–40.

336 Malone, *Steppin' on the Blues*, 2.

337 Malone, 33.

338 See also Gottschild, *Digging the Africanist Presence*, 11.

339 See, for instance, Malone, *Steppin' on the Blues*, 5–6.

the period are greater than the differences with regard to representations of African American music and dance. To an extent, all the era's screen images of Black performance relied on stereotypical ideas of a natural Black musicality, though performers often found ways to subvert these stereotypes to varying degrees with their skill and individualism. However, Soundies' modes of production, exhibition, and consumption – perhaps inadvertently – allowed for somewhat less strictly controlled performances than many Hollywood productions.

Many early bandstand Soundies seem like low-budget versions of the jazz shorts from the early sound era, framing their snapshots of show business as sophisticated and professional performances while also heavily drawing on the exoticist clichés of the previous decades' "Harlemania". But beginning as early as 1942, Soundies' increasing tendency towards small-scale, intimate settings did more than just mirror the positioning of the Panoram as "ambient, unobtrusive entertainment" in similarly mundane, everyday locales.[340] Given the informal origins of Black vernacular music and dance, the everyday ordinariness of Soundies' representations also relates to Black culture as an omnipresent everyday practice. In an essay comparing conventional Hollywood musicals with Black cinema, Richard Dyer argues that African American culture employs music as an always available source of creativity and energy rather than as a utopian escape: "Such dipping in and out of the always available music needs to be distinguished from the construction of Black musicality – the all-blacks-got-rhythm syndrome – of White cinema".[341] This "syndrome", which is evident in Hollywood films from the studio era and beyond, generally also informs representations of Blacks in Soundies. But Soundies' intimate settings and the Panoram's atmospheric presence in mundane locales often mitigate the stereotypical constructions of Black musicality as a spectacle for (predominantly) White consumption. The Panoram's ambient function as a movie machine that can – but doesn't have to be – watched ties in with the function of Black vernacular culture as a constantly present resource that can – but doesn't have to be – used, something that is always there for people to draw inspiration from while pursuing everyday activities.

As various dance scholars have pointed out, Black vernacular dance does not originate in formal "academic" institutions but is taught and learned in informal contexts, such as "dance halls, house parties, social clubs, and the streets".[342] Thus, if we conceive of Black vernacular music and dance as a sorf of street culture, then

---

340 Kelley, "Dynamics of Site and Screen", 82.

341 Dyer, "Is *Car Wash* a Musical?", 98. Dyer's example here is the feature-length comedy *Car Wash* (1976), and the author links the film's use of music to the circularity of its narrative, contrasting these aspects with the utopian transformations and linear narratives that are typical of White musicals.

342 Malone, *Steppin' on the Blues*, 28.

Black-cast Soundies, circulating in public everyday spaces, in a sense brought this street culture back into the street. Many Black Soundies depicted everyday scenes in comparatively intimate settings, with people playing music and dancing at home, in the street, or at private parties. While even improvised dancing is tied to a context of professional performance in early bandstand Soundies like *Air Mail Special*, later Soundies tend to frame their dance scenes as a private or semiprivate social activity in informal contexts (although the bandstand format also remained popular in Soundies).

Three Black Soundies with boogie-woogie pianist Lynn Albritton can serve to exemplify how Soundies negotiate prevailing stereotypes with representations of an everyday Black vernacular and its interactive, improvisational, and individualistic aesthetic.[343] *Dispossessed Blues* (1943) offers a literal (if somewhat clichéd) illustration of the street dance notion, with Albritton playing piano on the sidewalk, among piles of furniture and household goods. As more people show up and couples start dancing, the scene evolves into a full-blown street party. The film alternates between close-ups of Albritton's smiling face, medium shots of her playing the piano, and long shots showing dancers, a guitar player, and a few bystanders. The film's title and setting suggest that Black people are always in the mood to party, even if they have just been evicted from their homes and dispossessed of their belongings. On the one hand, the Soundie thus follows in the footsteps of Black specialty numbers in feature-length musicals like *Hooray for Love* (1935), implicitly justifying social injustice by depicting African Americans as happy-go-lucky entertainers. On the other hand, these ideological-narrative elements are often condensed to a mere allusion in Soundies or even missing altogether.

The dancing in *Disposessed Blues* is simultaneously an attraction – for audiences *in* and *of* the film – and an everyday activity. It is identifiable as the Lindy hop, which was professionalized as a performance art during the swing era, mainly by Whitey's Lindy Hoppers. But just like the earlier *Air Mail Special* with Whitey's group, *Dispossessed Blues* does not show the dance in its spectacular acrobatic form, nor does it offer the sexualized, exoticized imagery of Harlem as seen in some early Black sound shorts and Hollywood specialty acts. Instead, the Soundie is a rare instance of Black Lindy hop on film showing what the dance might have

---

343 The opening credits are missing from surviving versions of *Backstage Blues*, but William Forest Crouch, who made dozens of Black-cast Soundies, is credited in *Dispossessed Blues* and *Block Party Revels*. The overlap of performers and the close release dates (June and July 1943) suggest that all three Soundies were shot during the same session and directed by Crouch. I have found no other information about Lynn Albritton: she "appears to have never commercially recorded and all attempts to discover any biographical detail have been in vain". Dave Penny, "Half-Past Jump Time", booklet for *Half-Past Jump Time*, The Swingtime Collection, vol. 1 (Charlie Films, 2009), DVD.

Figure 30. Lindy hoppers in a street setting in *Dispossessed Blues* (1943). Pianist Lynn Albritton is in the background.

looked like in its social dance incarnation (fig. 30). While the performers here are undeniably quite proficient, their dancing is not overly flashy or spectacular, nor does it appear to be choreographed. The steps are not coordinated between the three couples. The women, wearing knee-length skirts and high heels, twist their hips and sometimes wave their arms, while the men occasionally do some tricky slides. There are brief moments with more showy moves (for instance, a male dancer spinning on one leg), but these seem almost incidental, as they either remain in the background or are quickly interrupted by cuts. As often in Soundies, the staging and editing appear a little careless and hastily executed. But rather than constituting a deficiency, the absence of a grand cinematic spectacle lends the Soundie an improvisational quality and ordinariness that is quite different from the carefully scripted and staged impressions of "authenticity" found in many large-scale Hollywood productions. While performed by obviously experienced dancers, the Lindy hop in *Dispossessed Blues* very likely *was* improvised.

In *Block Party Revels* (1943), Lynn Albritton plays for a party crowd, accompanied by a small band. Dancers take turns, dancing solo, in couples, and in groups. Though the set is evidently constructed in a studio, it suggests a semiprivate backyard space. Implications of social problems are missing altogether here; the only thematic content appears to be the social situation of people having a party, as indicated by the Soundie's title. The dancing is of a more explicitly performative nature than in *Dispossessed Blues*, featuring several brief choreographed sequences in combination with apparently improvised dancing. The Soundie opens with a male dancer somersaulting and whirling around in circles, foreshadowing the advent of break dancing decades later. Next, two jitterbugging couples are briefly featured, again without any apparent choreography. The Harlem Cuties, five light-skinned women in heels and knee-length dresses, dance partly together, but their routine allows for individual variations and turn-taking, lending the performance an improvisational, relaxed quality. Two dancers credited as Billy and Ann (who appeared in several Soundies) continue in the same vein during their brief showcase before the women's group joins them again.

On the one hand, the performances here are obviously staged and rehearsed with the aim of *constructing* an impression of spontaneity, as musical films conventionally do. Especially in terms of coordinating the music with the film's editing, this Soundie is comparatively well made, which suggests that some effort went into its planning and execution. On the other hand, there is a kind of casual, improvised quality to this jukebox short that is virtually nonexistent in Hollywood productions. The dancers in *Block Party Revels* seamlessly transition between performance and spectatorship, casually entering and exiting the central space that serves as a dance floor and stage, thus illustrating the dynamic and interactive nature of vernacular dance, which knows no strict division between the active performer versus the spectator as a passive consumer. The film's audience of dancers remains engaged in the performance throughout: all dancers not currently featured in the central space keep moving on the edges and in the background, alternately joining for brief segments of line dance choreography or simply grooving in their own individual fashion. The variety of dance moves and performance formats – solo, partnered, and in groups, variously acrobatic and elegant, improvised as well as choreographed – highlights individuality as much as collectivity. As Jacqui Malone notes, in the African American tradition, "the idea of executing any dance exactly like someone else is usually not valued"; instead, the focus is on "creating diversity within unity", even in the case of rehearsed group routines.[344] This principle is especially evident here in the line dance routine of the Harlem Cuties: they are obviously all familiar with the same sequence of steps, but just as obviously, they are not aiming for a streamlined chorus line display that would unite and unify the group into a single "collective body" as seen in many White Hollywood musicals. Instead, every single dancer

---

344 Malone, *Steppin' on the Blues*, 34.

maintains and emphatically displays her individuality, contributing to and interacting with the group as a whole.

In *Block Party Revels*, the diversity of dance performances and the casual alternation between them are almost overwhelming in the sense that they defy detailed description: there's simply too much going on, with constantly changing constellations creating a highly dynamic, fluid picture. Background and foreground, performers and spectators, improvised and choreographed segments are not neatly separated; instead, they shift, merge, and regroup, without ever settling into distinct, clearly delineated categories. Thus, instead of the obviously produced perfection of more elaborate, streamlined dance numbers, this Soundie illustrates what dance scholar Brenda Dixon Gottschild calls "embracing the conflict", with a strong focus on "difference, discord, and irregularity".[345] Last but not least, the Soundie's quality to a great extent rests on the dancers' embodiment of the African American aesthetic of the cool, which "combines composure with vitality".[346] Loose-jointed and relaxed, interactive and playful, but also rhythmically precise and elegant, the dancers are equal parts cool and controlled, casual and classy, seemingly dancing for their own enjoyment as much as for the entertainment of the party crowd. While obviously indebted to the Hollywood musical's mythology of spontaneous expression as well as to clichéd notions of Black musicality, *Block Party Revels* offers a remarkable manifestation of the Black vernacular in its emphasis on audience interaction, improvisation, individualism, and the aesthetic of the cool.

The third Soundie from this filming session, *Backstage Blues* (1943), also features the Harlem Cuties and several solo dancers centered around Lynn Albritton's piano performance. Here, the backstage environment suggests a professional showbiz context, thus drawing on the backstage musical's myth of entertainment, according to which even rehearsed professional performances originate from a spirit of improvised spontaneity.[347] In comparison with the two other Albritton Soundies, the performers here seem more aware of the film's absent but implied audience, deliberately facing and smiling at the camera, at times a little awkwardly. In addition, the dancing women are more explicitly sexualized in their skimpy costumes, showcasing bare legs and pronounced hip and upper-body motion to the piano's slow boogie-woogie beat. A much more stereotyped representation of Black musicality in combination with sex appeal, *Backstage Blues* has fewer redeeming qualities than some other Black-cast Soundies, and it inadvertently displays its constructedness. Nevertheless, the setting resonates with

---

345 Gottschild, *Digging the Africanist Presence*, 13.
346 Gottschild, 16. See also Malone, *Steppin' on the Blues*, 34.
347 See Feuer, "The Self-Reflective Musical".

one of the functions of the Panoram as a device offering entertainment during breaks between work hours (whether or not the backstage areas of theaters were among the actual exhibition sites of Soundies).

Other Black Soundies – for instance, *Rhythmania* and *Rug Cutter's Holiday* (1943) – are contained in entirely private settings, simply showing people having a party in somebody's living room. However, while these films offer non-narrative, matter-of-fact representations of Black music and dance culture, they also evidence the limitations entailed by Soundies' production processes. The presence of dancers can make the occasionally sloppy synchronization of image and soundtrack painfully obvious. *Rug Cutter's Holiday* offers an especially jarring example of this, as the dancers onscreen seem entirely disconnected from the accompanying soundtrack, a recording of "Panama" by Henry "Red" Allen and Jelly Roll Morton. Played in an early traditional jazz style, the song in no way matches the 1940s swing-era aesthetic of the dancing seen onscreen. The disjunction is additionally emphasized by the absence of diegetic sounds, such as voices, clapping of hands, or stomping of feet. Where the visual presence of musicians or a jukebox in other Soundies manages to divert attention from such missing sounds, the mismatch here is too glaring to be ignored. The piano player in the background provides the only visible source of music, at odds with the full band heard on the soundtrack. Similarly, the pianist in *Rhythmania* is shown enthusiastically playing his instrument and grinning into the camera, yet he remains inaudible except for a brief solo, whereas the rest of the band heard on the soundtrack is nowhere to be seen. While such improbabilities and inconsistencies tend to be carefully disguised in more elaborate Hollywood productions,[348] in these cheaply made Soundies, they can certainly make the image appear "discordant", to use media scholar Amy Herzog's term.[349]

Rather than completely dispensing with the usual Hollywood clichés, Soundies tend to condense the conventions established in more elaborate productions, so that titles, settings, costumes, and (often literal visualizations of) song lyrics serve as fragmentary codes demonstrating how much Black performance had become codified and commodified. Nevertheless, at their best, Black Soundies distance themselves both from the folk musical's romantic "music is in the air" myth, which located a natural Black musicality in the nostalgic rural South, and from the modern, urban exoticism that Black Harlem represented for Whites. While Black-cast shorts from the early sound film era often focused on professional show business, offering images of sophistication, competence, and abundance, many

---

[348] For a discussion of the "audio dissolve" used in musicals to inconspicuously transition between diegetic and nondiegetic sounds, see, for instance, Altman, *The American Film Musical*, 62–74.

[349] See Herzog, "Discordant Visions".

Black-cast Soundies frame Black vernacular music and dance as an ordinary part of modern, urban everyday life. With their simple sets, reduced or absent narratives, and their screening contexts reflecting onscreen activities, Soundies occasionally offer a comparatively cliché-free representation of a Black music and dance culture that is simultaneously modern, vernacular, and commonplace.

The generally favorable reviews of Black Soundies in *Billboard*'s "Movie Machine Reviews" indicate that they were a selling point for Soundies reels; at the same time, the reviews also confirm the ordinariness of Black Soundies. *Block Party Revels*, for example, is said to present "hot music in a highly acceptable way. Lynn Albritton, an excellent pianist; Billy and Ann and the Harlem Cuties in a good dance routine and a novelty musical group, the Six Knobs, show what goes on at a Harlem block party".[350] The adjective "hot" here is reminiscent of the discourses on Black performance in early sound film. While commending the quality of the performances, the review also implies that the Soundie just shows things "as they are" at a Harlem block party, suggesting a certain ordinariness. The listing for *Dispossessed Blues*, in turn, lacks any reference to race, stating matter-of-factly that the film "features the piano playing of Lynn Albritton, plus the jitterbugging of the Four Knobs. A tenement street is the background".[351] Here, the absence of color-coding suggests that Black Soundies were commonplace and expected, so that they didn't *need* to be marked as different from the rest of a Soundies program.

"You Do It Any Way You Will": Soundies' Black Women

Perhaps the most remarkable aspect of race in Soundies is that these short films gave significantly more exposure to African American women than Hollywood productions of the time. The AFM recording ban contributed both to a stronger African American presence and to the use of more dancers in Soundies. At the same time, the war generally brought female performers to the fore in a variety of entertainment contexts.[352] This is not to downplay the fact that Soundies – across all musical genres, races, and ethnicities – were full of eroticized images of scantily clad showgirls executing rather unimpressive dance routines or simply showing their legs and smiling. But at the same time, Soundies also showcased women as bandleaders, instrumentalists, and solo dancers more prominently than Hollywood films, and the women were often given screen credit.[353]

350 Review of *Block Party Revels*, Movie Machine Reviews, *Billboard*, June 5, 1943, 66, Google Books.
351 Review of *Dispossessed Blues*, Movie Machine Reviews, *Billboard*, July 24, 1943, 66, Google Books.
352 For a comprehensive history of all-female swing bands during World War II, see Tucker, *Swing Shift*. On film appearances by female jazz musicians during the period, see McGee, *Some Liked It Hot*, chapters 5–7.
353 For a discussion of some Soundies featuring White female bandleaders who also danced in front of the band, see McGee, *Some Liked It Hot*, 145–167. McGee points out that "the physical appearance of female bandleaders became the selling point for these groups as lead women sang, danced, and wore dresses and costumes that augmented their female sexuality" (166–167).

For Black women, in particular, the small screen of the Panoram offered more opportunities and also a more diverse range of images than the big screen, despite the fact that Soundies generally continued the objectification of light-skinned African American women as sexualized showgirls. As performer Jackie Lewis Parton recalls, producers hired mostly "very fair girls" for their Black-cast Soundies, perpetuating the intraracial hierarchy between light-skinned and darker-skinned performers that applied (and still applies) to African American women in the culture at large.[354] Typically, these "very fair girls" served a mainly decorative function in Soundies starring prominent men like Cab Calloway and Fats Waller, and their job was to admire these stars and flirt with them as well as with the films' audience. Nevertheless, the jukebox films also had several Black women "stars", including singers, instrumentalists, and dancers, who offered ambiguous embodiments: simultaneously sexualized, racialized attractions and individualized, independent, competent performers.

The most prominent Black female performer in Soundies was Dorothy Dandridge, who is mostly remembered for her tragic mulatto roles in Hollywood films of the 1950s, notably the operatic musicals *Carmen Jones* (1954) and *Porgy and Bess* (1959).[355] But much earlier in her career, Dandridge appeared in a series of ten Soundies that showcased her as a multitalented singing and dancing spectacle.[356] Though her decidedly sexy performances obviously catered to male heterosexual desire, Dandridge's persona is not one-dimensionally sexual, as Andrea Kelley shows in her acute analysis of Dandridge's emerging star persona in Soundies: while some Soundies frame her as a sexualized, exotic object of male fantasy and a marketable commodity constrained by her race and gender, others present her variously as a self-made artist, a "fantasy of leisure and prosperity",[357] and a symbol of Black class mobility, "circulating images of black leisure and conspicuous consumption".[358] Kelley outlines Dandridge's status as a hybrid figure with considerable crossover appeal, discussing how several Soundies

---

354 Jackie Lewis Parton, interviewed in the documentary *Soundies: A Musical History*, directed by Chris Lamson, 2007.

355 In both, Dandridge's singing voice was dubbed.

356 Prior to her Soundies career, Dandridge had appeared in a few specialty acts in Hollywood films, for instance in the "Chattanooga Choo Choo" number with the Nicholas Brothers in *Sun Valley Serenade* (1941), a star vehicle for Glenn Miller and his hugely popular big band. Dandridge's ten Soundies from 1941/42, in chronological order, are *Swing for Your Supper*; *Jungle Jig*; *Yes, Indeed!*; *Lazybones* (with Hoagy Carmichael); *Easy Street*; *A Zoot Suit with a Reet Pleat* (with Paul White); *Congo Clambake*; *Blackbird Fantasy*; *Cow-Cow Boogie*; and *Paper Doll* (with the Mills Brothers).

357 Kelley, *Soundies Jukebox Films*, 100.

358 Kelley, 103.

articulate her liminal status by showing her "in the act of identity transformation".³⁵⁹ It is important to note that even when she is framed as a servant or an object of male desire, Dandridge's body language and expression counteract whatever demeaning role is implied by the context: her facial expressions come across as self-assured, her enunciation during songs is deliberate and clear, and her dance movements are precise and confident.

While Dorothy Dandridge may be Soundies' most complex Black female figure, numerous lesser-known performers contributed to a remarkable diversity of screen images. African American dancer and singer Mabel Lee, dubbed "Queen of the Soundies" by her fans, also embodies an ambiguous image, both highly sexualized and confidently competent. A former member of the Apollo Theater's chorus in Harlem, where she was soon given a spot as a soloist, Mabel Lee seems to have appeared in dozens of Soundies as an extra and was featured in about ten.³⁶⁰ Unlike Dorothy Dandridge, she did not go on to have a Hollywood career. Her moderate fame onstage and on the Panoram's small screen supposedly rested on her slim legs, displayed liberally in her Soundies. Usually wearing very short dresses and also showing her flat belly, she would always feature pronounced hip motion and other moves with strong sexual connotations, such as shimmies, in her dances. At the same time, these explicitly sexy performances also reveal her versatility as a jazz dancer who has mastered the vocabulary of Black vernacular dance movement.

In *Rhythmania* as well as in *Chicken Shack Shuffle* (1943), Lee shares screen time with other dancers, notably with male tap dancers (in addition to the Harlem Honeys in the former and an uncredited jitterbugging couple in the latter). In both Soundies, the highly rhythmic footwork of all the dancers is evident from the film footage, which makes the absence of the corresponding tap sounds quite conspicuous. In the case of the male dancers (Harris and Hunt in *Rhythmania*, an unnamed dancer in *Chicken Shack Shuffle*), this mismatch between image and sound arguably diminishes the power of their performance. But in the case of female dancer Mabel Lee, the missing sounds distract from her rhythmic competence in favor of underscoring her sexuality, which is additionally emphasized by the costumes and cinematography. In *Rhythmania*, Lee lifts her knee-length skirt

---

359 Kelley, 98.

360 See Hill, *Tap Dancing America*, 144–145; MacGillivray and Okuda, *The Soundies Book*, 154–155; and Brian Seibert, "Mable Lee, Tap-Dancing 'Queen of the Soundies', Dies at 97", *New York Times*, February 14, 2019, https://nyti.ms/2UY2Mqs. Lee's first name was alternately spelled Mable and Mabel, with the latter appearing more frequently in historical sources, such as press reports.

while the camera pans down from her torso to her legs. A cut to the piano player, whose wide-eyed and grinning face is simultaneously buffoonish and lewd, reinforces Lee's function as an object of the male gaze while simultaneously ridiculing the male performer by minstrelizing him. In *Chicken Shack Shuffle* (allegedly a reference to the popular Harlem restaurant Tillie's Chicken Shack), Lee sings and dances in an extremely sexy feathered bikini, while restaurant patrons in regular street clothes watch her (fig. 31). Her strongly sexualized appearance and performance are more suited to a nightclub setting than to the unassuming eatery represented here.

Despite all of this, Lee is far from being *only* objectified. With a radiating smile that exudes confidence and a moving body that demonstrates competence, she delivers commanding performances in several of her Soundies. In *Chicken Shack Shuffle*, she also commands participation through the song lyrics, which are mock instructions for the supposed eponymous dance: "There's a riffle and a ruffle, chicken shack shuffle, you do it any way you will / you jump to the left, and you cross your legs, and tip along like you're walking on eggs / do anything but a pigeon wing, strut like a rooster but you gotta swing".[361] As silly as these lines may be, they assert creative freedom and control ("you do it any way you will"), and Lee's delivery is engaging. Going into her dance, she combines leg wiggles, upper-body shimmies, an undulating torso, and over-rotated twists of hips and legs with distinctly rhythmic footwork. Her animated face additionally accentuates individual motions in a deliberate and precise manner, directing the viewers' attention to her agency and control. Outright demanding to be looked at, Mabel Lee draws attention to her skill as much as to her sexuality, as if to say, "look at what I can do".

The power implicit in competent dance performance is made even more explicit in Mabel Lee's later Soundie *Cats Can't Dance* (1945). Here, Lee mockingly sings about all the men who are interested in her but whom she finds unappealing because they don't know how to dance. The male musicians in the small swing combo (led by Deryck Sampson) throw appreciative glances at her as she twists her hips, wiggles her shoulders, and flings her legs and arms in the air (fig. 32). While she faces the camera most of the time – except for a few cutaways to the band and the piano player's hands – the band members also function as stand-in spectators who get a view of her butt's undulating motions. Yet once again, despite

---

361 Dance songs with more or less detailed descriptions or instructions first became a popular trend in the 1910s and were used to market sheet music for "danceable" tunes. While many early dance songs referenced actual dance moves from the African American vernacular, later swing-era examples often simply invented names for the alleged latest dance fads that nobody had ever seen. See, for instance, Stearns and Stearns, *Jazz Dance*, 95–114.

Chapter 4 Jumpin' at the Jukebox, Dancin' in the Street

Figures 31 and 32. "Queen of the Soundies" Mabel Lee dances in *Chicken Shack Shuffle* (1943) and *Cats Can't Dance* (1945).

being partially objectified by the camera, costume, and mise-en-scène, Lee's performance demonstrates agency, independence, and choice.

Marie Bryant, another exceptional Black dancer who was woefully underrepresented in films, appeared in the Soundie *Bli-Blip* (1942), performing a comic song and dance routine with Paul White to a soundtrack recorded by Duke Ellington (who doesn't appear onscreen here).[362] The film frames Bryant and White as employees of a bar after closing, and the song serves as a flirting vehicle for them. They deliver the song's nonsense lyrics with exaggerated grimacing that is emphasized in close-ups, with a stronger focus on White. While such minstrelsy-inspired mugging was common for Black men onscreen, it was less often seen in performances by women, and here too, it is mostly Paul White's rather buffoonish delivery that panders to demeaning stereotypes, while Marie Bryant's performance comes across as more ironically comic. The choreographed dance, filmed mostly in full shot, is an expressive and highly rhythmic modern jazz routine that frames the pair as equal partners engaged in playful flirtation. Bryant is not excessively sexualized, thus offering an alternative to the sexy jungle dancer cliché. The absence of rhythmic footwork sounds is less conspicuous than in many other Soundies, largely due to better coordination between Ellington's recording and the dance routine, which functions as a redeeming counterpoint to the performers' stereotypical servant roles and the buffoonery of the song.

Many other Black-cast Soundies showcased largely forgotten dancing women, whether they appeared solo or as part of a group, often in ways that oscillate between fetishizing looks at their bodies, especially their legs, and confident demonstrations of classic vernacular jazz dancing. All in all, the Soundies of the 1940s probably contained more images of Black dancing women than all Hollywood feature films from the late 1920s through the mid-1940s combined. While the most prominent of these women were undoubtedly successful due to their looks, which conformed to the ideal of the light-skinned dusky belle, they nevertheless articulated the "tensions between feminine subjectivity and objectivity".[363] They functioned simultaneously as sexualized objects of desire and as individualized, charismatic women performing with humor, skill, and agency. In a sense, the Black dancing women in the Soundies of the 1940s pick up where Nina Mae McKinney and Fredi Washington left off in 1929, continuing the tradition of fetishizing the light-skinned African American beauty. But the three-minute jukebox films dispense with tragic narratives and refrain from punishing their protagonists. Having shed the narrative framework of Holly-

---

362 For a short biography of Marie Bryant, see Almonte, "Know Your Jazz Dancer".

363 McGee, *Some Liked It Hot*, 31.

opportunity.[368] This discourse of economic opportunity echoes discussions from the early sound film era, when the brief trend of Black-cast musicals elicited enthusiastic reactions from commentators who hoped for increasing African American participation in the film industry – hopes that didn't materialize to the expected degree.[369] With the Soundies of the 1940s, this history arguably repeated itself to some extent. After all, the jukebox shorts did not bring about revolutionary changes in the mainstream film industry. But the novel exhibition and viewing practices of Soundies included and integrated African Americans in a transitional moment of media history that changed film-audience and performer-audience interaction in public spaces.

Considered as individual films, Black Soundies offer utopian spaces of fun and freedom beyond the confines and control of the White world. As with other all-Black-cast films, these segregated fantasy spaces also erase the signs of segregation and White privilege – in the entertainment industry and in society at large. But Soundies' mode of exhibition desegregates their self-contained worlds by reintroducing the White "outside world" in a twofold manner: one, by showing Black-cast Soundies next to the White Soundies on the same film reel; two, by circulating them in – often racially integrated – public spaces, which frequently resembled the spaces shown on the small screens of the Panoram jukebox. In this context, the frequent appearance of dancers and the often casual, improvised, almost incidental staging of Black vernacular dance are significant: Soundies' mirroring of screen content and screening context suggests an opening for new possibilities, the possibility of a similarly casual, improvised, almost incidental presence of African Americans *moving* in and into public everyday spaces in new ways and to a new extent.

Despite Soundies' novelty, however, it is important to note that there is no absolute boundary between Soundies and big-screen Hollywood productions with regard to the content and aesthetics of music and dance performances. In the late 1930s and early 1940s, swing culture also plays a curiously contradictory role in Hollywood productions. Especially with regard to dance, swing in Hollywood is simultaneously – and paradoxically – ubiquitous and marginalized. In the final two chapters, I look at images of swing dancing in a variety of films, focusing on Black and White dancers, respectively.

---

368 Kelley, unpublished manuscript (outtakes from *Soundies Jukebox Films*, chapter 5).
369 See Friedman, *African American Films*.

CHAPTER 5 Harlem to Hollywood: Whitey's Lindy Hoppers and the Crossover Success of a Black Dance

From the 1920s through the early 1940s, tap dance was the key performance mode of vernacular jazz dance. During the swing era of the 1930s and early 1940s, jazz-inspired styles derived from the African American vernacular also came to dominate partnered social dancing. The new swing – or jitterbug – styles brought a departure from traditional gender roles and European-based aesthetics in social dance, as well as a shift in the perception and representation of Black dancers, who came to stand for a rejuvenated, modern American popular culture. A significant influence in this respect was the Lindy hop, a highly expressive Black partner dance. According to all available evidence, the Lindy originated at the Savoy Ballroom in Harlem around 1927, evolving from earlier jazz dances, including the Charleston.[370] In the 1930s, the Lindy became professionalized as a high-speed, high-energy, and often acrobatic spectacle. Along with other swing dance styles, it was also popularized as an amateur dance among young swing fans during the time when big band swing was the nation's dominant dance music. Eventually, swing dancing also spread internationally, and during World War II, swing culture came to symbolize American values overseas. In 1943, *Life* magazine called the Lindy hop America's "true national folk dance" in a cover story featuring photographs of both Black and White dancers.[371]

But despite their enormous popularity, swing dance styles never became as prominent in film as tap dancing. This is not to say that there was no swing

---

370 Legend has it that the name was a reference to aviation pioneer Charles Lindbergh's historic "hop" across the Atlantic in 1927. See, for instance, White, "Birth of Lindy Hop". The Lindy hop was rediscovered in the 1980s and has been experiencing a large-scale revival ever since, accompanied by extensive efforts to research and document its history. For the history of the Lindy hop and the Savoy Ballroom, see, for instance, Dinerstein, *Swinging the Machine*, 250–282; Engelbrecht, "Swinging at the Savoy"; Hubbard and Monaghan, "Negotiating Compromise"; Malone, *Steppin' on the Blues*, 100–106; Manning and Millman, *Frankie Manning* (hereafter cited as Manning); Miller with Jensen, *Swingin' at the Savoy* (hereafter cited as Miller); and Stearns and Stearns, *Jazz Dance*, 315–334.

371 "The Lindy Hop: A True National Folk Dance Has Been Born in U.S.A.", *Life*, August 23, 1943, 95–103, Google Books.

dancing onscreen. There was, in fact, quite a lot of it, but it never evolved into a major trend in the movies. Feature films rarely framed swing dance scenes as a central attraction, and the dance numbers were not usually performed by the films' protagonists and stars. Accordingly, none of the swing dancers who appeared in films became major movie stars in the way that some tap dancers did. While proficiency in swing dancing offered some employment opportunities in the film industry, it did not lead to full-fledged stardom.

It is all the more remarkable that the swing dancers who arguably came closest to movie stardom were African Americans: Whitey's Lindy Hoppers, a group of professional Black dancers based at the Savoy Ballroom in Harlem, whose success led to a handful of remarkable performances in Hollywood films of the late 1930s and early 1940s. While this group of Black dancers operated within the usual confines imposed on African Americans during Hollywood's studio era, their scenes in feature films also testify to the tensions within that system, evidencing subtle but significant shifts in Black screen images. Especially in the context of slapstick comedy, the dance numbers of Whitey's Lindy Hoppers take on a subversive function, inadvertently and ambivalently highlighting and confirming Black/White power hierarchies. The group's final Hollywood appearance in *Hellzapoppin'* (1941) is a climactic achievement in terms of capturing the aesthetics of the dance on film, even if it remains within the usual conventions for Black specialty acts in terms of narrative framing.

Swing culture's most progressive aspects found expression in marginal forms, such as theatrical short films, Soundies, and low-budget B movies, rather than in big-budget feature films. Overall, Hollywood's reaction to the nation's jitterbug craze was slow and limited. Nevertheless, by the early 1940s, the mainstream success of swing music and dance with a young (White) mass public was hard to ignore and started feeding back into screen representations of swing dancing. A small number of mock-educational, comic short films are among the most interesting productions from the period. Parodic shorts like the Soundie *The Outline of Jitterbug History* (1942), with Whitey's Lindy Hoppers, and the nine-minute *Groovie Movie* (1944), which features prominent White dancers, evidence the growing social acceptability of jitterbug dancing as well as its crossover appeal, and they present (Black) vernacular jazz culture as a modern all-American culture in ways rarely seen in feature films.

Rewriting Rules, Shifting Perceptions

In the 1920s, the Charleston had come to symbolize the Jazz Age in general and the liberation of (White) women in particular, and the decade saw a number of other dance fads, many of African American origin, come and go. But it was in the swing era of the 1930s and early 1940s that the aesthetics of African American vernacular jazz dance really became prevalent on the social dance floor. While the previous generations kept fox-trotting and waltzing, the high-school- and college-age crowd embraced the new swing styles, increasingly infusing their "collegiate" versions of ballroom dances with a Black vernacular aesthetic. From the mid-1930s on, with the enormous success of big band swing music, partnered swing dancing became a mainstream phenomenon. As young people across America came up with countless, often short-lived dance fads, there was a lot of local and regional variation in social dance styles. The precise origins of many specific steps – and of their names – remain obscure or anecdotal at best, and the inconsistent use of swing dance terminology often adds to the confusion.[372] This is not the place to untangle and retrace the complex history of swing dances and their names in detail. But it is important to note that, for all their variations and constant evolution, swing-era social dance styles had some crucial traits in common. These include the break with traditional social dance etiquette and its corresponding gender roles. In the so-called breakaway, partners broke away from the traditional close embrace, leaving room for improvisation and individual expression. The breakaway was allegedly introduced as a Charleston variation by "Shorty" George Snowden, one of the most prominent dancers at the Savoy in Harlem during the first few years of the ballroom's existence (it opened in 1926). Variously described as a Charleston variation and as a dance in its own right, the breakaway is often considered a precursor to the Lindy hop.[373] While the Lindy itself incorporated numerous elements from other dances, it was based on "an eight-count box-step syncopated on the offbeat, where the couple followed a circular path around a shared central axis".[374] The Lindy's trademark move is the swing-out, which "involves the leader letting the partner out and away by extending the hand. At that point, either or both partners can improvise".[375]

This emphasis on individuality – for both partners – runs like a common thread through new styles of partner dancing from the 1920s onward. Especially for women, who had previously been restricted to the more passive role of the follower in social dance, this freedom was all but revolutionary. Unlike tap,

---

372 In general, "swing dance" and "jitterbug" are both umbrella terms that encompass any type of dancing done to the swing music of the 1930s and 1940s. However, the term "jitterbug" is sometimes also used as a synonym more specifically for the Lindy hop. Stearns and Stearns speak of the "Jitterbug, or Lindy" in their book (*Jazz Dance*, 1). To further confuse matters, the word "jitterbug" initially referred not to a dance style but to swing dancers and, even more generally, to fans of swing music. With the growing popularity of swing culture, the term "jitterbug" was increasingly used to refer to dancing, both as a verb ("to jitterbug") and as a noun ("to dance the jitterbug"). See also Hubbard and Monaghan, "Negotiating Compromise", 145n35; and Outman, "'Jitterbug' and 'Swing'".

373 See also Manning, 49–50; and Stearns and Stearns, *Jazz Dance*, 323–324.

374 Dinerstein, *Swinging the Machine*, 257.

375 Dinerstein, 257.

partnered swing dancing was by no means "a man's world" but a sphere of gender equality, or at least near equality. Swing dance styles generally uphold the traditional social dance roles of male leaders and female followers as an overall principle – though even back in the day, women would sometimes lead and men sometimes follow. But within this general framework, the female follower's role is as active and as creative as the male leader's role, with plenty of room for improvisation and individual expression. In fact, partner dancing in the swing idiom was rarely partnered throughout. Instead, dancers would often let go of each other entirely, making room for solo movement, which incorporated a wide range of steps from the Black vernacular tradition and which sometimes originated in or led to brief dance fads.

Further, swing dances are relatively athletic and often danced at fast tempos, requiring a good deal of physical stamina. In contexts of performance and competition, the music tended to be fast and, from the mid-1930s on, the dancing often featured acrobatic elements.[376] While true acrobatics were introduced for and restricted to performance and competition settings, a general athleticism pervaded social dancing too, at least in comparison with more traditional ballroom dances, and relatively high tempos were vital to swing dancing.[377] Women therefore often (though not always) danced in lower heels and wore shorter skirts or dresses to allow for better freedom of movement. Inventiveness, originality, and expressivity were valued over conventional ideas of elegance or compliance with rules, and comic elements often subverted older standards of grace and perfection. As Joel Dinerstein notes, "swing-era dance culture broke down the European mask of sophistication, the lindy deemphasized the idea of good form or dance rules and empowered individual self-expression and the judgment of the audience".[378] As with all forms of vernacular jazz dancing, the aesthetics of social swing dancing generally included a grounded posture, an emphasis on hip motion, polycentric isolation, and syncopated rhythms.

Robert P. Crease notes that the Lindy hop sometimes caused concern among self-declared guardians of public morals, who considered it "disruptive, barbaric, and obscene".[379] And with regard to swing music, jazz and film scholar Krin Gabbard argues that

---

376 Dancer Frankie Manning, who took on something of a lead role within Whitey's Lindy Hoppers, is generally credited with introducing acrobatics (so-called air steps) and ensemble dancing into the Lindy hop in 1936. See Manning, 93–104; and Miller, 98–10.
377 See also Stearns and Stearns, *Jazz Dance*, 323.
378 Dinerstein, *Swinging the Machine*, 280.
379 Crease, "Divine Frivolity", 211.

> many white Americans embraced swing because it contained elements associated with African American spontaneity, transgressiveness, and, most importantly, sexuality. These elements were clearly implied even when the music was played by an entirely white big band. ...
>
> Although the white swing of the 1930s made black music seem less "dangerous", the African American underpinnings of swing may still have made a large portion of the white audience uncomfortable.[380]

While these elements no doubt resonated with swing fans as well as opponents, connotations of sexuality are often secondary in swing dancing, where rhythm, high energy, and humor generally outweigh the potential eroticism of the dance (as well as of the music). Music historian Lewis E. Erenberg also considers social swing dances an "important part of interaction between the sexes, ... [which] featured honest emotional expression more than overt sexuality or obsessive sentimental love".[381]

Whereas partnered swing dancing in general is noteworthy for redefining gender roles, the Lindy hop, as the most prominently publicized and professionalized of swing dances, is remarkable for the dominance of Black dancers. This is true not only in terms of the dancers' skill but also regarding their presence and perception in public discourses concerning the dance. Joel Dinerstein points out that the dance was distinguished "from the assumed primitive sensuality and 'natural' rhythmic ability of blacks" and that this distinction "represented a major breakthrough in the white gaze".[382] The perception of the Lindy hop as an African American dance went hand in hand with its valuation as a modern, urban form of expression, part of the kind of popular vernacular modernism that played an important role in representations of a democratic, modern American mass culture.[383] Dance historians Karen Hubbard and Terry Monaghan suggest a connection between the racial and gender aspects:

> The Lindy Hop also involved a redefinition of gender relations that struck at the core of prevailing derogatory and demeaning racial characterizations of African Americans. Developing into a comprehensive and rhythmically charged critique of the European partner-dancing tradition, it articulated a new aesthetic of cultural equality. ... The driving reciprocal dynamic of both partners characterized the essential vitality of the dance that paid minimal deference to the ballroom conventions of leaders and followers. ... The new Lindy Hoppers made a major contribution to transforming the way these dancing African Americans not only saw each other but also how other blacks and whites perceived them. ... Black dancing bodies became "hep" and respectfully imitated.[384]

380 Gabbard, *Jammin' at the Margins*, 27.
381 Erenberg, *Swingin' the Dream*, 51.
382 Dinerstein, *Swinging the Machine*, 251.
383 On swing music and dancing as "African American popular modernism", see Dinerstein, *Swinging the Machine*, 106. On the concept of vernacular modernism more generally, see Hansen, "Mass Production of the Senses".
384 Hubbard and Monaghan, "Negotiating Compromise", 133.

Hollywood, however, was not "hep" to the new trend from the beginning. As much as early sound cinema liked to showcase Black dancing bodies, the Lindy hop developed in Harlem largely ignored by the film industry, and film footage from the early years of the dance's history is rare.

From the Savoy to the Screen

Among today's swing dance "revivalists", the short film *After Seben* (1929) has canonical status as the first known cinematic document of the Lindy hop, featuring "Shorty" George Snowden, one of the Savoy's preeminent dancers in the early years.[385] The film's Harlem cabaret/nightclub setting is typical of the early sound era's Black-cast films, depicting a stereotyped milieu of gambling and musical entertainment. Rather atypical is the fact that it is a racially mixed film, featuring White vaudevillian James Barton in blackface among an otherwise African American cast.[386] What little plot there is concerns Barton as a cabaret manager, who argues with his wife over money and suspects her of cheating on him. The second half of the fifteen-minute film is dedicated to music and dancing. A trade press review assessed the dance scene as follows:

> There are some dancing scenes in which negro energy just overflows. Several couples swing into typical "n— dances" and Barton himself does a characteristic step. …
>
> Then again some of the negro dancing is liable to offend some, for it is a fact that one of the dances bordered for a few seconds on the obscene.[387]

The scene consists of three brief consecutive performances by three couples, narratively framed as a dance contest in the nightclub. For today's viewers, the "obscene" might be rather hard to detect, but the reviewer most likely referred to a few moments of hip motion that the first two couples do in close embrace. A quick-quick-slow step pattern provides the rhythmic base of the dance, with couples alternating between close embrace and open position. This breakaway principle unmistakably resembles the swing-out of the later Lindy hop, although the rhythmic pattern is not the same. A syncopated triple step was later added to the swing-out, and compared with the more bouncy, up-and-down styles of the 1920s, the Lindy of the 1930s "flowed more horizontally and smoothly".[388] While all three couples here do essentially the same type of dance, they each display

---

385 Lindy hop pioneer "Shorty" George Snowden has also been widely credited with naming the dance (see Manning, 245), though this is a matter of some controversy (see, for instance, White, "Birth of Lindy Hop"). None of the other five dancers in the film have been identified to date, but according to Ernie Smith, they were all recruited from the Savoy; see Smith, "Portrait of the Swing Era," xx; and Manning, 263n2.

386 On James Barton, see Stearns and Stearns, *Jazz Dance*, 197–203.

387 Raymond Ganly, Review of *After Seben*, *Motion Picture News*, October 5, 1929, 1261, Media History Digital Library.

388 Stearns and Stearns, *Jazz Dance*, 325.

individual specialties, and male and female dancers contribute as equal partners. The last couple performs a dip foreshadowing the Lindy's later acrobatics and then exits with a high-kicking strut reminiscent of the cakewalk.

While attracting little interest from the film industry, the large-capacity Savoy Ballroom became one of Harlem's hot spots, drawing remarkably diverse – and racially mixed – crowds, who came to hear the popular big bands, socialize, and dance. The ballroom's best regular amateur dancers increasingly turned into an attraction in their own right, adding to the Savoy's growing reputation and introducing the general public to the latest innovations in (Black) social dance. Cinema played a marginal role in spreading awareness of the new dance trends emerging from the Savoy. Only a handful of – mostly unidentified – Savoy dancers were captured on film in the early years, appearing in both documentary and fictional shorts, usually just for a few seconds. For example, the documentary *Manhattan Medley* (1931), a ten-minute "city symphony", shows a couple, possibly George Snowden and Mattie Purnell, for about three seconds, doing a dance very similar to that in *After Seben*. These kinds of short dance scenes were few and far between, only offering a fragmentary idea of how the new dance evolved during the first half decade of its existence.[389]

In the mid-1930s, when big band swing became firmly established in the mainstream, it was newsreel footage of the Harvest Moon Ball – rather than Hollywood movies – that began disseminating moving images of the Lindy hop (and from 1937 on, also of the collegiate shag, another popular partner dance of the swing era). The first Harvest Moon Ball dance contest was held in New York's packed Madison Square Garden in 1935, and the event would continue to sell out year after year. While the origins of the contest and the motivation for including the Lindy hop remain somewhat obscure, the popularity of swing was key in the event's reception. More traditional ballroom styles – namely, the fox-trot, waltz, tango, and rumba – made up most of the contest, but the Lindy hop was the real crowd-pleaser, presented as the final climactic section. While coverage in the *New York Daily News*, the event's sponsor, focused on the White winners in the other divisions, newsreel reports tended to prominently feature

---

[389] I have not been able to find any information on a 1931 Pathé News segment titled "It Takes 'Hot Dogs' to Win the Lindy Hop", which is mentioned in various sources (see, for instance, Crease, "Divine Frivolity", 212; and Manning, 255). Some footage that seems to have been shot at the Savoy later in the decade appears in newsreels and short documentaries, notably in "Dance Contest at Savoy Ballroom" (New York City Paramount News, 1938) and in *Life in Harlem – A Documentary Film of America's Negro Metropolis* (Colored America on Parade series, 1940). The Vitaphone short *Rufus Jones for President* (1933) features one couple for a total of about twenty seconds in an eclectic mix of partnered and solo dancing that includes breakaway patterns and high-kicking Charleston steps. This is arguably a version of the Lindy hop, and according to dancer-historian Peter Loggins (personal conversation with the author), the male dancer is probably "Twistmouth" George Ganaway, a prominent first-generation Savoy dancer. The two dancers are later briefly joined by a second couple, likely also from the Savoy.

the spectacle of the Lindy hop, which was unquestionably dominated by Black dancers.[390]

The first Harvest Moon Ball also marked the beginning of the professional careers of Whitey's Lindy Hoppers, many of whom were still in their teens when they won the contest's first edition.[391] The Black dance group was formed that year by Herbert "Whitey" White, formerly a prizefighter, later a bouncer at the Savoy Ballroom, where he discovered the Lindy hop's potential as a business.[392] White had been scouting talent among the Savoy's best regular amateur dancers, who developed into a professional performance group under his supervision and management. Based at the Savoy, where they would social dance, compete, and perform regularly, members of the group also began touring nationally and internationally with prominent musicians, and they appeared in Broadway productions and films. Dozens of dancers were members of Whitey's Lindy Hoppers at one time or another between 1935 and 1943, with various subsets of the group performing under different names, including Whitey's Hopping Maniacs, the Harlem Congeroo Dancers, and the Hot Chocolates (to avoid confusion, I will use the name Whitey's Lindy Hoppers to refer to all of the subgroups).[393]

According to Robert P. Crease, "nearly all show-business jobs for Lindy Hoppers were filled by members of Whitey's Lindy Hoppers because of the dominance of New York Lindy Hopping over Lindy Hopping elsewhere, of Savoy Lindy Hopping over that of the rest of New York, and of White over the Savoy".[394] This dominance eventually extended to film screens, and dancers from Whitey's group were hired to perform in a total of five feature films produced by Hollywood studios: MGM's *A Day at the Races* (1937) and *Everybody Sing* (1938), Republic's *Manhattan Merry-Go-Round* (1937), RKO's *Radio City Revels* (1938), and Universal's *Hellzapoppin'* (1941). However, their dance number in *Everybody Sing*, an early star vehicle for Judy Garland, was cut from the film. In addition to

---

390 For a general history of the Harvest Moon Ball and how it was covered in the press, see Dinerstein, *Swinging the Machine*, 268–276. For an example of a newsreel report on the event, see "Dancing: Broadway Stages Big Orgy of Ball-Room Eccentricities", British Movietone News, 1937, YouTube video, https://youtu.be/hOpKWJDczpc.

391 For accounts of the Harvest Moon Ball from dancers Frankie Manning and Norma Miller, see Manning, 88–91; and Miller, 65–82.

392 The (auto)biographies of members Frankie Manning and Norma Miller offer the most comprehensive histories of Whitey's Lindy Hoppers. For more about Herbert White's early career, see also Stearns and Stearns, *Jazz Dance*, 317–320.

393 According to Stearns and Stearns, Whitey "employed around seventy-two dancers" (*Jazz Dance*, 331). As of August 2020, Wikipedia lists forty-nine members by name; see "Whitey's Lindy Hoppers", Wikipedia: The Free Encyclopedia, https://en.wikipedia.org/w/index.php?title=Whitey%27s_Lindy_Hoppers&oldid=971589015.

394 Crease, "Divine Frivolity", 212. Accounts by contemporary witnesses add up to suggest that Whitey effectively monopolized the business of Black Lindy hop and exploited the dancers. See Stearns and Stearns, *Jazz Dance*, 331–332; and Miller 58–64, 121–132, 149–155. Frankie Manning expresses a more moderate view of Whitey's business approach and treatment of the dancers; see Manning, 140–142.

these Hollywood features, Whitey's Lindy Hoppers appeared in the race movie *Keep Punching* (1939) and in several Soundies in the early 1940s. The group disbanded in 1943, after many of the male dancers had been drafted. Following the war, their leading dancer and choreographer, Frankie Manning, founded the four-piece group the Congaroos, whose only screen appearance was in a race movie.

The feature film appearances of Whitey's Lindy Hoppers are typical of classical Hollywood's Black specialty acts in that they hint at White America's dependence on African Americans, with the latter taking the role of servants and/or entertainers. Within this framework, however, some of their numbers also negotiate and, to a degree, subvert Hollywood's standard formula. This is especially the case in the group's two most elaborate dance scenes, which are also their best known. They occur in the group's first and last feature films, *A Day at the Races* and *Hellzapoppin'*, and it is conspicuous that these two films also share a number of other characteristics. Both contain several musical numbers, but neither is primarily a musical. Rather, they are anarchistic comedies, in which slapstick, wordplay, and general mayhem outweigh narrative logic and coherence. In both cases, the African American musical number shares the film's anarchistic spirit, high energy, and focus on the physical. The two films are also similar in how they stage and narratively frame the Lindy hop: in both, the dance serves as an inspiration for White characters, yet it also occurs somewhat surreptitiously, which lends it a strong note of the illicit and subversive.

Star Turns in *A Day at the Races*

MGM's Marx Brothers vehicle *A Day at the Races* costars Allan Jones and Maureen O'Sullivan as the lead romantic couple, Gil and Judy. Compared with the Marx Brothers' earlier films at Paramount, *Races* has a more coherent storyline, with the comedians' antics frequently at the service of plot development. Nevertheless, there is still plenty of room for narratively unmotivated and unintegrated gags.[395]

The Lindy hop is part of an African American sequence set in a kind of picturesque, stereotypically "folksy" Black ghetto. Unusually long at eight minutes, the sequence occurs at a point of crisis in the White-dominated plot and leads to a solution, at least symbolically: the sanitarium owned by Judy is in financial trouble, so she is hiding from the sheriff in a horse barn with boyfriend Gil and their friends Tony, Stuffy, and Dr. Hackenbush (the Marx Brothers). Gil tries to cheer up his sweetheart with the ballad "Tomorrow Is Another Day".

---

[395] For an in-depth analysis of the increasing narrative integration in the later Marx Brothers comedies, see Jenkins, *What Made Pistachio Nuts?*

Before breaking into song, he points to the children playing outside: "Look at those kids, laughing, happy". The corresponding shot through the window reveals what we could call a pastoral Black ghetto setting: a group of Black children are skipping rope amidst simple but picturesque little cabins.[396] Gil's song is followed by a rollicking tour through this scenery, initiated and headed by Harpo Marx, whose tin whistle draws a veritable catalog of Black stock characters from their humble abodes: little kids who clearly have rhythm in their blood, hardworking Christians (identified by way of some "Hallelujahs" and a few notes from the spiritual "Nobody Knows the Trouble I've Seen"), crapshooters, and the musicians and patrons of an overcrowded jazz bar, whose walls are literally shaking from the hard-swinging music and dancing. They all join Harpo, and the growing crowd euphorically sings and dances through the streets and eventually back into the barn, where vocalist Ivie Anderson delivers the scene's message in song: "All God's children got rhythm, all God's children got swing, maybe haven't got money, maybe haven't got shoes, but all God's children got rhythm, to push away the blues, yeah!" At the end of the song, there is a smooth transition into the Lindy hop. Only about ninety seconds long, the Lindy is staged as a spontaneous jam session and danced at a high speed. The dancers emerge from the crowd, which forms a circle around them, and at the end, they return to the circle and merge back into the crowd before the number ends with more singing and dancing by the large ensemble.

The entire Black sequence, and the climactic Lindy hop in particular, exemplify the African American star dance as described by Arthur Knight in an essay on Black stardom in Hollywood. According to Knight, the structure of star dancing has West African roots and runs like a common thread through all of African American dance history:

> In all these dances, performers emerge – or break – into the center of the circle, perform their "star" turn, and then return to the circle to support the next star. Star dancing … existed as a structure, a relation of individual and group, rather than as a content or specific series of moves with a fixed meaning. …
>
> The turn is simultaneously a horizontal trip into the center of the circle of culture and community *and*, in terms of the quality and merit of the individual's performance, a break, an ascension.[397]

---

396 See also the concept of the "idyllic chronotope" as employed by Paula Massood to describe Hollywood representations of Black life in a timeless and static rural space (*Black City Cinema*, 14–16).

397 Knight, "Star Dances", 398 (italics in the original). Knight uses the concept and structure of star dancing as a metaphor for the problematic nature of African American stardom in classical Hollywood cinema: through their success, Black film stars often break away from and lose touch with their community without ever ascending to the same star status as White movie stars.

In *A Day at the Races,* everybody from the smallest child to the overweight pianist is seen dancing at some point, and in addition to singer Ivie Anderson, various musicians and dancers get their brief star turns while also staying connected with the whole community. The short but impressive display by Whitey's Lindy Hoppers is the climax in this respect, both in terms of the group's breaking out from the larger community and in terms of the dance itself, which emphasizes the individual dancers' specialties as much as the collaborative spirit of ensemble dancing. Robert P. Crease characterizes the Lindy hop in similar terms regarding the relation between individual and group:

> As a jazz dance, it (like jazz music) is both an improvisational and individualistic practice and a collaborative one. To capture that antinomic character involves somehow representing the performer both as individually creative and as involved in a give-and-take with a community of other performers.[398]

Crease argues that the "Lindy does not lend itself readily to representation through traditional cinematic methods" because of these characteristics and because "vernacular dances like the Lindy are unlike stage dances in that they are not composed to be performed on stage before an audience from a privileged perspective", which makes it difficult to effectively capture the spirit of the dance.[399] However, as Crease himself goes on to show in his analysis, some film scenes *did* capture the Lindy's vernacular qualities along with the spectacular aspects of its professionalized form.

The Lindy routine in *A Day at the Races* begins with the four couples briefly dancing together, then one couple after another takes the spotlight, demonstrating individual signature steps: Dorothy Miller and Johnny Malls get the first and shortest star turn, doing several swing-out variations before they exit with a drag – that is, with Miller being dragged off the floor as she leans against Malls; Norma Miller somersaults over Leon James after several swing-outs; Snookie Beasley solos with a syncopated lock step, in which he crosses and momentarily locks his legs in a freeze before throwing his partner Willamae Ricker in the air; the last couple, George Greenidge and Ella Gibson, perform variations of the Lindy Charleston, moves adapted from the 1920s dance with a stronger emphasis on leg kicks (fig. 33); then they also add in some acrobatics and eventually exit with a drag. Wearing "respectable" outfits of low-heeled shoes, below-the-knee skirts, and sweaters, the female dancers are not eroticized, nor are they in any way presented as inferior to their partners. Instead, each couple performs as a team of equals in terms of their rhythmic ability, expressivity, and athleticism. At the end, everybody joins in again for some ensemble dancing (fig. 34), which ends with an acrobatic exit of

---

398 Crease, "Divine Frivolity", 209.

399 Crease, 208–209.

Jumping the Color Line: Vernacular Jazz Dance in American Film, 1929–1945

Figures 33 and 34. Star turns and ensemble dancing in the Lindy scene from *A Day at the Races* (1937) with Whitey's Lindy Hoppers.

dancers piled on top of each other as they rejoin the crowd – that is, the circle – of spectators.

Only rarely has this kind of integration of community and individuality, of structure and improvisation, which is so characteristic of African American vernacular culture, found similar expression in studio-era Hollywood cinema. To be sure, the heavy-handed stereotyping of the setting and narrative context compromises the qualities of the scene, as do the brief close-ups of dancers Norma Miller and Leon James pulling funny faces. These function as instances of visual minstrelization, a common aesthetic strategy for Black specialty acts, which serves to "contain the expressivity of African American jazz performance", as Corin Willis has convincingly argued.[400] Slapstick-style sound effects accompanying the music and accenting the close-ups additionally enhance this minstrelization.

In spite of all these distractions, both the vernacular social dance origins of the Lindy hop *and* the way the dance had evolved into a professional performance practice seem to have been translated quite faithfully to the screen. Dancer Frankie Manning, who didn't appear in the film himself, relates the routine's creation in his characteristically modest way:

> Some people think that I choreographed *A Day at the Races*, but I don't say that. Before the Ethel Waters group left New York, each couple did their own solo, and I coached them and gave them suggestions about where to put steps. This is where their individuality came out.
>
> Then I gave them the ensemble section, which included the horses that are done at the end of the scene. ...
>
> The routine was shortened in the movie, so I can't say they did exactly what I choreographed, but it's fair to say that I was partly responsible.[401]

This description is consistent with other accounts (by Manning as well as other dancers) about the group's typical approach and work process. As Whitey's top dancer and innovator, Manning was often the one to choreograph routines for the various performance groups, although – as he and others have pointed out – choreography was not a term they used at the time. In these routines, however, Manning didn't simply impose his ideas on his fellow dancers. Instead, the numbers would showcase each dancer's or couple's individual creations and trademark moves in the solos, and the ensemble sections also incorporated the ideas and inventions of various dancers. In other words, the final product was always a result of both collaboration and individual innovation. What we see

---

400 Willis, "Blackface Minstrelsy", 55.

401 Manning, 130–131. Three couples from Whitey's Lindy Hoppers were touring with Ethel Waters's stage show, and it was while performing in Los Angeles that they were hired for *A Day at the Races*. The "horses" refers to the acrobatic exit at the end of the scene, where one dancer carries two others.

onscreen in *A Day at the Races*, and in all films with Whitey's dancers, thus mirrors the actual production process in a way that is rather unusual for studio-era film musicals.

A Day at the Races juxtaposes its Black musical act with a White foil in the form of an elaborate balletic production number set in a luxurious health resort, the narrative's main location. The featured ballerina, Vivien Fay, appears under her own name, and while she has no role outside of this number, she and her dance company are announced as the evening's main attraction in a diegetic playbill. Unlike the Lindy dancers, Fay is also mentioned in the film's opening credits.[402] The ballet presents the greatest possible contrast to the African American number. As Richard Dyer has argued in his seminal book *White*, the romantic ballerina of the nineteenth century perfectly embodies the ideal of the angelic White woman, presenting a "translucent, incorporeal image".[403] The aesthetic of the ballet in *A Day at the Races* clearly stems from this tradition: dancing in light, transparent, and mostly white costumes, the female dancers seem to move weightlessly through the glamorously illuminated, sterile, white fantasy space, a gigantic stage in the middle of an artificial pond (fig. 35). In their pointe shoes, the ballerinas are an ethereal presence that could not be further removed from that of the Black dancers, whose performance in unglamorous everyday clothes is presented as a down-to-earth, physically challenging spectacle. As Crease observes, "By the end they are sweating, with perspiration under their arms testifying to how physically taxing that ninety seconds of performance had been".[404] The ballet, by contrast, clearly aims to conceal the physical strain that went into its production. While the ballerinas seem to – literally – aspire to greater heights, the Lindy hoppers never lose touch with the ground, even when they fly through the air performing acrobatic feats. And in contrast to the harmoniously synchronized ballet movements, the Lindy hop also allows for individualized expression within the group. Even in the ensemble parts at the beginning and end of the routine, when all the Lindy hoppers execute the same steps, their timing is not as precisely synchronized, their appearance as a group never as homogenous as that of the ballet ensemble. But rather than being a deficiency, maintaining individuality within collective expression is desirable here – it is exactly what African American vernacular dance is *about*.

---

402 While the dancers remain uncredited, both opening and end credits do mention "Ivie Anderson and the Crinoline Choir"; Anderson was quite famous as a vocalist with Duke Ellington's band during the 1930s.

403 Dyer also mentions the ambiguity of this image, pointing out that the "ballerina was also always a flesh and blood woman showing her legs" (*White*, 130–131).

404 Crease, "Divine Frivolity", 216.

Chapter 5 Harlem to Hollywood

Figure 35. The elaborately staged White ballet in *A Day at the Races* (1937) provides the maximum possible contrast to the Black dance number.

It is also noteworthy that the White ballet narratively takes the place typically accorded Black musical numbers. It is entirely excessive in terms of narrative and could easily be cut without affecting the plot. The Black number, by contrast, is more integral to the film as a whole, since the performers have at least a symbolic narrative function as the protagonists' allies and aides. While the ballet's seamless, synchronized precision appears out of place in this anarchistic slapstick comedy, the Black scene has a transgressive function within the plot: after all, the number occurs while the protagonists are hiding from the law. When the sheriff and his buddies appear at the end of the scene, general turmoil ensues as soon as the crowd becomes aware of being discovered and exits in a hurry. Crease suggests that "in their sudden terrified exit the crowd acknowledges guilt that, instead of dancing, they should have been at work. The scene thus shares the same spirit as that of the Marx Brothers themselves".[405] I would argue that the significance of the scene's ending goes further. Before everyone's "terrified exit", a Black man is seen exclaiming "the sheriff!" in a close-up that shows his alarmed facial expression, with eyes wide open. This is both another stereotypical minstrelizing shot and a telltale moment with regard to power relations, going well beyond the issue of

405 Crease, 216.

171

not having been at work. As far as the narrative discloses, only the White characters have violated any laws, yet the African Americans behave as if their mere presence in the company of Whites – perhaps even their very existence – were unlawful. That the entire Black crowd's impulse is to run and hide from "White law" speaks volumes about power and control as well as betraying the film's anxiety about racial integration.

As was common for Hollywood films of the time, *A Day at the Races* is ambiguous in its celebration of Black culture. Ivie Anderson's song declares rhythm and swing to be universal properties that unite "all God's children" while also suggesting that these are the things that Whites could and should learn from Blacks. Yet much in this depiction of Black musicality remains cliché, especially the idea that Blacks are happy despite social and economic discrimination. The message that collective singing and dancing is the best remedy for misery certainly points to the important role these forms of expression have played throughout African American history. But the scene also implies that music and dance are *all* that Black people need, and by showing their life as one big party, it justifies their inferior social and economic status.[406]

The inequality between Blacks and Whites is also underlined by the respective allocation and use of narrative spaces. As Richard Dyer has argued, the "movement of expansion and incorporation" that is so typical of the musical's song and dance numbers is generally the privilege of White performers, while Blacks remain within clearly confined spaces.[407] Whites are allowed to conquer and control any space, whether private or public, but "Black people doing the same thing would in the white imagination seem like a terrifying attempt to take over".[408] The sequence in *A Day at the Races* might seem like such an attempt, with its growing crowd of African Americans expanding into and taking over the streets. But the film defuses the potential threat of the situation in at least three ways: One, the entire sequence is initiated and spearheaded by Harpo Marx, who thus functions as a stand-in for the film's director. Two, the neighborhood is clearly marked as a (timeless and idyllic) ghetto space that is geographically and narratively separate from the film's main settings. Three, the interaction and exchange between Blacks and Whites remains lopsided – Black rhythm and swing have a positive effect on the White characters, who visit the Black ghetto at the low point of their financial crisis to draw new hope from the vitality of those who are even worse off in

---

406 This is similar to the Harlem scene with Bill Robinson, Jeni LeGon, and Fats Waller in *Hooray for Love* from 1935 (see chapter 3 in this book), which reassures its (White) audience that the performers are "living in a great big way" despite living in poverty.

407 Dyer, *Only Entertainment*, 41.

408 Dyer, 41.

material respects. By contrast, the Black characters receive no reward for their musical gift. When the protagonists head towards the happy ending, leaving behind the Black neighborhood, its inhabitants simply return to their unchanged daily routine. It is the common contradiction in Hollywood representations of Black people: they are shown moving and expressing themselves physically, yet this vitality is associated with social stasis and immobility. By confining the Black characters to an unspecific, timeless idyll, the film denies them the possibility of progress and development.[409]

But confinement is never complete, and it is the Lindy hoppers who most powerfully challenge the spatial and narrative constraints imposed on African Americans. Crease attributes "a margin of independence and integrity" to the scene, arguing that "with the entry of the Lindy Hoppers and the departure of Harpo, it is finally black performers calling their own tune".[410] The margin may be small, but it is significant. While the dancers had no control over the musical tune used on the soundtrack (which was added later), they largely called their own tune of dance steps, as described by Frankie Manning above. While Black narrative agency is limited to serving the White protagonists, the dance scene in particular allows for a degree of creative physical agency.

Ironically, though not surprisingly, this kind of behind-the-scenes authorship was often erased, made invisible in Hollywood. White dance director Dave Gould was nominated for an Academy Award in the short-lived Dance Direction category for his staging of the Black number in *A Day at the Races*.[411] There is, however, a brief moment of implicit acknowledgment of the Black contribution to White success when the Black performers somewhat unexpectedly reappear during the film's final moments and everybody reprises Ivie Anderson's song (which also plays over the opening credits).

The mainstream press paid little attention to the African American sequence in *A Day at the Races*, and even less to the Lindy hop routine. The screen performances of Whitey's Lindy Hoppers generally garnered very few mentions from film critics. What sparse reactions there are suggest that, in the eyes of journalists, there was nothing new or very surprising about the Lindy's presence in films.

409 See also Friedman, *African American Films*, 19, 195.

410 Crease, "Divine Frivolity", 216.

411 The Dance Direction category only existed from 1935 to 1937. The "Swing Is Here to Sway" number with Jeni LeGon from *Ali Baba Goes to Town* (1937), staged by Sammy Lee, was nominated the same year. However, the award went to Hermes Pan for the "Fun House" number in *A Damsel in Distress* (1937), which featured Fred Astaire, Gracie Allen, and George Burns. See Academy Awards Database, Academy of Motion Picture Arts and Sciences, http://awardsdatabase.oscars.org. Dave Gould was also the dance director for the Lindy hop scene in *Everybody Sing*, which Whitey's Lindy Hoppers filmed the following year, and which would be cut from the film.

Variety's review of *A Day at the Races* is one of the few press reports devoting more than a few words to a film scene featuring Whitey's dancers:

> One other musical highlight is a Harlemania sequence with Harpo leading the dusky cavalcade in a goofy Pied Piper number, 'All God's Children Got Rhythm', easily the best tune in the score. While the Negroes are more or less dragged in by their bojangles, the ensuing business more than extenuates the irregular pacing. Camera angles and Sam Wood's direction here run the gamut of all the colored lexicon from 'Porgy' to 'Blackbirds', with plenty of that 'St. Louis Blues' motif for backgrounding, capped by a fast and furious Lindyhopping finale, probably the first of that school of hoofing to hit the screens. Ivie Anderson (who used to sing with Duke Ellington's band) and the Crinoline Choir are standouts in the Harlem stuff.[412]

Like many press reports from the period, the review confirms how much Black entertainment had become a common production feature of Hollywood films, with the author apparently assuming a familiarity with all things "colored" on the part of the reader. The elements of the "colored lexicon" listed here are obviously meant to evoke every possible Black stereotype of stage and screen, rather than describing anything that's specific to this film. In fact, it is entirely unclear what elements of "Porgy", "Blackbirds", or "St. Louis Blues" are supposed to be found in the scene. The term "Harlemania" is indicative of how Black musical performance had become associated with the modern, urban environment of Harlem – despite this scene's more rural setting. At the same time, it indicates that the performance transcends the confines of its idyllic setting and is instead perceived as the product of Harlem's professional entertainment industry. The review also underlines that Hollywood representations of the Lindy hop were the result rather than the cause of the dance's growing popularity. For all we know, the author is right that this is the first instance of the Lindy to hit the screens, at least with regard to mainstream *feature* films, yet the phrasing implies that the public is already familiar with the dance and that no further explanation is needed.

Perhaps more surprisingly, the film appearances of Whitey's Lindy Hoppers were also often ignored in the African American press. In the case of *A Day at the Races*, Black press coverage highlighted the participation of popular vocalist Ivie Anderson, rather than the dancers. Throughout the 1930s and early 1940s, the *Chicago Defender* and the *Pittsburgh Courier* would mention Whitey's dancers here and there with a kind of casualness implying that readers were expected to already know the group, but their film appearances were not treated prominently in the Black press.

In part, the sparse press response simply mirrors the group's scant presence onscreen. Whitey's Lindy Hoppers continued to dominate the world of live Lindy

---

412 Review of *A Day at the Races*, *Variety*, June 23, 1937, 12, Media History Digital Library.

hop, performing in nightclubs and theaters with prominent Black bands, and members of the group kept winning the hugely popular Harvest Moon Ball in New York, which had become institutionalized as an annual event.[413] But their remaining Hollywood appearances of the 1930s failed to give them much prominence, and the Lindy hop generally remained relatively rare on movie screens – as did other swing dance styles.

Sidelined: The Forgotten Films

After *A Day at the Races*, a different set of dancers from Whitey's group appeared in *Manhattan Merry-Go-Round*, a little-known revue musical, where the Lindy hoppers are briefly seen as part of a specialty number set in Cab Calloway's Cottonpicker's Club. One of Whitey's groups, which included Frankie Manning, performed with Calloway at the Cotton Club for six months in 1936/37 before they took the show on the road.[414] Judging from Manning's account, the short number in *Manhattan Merry-Go-Round* is loosely based on the much longer performances in these live shows.[415] Like its real-life model, the club in the film has a White audience enjoying a floor show of African American acts. Calloway sings "Mama, I Wanna Make Rhythm" with his band, and we see him bounce and twist his legs in his characteristic way. When he finishes singing, the tempo speeds up for the following dance number. Less than a minute long, it is the shortest scene with Whitey's Lindy Hoppers, who are actually only seen during a fraction of that minute and accordingly don't receive any screen credit.

Calloway's status, on the one hand, and the scene's aesthetics, on the other, detract from the performance of the dancers. Calloway was one of the best-known Black entertainers at the time, widely successful with mainstream (White) audiences, and the Black scene here is constructed entirely around his renown. A double-page advertisement for the film in the trade magazine *Motion Picture Daily* names and depicts fifteen performers standing side by side, with Calloway in the middle.[416] This kind of inclusion of a Black performer as both central and equal to Whites is quite unusual for the time, speaking to Calloway's exceptional market value and star power. His status is additionally boosted by the film's variety format, which mitigates the usual discrimination against Black performers in feature films. Instead of a clear hierarchical division between White stars and Black specialty performers, there is more of a side-by-side of White *and* Black specialty

---

413 See Dinerstein, *Swinging the Machine*, 302–304; Manning, 160–164; and Miller, 133–147.
414 The Cotton Club moved from its original Harlem location to Midtown Manhattan in 1935.
415 See Manning, 125–132.
416 Advertisement for *Manhattan Merry-Go-Round*, *Motion Picture Daily*, November 18, 1937, 10–11, Media History Digital Library.

performers, who are equally disconnected from the narrative, and Calloway is billed prominently in the opening credits. With singing cowboy star Gene Autry, several "name bands", vocalists, and a cameo by baseball player Joe DiMaggio, it is obvious that more effort went into assembling the film's lineup of performers than into writing a coherent script.[417] In the words of *Variety*'s reviewer, the film is "a piece-together of various specialties dangled on a perilously fragile story idea".[418] Frank S. Nugent of the *New York Times* had little patience for what he called "another of those courteously called musical pictures in which a thread of banal plot is compelled to suspend practically everything but the kitchen sink".[419]

The status of the Lindy hoppers as mere support for Calloway is underlined by the cinematography and editing. The Black nightclub scene is heavily edited, and the cutting rate is even higher during the Lindy hoppers' dance routine, with variously shaped wipes between shots creating a time-lapse effect. While the seamless soundtrack holds the images together, the editing suggests that we only see an excerpt from the full number. Clearly, the purpose of this short, high-speed montage sequence is not to showcase the dancing per se but to capture the tempo and excitement of Harlem nightlife. The effect is enhanced by the use of tilted camera angles, a common device in representations of New York nightlife in general and Harlem jazz culture in particular. With expressionist visuals reminiscent of Black-cast films from the earliest years of sound cinema, the number is meant to capture the speed and excitement of city life as well as the supposedly excessive physicality of Black performance.[420] The Lindy hoppers are mostly seen in full shot, with a few acrobatic elements filmed in waist shot. These closer views of body parts accent the dancers' strong physical presence, but they also prevent the display of the full extent of their skill. The dance is additionally fragmented by inserted close-ups of musicians and a waist shot of Calloway "conducting" the band by frantically wiggling his head and waving his arms. Calloway's commercialized public image emphasized his showmanship over his musical proficiency as the leader of a first-rate big band. The dance scene here serves to underline his exuberant performance style, which almost always included some dance moves. At the end, Calloway joins the dancers with a chorus girl who is clearly not a proficient Lindy hopper, whereas the real Lindy dancers serve as atmospheric entourage for Calloway rather than a featured specialty in their own right.

---

417 *Manhattan Merry-Go-Round* was produced by Republic Pictures, a company specializing in low-budget Westerns and serials; the film was among the studio's more ambitious projects.

418 Review of *Manhattan Merry-Go-Round*, *Variety*, November 10, 1937, 10, Media History Digital Library.

419 Frank S. Nugent, "At the Criterion", review of *Manhattan Merry-Go-Round*, The Screen in Review, *New York Times*, December 31, 1937, TimesMachine.

420 See also chapters 1 and 2 in this book; and Friedman, *African American Films*, 42–56, 85, 110.

Next, Whitey's Lindy Hoppers filmed a dance number for *Everybody Sing*, which starred a young Judy Garland. The dance scene, however, was cut from the film, allegedly due to a dispute between the dance group's manager, Herbert White, and the film's director, Edwin L. Marin.[421] The scene, which seems to have followed the standard narrative formula for Black specialty numbers, appears to be lost. But from Manning's descriptions we know that it included the Lindy hop as well as a version of a big apple group routine similar to that in *Keep Punching*, the race movie in which the dancers appeared the following year.[422]

The group's next film was *Radio City Revels*, in which the Lindy hoppers appear as one of a series of attractions in an extended, racially mixed specialty sequence that includes a White female contortionist dancer (Melissa Mason) as well as a White male tap dancer (Buster West), whose floor moves anticipate the break dancing of the 1980s. Here, the Black performers are not alone in appearing without any plausible narrative motivation, since the entire sequence is itself a narratively implausible excursion to the countryside. The singing and dancing occur as part of a massive outdoor barbecue party, with the setting naturalizing the African Americans as a seemingly organic part of rural life. Like in *A Day at the Races*, the dancing is staged as a spontaneous outgrowth of this community event, with the first Lindy couple dancing in the background, while people are busy singing, eating, and frying corn in the foreground, before a cut puts the dancers center stage. The arrangement is similar to the scene from *A Day at the Races* in that the dancers appear to emerge from the crowd into the circle, where they take turns soloing while the others cheer them on. But unlike in the earlier film, the nondancing audience here consists mainly of Whites. The other difference is the sloppy editing and coordination with the music. While the nightclub scene in *Manhattan Merry-Go-Round* was too heavily edited to really showcase the dancers' skill but managed to convey a sense of the performance's physical power, the dance number in *Radio City Revels* is both too short and too carelessly staged and edited to do much of either. Barely over a minute long, it contains a few highlights in each couple's solos, with some of the same trademark moves as in *A Day at the Races*, and heavyweight dancer John "Tiny" Bunch (in chef's costume) can be seen throwing his diminutive partner Dorothy "Dot" Johnson around. But the poor choice and editing of the music detract from the scene's effect, and the final ensemble sequence, with a few Charleston moves and an

---

421 See Manning, 149–150; and Miller, 158.

422 See Manning, 142–149. The dancers were the same four couples as in *Manhattan Merry-Go-Round*: Frankie Manning and Lucille Middleton, George Greenidge and Eleanor "Stumpy" Watson, Eddie Davis and Mildred Pollard, and John "Tiny" Bunch and Dorothy "Dot" Johnson.

over-the-back air step, fails to turn into a climactic moment.[423] The press took hardly any notice of the Lindy scene (the only Black number in the film), though *Variety* briefly mentioned the dancers favorably: "a highlight is developed through the shagging routines of four colored couples in character. They stand out strongly".[424]

Whitey's Lindy Hoppers would not return to Hollywood until 1941. Meanwhile, they performed in stage musicals, including *The Hot Mikado* (1939) and *Swingin' the Dream* (1939), as well as at the 1939/40 New York World's Fair.[425] In 1939, they also appeared in their only race film, *Keep Punching*, a boxing movie set in Harlem. This film employs the dancers in much the same way as a Hollywood production – that is, as an "only entertainment" specialty act with no narrative function. They appear twice in the context of nightclub scenes. Their first performance is announced as "the big apple contest", although it is clearly not a contest but a choreography. The routine was one of many big apple versions that Frankie Manning would choreograph over the years. The first was for the excised scene in *Everybody Sing*, which Whitey had asked Manning to create as a response to the fad for the dance, which is only loosely defined as a variety of vernacular (solo) jazz moves danced in a circle that moves counterclockwise. In *Keep Punching*, all ten dancers do the same steps in a group routine that includes circle and line formations but no partner dancing.[426] In a later scene set in the same location, the instrumental track from the big apple routine is simply reused for the "jitterbug contest", in which six couples from Whitey's Lindy Hoppers mix in with a larger crowd of less proficient dancers. This scene has a more atmospheric function, with several cutaway shots to characters in the audience. The seemingly spontaneous yet highly skilled dancing by alternating couples may be a good approximation of what the professional Lindy dancers would do at the Savoy in Harlem. As dancer Norma Miller recalled, "when the tourists came to the ballroom, they saw what they thought was a spontaneous exhibition by a regular group of dancers, simply in a ballroom to enjoy social dancing. But that wasn't the case, what they were watching was a rehearsed and choreographed

---

423 Crease describes the music as a hybrid of square dance and swing (see "Divine Frivolity", 217–218), whereas Manning said that "the music, 'Swingin' in the Corn', didn't swing, but it *was corny*" (Manning, 153, italics in the original).

424 Review of *Radio City Revels, Variety*, February 2, 1938, 15, Media History Digital Library.

425 See Manning, 140, 160–164; and Miller, 133–148. For a detailed discussion of swing at the World's Fair, see also Dinerstein, *Swinging the Machine*, 283–311.

426 The history of the big apple remains somewhat obscure. Supposedly, a group of White college kids from South Carolina discovered the dance in a Black club called the Big Apple, adapted it, and eventually brought it to New York, where it became a big fad in 1937/38. See Manning, 142–152; and the documentary *Dancing the Big Apple 1937: African Americans Inspire a National Craze*, directed by Judy Pritchett, 2010.

dance".⁴²⁷ *Keep Punching* is thus another example of how the vernacular origins of the Lindy hop would sporadically translate to film screens.

Hellzapoppin'

The 1941 film *Hellzapoppin'* would be the last feature film appearance of Whitey's Lindy Hoppers, and it is generally considered the apex of the Lindy hop's history both on- and offscreen. The movie shares the irreverent, anarchistic spirit of *A Day at the Races*, providing a similarly appropriate context for a spectacular display of fast and acrobatic Lindy hop. Some of Whitey's dancers had appeared in the 1938 Broadway revue of the same title, which was written by and starred the comedy team Olsen and Johnson (John "Ole" Olsen and Harold "Chic" Johnson), who also headed the cast of the film version. Though only loosely based on the stage show, the film retained the same zany "anything can happen" spirit, adding cinematic special effects that were not possible onstage. *Hellzapoppin'* stands out from the era's standard film fare through its extraordinary use of self-reflexivity, repeatedly breaking the fourth wall. It tells the story of the making of a movie, which in turn tells the story of the production of a stage show. The film is replete with self-reflexive jokes about filmmaking, with the opening credits pointing out that "any similarity between *Hellzapoppin'* and a motion picture is purely coincidental". In the frame story, the creative heads of a film studio poke fun at Hollywood conventions with remarks like "we've got to have a love story, every picture has one" or "not another picture with a show in it, please!" The subsequent film-within-the-film is set at a fancy Long Island estate; it does indeed have a show in it as well as the obligatory love story, with rich girl Kitty (Jane Frazee) and poor producer Jeff (Robert Paige) bridging the class gap. But this embedded narrative departs from the conventions of the backstage musical in that it keeps being interrupted and influenced by events occurring in the frame story – for instance, when the film slips out of position during projection, cutting the characters in half, much to their distress; or when characters ask the projectionist to rewind the film, so that they can get another shot at manipulating the course of events in their favor. Much of the film's comedy results from such self-reflexive gags and their "impossible" mixing of diegetic levels. In addition, *Hellzapoppin'* contains heavy doses of slapstick, wordplay, and elements of screwball comedy.

The musical numbers are generally kept in a comic vein too: in "Watch the Birdie", for instance, performers fall into a swimming pool, and the romantic ballad "Heaven for Two" is interrupted by comic text slides projected over images

427 Miller, 63.

Jumping the Color Line: Vernacular Jazz Dance in American Film, 1929–1945

Chapter 5 Harlem to Hollywood

Figures 36–38. With *Hellzapoppin'* (1941), the Lindy hop reaches its apex as a performance dance, filmed simply but effectively. Whitey's Lindy Hoppers combine spectacular acrobatics, group interaction, and ensemble dancing at breakneck speed.

of Jeff and Kitty swooning. By contrast, the only Black musical number is in some ways remarkably – if not surprisingly – conventional in the context of this highly unconventional film. As is often the case, the Black performers suddenly appear out of nowhere, only to disappear again after their number. Framed as a spontaneous jam session occurring behind the scenes of the show on which the film-within-the-film centers, the number follows the generic conventions of the backstage musical. Two Black porters (musicians Slim Gaillard and Slam Stewart) deliver the musical instruments for the planned stage show. Unaware of any observers, they cannot resist the temptation to try the instruments out. In an apparently incidental fashion, additional Black servants/musicians join them, until a six-piece band is in full swing. Meanwhile, various Black servants in other rooms of the mansion are shown – through parallel editing – to be distracted from their work by the music. The show's producer Jeff and his prop men (Olsen and Johnson) also happen to pass by and take notice of the music. While the audience of the film sees how these three White characters pull aside a curtain and watch the jam session, the musicians are unaware of their audience in the film.

181

When the relaxed but swinging tune is wrapped up, the tempo suddenly speeds up, and after a drum solo, a quick panning shot leads away from the band – which immediately evolves into a full-blown orchestra on the soundtrack – to the first of four dance couples. The following two minutes belong entirely to Whitey's Lindy Hoppers, now at the high point of their career.[428] Dressed in a range of stock servant costumes, the eight dancers perform one of film history's fastest and most challenging dance numbers, which no description could do justice to. Each couple gets a chorus-length solo demonstrating remarkable athletic prowess in spectacular acrobatics, as well as rhythmic precision (fig. 36). The swing-out, generally considered the Lindy's trademark move, is featured more prominently than in the group's earlier film scenes, danced by each couple at the start of their solo. The dancers' low, crouching posture enables the momentum required for doing the swing-out at the breakneck speed of over three hundred beats per minute. Some of the men, in particular, assume an almost horizontal position at moments when they're furthest apart from their partners and getting ready to pull them back in for the next move. A Charleston variation performed by Al Minns and Willamae Ricker facing each other and holding hands also emphasizes low-down body posture and horizontal full-leg kicks. All but one of the couples' spotlights include moments where partners separate from each other completely, letting go of each other's hands. William Downes and Frances Jones incorporate a brief eight-bar solo routine, illustrating how a focus on rhythmic precision is by no means dependent on wearing tap shoes. The transitions between the solos are smooth and interactive (fig. 37), with couples egging each other on and reacting to each other before they all come together for the ensemble ending (fig. 38).

Couple spotlights as well as the concluding ensemble section also feature a wide variety of acrobatic air steps, among them several where the man is lifted by or jumps over his respective female partner. Landing from their leaps, the dancers rebound and hit the next dance move with impeccable timing. Yet for all the speed, strength, and agility, the performers never sacrifice the quality of what is primarily highly original and expressive vernacular dancing. At no point do they privilege the physical spectacle of acrobatics over rhythmic expression. In fact, the fast-moving feet, especially the women's, are among the most fascinating things to watch during the final team routine: with couples lined up across the room, they wait in line, so to speak, getting ready for their turn in a series of staggered air steps, relentlessly stepping in place without ever missing a beat. The routine ends with the four couples collapsing on the floor, in sync. When the

---

428 The four couples, in order of appearance, are William Downes and Frances "Mickey" Jones, Billy Ricker and Norma Miller, Al Minns and Willamae Ricker, and Frankie Manning and Ann Johnson.

subsequent applause makes them aware of their audience, they are back on their feet within seconds and hurry away.

Frankie Manning choreographed the dance routine, as usual incorporating moves from various sources, though it was staged in collaboration with renowned White dance director Nick Castle. Castle was known from his work with the Nicholas Brothers, among others, and was highly respected among Black dancers. According to Manning's memory of the filming, however, Castle's contribution was minimal, although he was, of course, credited for staging the scene.[429] As Crease points out, "the dance is filmed as a seamless whole, one continuous discharge of energy".[430] The solos of the four couples are filmed in full shots and almost uninterrupted by editing. There are only nine cuts in total, four of them during the ensemble section, which takes up the final twenty seconds. Camera angles are for the most part realistically motivated. A small level of stylization or abstraction occurs towards the end, when the four dancing couples form a diagonal line within the frame. This hints at the presence of the camera, but overall, the camera is at the service of the choreography. The accent is on the dancers' physical performance, not on the technical performance of the camera or filmmakers. Like almost all film scenes with Whitey's dancers, the number thus belongs to the category of "moving-picture dance reconstructions" in film scholar Noël Carroll's terminology[431] – that is, combinations of dance and film that make use of the medium of film to highlight the characteristics of a dance (rather than producing a new dance work mainly through cinematic means). The unobtrusive film style amplifies the effect of authenticity, lending credibility to the dancers' impressive physical display.

It is with reference to this scene that author Robert P. Crease qualifies his own prefatory statement that the Lindy hop doesn't lend itself to cinematic representation:

> With its careful filmwork, the sequence owes as much to Hollywood as it does to the Savoy Ballroom floor. It would be difficult to represent the entire sequence, solo and support couples, in front of a live audience to the right effect. … On film, the camera can catch the solo couple from different angles, while still picking up interaction with support couples. … The sequence manages to preserve the feeling of simultaneous improvisation and collaboration.[432]

429 See Manning, 176–177.
430 Crease, "Divine Frivolity", 220. See Manning, 171–179, on choreographing and filming the routine.
431 Carroll, *Engaging the Moving Image*, 245. The one exception is the short scene in *Manhattan Merry-Go-Round*, which is closer to the category of "moving-picture dance constructions" (245) – that is, scenes where cinematic devices contribute as much to giving the impression of a dance as the performance in front to the camera.
432 Crease, "Divine Frivolity", 221.

The scene also preserves a few moments of actual improvisation among the dancers who support the soloing couples, as Manning recalled: "By the way, the movements we did in the background were not choreographed and they were not repeated exactly for each take".[433] There is, in fact, a moment where Manning bumps into Willamae Ricker as he tries to get out of the way for her spotlight with Al Minns. In sum, with *Hellzapoppin'*, the Lindy hop comes of age as a professional cinematic dance – but one rooted in live performance, social dancing, and improvisation.

While the scene marks a level of aesthetic emancipation in terms of staging the dance, the narrative framing, by contrast, is far from emancipatory. In the context of a film that isn't too scrupulous about narrative logic, the instrument delivery and the servant roles provide ample justification for the presence and performance of the African Americans, who have no part in the film before or after. That their outbreak of improvisational energy occurs during an unauthorized break from work, which they believe goes unnoticed, lends the number a subversive note, much like in *A Day at the Races*. It is not much of a stretch to see this as echoing the function of recreational music and dancing in the era of slavery. The dancers' hurried exit when they realize that they've been discovered illustrates the hierarchy between Blacks and Whites in general and the power structures within show business in particular. Producer Jeff admiringly exclaims, "wow, too bad they're not in the show", to which one of his prop men replies with the suggestion to "put them in the next one". The brief dialogue clearly identifies the White producer as the decision maker and the person to profit from the show. It is not hard to imagine Hollywood executives of the era looking at Black musical performers and deciding to "put them in the next show" – that is, the next movie.

As Jane Feuer has argued, the classical backstage musical's "use of theatrical audiences *in* the film provides a point of identification for audiences *of* the film", often by aligning their respective points of view through camera perspectives.[434] In addition, musicals regularly use "natural, spontaneous audiences which form around offstage performances", and which offer "a vicarious sense of participation for the film audience", suggesting its involvement in the production of entertainment.[435] The Lindy dancers' three diegetic spectators in *Hellzapoppin'* are such a natural and spontaneous audience. But since they watch the performance secretly, they are also representatives of the voyeuristic gaze, which has been associated with a more general idea of classical Hollywood film spectatorship.[436] Rather than

---

433 Manning, 177.
434 Feuer, "The Self-Reflective Musical", 170 (italics in the original).
435 Feuer, 170.
436 See, for instance, Baudry, "Ideological Effects".

becoming involved in the performance, their initially unnoticed spectatorship suggests surveillance and control here.

Hellzapoppin' repeatedly exposes the classical cinematic illusion as an artificial convention, pointing to the film's materiality and constructedness. But in the Black specialty number, there are no self-reflexive jokes making fun of formulaic filmmaking. Instead, we are given a supposedly transparent view of the dance scene, which makes us forget that the whole world of the film is artifice. While cinematic conventions are parodied and turned upside down in *Hellzapoppin'*, the conventional cinematic representation of the hierarchy between Whites and Blacks is simply reproduced. In its implied naturalness, the Lindy scene is thus a moment of classic "invisible ideology": it confirms social hierarchies by mirroring the film industry's racial segregation without questioning it. The subversive act of playing music and dancing during work hours is endorsed at the plot level (by the diegetic audience) insofar as it represents a potentially profitable spectacle, and this subversiveness is consistent with the film's overall riotous spirit. But it is also in tension with the tacit affirmation of existing power relations. The stage show at the end of *Hellzapoppin'*'s film-within-the-film only features White performers. It naturally turns out to be a big success – from which the African Americans remain excluded.

Ultimately, the Lindy hop is also overshadowed by the film's very unconventionality. Whitey's Lindy Hoppers received screen credit for the first time here (as the Harlem Congeroo Dancers), which points to the group's popularity, and Norma Miller recalled being given "the star treatment" on the set.[437] Yet the press once again hardly took any notice of the dancers. In light of the movie's excesses of parodic self-reflexivity, critics mostly overlooked the comparatively conventional occurrence of an African American music and dance number, despite the fact that this was an exceptionally spectacular dance performance. The *New York Times* mercilessly described the film as "an anarchic collection of unfunny gags" and "a jerky sequence of third-rate gags punctuated by gunfire"[438] without mentioning the dance number, whereas *Variety*'s more favorable review merely noted that the "plentitude of slapstick hokum … even drags in a colored lindy-hopping troupe".[439]

Overall, the appearances of Whitey's Lindy Hoppers in Hollywood feature films are typical of their times as far as their framing and function is concerned: they

---

437 Miller, 160.

438 T. S., "At the Rivoli", review of *Hellzapoppin'*, The Screen in Review, *New York Times*, December 26, 1941, TimesMachine.

439 Review of *Hellzapoppin'*, *Variety*, December 24, 1941, 8, Media History Digital Library.

are moments of Black musical spectacle, largely disconnected from the otherwise White-cast narratives but performed for White audiences both of and within the films. Framed as servants and/or entertainers, the Black dancers are presented as objects of the White gaze, which keeps them under control and denies them narrative agency. But control does not extend to their creative agency, and their dancing denotes improvisational creativity, spontaneity, high energy, and exceptional physical dexterity. Notably, what is lacking from this emphasis on the physical is any connotation of the erotic or sexual. Even when the female dancers' underwear becomes briefly visible in *Hellzapoppin'*, it is clear that they wear short dresses for reasons of agility rather than for seductive purposes. In all film scenes with Whitey's dancers, the women are the men's equals, displaying the same high skill level in terms of rhythmic footwork, athleticism, and expressivity. In principle, the men still take the traditional leader role of partner dancing, but that hardly matters here. Throughout, the women unmistakably stand their own ground, literally and figuratively, very much doing their own dancing, and their partners depend on them as much as vice versa. This is even true in some of the air steps, with the women sometimes lifting their male partners, and in a moment of physical comedy in *Hellzapoppin'*, Ann Johnson even kicks Frankie Manning in the butt, which sends him flying across the floor and landing facedown.

Through the dancers' highly expressive but asexual physicality, the presence of African Americans in the White world is mostly unthreatening, posing no danger to White unity and purity. This relative harmlessness in combination with the narrative and spatial confinement of Black performances allows the White protagonists – and by extension the film industry – to be inspired by and profit from Black talent without getting too involved with Black people. As Richard Dyer has argued, "through the figure of the non-white person, whites can feel what being, physicality, presence, might be like, while also dissociating themselves from the non-whiteness of such things".[440] There could hardly be a better illustration of these racial dynamics than the performances of Whitey's Lindy Hoppers in their Hollywood films.

Jitterbug Dancing in Mock-Educational Short Films

After *Hellzapoppin'*, the dancers' contract at Universal called for another film. But as the project didn't materialize and war was looming, White managed to get out of the contract, and the dancers went on tour again.[441] *Hellzapoppin'* would be their last feature film appearance, but in the early 1940s, subgroups of Whitey's

---

440 Dyer, *White*, 80.

441 See Crease, "Divine Frivolity", 221; and Manning, 180–181.

Lindy Hoppers performed in several Soundies. Three of these feature all-Black onscreen casts – namely, *Hot Chocolate* (a.k.a. *Cottontail*) with Duke Ellington (1941), *Air Mail Special* with Count Basie (1941), and *Sugar Hill Masquerade* (1942), where White drummer Gene Krupa's band provides the soundtrack but doesn't appear onscreen. By contrast, *The Outline of Jitterbug History* (1942) has a racially mixed cast. *Air Mail Special* shows the dancers as contestants in a social dance competition, testifying to their improvisational skills.[442] In the other Soundies, the dancing adheres to the group's now-familiar pattern of combining couple spotlights with an ensemble section.[443] Unlike the Hollywood films, the Soundies with Whitey's Lindy Hoppers lack the flimsy excuses for their appearance as servants/helpers to White people, leaving their dancing unencumbered by such narrative framing. However, the most remarkable of the group's Soundies is in fact the one with the most elaborate narrative: *The Outline of Jitterbug History* is not only noteworthy for its racially mixed cast but also for the way it transgresses and inverts Hollywood's usual narrative formulas around Black performance. In addition to testifying to swing culture's crossover appeal and mainstream success, the comic Soundie elevates the status of Black culture by framing Black dance as a crowning achievement and a positive modernizing force in American culture.

By the late 1930s, swing culture was a mass phenomenon, with a veritable industry promoting big band swing as the primary dance music for the nation's youth. The Lindy hop, once a Black subcultural practice, had also gained mainstream popularity (even though the casual styles of swing dancing practiced by a relatively wide segment of the population were a long way from the acrobatic, breakneck-speed spectacles presented by Whitey's Lindy Hoppers). With the crossover success of swing dancing came an increasing social acceptability, and in the 1940s, dance schools began incorporating jitterbug styles into their curricula, however reluctantly.[444] Though swing dancing remained relatively marginal in the movies, the new trend for teaching it brought forth a small number of mostly comic, mock-educational short films, ranging from newsreel-style pseudodocumentaries to Soundies. An early example of this minitrend is the "instructional" short *How to Dance the Shag* (1937), featuring White dance entrepreneur Arthur Murray with a group of dancers. After a very upright and uptight Murray teaches the basic shag steps to a group of "beginners", he relies on several young couples to demonstrate what the bouncy dance with the fast footwork really looks like. Having completed their single lesson, the "students" miraculously go on to give

---

442 See also chapter 4 in this book.

443 According to Frankie Manning, the dancers reused parts of the *Hellzapoppin'* routine in the Soundie *Hot Chocolate* (see Manning, 180–181).

444 See Crease, "Divine Frivolity", 224; and Dinerstein, *Swinging the Machine*, 277–278.

a perfect choreographed shag performance at an elegant club the very same night. The somewhat cartoonish dance with its step-hop pattern featured here – often referred to as the collegiate shag – was a swing-era favorite and can also be seen in some of the surviving newsreel footage from the Harvest Moon Ball competition in New York.[445] In the Arthur Murray film, it is introduced as "the dance sensation which is sweeping the country". Produced by the Educational Films Corporation of America, the short clearly aims to promote the shag as a legitimate social dance that can be learned formally, but at the same time, the movie is also clearly tongue-in-cheek.

Similarly, the big apple fad of 1937/38 also received comic treatment in film – for example, in a short from the Paramount Headliner series titled *From the Minuet to the Big Apple* (1937). With remarkable honesty, the film half-mockingly admits that this latest dance craze is really nothing but a mash-up of various vernacular jazz dances, as the evening's host in the film announces: "Thanks to the birth of jazz, new dances caught the public fancy, among them the Charleston, the black bottom, and lately the truckin', the Lindy hop, the shag, and what not. Somebody scrambled them up, threw them together and what came out: you tell 'em kids, it's the big apple!" These short films function to promote the dances they showcase while also poking fun at them. Later examples of the mock-educational swing dance short film – which constitutes a sort of minigenre – continue to simultaneously ridicule and promote jitterbug dancing; increasingly emphasizing comic narratives and slapstick, they also explicitly make fun of traditional dance and dance teaching.

The Soundie *The Outline of Jitterbug History* claims to present a historical outline of jitterbug dancing. In a three-minute parody of a history lesson, an elderly White professor (Tom Herbert) at a blackboard introduces the various influences that have contributed to the dance's contemporary form. Each of the explanations on the blackboard – which function as intertitles in the dialogue-free Soundie – is followed by a short dance scene illustrating the supposed origins of the modern jitterbug. The first of these dance scenes is the rather violent "cave hop" of prehistoric times. A scantily clad couple of cave people are seen hitting each other before they go into a frantic dance with widely waving arms and pelvic thrusts. The second of the jitterbug's alleged predecessors is the "minuet jive", demonstrated by what appears to be an upper-class couple of the early 1800s, wearing white wigs, hoop skirt, and breeches. After curtseying formally, they suddenly go into a modern jitterbug in open position, with shimmies and wiggling hips and eventually a few swing-outs. The next step in the dance's evolution, the "square

---

445 For a brief overview of the collegiate shag's spotty history, see Loggins, "History of Collegiate Shag".

dance shiver", seems to be associated with the American West. Two couples – men in overalls and cowboy hats, women in "traditional" skirts and blouses with puffy sleeves – hop around in circles, an activity which we are to understand as traditional square dancing. When a drunken third woman introduces jazzy hip twists and shaking shoulders, the new fashion immediately catches on with the other dancers. And finally, the professor's blackboard informs us, "they then started 'cutting the rug' in 1912". In this last bit of jitterbug prehistory, we see a White, urban middle-class couple in their living room doing the falling-off-the-log, a classic vernacular jazz step that consists of a leaning body posture and leg kicks.

All of the dancers demonstrating the jitterbug's supposed antecedents are White. The four vignettes – each lasting twenty seconds or less – are followed by about one minute of dancing by Whitey's Lindy Hoppers. This dance scene's general setup and structure is familiar from the group's previous appearances in feature films. Again, four couples take turns demonstrating various acrobatic air steps, while the others clap and cheer them on. And again, the number ends with some synchronized ensemble dancing.[446] Introduced by the professor as "jitterbugging as you have never seen it!" this Black version of the jitterbug is presented both as the film's climax and as the historical end in the evolution of the dance.

The Soundie's mininarrative, with its series of made-up comic dances, is obviously tongue-in-cheek. But the comic form allows for a remarkable inversion of classical Hollywood's standard jazz narrative, according to which a talented White (and usually male) protagonist is inspired by the "raw" vitality and "wild" rhythms of African American music and dance, which he then "refines" and elevates in status. In classical Hollywood films with contemporaneous settings, Black culture is generally valued as a commodity for White consumption, whereas historical narratives value it as a source of inspiration, which needs the skill and intellect of White artists and the sophistication of Euro-American culture in order to be "lifted" to the level of mainstream – that is, White – acceptability. This pattern occurs consistently in musicians' biopics and musicals of the 1930s, '40s, and '50s, whether their protagonists are fictional or based on historical figures.[447]

The Outline of Jitterbug History in a sense reverses this formula, with "primitive man" appearing in the form of the White cave people. In each of the brief White dance scenes, the dancers' body movement is replete with markers of Blackness, such as low-down posture, shimmying shoulders, and pronounced hip motion.

---

446 According to Manning, who had no recollection of making the Soundie, this is the same group as in *Hellzapoppin'*: "I also don't remember making *Outline of Jitterbug History*, which we filmed in the early '40s, before *Hellzapoppin'*. It's the same dancers in both pictures". Manning, 161.

447 See Gabbard, *Jammin' at the Margins*, 76–87.

The "Cave Hop" is the only one of the dances associated with sexuality as well as with uncivilized, even violent behavior. All the scenes employ expressive jazz dancing primarily for comic effect, which mainly results from the incongruity of the dancing with the costumes and settings. In this comic juxtaposition of "traditional" settings and dance styles (minuet, square dance) with the modern jitterbug, the joke is at the expense of the old, which is presented as uptight and outdated.

By the time the film's history lesson reaches its climax with Whitey's Lindy Hoppers, there is no trace of primitivist stereotypes. Hollywood's usual signifiers of Blackness at the level of character, setting, or narrative structure are absent from the representation of Black people in this particular Soundie: there are no stereotypical stock characters of blackface minstrelsy, no essentialized Black bodies, no nostalgic "folk" settings, such as the Southern plantation, no exoticized, eroticized images of Harlem. And perhaps most importantly, there is no suggestion of Black servitude to Whites. Instead, the African American Lindy hop is presented as the most modern form of jitterbug dancing and the one requiring the highest skill level. The segment with Whitey's Lindy Hoppers is the longest one, and it contains the most impressive dancing of all the short scenes. Their performance has all the elements of Black vernacular jazz dancing without any of the narrative confinement and denigrating context usually found in White-produced films. The Soundie's last segment also has the simplest mise-en-scène, lacking pseudohistorical costumes and props. The basic set is rather unspecific, possibly representing the interior of a train station or a theater lobby. In any case, the suggestion is that the dancing occurs in a public urban space and that the dancers are thus neither hiding from anyone (as in *A Day at the Races* and *Hellzapoppin'*) nor being exhibited on a stage for the pleasure of a White audience (as in *Manhattan Merry-Go-Round*). Instead, they occupy a public – potentially integrated – space, and the Soundie may very well have been screened on Panoram jukeboxes located in similar public spaces.[448] Presented in an everyday urban environment, performing in everyday and contemporary urban clothes, the Lindy dancers appear as nothing less than ordinary Americans – with extraordinary abilities. *The Outline of Jitterbug History* is thus an explicit testimony to swing culture's crossover appeal, integrating Black dance culture into the American mainstream. It is also racially integrated, at least in the sense that it presents Black and White dancers side by side, albeit never within the same image, let alone dancing together.

---

448 On the exhibition and viewing practices of Soundies, see also chapter 4 in this book.

The Outline of Jitterbug History also inverts another convention of classical Hollywood cinema – namely, that of the invisible Black soundtrack for White images. Countless films of the period featured (often uncredited) African American musicians on the soundtrack, invisibly providing music for White bands that were seen – but not heard – onscreen. In this Soundie, White bandleader Stan Kenton's orchestra provides the soundtrack for both White and Black dancers, with one continuous recording played over the montage of images. As usual in Soundies, there is neither dialogue nor any other sound with a diegetic source. In narrative and aesthetic terms, the music's function is to hold the disparate images together, not to suggest that it emanates directly from them. In economic terms, Soundies were also a means to promote recording artists and sell their records. Kenton receives screen credit – the words "recorded by Stan Kenton and His Orchestra" appear right under the film title – but the musicians are never visible onscreen, nor is the song title, "Harlem Folk Dance", mentioned.[449] The music is thus put at the service of the dancers' performance, and Whitey's Lindy Hoppers are announced in the title credits, whereas none of the White dancers are listed.[450]

The Outline of Jitterbug History values and embraces Black jitterbug dancing as the embodiment of a youthful, modern, and all-American spirit. When even the older White professor starts swinging at the very end, this is a fairly obvious hint at how African American swing culture has rejuvenated American culture. The film's White jitterbug prehistory doesn't serve as a myth of origin but simply as a comic means to an end. While the mock-historical mininarrative portrays the dance as a culturally hybrid form, the Soundie showcases the Black Lindy hoppers as a positive modernizing influence in American culture and, however tentatively, suggests a racially inclusive attitude.

If the mock-educational swing dance short film constitutes its own minigenre, then its history culminates in 1944 with the MGM production *Groovie Movie*. Part of the studio's popular Pete Smith Specialty series, this nine-minute theatrical short film is a much more elaborate production than *The Outline of Jitterbug*

---

449 This song title resonates with White views of Black culture in ambiguous ways. Implying that it was the Lindy hop – the "Harlem Folk Dance" – that inspired Kenton to write the song, the tune presumably aims to evoke and match the dance's rhythmic pulse and energy. On the one hand, the title has a distancing effect in an ethnographic sense, marking the "Harlem Folk" as Other. As in many White discourses about African American culture, nostalgic ideas of an idealized Black folk culture both clash and merge with the modern and urban imagery of Harlem. On the other hand, "Harlem Folk Dance" registers the shifts in these discourses, as the war recast swing as America's very own folk culture and the Lindy hop as its "true national folk dance", as the cover story in *Life* magazine would claim the following year ("The Lindy Hop: A True National Folk Dance Has Been Born in U.S.A.", *Life*, August 23, 1943, 95, Google Books). Since the song title is not mentioned in the film itself, these associations remain hidden from the audience. Nevertheless, they inform the Soundie's content, with its cautious move towards racial integration.

450 Whitey's Lindy Hoppers also received screen credit in the Soundies *Hot Chocolate* and *Sugar Hill Masquerade*. The credits for *Air Mail Special* are missing from all versions I have been able to view.

History.[451] Unlike *Outline*, it focuses on White dancers, yet it shares some key features with the earlier Soundie. *Groovie Movie*'s voice-over narration further develops the idea of the mock-historical narrative, again providing comic illustrations of the supposed origins of jitterbug dancing. While a White couple dances on a stage, the narrator (Pete Smith) explains that "the dance these kids are doing is strictly modern, yet many swing steps come from dances of long ago". He goes on to give examples, such as the waltz, ballet, and even an "old Javanese dance", again adding a multicultural aspect to the mock history. The narration then proceeds with examples of "original" steps that have come about "by accident", while the dancers' corresponding demonstrations provide some slapstick. As in *The Outline of Jitterbug History*, the young dancers are contrasted with an older character – here a boogie-woogie pianist (Buster Brodie) – for comic effect.

In addition to dance history, *Groovie Movie* also parodies dance instruction with a lesson that is impossible to follow – with marks on dresses and a white line tracing the dancers' steps on the floor – and which leads to an interesting conclusion: "Having learned the basic steps, you now forget them completely" (figs. 39 & 40). Poking fun at the recent trend of formally teaching the formerly disreputable jitterbug in dance schools, *Groovie Movie*'s mock lesson obviously favors improvisation and individual expression over the standardized patterns of more traditional social dance styles. It suggests that it is rather pointless to learn the "dance of modern youth" formally. Rather, the way to learn it is to do it, and thus the narrator concludes: "Anyway, when done right, the dance is rather delectable, even though quite inexplainable".

The parodic history and instruction take up the first five minutes of the short film, and they are dedicated to prominent White dancers Arthur Walsh and Jean Phelps Veloz. The voice-over introduces Walsh by name as "winner of more than a hundred rug-cutting contests" and "top-flight hep cat", but his female partner is not named, despite being one of the era's most prominent White swing dancers on- and offscreen. The couple's demonstrations are explained by narrator Smith (the only performer credited in the opening titles) and accompanied by a piano playing in a boogie-woogie style at a moderate tempo (the only arguably diegetic sound in the film).

For the second part, the soundtrack swells from solo piano to a full (invisible) big band. There is a cut to three couples rocking and bouncing in place as they're getting ready to swing out, and Smith announces "the group precision jitterbug,

---

451 Pete Smith produced and narrated about 150 shorts for MGM, mostly comic (pseudo)documentaries. He received an Honorary Award at the 1953 Academy Awards. See Academy Awards Database, Academy of Motion Picture Arts and Sciences, http://awardsdatabase.oscars.org; and Maltin, *The Great Movie Shorts*, 140–155.

Chapter 5 Harlem to Hollywood

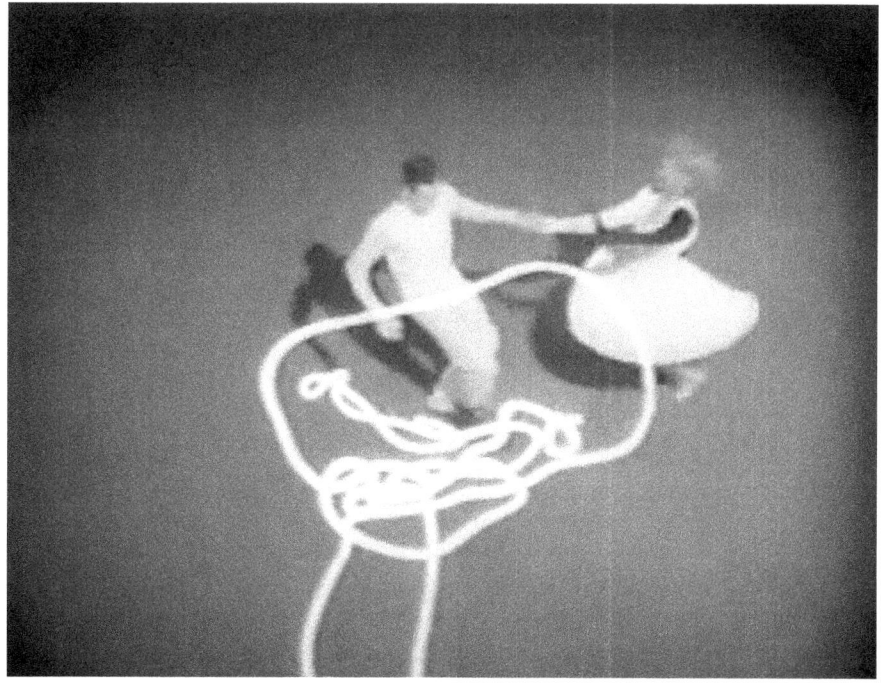

Figures 39 and 40. A parody of a dance lesson in the comic, pseudo-instructional short film *Groovie Movie* (1944) with Arthur Walsh and Jean Phelps Veloz.

193

in which the steps are executed on command, as was the custom in the old country square dance", thus claiming a link to earlier American traditions (as in *The Outline of Jitterbug History*). After calling out the moves of the group routine, Smith challenges the dancers to "hit that jive!" The voice-over then ceases, and the remaining three minutes consist of a montage sequence to a continuous soundtrack of the extradiegetic big band playing an up-tempo version of "One O'Clock Jump".[452]

This final sequence cuts between various couples, with two couples from the preceding group routine doing a very smooth Lindy hop, while the third couple dances the (collegiate) shag.[453] Additional performers with different physiques are juxtaposed for comic effect: a woman in high heels stands stoically while her much shorter male partner is frantically hopping around and holding on to her hand; a very tall man dances with a little girl, leading her by her head and having her slide down his leg. There are moments of mock violence between couples, including a man banging on his female partner's head and another woman poking her partner's face. Film scholar Miriam Hansen has noted the role of slapstick as a response to the challenges of modernity and modernization, arguing that "slapstick comedy allowed for a playful and physical expression of anxieties over changed gender roles and new forms of sexuality and intimacy".[454] *Groovie Movie*'s comic representation of social swing dancing as a sphere of gender equality illustrates this by staging a playful battle of the sexes by means of slapstick and mock fights. Additional comic elements are grimacing faces and shots of the dancers filmed from below through a glass floor, showing their fast-moving feet. For the film's final minute, the cutting rate increases, as does the overall energy of the music, and the three main couples take turns performing a series of acrobatic moves. Their final synchronized jump is stopped in a freeze-frame before they land and collapse on the floor and "The End" appears onscreen.

Unlike in *Outline,* the emphasis in *Groovie Movie* is clearly on White dancers. The only Black performers are two little kids, dressed all in white, who appear briefly (about twenty seconds in total) during the final montage sequence but never within the same image as any of the White dancers. In this respect, *Groovie Movie* follows the standard Hollywood formula of vaguely hinting at jazz culture's Black roots, in this case through the unthreatening presence of two children. By

---

452 The soundtrack was recorded by Jimmy Dorsey and his orchestra, according to Meeker, *Jazz on the Screen*, 849.

453 The three couples are Arthur Walsh and Jean Phelps Veloz, Charles "Chuck" Saggau and Irene Thomas, and Lennie Smith and Kay Vaughn; see Tom Koerner and Debra Sternberg, "About Jean", JeanVeloz.com, http://www.jeanveloz.com/about.

454 Hansen, "Mass Production of the Senses", 343.

only half-heartedly acknowledging the contributions of African Americans, the film inadvertently lays bare the entertainment industry's practice of "love and theft", engaging in the same kind of cultural colonialism as countless other Hollywood productions. In terms of racial representations, this theatrical short film is thus much more ambiguous and problematic than *The Outline of Jitterbug History*. Like the earlier Soundie, *Groovie Movie* also endows its White performers with markers of Blackness, especially with regard to the dancers' movement qualities, which include a generally grounded posture with bent knees, pronounced hip motion, isolation of other body parts, and, of course, highly rhythmic footwork. All of these elements, which define African American jazz dancing, were also present in the Soundie, where all the dancing was filmed in long shots. In *Groovie Movie*, they are additionally highlighted through some close-ups of individual body parts (wiggling toes, twisting hips) and in the voice-over's corresponding comments. The narrator also uses the slang of jazz ("hep cats", "solid") without explicitly referencing Black culture. Instead, this so-called jive talk indicates hepness, and as a marker of the current swing youth culture, it serves to exclude those not in the know. While the word jazz is never mentioned, the film clearly showcases and endorses an African American jazz aesthetic. The erotic aspect is largely defused through the use of physical comedy. The girls' knee-length skirts and dresses are typical teenage jitterbug attire – feminine but not provocatively sexy. The male dancers wear uniforms, likely as an allusion to the popularity of swing dancing among soldiers during World War II.

Unlike the various film scenes with Whitey's Lindy Hoppers, *Groovie Movie*'s aesthetic is closer to what film scholar Noël Carroll calls "moving-picture dance constructions", with sound effects, cinematography, and editing contributing substantially to the overall effect of a cinematic dance.[455] Extradiegetic sound effects in the style of silent slapstick comedy are added on top of the music to emphasize especially comic moments. Additionally, the film fragments the dance by inserting close-ups of faces, feet, and other body parts, also for comic effect. As Arthur Walsh is shown grimacing in a close-up, Smith's voice-over ironically claims that "facial expressions are always dignified". There is also a minstrelizing shot of the little Black girl shaking her pigtailed head in a close-up. Yet this is put into perspective by Walsh's mugging which, in a sense, amounts to the minstrelization of a White performer. In the context of this film, which makes everybody look quite silly, the African American kids don't particularly stand out as Other, although they are clearly subordinate as far as their time onscreen goes.

---

455 Carroll, *Engaging the Moving Image*, 245.

Neither *The Outline of Jitterbug History* nor *Groovie Movie* directly acknowledges the possibility of racial integration. Black and White people are neither dancing together nor sharing the same space, and they are never shown within the same image. While Black and White dancers did share the same dance floor at Harlem's Savoy Ballroom and occasionally at other venues, these instances of public desegregation were still rare, and the film industry was extremely reluctant to show any kind of interracial interaction that did not place Black people in clearly subservient positions. Nevertheless, these short films' comic narratives allude to the exchange between and coexistence of Black and White cultures. They represent the expressivity of a modern African American vernacular jazz culture in ways that are just as appreciative but less patronizing, essentializing, or racially stereotyped than was the case in many of Hollywood's feature-length productions. The dance's positive connotations of youthful playfulness and high-energy, asexual physicality come to replace Hollywood's old primitivist, racist stereotypes. Through the films' focus on an improvisational jazz aesthetic and on individual expression, jitterbug dancing is comically hailed as a modernizing force that rejuvenates the old and connects people across generations and races – even if only through film editing. As much as these films represent the dance by means of irony and slapstick comedy, the joke is ultimately at the expense of the old: traditional dance styles and uptight movement are presented as passé, whereas the rug-cutting of the young hep cats is what everyone should aspire to. With their comic, mock-educational discourses of multicultural history, these films embrace the integrationist tendencies of swing's youth culture and testify to the fact that jitterbug dancing has reached mainstream acceptability.

Overall, however, Hollywood still remained rather hesitant to prominently showcase swing dancing, even during the time of swing's greatest media presence. When MGM advertised *Groovie Movie* to exhibitors, promising that audiences would "buy tickets when you book this fast-paced demonstration of the Jitterbug Joy Wave that's sweeping the country", this "Joy Wave" was not exactly news.[456] During World War II, swing culture was instrumentalized as America's national treasure and a symbol of personal freedom. By 1944, the jitterbug had long swept past the country's borders and was being exported overseas by soldiers and performers entertaining the troops. When Black Lindy hopper Frankie Manning, who was deployed overseas in 1943, was called onstage to dance with blonde movie star and pinup girl Betty Grable on her USO tour in New Guinea, "the dance was now much more than a hot and exciting black vernacular dance; it had

---

456 Advertisement for *Groovie Movie*, *Motion Picture Daily*, May 5, 1944, 7, Media History Digital Library.

become a symbol of America, the great melting pot".[457] As Robert Crease further observes, the year 1943 was the "high-water mark of the Lindy's respectability", when professional dance teachers started to teach it, and when *Life* magazine featured it as a popular dance of national importance.[458] Significantly, the *Life* cover story focused on White *and* Black dancers, featuring photographs of two couples: White professional dancers Stanley Catron and Kaye Popp as well as Leon James and Willamae Ricker of Whitey's Lindy Hoppers.[459]

The Lindy hop is a unique case of a popular vernacular dance that was not only created by African Americans but also remained dominated by them in its most professional manifestations. That this dominance extended beyond contests and stage performances to the big screen of Hollywood's conservative and racist feature film industry – however briefly and incompletely – is nothing short of sensational. The Lindy hop provided its most prominent African American practitioners with rare but significant opportunities for aesthetic self-expression on the movie screen, where they retained a comparatively high degree of creative control over the material they performed. In their film performances, Whitey's Lindy Hoppers challenge stereotypes, negotiate narrative boundaries, and present new images of hip dancing bodies. Male and female Lindy dancers share the screen and partake in the creativity of the dance as equals. Remarkably, this gender equality is presented as a matter of course, and unlike most other dancing women onscreen, female swing dancers are generally not eroticized. What's more, the common intraracial hierarchy among female dancers, with its preference for lighter-skinned women, does not apply here.

Yet when Whitey's Lindy Hoppers disbanded after many of the male members had been drafted, that pretty much spelled the end for Black Lindy hop in film. After the war, Frankie Manning had one more screen appearance in the race movie *Killer Diller* (1948) with his new dance group, the Four Congaroos, which included former Whitey's dancers Ann Johnson, Russell Williams, and Willamae Ricker. A number of other Black Lindy hoppers appeared in Soundies, theatrical shorts, and race films over the years. But most of these productions didn't showcase the dance as prominently as those with Whitey's group, nor did they credit the dancers, many of whom remain unidentified to this day.[460]

457 Crease, "Divine Frivolity", 224; see also Manning, 198–201.
458 Crease, 224.
459 For a short discussion of the photographs in *Life*, see also Dinerstein, *Swinging the Machine*, 266.
460 A notable Hollywood number with Black dancers who were not part of Whitey's group is a nightclub scene from MGM's all-Black-cast musical *Cabin in the Sky* (1943), which features Lindy hoppers dancing a highly stylized choreography to a slow song played by Duke Ellington's band. For additional examples of films showing Black dancers, mostly in independently produced race films, see also White, "Classic Black Lindy Hoppers".

In the early 1940s, Hollywood feature films began employing increasing numbers of White swing dancers, but they were mostly used as atmospheric background rather than as central attractions. In fact, the short *Groovie Movie* is quite an anomaly in terms of its elaborate mise-en-scène and cinematography. Even in the case of the best White swing dancers, such efforts to showcase their skills remained rare in feature-length films. When jitterbug dancers were the focus, it was often in low-budget films, which for the most part ignored the dance's African American roots and only occasionally hinted at an exchange between Black and White people. The potentially subversive function of the music and dance was recast in generational – rather than racial – terms by having young White swing fans rebel against their more conservative elders, albeit in rather harmless ways. In 1942, Universal Studios assembled a group of teenage dancers, the Jivin' Jacks and Jills, who would appear in a series of low- and medium-budget musicals over the next couple of years. These teen films are the subject of the last chapter.

CHAPTER 6 "A Savage Exhibition"? Swing and White Youth Culture in B Movies

For this final chapter, I shift my focus away from cinematic images of Black dancers to films featuring White dancers, discussing some of the ways in which Hollywood productions reflected the mainstreaming of swing music and dancing through representations of a hip White swing culture. By the late 1930s, big band swing had become a mainstream industry. Most dance bands didn't play swing exclusively; typically, their repertoire also included more traditional styles of dance music, such as waltzes, as well as "sweet" music. Nevertheless, swing became the nation's favorite dance music, especially among young people. Not only was swing the most popular music for social dancing, it also pervaded all areas of popular culture – stage and screen, radio and records, fashion and language. Two aspects of swing as a mainstream cultural phenomenon are particularly noteworthy, both in and of themselves and in how they find expression in films of the period.

The first is swing's young audience. Teenagers and young adults played an important role in swing fandom as dancers, as radio listeners and consumers of recorded music, and as fans whose behavior at concerts significantly increased the media attention given to swing. Through enthusiastic dancing – but also through fashion, language, and record collecting – high school and college students helped democratize the consumption of music and transformed the role of the audience from passive consumers into active participants. Almost two decades before rock 'n' roll, swing music and dance created America's first mass youth culture, which was often perceived as rebellious by older generations.[461] As Joel Dinerstein observes with respect to the Lindy hop:

> The lindy also furthered the development of a new youth culture, especially as women developed their own uniforms to enable more athletic dancing; the now-famous saddle shoes, full skirts, and sloppy sweaters evolved for dancing the lindy, not rock and roll.

---

461 See Dinerstein, *Swinging the Machine*, 250–282; and Erenberg, *Swingin' the Dream*, 35–64.

> The familiar cluster of youth culture – new slang, hip clothing, a new rhythmically driven form of music, sexual liberation – began with jazz and the Charleston in the 1920s but became codified through swing music and dance.[462]

The second aspect concerns swing culture's connections with progressive attitudes regarding issues of race and class. Overall, the various entertainment industries continued the old pattern of the White appropriation and commercialization of Black cultural forms, and this pattern has often dominated histories of swing. Yet at the same time – and just as importantly – swing culture functioned as an important arena of racial integration (even if segregation remained the norm overall). Black and White musicians and dancers publicly played music and danced together, sometimes consciously pursuing the cause of racial equality, supported by like-minded journalists, politicians, patrons, and activists. The fight for racial equality was paralleled by and interlinked with class struggle, as evidenced by swing culture's various connections with the Communist Party and other leftist organizations.[463] Music critics who were allied with the Popular Front and the New Deal advocated swing as a pluralist and democratic art form for the masses, and they often used their influence as impresarios and talent scouts to push the music industry to include Black artists. As music historian Lewis A. Erenberg writes: "Swing's audience was mass not class, and its popular appeal challenged the cultural authority of class itself".[464]

Both swing's youth culture and its pluralist-democratic tendencies found their way onto the big screen (as well as onto the small screen of the Panoram movie jukebox), albeit moderated by the film industry's more conservative ideological disposition. Unsurprisingly, Hollywood's response to the nation's swing craze downplayed the culture's radical tendencies with regard to class struggle and racial desegregation. In general, feature films either literally whitewashed the music and dancing by ignoring its African American roots, or they relegated it to the ghetto of the Black specialty act. In the former case, swing's subversive potential is often displaced from racial to – very mild – generational conflicts. In the latter, the Black performers sometimes unsettle racial stereotypes and hierarchies, even if only momentarily, as I have suggested with regard to Whitey's Lindy Hoppers. An often subtle but undeniable hint of subversion thus links young White "swingsters" with their African American counterparts: each group challenged and shifted social norms and hierarchies, as can be observed both at the level of sociocultural realities and of cinematic representations.

462 Dinerstein, *Swinging the Machine*, 280.
463 See Erenberg, *Swingin' the Dream*, 120–149.
464 Erenberg, 153. See also Stowe, *Swing Changes*.

Chapter 6 "A Savage Exhibition"? Swing and White Youth Culture in B Movies

In cinema, the films with the Jivin' Jacks and Jills – a group of White teenage dancers who appeared in a dozen low- and medium-budget productions in the early 1940s – offer especially intriguing objects of study with regard to swing's youth culture. Emphasizing the connection between swing and its young devotees, these films frame swing music and dancing as a youthful and sometimes subversive activity. With their relatively loose narrative structures, they prioritize physical performance – through dance, music, and comedy – over coherent storytelling intended to convey clear ideological messages (as Hollywood films are often said to do). The group's most prominent members, Peggy Ryan and Donald O'Connor, articulate identities that deviate considerably from the era's conventional gender roles, and Ryan embodies a highly unusual dance aesthetic for a White female dancer. In addition, the discourses of publicity and reception that accompanied the films also reveal a focus on the fashions of swing's youth culture rather than on (ideologically charged) storytelling, and in many ways, these swing youth musicals anticipate Hollywood's later shift towards addressing a distinct teen market.

Swing, Youth Culture, and Racial (De)Segregation

In her study of the emergence of a teenage girls' culture, Kelly Schrum finds that teenagers, both male and female, were among the most avid fans of swing music. Swing was "teenagers' favorite music, though slightly less for white girls than for white boys or African American girls or boys".[465] According to Schrum, swing "influenced high school life deeply",[466] and by the late 1930s, it was the most important music for high school students. The study also gives ample evidence of the centrality of dancing to teenage social life during the period: practicing dance steps became an important peer activity, and students often danced in gymnasiums, at home, or in public spaces, such as drugstores.[467] In the late 1930s, swing bands began placing ads in high school yearbooks, and students were frequently described as "swingsters", "jitterbugs", or "rug cutters".[468] The dances mentioned most frequently in high school yearbooks are of African American origin, starting with the black bottom and the Charleston in the 1920s and

---

465 Schrum, *Some Wore Bobby Sox*, 104.

466 Schrum, 110.

467 See Schrum, 113–119. Schrum's study encompasses the years 1920–1945, arguing that the period was crucial for the emergence of a teenage girls' culture and that "dance and dance music were integral to teenage culture from the 1920s through the 1940s, playing an important role in leisure time activities, peer group formation and individual friendships" (98). While the jazz of the 1920s was a major influence in making music and dance central to teenage life, this trend increased exponentially with the swing culture of the 1930s. Although Schrum's focus is on teenage girls, boys are implicated in a substantial part of her evidence. Other histories of swing culture also indicate that the era's dance craze involved both male and female adolescents; see Dinerstein, *Swinging the Machine*; and Erenberg, *Swingin' the Dream*.

468 Schrum, *Some Wore Bobby Sox*, 110, 114.

shifting towards the swing idiom in the 1930s, with numerous references to the big apple, the jitterbug, the shag, or more generally, "fast swing steps".[469] Meanwhile, more traditional dances went out of fashion, and "by the late 1930s, the waltz and fox trot did not attract much teenage interest".[470]

The jitterbug's possibilities for emotional release and individual self-expression played an important role for White youth from varied class and ethnic backgrounds, who were looking to define their own American identities. As Erenberg writes, "swing attracted young people aspiring to establish their independence from their families and to affirm a more vigorous personal experience that cut across ethnic, class, and, at times, racial lines. ... For many, swing defined an American world of personal freedom different from their immigrant roots".[471] Ernie Smith, who later became known as an authority on jazz and a collector of jazz films, was one such immigrant kid. The son of Hungarian show business parents who toured the "ethnic" theater circuit, he discovered swing at age fifteen, frequenting Black dance halls in Pittsburgh's Hill City neighborhood, where few White people went. He recalled becoming obsessed with the Lindy hop, which he learned by watching and copying Black dancers and by going out to dance about five times a week.[472]

White youngsters adopted and adapted the Black dance styles as well as the era's jive talk – that is, the slang associated with Black jazz culture – even if direct exposure to Black bands and contact with African Americans remained limited in what was still a largely segregated society. White teenagers' favorite swing bands and singers were predominantly White, and many fans might have been genuinely oblivious to the music's African American origins. The majority of dance halls and nightclubs were racially segregated, as was most sponsored commercial radio, especially "nationwide shows whose sponsors worried about losing the southern white market".[473]

But swing musicians and dancers also played an important role in transgressing racial boundaries. "Music had the power to overcome racial barriers and challenge restrictions because of the musicians' competence as artists", writes Erenberg.[474] Late-night local radio programs offered more chances to hear Black bands than the nationwide broadcasts. "King of Swing" Benny Goodman was a major force

469 Schrum, 114.
470 Schrum, 117.
471 Erenberg, *Swingin' the Dream*, 39.
472 See LeGon and Smith, interview, Gray; Smith, interview, Murray; and Stearns and Stearns, *Jazz Dance*, 329–330.
473 Erenberg, *Swingin' the Dream*, 43.
474 Erenberg, 116.

Chapter 6 "A Savage Exhibition"? Swing and White Youth Culture in B Movies

in integrating bands and among the first White bandleaders to publicly play with Black musicians. Supported by rich impresario and leftist jazz critic John Hammond, who promoted both Black and White musicians and fought for equal rights in the music business, Goodman brought swing to respected venues. His legendary 1938 concert at Carnegie Hall in New York City is considered a milestone in this respect.[475]

While musicians, jazz critics, and leftist politicians advocated racial equality, the bands' predominantly young following increasingly transcended barriers of class, ethnicity, and race. Without an explicitly political agenda, young swing fans thus created social environments with more interaction between Blacks and Whites than ever before. Especially in urban centers like New York and Chicago, Black bands played for White dancers, even though Black patrons were usually not welcome in dance halls intended for White customers. While segregated venues remained the norm, there were exceptions, most notably the Savoy Ballroom in Harlem, which attracted large crowds of young working- and middle-class customers (as well as many White celebrities). With both Black and White bands playing for a racially mixed audience, the Savoy became "a unique model of a public integrated space, arguably the *only* desegregated national institution".[476] Another temporarily integrated space was the outdoor dance floor at the 1939 New York World's Fair, as evidenced by some amateur film footage, which shows Blacks and Whites sharing the same space, although there are no interracial couples dancing together.[477] Many onetime events also drew racially mixed crowds, although they were the exception rather than the rule.[478]

Teenage swing fans' behavior was at least partly responsible for the extensive media attention given to the music. Benny Goodman's now-legendary 1937 appearance at New York's Paramount Theatre brought swing and its fans – who danced in the aisles – into the national spotlight, and henceforth, "high school students received special media notice as enthusiastic *dancers*".[479] However, musicians and music critics didn't always react favorably to the young jitterbugs;

---

475 See Erenberg, 65–71, 120–130.

476 Dinerstein, *Swinging the Machine*, 258–259. On the Savoy Ballroom, see also Engelbrecht, "Swinging at the Savoy", Erenberg, *Swingin' the Dream*, 48–52; Malone, *Steppin' on the Blues*, 100–106; Manning and Millman, *Frankie Manning*, 61–107; and Miller with Jensen, *Swingin' at the Savoy*.

477 See "1939 New York World's Fair: Savoy Ballroom Exhibit", silent amateur footage, 1939, YouTube video, https://youtu.be/T9zb7KGWXvc.

478 Erenberg relates the story of a free swing jamboree in Chicago, which attracted a racially mixed audience of a hundred thousand young people, who danced to both Black and White bands; see *Swingin' the Dream*, 35–36. On the Harvest Moon Ball, see Dinerstein, *Swinging the Machine*, 268–276; Manning and Millman, *Frankie Manning*, 88–92; and Miller with Jensen, *Swingin' at the Savoy*, 65–82.

479 Schrum, *Some Wore Bobby Sox*, 119 (my italics).

instead, they sometimes deplored the fans' excessive enthusiasm, which they thought detracted attention from the music's artistry.[480]

Adult discourses – from film narratives to music journalism to writings by social critics and educators – clearly betray the White public's ambivalent fascination both with Black culture in general and with swing's appeal to adolescents. Media coverage of Benny Goodman's second Paramount concert in 1938 is an excellent case in point. A *New York Times* article reported that the fans "danced in the aisles, clambered upon the stage, waggled their hands, shook their shoulders, whinnied, whistled, clapped and sang. It was a savage exhibition, as animalistic as a monkey's or an elephant's rhythmic swaying to the beat of a tom-tom".[481] The nonhuman and non-White imagery used to portray the young – presumably mostly White – fans associates them with the supposedly primitive physical musicality often attributed to Black people. The disruptive power of such a "savage exhibition" thus suggests a parallel between racial and generational tensions. This is also true of many cinematic uses of swing music and dancing. Even though Hollywood downplayed the larger swing culture's progressive tendencies, dance in swing-themed musicals is often disruptive and unruly, posing a challenge to the normative White identities and ideologically conservative narratives that have often been associated with studio-era musicals.

Swing Kids Go to Hollywood

Inevitably, the nationwide swing fever spread to Hollywood. Beginning with RKO's Astaire-Rogers feature *Swing Time* (1936), the word "swing" appeared more and more often in movie titles. In *Swing Time*, Fred Astaire infamously paid his blackface tribute to Black tap dancer Bill Robinson in the much-discussed "Bojangles of Harlem" number.[482] The film's title, however, is taken from one of Astaire's duets with Ginger Rogers, the "Waltz in Swing Time", but neither this syncopated waltz nor any of the film's other Jerome Kern tunes have much to do with swing music (despite the uncredited participation of Black swing pioneer Fletcher Henderson as an arranger). The film's lush art deco settings are Hollywood versions of the types of swanky Midtown Manhattan hotels and supper rooms where society dance orchestras played for upper-class customers, rather

---

480 See, for instance, Erenberg, *Swingin' the Dream*, 56–59.

481 Frank S. Nugent, "Vendetta, or A Clarinetist's Revenge", *New York Times*, January 30, 1938, TimesMachine. For more about press reports on this event, see also Schrum, *Some Wore Bobby Sox*, 99.

482 For commentary on this Astaire number, see, for instance, Rogin, *Blackface, White Noise*, 184; Dinerstein, *Swinging the Machine*, 226; and Gubar, *Racechanges*, 88–90.

Chapter 6 "A Savage Exhibition"? Swing and White Youth Culture in B Movies

than the more inclusive ballrooms where swing big bands entertained the masses.[483]

To some extent, the film industry thus capitalized on swing's popularity by mere association, since many productions that reference swing arguably didn't contain any. Nevertheless, swing culture did make its way into the movies. From the late 1930s through the mid-1940s, swing bands were a relatively common screen presence, with a number of feature films constructed around the appearance of a prominent White band.[484] But despite swing's enormous popularity, jitterbug dancing never became a principal cinematic attraction like tap, nor did it produce any major movie stars. As a spectacle in Black specialty acts, it was rare. As a White phenomenon, it became a frequent – yet almost always marginal – screen presence, often in B movies.

The college musicals *Start Cheering* (1938) and *College Swing* (1938) are among the earliest films to show swing as a rebellious youth culture frowned upon by older generations. In Paramount's *Start Cheering*, the school's dean is outraged to find a jazz band (featuring Louis Prima) playing in students' rooms in the middle of the night. Yet at the end, a Friday night dance at the gym – complete with partnered jitterbug, tap solos, and a big apple routine – establishes swing dancing as a legitimate pastime for the White youngsters.[485] Columbia's slapstick-laden *College Swing* starts with an eighteenth-century frame story in which an unruly choir boy anachronistically breaks into jazzy scat singing, explaining to the shocked headmaster that "it's Benny Goodman". The film's title number, sung by Betty Grable, leads to spontaneous dancing at the college bar. It involves a lot of pecking, a move that consists of a backward and forward motion of the head meant to imitate a chicken. Like other dance moves from the Black vernacular tradition of animal dances, pecking became part of the swing repertoire. The music in this number, however, is swing-inflected at best, and Grable's dance is a rather stiff attempt at the Black movement idiom. The film's remaining musical numbers include sappy love songs, comic routines, and a rumba – but no more swing. *College Swing* thus illustrates Hollywood's abovementioned tendency to use the term "swing" as a marketing tool without actually giving much prominence to the music and dance culture in question. Nevertheless, with their school setting and the mildly subversive function of swing, these two films prefigure the themes that would become codified with the 1940s cycle of teen swing musicals.

---

483 See Erenberg, *Swingin' the Dream*, 48–49, 152–153.

484 For a brief historical overview of the big band musical, see Chapman, "Big Band Musical".

485 A Black musical number featuring tap dancer Jeni LeGon with the Four Blackbirds was cut from this film (see chapter 3 in this book).

Kelly Schrum observes that the music industry "did not create a teen market for popular music as much as they responded to one".[486] The same is true of the film industry, as Hollywood picked up on swing's popularity with youngsters rather late and only started portraying teenage swing fans and dancers somewhat regularly in the 1940s. During this period, the film industry generally still catered to a broad intergenerational audience rather than targeting specific groups with specific products. But the teen swing musicals that emerged from the period's new mass youth culture foreshadow the age-specific film production and marketing of post-World War II teen films.[487]

Hep to the Jive: The Jivin' Jacks and Jills at Universal

Universal Studios' series of low-budget musicals featuring the Jivin' Jacks and Jills, a White dance group, best exemplifies Hollywood's interpretation of and reaction to swing's youth culture. Noteworthy for their portrayal of young White swing fans as well as for their reception by a young audience, these films indicate the industry's growing awareness of the market potential of teenagers and young adults – the demographic groups who made up the most substantial audience segment.

The Jivin' Jacks and Jills were assembled by Universal's dance director Johnny Mattison in 1942. Mattison staged the group's dances in their first three films, *What's Cookin'* (1942), *Private Buckaroo* (1942), and *Give Out, Sisters* (1942), after which he was replaced by White tap dancer Louis DaPron, who would be responsible for their dance numbers throughout the remainder of the series, with the exception of *Moonlight in Havana* (1942).[488] Initially, the group consisted of twelve dancers, mostly aged twelve to seventeen. Though they were primarily tap dancers, their routines usually included sequences of partnered jitterbugging, and many scenes had a social dance setting that emphasized youth culture. The group performed their unique blend of tap and jitterbug – sometimes mixed with elements of ballroom and ballet – in about a dozen films over the short period

---

486 Schrum, *Some Wore Bobby Sox*, 127.

487 For general introductions to and historical overviews of teen films, see Driscoll, *Teen Film*; and Shary, *Teen Movies*. As these and other authors point out, the concept of adolescence developed in the twentieth century in a variety of contexts, ranging from social science to popular culture. As with music and many other industries, the film industry only began to specifically target teenagers on a large scale in the 1950s. See also Klein, *American Films Cycles*, 100–137; and Mundy, *Popular Music on Screen*, 97–99.

488 See Billman, *Film Choreographers*, 286–289, 413. Louis DaPron was a tap dancer in numerous films throughout the 1930s and 1940s, but he never attained star status and is mostly remembered as a choreographer. He was under contract as Universal's dance director for four years, during which period he spent a lot of time rehearsing with Donald O'Connor. Tap dancer Peggy Ryan considered DaPron one of the best dancers, one who "should have been a star himself"; quoted in Frank, *Tap!*, 209. After the Jivin' Jacks and Jills were disbanded, DaPron kept working as Donald O'Connor's choreographer as well as being head choreographer at Universal into the 1950s. See DaPron, interview, Daniels; and Frank, *Tap!*, 203.

from 1942 to 1944, with the number of dance scenes ranging from one to eight per film. Many of the dancers had their own style and trademark moves, which were showcased in solos within the larger group's dance numbers. Donald O'Connor and Peggy Ryan quickly became the group's most prominent members and were often given significant speaking parts as well as additional, usually comic, dance numbers.[489] Musical performers who appeared in their films repeatedly included the teenage soprano singer Gloria Jean, usually cast as Donald O'Connor's love interest, and the vocal trio the Andrews Sisters, whose enormous popularity reached its peak during the war years and who always appeared as themselves.[490] Several of the films also featured White big bands whose leaders used their real names, whereas male and female singers of "sweet" ballads usually played fictional characters. A few of the films included Black specialty performers, most notably the Four Step Brothers in *When Johnny Comes Marching Home* (1942) and the Count Basie orchestra in *Top Man* (1943).

The notion of film cycles as described by genre theorist Rick Altman in *Film/Genre* provides a useful framework for considering these films as a group. Altman shows how "studios prefer to establish cycles rather than genres", thus creating "successful, easily exploitable models associated with a single studio".[491] Universal created its own cycle of low-budget musicals with its own team of adolescent dancers. At the same time, the studio also capitalized on the national swing craze by featuring some of the era's most popular musical acts. Robert "Bobby" Scheerer, a member of the Jivin' Jacks and Jills, stated in an interview, "I don't know that it was even thought of to be a series at that point [when he auditioned for the first film], although I do feel they were in some ways trying to duplicate what was happening with the MGM Mickey Rooney/Judy Garland pictures, the success of them".[492] Like the Rooney-Garland youth musicals by MGM and RKO's 1930s cycle of Astaire-Rogers features, Universal's teen musicals are not a coherent series, as they lack continuity of setting and character. But the repeated use of themes, performers, narrative formulas, and music and

---

489 The group's composition would vary somewhat between films. According to Rusty Frank, the initial lineup consisted of Jack McGee, Roland Dupree, Robert "Bobby" Scheerer, Joe "Corky" Geil, David Holt, Dolores Mitchell, Dorothy "Dottie" Babb, Jean and Jane McNab, Grace McDonald, Donald O'Connor, and Peggy Ryan. See Frank, *Tap!*, 203. The exact film count depends on what one includes: apart from the ten films with a version of the Jivin' Jacks and Jills as an ensemble, *When Johnny Comes Marching Home* (1942), *Top Man* (1943), and *This Is the Life* (1944) feature Donald O'Connor and Peggy Ryan without the rest of the group. These films are included in my discussion because they have enough in common with the other productions to be considered part of the cycle. Additionally, O'Connor and Ryan appear as a team in two films set on the vaudeville stages of yesteryear rather than in the swing era, *The Merry Monahans* (1944) and *Bowery to Broadway* (1944).

490 From 1940 to 1945, the Andrews Sisters appeared in thirteen films for Universal as well as in *Hollywood Canteen* (1944) for Warner Bros.

491 Altman, *Film/Genre*, 58–60.

492 Scheerer, "Hollywood to Broadway", 22.

dance styles lends them a high degree of consistency, making them recognizable as a cycle, in which the same elements reappear in a variety of combinations.

Film scholar Amanda Ann Klein takes up Altman's definition, modifying and expanding it for her own study of American film cycles. What she considers typical of film cycles in general is also true of Universal's teen musicals: they are "associated with commercialism and artlessness", and they have generally been treated as "cultural ephemera cranked out to capitalize on current events, trends, fads, and the success of other films".[493] The short-lived cycle of Universal's teen musicals was obviously cranked out to capitalize on the trend for all things swing, reflecting the historical context of the late swing era, when swing music and dancing was a widely accepted mainstream phenomenon.

The Jivin' Jacks and Jills' first film, *What's Cookin'*, sets the tone for the entire cycle, offering a sort of prototypical template against which to read the films as a group.[494] The Jivin' Jacks and Jills play a group of penniless aspiring dancers. The formulaic story concerns the attempt to replace a classical music radio program with the more modern sounds of big band swing. This requires a sabotage plot against a stereotypically uptight, middle-aged lady named Agatha, whose sponsorship of the program makes her the final authority on its content. Luckily, her husband bonds with the group of youngsters assembled by his daughter Sue, played by young classical soprano singer Gloria Jean. The swing/classical opposition is thus paralleled by a generational conflict. The two musical worlds are also associated with different social classes, juxtaposing Sue's upper-class family with the broke swing kids. The rich but unspoiled singer acts as the integrating force, linking the young showbiz hopefuls and their modern swing culture, on the one hand, to the older generation and its taste for classical music, on the other. Additional grown-up help comes from the Andrews Sisters and from Woody Herman and his orchestra, who play themselves. As representatives of the White mainstream version of swing, they help to pursue the film's central narrative goal – namely, to legitimize swing as an acceptable cultural form – by joining forces with the adolescent White dancers (fig. 41).

---

493 Klein, *American Film Cycles*, 6. I agree with Klein's view that film cycles are not necessarily the product of a single studio; rather, they can be created by multiple studios releasing similar movies simultaneously (see 79). Using a very inclusive definition, the cycle of teen swing musicals might thus comprise every musical from the late 1930s and early 1940s that features adolescent swing fans and/or dancers. Universal Studios' films with the Jivin' Jacks and Jills would then form the core of this broadly defined cycle, its most typical or representative examples.

494 In genre theorist Rick Altman's terminology, it condenses and prefigures the central semantic and syntactic elements found in the other films – that is, the films' building blocks and their structural relationships. See *Film/Genre*, 216–226.

Chapter 6 "A Savage Exhibition"? Swing and White Youth Culture in B Movies

Figure 41. The Jivin' Jacks and Jills as adolescent swing fans and showbiz hopefuls in their first film, *What's Cookin'* (1942), with bandleader Woody Herman. Credit: Universal Pictures/Photofest.

Like countless musicals from Hollywood's studio era, *What's Cookin'* integrates opposites, promotes an indigenous American popular culture and its mass appeal over highbrow European culture, and addresses American Dream fantasies of self-made success.[495] With its showbiz success story, it is typical of the backstage musical subgenre, to which most of the Jack-and-Jill movies belong. However, the ways in which these films deviate from what is generally considered the classical Hollywood musical are more interesting than the ways in which they correspond with that model. This concerns both the textual and the contextual levels – that is, the films themselves as well as the circumstances of their publicity and reception. At the textual level, a heterogeneous assortment of musical, physical, and comic performances usually overshadows the weak narratives. While most of the films with the Jivin' Jacks and Jills have an all-White cast, the musicians and dancers embody class, age, gender, and race in unconventional ways that depart from Hollywood's usual representations. Further, through the portrayal of an increasingly independent youth culture, the films appealed to a young audience of White swing fans.

---

[495] For general analyses of the structure of classical Hollywood musicals, see Altman, *The American Film Musical*; and Feuer, *The Hollywood Musical*.

In its brief sixty-nine minutes, *What's Cookin'* addresses a wide range of discourses, themes, and performance styles, including classical music and big band swing, traditional family values and a rebellious youth culture, individualism and patriotic unity. Despite the focus on music suggested by the film's radio setting, dance is at least as important, with no less than five numbers spotlighting the terpsichorean skills of the Jivin' Jacks and Jills. The strong presence of the dancers establishes the central role of non-narrative physical performance, which would continue to dominate these teen films.

The film's overall narrative, as well as the framing of individual music and dance numbers, lends all things swing a hint of rebellion. *What's Cookin'* starts with the young dancers trying to sneak out of their boarding house – because they can't pay the rent – which they do quite improbably by dancing on the staircase. Up next is a live radio broadcast featuring Woody Herman's band. During this, a ballad by vocalists Robert Paige and Jane Frazee is followed by a medium-slow, slightly swinging tune by the Andrews Sisters, who underscore the song's rhythmic flow with a laid-back bounce while a group of young spectators chew gum in unison with the beat. The Jacks and Jills then start to jitterbug, but they are quickly stopped by employees – an occurrence that is repeated at the end of the song. With the seated radio audience, dancing kids, and adults trying to restore order, the scene epitomizes the crucial and active role of adolescent audiences: by appropriating performances that were aimed at a general audience, teenagers fashioned swing into their own youth culture.

Through far-fetched plot developments, the swing gang then winds up at a fancy mansion, whose new owner, Woody Herman's singer Anne Payne (Frazee), complains to her manager that the house is too big. The brief dialogue – the manager answers, "I pick this joint up to give you a little class and you don't appreciate it" – is revealing in terms of class issues, introducing the improbable upper-class setting, only to democratize it through the arrival of the teen dancers and the big band. Following mild complications and youthful scheming, the inevitable happy ending ensues. After a classical violinist is sabotaged and ridiculed, the final show starts with some operatic singing by Gloria Jean – who is in on the joke – before the Andrews Sisters and Woody Herman's band take over by literally pushing the symphony orchestra off the stage. A brief exchange of scat syllables between Gloria Jean and Patty Andrews seals the musical deal, and after the initial shock, even stuffy old Agatha is persuaded by the irresistible swing rhythms and – in the best movie cliché fashion – starts bouncing to the beat against her will.

Chapter 6 "A Savage Exhibition"? Swing and White Youth Culture in B Movies

The musical, class, and generational oppositions that structure the narrative of *What's Cookin'* run through the entire film cycle. For instance, *Give Out, Sisters* (1942), *Get Hep to Love* (1942), *Mister Big* (1943), and *Patrick the Great* (1945) all tie a "swing versus classical music" narrative to generational conflict. While these White narratives erase the Black roots of swing, African American elements remain present by association. They are implied in the music and especially in the dance performances but also in the young generation's frequent use of jive talk, the Black-originated jazz slang that indicates hipness and betrays "a racialized notion of popular culture", as Kristin McGee notes.[496] In *Mister Big*, Donald O'Connor, Peggy Ryan, and Gloria Jean play students at a traditional school of performing arts, where rebellious O'Connor causes the school band to break into a swing jam session as soon as the music teacher leaves the classroom. While the school's elderly owner doesn't want to encourage the kids in their "low taste for jazz music", as she says, two younger teachers endorse the youth culture, and the "good girl" teacher finds herself inadvertently (and rather unconvincingly) talking jive. The kids eventually get to perform their swinging musical instead of Sophocles's *Antigone*, and in the final number, they break into an electrifying jitterbug and tap routine in their "ancient Greek" costumes. The victory of a jazz-inflected, Black-originated American vernacular over the White, European classics could hardly be more explicit. In *Give Out, Sisters*, heiress Gracie Waverly (Grace McDonald) has to hide her dancing ambitions and performances from a trio of conservative elderly aunts. Help comes from the Jivin' Jacks and Jills, playing students of a tap school, whereas the Andrews Sisters again fulfill a mediating function as adults whose streamlined popular swing appeals to a White mass audience. Gracie's double life between musical worlds, social classes, and generations again epitomizes the overall penchant of the teen swing musicals: popular culture is associated with youth, renewal, and an inclusive and democratic – rather than an exclusive and elitist – stance. More specifically, the right to dance drives the flimsy narrative, and physical expression through dance stands for individuality and personal freedom. In *Get Hep to Love*, Donald O'Connor and Gloria Jean play the lead roles of juvenile wannabe hep cat Jimmy and overworked child prodigy opera singer Doris, respectively. Doris, having run away from her strict and overambitious aunt's tutelage in search of a normal life and some fun, is introduced to small-town high school life by Jimmy. A swinging number in a burger bar, preceded by a dialogue full of exaggerated, corny slang, serves as a sort of initiation ritual for Doris, introducing her to the language, music, and dance of modern youth culture as well as sending her on her path to romance. The classical/swing musical dichotomy is again paralleled by class contrast, and the

---

496 McGee, *Some Liked It Hot*, 89.

(highly implausible) plot favors a normal middle-class life over Doris's upper-class background, which is depicted as full of hypocrisy and unwholesome stress. *It Comes Up Love* (1943), another pairing of teen stars Donald O'Connor and Gloria Jean, doesn't have the Jivin' Jacks and Jills, but it does have a classical/swing opposition, with O'Connor playing boogie-woogie piano and teaching the uptight singer – who doesn't "care for modern music" – some dance steps and jive talk.

The context of World War II provided additional ideologically tinged subject matter. Military institutions also become a target of adolescent rebellion, as in *Chip Off the Old Block* (1944), where O'Connor plays a Naval Academy student, whose disobedience is again expressed through music and dancing. The movies with war-related settings all juxtapose fun with military discipline, only to paradoxically integrate the two, thereby legitimizing the role of entertainment in the war effort. *Private Buckaroo* shows big band leader Harry James and the Andrews Sisters as key figures of American patriotism (unlike James, the Andrews Sisters extensively entertained the Allied forces in real life, too, which lends their film appearance a high degree of credibility). The bluntly propagandistic film wraps its call for enlistment in a wide variety of popular entertainment, with a dozen music and dance numbers clearly dominant over the plot, which is even weaker than usual and centers on teaching the merits of discipline and obedience to singer Lon (Dick Foran). The message is that showbiz and the army – entertainment and discipline – are compatible rather than mutually exclusive.

While expressions of patriotism were not limited to any specific musical style, swing did play an especially prominent role in wartime popular music. Erenberg points out that swing was much more successful than patriotic marching songs when it came to boosting wartime morale. He argues that swing ideologized the war as a defense of a superior American culture, representing the American way of life at home for soldiers abroad. It also conveyed ethnic and racial cosmopolitanism, and in many films, such as *Stage Door Canteen* (1943) or *Air Force* (1943), "swing embodied an American way of life – democracy, pluralism, and personal freedom – under attack".[497]

With regard to the Jivin' Jacks and Jills, swing culture's democratizing impulse is perhaps most apparent in the "Golden Wedding" number from *What's Cookin'* (the title of this instrumental piece, performed by Woody Herman's band, is not related to anything happening in the film's plot). With its extensive clarinet and drum solos, the high-energy tune is reminiscent of Benny Goodman's famous rendition of "Sing, Sing, Sing" at his 1938 Carnegie Hall concert – one of the

---

[497] Erenberg, *Swingin' the Dream*, 184.

central real-life precedents for the swinging democratization of upscale venues. A similarly symbolic democratic takeover of an elite space occurs in this number, as the Jivin' Jacks and Jills, spearheaded by Peggy Ryan, spontaneously invade the outdoor dance floor of the upper-class estate.

The number showcases a variety of dance styles. Individual dancers are spotlighted in solos and in teams of two or three, alternating with sections that involve the whole group. A comparison between the two main female soloists is instructive. Grace McDonald, the only adult member of the Jivin' Jacks and Jills, was cast as the romantic lead in three of their films, and her dance solos usually showcased her capacity for multiple consecutive spins. With her upright, controlled posture, elegant ballroom-style lifts, and nearly balletic pirouettes, she embodies a normative White dance aesthetic. Peggy Ryan, by contrast, energetically throwing her limbs and head around with little restraint, knees bent low, shoulders forward, and legs often apart, reveals her roots to be in the Black vernacular. With her second entrance in this number, Ryan first makes fun of McDonald's pirouettes, only to steal the show with an even more impressive display of spinning skills. As a group, the Jivin' Jacks and Jills encompass the entire range between the antithetical extremes of a European-based upright and linear dance aesthetic, on the one hand, and the crouching position of African American vernacular dance, on the other. While the number also has a ballet component, especially in some of the boys' pirouettes, tap and swing elements dominate the overall picture.

In line with the musical aesthetic of big band swing, the "Golden Wedding" number combines ensemble collaboration with the freedom of personal expression in a series of individual spotlights. Although choreographed tap dominates, it is interspersed with references to improvised social dances, such as the collegiate shag or the Charleston, with Ryan doing some high Charleston kicks, for example. Combining Black and White traditions, social and performative dance styles, individual self-expression and collective drive, the number blends seemingly opposed aesthetic principles effortlessly. Despite the lack of explicit references to racial and ethnic diversity, the result implicitly reflects swing culture's pluralist and democratic tendencies, presenting a heterogeneous coexistence more than a homogenizing melting pot.

At a purely aesthetic level – beyond concerns of narrative framing and function – this tendency towards an eclectic pluralism can be found in most of the Jivin' Jacks and Jills' dance routines: they combine tap, various social jitterbug styles, solo moves from the Black vernacular jazz idiom, elements of ballroom dance, and even ballet. Most dance numbers in these films have little or no narrative function in terms of driving the plot forward. They do, however, serve to express identities. Specific dance styles and moves, costumes, settings, and mise-en-scène mark the performing bodies in terms of age, class, gender, and race in ways that frequently challenge Hollywood's conventional identity constructions.

The first group routine in *Mister Big*, danced to a medium-tempo big band swing tune, alternates synchronized tap dancing with solo spotlights. Another diverse mix of dance styles, the number includes brief acrobatic lifts (Peggy Ryan and Donald O'Connor), balletic turns with tap rhythms (Tommy Rall), one girl's tap solo on the bar counter, and the knee-bending Shorty George by the whole group. Costumes (an oversized bow in Ryan's hair, short pants on one of the boys) and setting (an ice cream parlor) signify youth culture, and the number ends with everybody sitting down to sip milkshakes. A later rehearsal scene combines the group's partnered jitterbug with a brief sequence of two boys challenging each other with acrobatic flips, evoking the African American tradition of the challenge dance.[498] In the stage show at the end of the film, the dancers change from evening gowns and tailcoats into hip swing outfits by the magic means of a dissolve – a costume change that dissociates them from the adult upper class, instead associating them and their swinging dance style with popular youth culture.

The Jivin' Jacks and Jills' only dance routine in the propagandistic revue musical *Private Buckaroo* is one of their most elaborate numbers and undoubtedly the film's climax (fig. 42). It starts with comic moments of couples miming adolescent dating scenes on a bench, with much nervous giggling. The dancers' youth is further emphasized through close-ups of their faces as well as long shots that reveal the girls, in heels, to be taller than the boys. Yet another eclectic amalgam of contemporary popular dance styles, the high-energy dance number includes bits of partnered dancing with high kicks reminiscent of the collegiate shag, synchronized tap by the whole group, brief solo and couple spotlights, a lot of pirouetting (especially by some very young boys), acrobatic lifts and flips, and shimmying shoulders. In her solo, Peggy Ryan again stands out with comic facial expressions, strongly accented movements, and extremely low-down, angular hip twists, all of which sets her apart from the more upright posture and streamlined motion of the other dancers (fig. 43).

Always a Bridesmaid (1943) has the kids crash a party and perform a dance routine that stays entirely in the partnered jitterbug idiom, with a very grounded and groovy aesthetic, danced to a boogie-woogie/swing tune. There is talk of hep cats and jitterbugs among the adults standing by, whose stiff manner of observing and

---

498 See, for instance, Hill, *Brotherhood in Rhythm*, chapter 6; Hill, *Tap Dancing America*, 2–3; and Malone, *Steppin' on the Blues*, 5. There are also numerous references to the tradition of challenge dances in Stearns and Stearns, *Jazz Dance*.

Chapter 6 "A Savage Exhibition"? Swing and White Youth Culture in B Movies

Figures 42 and 43. An eclectic group routine with the Jivin' Jacks and Jills in *Private Buckaroo* (1942). In her solo, Peggy Ryan demonstrates her characteristic grounded posture and over-rotated hip twists.

speaking sets them apart from the lively swing kids. The "Madame Zam" number from *Patrick the Great* enumerates tap steps in the lyrics and incorporates the Jivin' Jacks and Jills as audience members who spontaneously join in, thereby both feeding into the musical's "myth of the audience"[499] and stressing the participatory nature of swing culture. In *Top Man*, the soda parlor serves as the central locus of a youth culture that revolves around dating, music, and social dancing – a world that is simultaneously separate from the world of adults and a sort of training ground for grown-up life and behavior.

To once again return to the group's first film: *What's Cookin'* climaxes with a dance to Woody Herman's biggest hit, "Woodchopper's Ball" (first recorded in 1939), a riffy big band tune with a propulsive, driving rhythm. While the Jivin' Jacks wear formal tailcoats, for which they clearly look too young, the Jills appear in somewhat exaggerated teenage girl attire, with knee-length white puffy dresses and giant bows in their hair. In contrast to their earlier rebelliousness, they are much more contained by their appearance as "proper" White kids here. Accordingly, the dance's African American aesthetic is less pronounced than in previous numbers, and the choreography stresses the ensemble more than individual expression in solos. The narrative context highlights youthful renewal as well as family and community, and the film ends with a finale of patriotic marching and everybody singing the World War I morale booster "Pack Up Your Troubles". But this allusion to the war is a pasted-on message coming out of nowhere, and the conservative ending, with its emphasis on family, community, and national unity, doesn't quite defuse the power of swing. Tapping in unison and beating small hand-held drums, the Jivin' Jacks and Jills emphasize big band swing's rhythmic drive. Despite the ensemble choreography, there is still some room for individuality, and Peggy Ryan is briefly spotlighted again, resisting integration into the streamlined group aesthetic with her idiosyncratic, charismatic dance style.

Crucially, the group routines of the Jivin' Jacks and Jills also deviate from the dominant ways of representing gender through dance in Hollywood musicals. The sexualization and objectification of dancing women is largely absent. Neither Busby Berkeley's uniformly dehumanized chorus girls nor eroticized seductresses, the girls are the boys' equals in terms of technical ability, and they are given as much opportunity for individualized self-expression.[500] A closer look at the dance

---

[499] See Feuer, "The Self-Reflective Musical".

[500] According to film and music historian Peter Stanfield, the persona adopted by White female vocalists also changed significantly in the late 1930s and early 1940s. The new singers of the swing era "did not identify with the masochistic psychic suffering of the torch singer and instead project an image of worldly independence and professionalism. Moreover, styled as 'one of the boys' along with the band produced an image of femininity that was not readily susceptible to victimhood" (*Body and Soul*, 135–136).

group's most prominent soloists sheds further light on how these films propose alternatives to classical Hollywood's conventional ways of representing White racial and gender identities.

The Alternative Embodiments of Peggy Ryan and Donald O'Connor

Dancer Grace McDonald, a few years older than the other dancers, appeared in only three of the films with the Jivin' Jacks and Jills: *What's Cookin'*, *Always a Bridesmaid*, and *Give Out, Sisters*. In each, she is set apart from the teenagers by her greater height, her wardrobe (with the occasional evening gown lending her a touch of glamour and clearly identifying her as an adult), and her language, which lacks the teenagers' use of slang. Though the social class of her characters varies from film to film, her appearance and her elegant ballroom-inflected dancing code her as White, middle class, and respectable – but never elitist. A conventionally pretty all-American blonde, her physical presence and dance ability remain unthreatening, and her romantic lead roles invariably end up domesticating her.

Dark-haired Peggy Ryan, by contrast, doesn't conform to any normative notions of either femininity or Whiteness. Ryan is, in fact, quite an anomaly among Hollywood's White female dancers of the period. The daughter of a ballroom dance couple, she first appeared onscreen at age five in Roy Mack's short film *The Wedding of Jack and Jill* (1930)[501] but afterwards didn't return to Hollywood until 1936. Her feature film debut was in Universal's *Top of the Town* (1937), in which she appeared as a pert ten-year-old specialty dancer impersonating Eleanor Powell. Explicitly copying Powell's tap style and costume (a shiny one-piece pantsuit), she effortlessly equals the older dancer, who was being promoted to stardom by MGM at the time.[502] But this promising stepping-stone for Ryan was followed by only a handful of nonmusical bit parts and appearances in short films – until the inception of the Jivin' Jacks and Jills in 1942.[503]

Initially, Universal's teen musicals gave Ryan opportunities to display her skills in spotlights within the group routines. As she became increasingly featured in solo numbers and duets, she might easily have joined the ranks of Hollywood's

---

501 The film also featured seven-year-old Judy Garland. According to Edwin M. Bradley (*Hollywood Sound Shorts*, 103), only the audio track of this short film survives.

502 Peggy Ryan's impersonation here is ironic, since MGM had previously offered young Ryan a seven-year contract and a role in *Born to Dance* (1936), which starred Eleanor Powell. But when seeing Ryan dance, Powell apparently saw her own star status under threat: she objected to Ryan's participation in "her" film, and the deal was off; see Ryan, quoted in Frank, *Tap!*, 204. In another twist of irony, a scathing review of *Top of the Town* called Ryan a "12-year-old Eleanor Powell protégée". Frank S. Nugent, "Universal Unveils Its Elaborate Revue, 'Top of the Town', at the Roxy – New Foreign Films", review of *Top of the Town*, The Screen, *New York Times*, March 27, 1937, TimesMachine.

503 For a short biography, see also Cullen, Hackman, and McNeilly, *Vaudeville*, 985.

foremost female dancing stars. Like Eleanor Powell, Rita Hayworth, or Ann Miller, she performed with virtuosic competence and creativity. Her numbers exhibited what Adrienne McLean, referring to Eleanor Powell, has called "an aesthetics of competence, the physical practices of virtuosity and skill".[504] In fact, it is instructive to compare Peggy Ryan's screen image with that of Eleanor Powell as analyzed by McLean. Just like Powell's, Ryan's active and creative persona as a dancer differs considerably from that of a conventional, objectified showgirl. McLean argues that "Powell was portrayed as being able to handle anything life threw at her with a minimum of fuss and bother, and her nonconformity … lay in her extreme competence and … the fact that she was also unutterably normal and healthy".[505] McLean then goes on to observe that Powell's performances, including those in male drag, were "fully integrated with a spectacular femininity".[506] It is in this respect that Peggy Ryan differs most from the era's other top female screen dancers: whether in narrative terms or in the way she presents herself in her dance numbers, Ryan's appeal never lies in a romantically or sexually defined femininity. When highly feminized dance styles like ballroom or ballet are included in her numbers, they are usually undermined by her mocking treatment of them. Instead of a "spectacular femininity", her performances present a spectacle of competence and comedy; in addition to its undeniable physical virtuosity, Ryan's dancing is also exceptionally comic and irreverent, displaying a high level of craft in slapstick and parody.

In the "Gremlin Walk" number from *This Is the Life* (1944), for example, Ryan sings and dances in striped pajamas, performing a series of comically exaggerated dance moves that belong as much to the vaudevillian tradition of eccentric dancing as to the African American vernacular, with lots of so-called legomania, as well as Black-originated moves, including the Shorty George and some especially unruly, high-energy Charleston variations.[507] In "Let's Hitch a Horsie to the Automobile" from *Get Hep to Love*, the jukebox in a diner inspires seemingly improvised jitterbugging by several couples before the scene turns into a showcase for Peggy Ryan, who first sings the silly song with her somewhat quacky voice and then leads everyone in a tap dancing circle. But it is especially in her dance solo towards the end of the number that she again defies all norms of White femininity with extremely high kicks, over-rotated hip twists, loosely dangling arms, pecking head moves, imitations of a horse, and grimacing. Eventually, multiple couples return to the floor for more jitterbugging, which

---

504 McLean, "Putting 'Em Down", 90.

505 McLean, 92.

506 McLean, 93.

507 On eccentric dancing, see Stearns and Stearns, *Jazz Dance*, 231–238.

includes an overly cartoonish version of the collegiate shag, with dancers leaning on each other and kicking high to the side. In "Samba Sue from Paducah" from *Top Man*, Ryan starts with a parodic allusion to the "exotic" Brazilian Hollywood star Carmen Miranda. But then she goes into a particularly frantic tap dance full of hip-wiggling that has little to do with the Latin American samba and much more with the boogie and Shorty George from Harlem.

In almost all of her numbers, Ryan's dance style betrays a strong African American influence through her grounded posture, bent knees and arms, angular movements, and a strong emphasis on hip motion. In fact, Ryan herself recalled meeting Bill Robinson, who told her that she danced like a Black person, which she took as a big compliment; and African American tap dancer Jeni LeGon mentioned teaching Ryan at Universal in the 1940s.[508] Although these kinds of stories often remain anecdotal, they are revealing. The full extent of behind-the-scenes interaction between Black and White dancers in the various entertainment industries will likely never be known, but there is a good deal of evidence suggesting that it was much more substantial than would have been publicly acknowledged at the time.[509] Regardless of how directly Ryan was exposed to African American dance and dancers – the absence of any "Whitening" in her style is highly exceptional for a White dancer in 1940s Hollywood. Whether she flicks her head, twists her hips, kicks her legs, flings her arms, or wiggles her shoulders – her posture is always more angular and each of her motions always more expressive, more expansive, and more rhythmically accented than is the case with any of the other dancers in these films. While other members of the Jivin' Jacks and Jills would be spotlighted as soloists or couples but conformed to a streamlined group aesthetic in the ensemble parts, Peggy Ryan resists containment and full integration into the unified aesthetic of synchronized ensemble dancing, even when she executes the same choreography as everyone else in a group routine. In other words, Ryan's dancing – even in an all-White context – is in line with the African American principle of preserving one's individuality within a collective performance.

In his book on jazz and blues in American film, Peter Stanfield shows how numerous films of the period use signifiers of Blackness to represent a vulgar – but also vital – American vernacular culture. Black art forms and artists are often used as a source of inspiration, serving

---

508 LeGon and Smith, interview, Gray; and Ryan, quoted in Frank, *Tap!*, 209.

509 Black tap dancer Willie Covan, for example, became head dance instructor at MGM, where he coached major stars, including Eleanor Powell and Ann Miller; see Frank, *Tap!*, 23–29; and Stearns and Stearns, *Jazz Dance*, 270.

to authenticate the appropriating performer. ... Each [White] artist takes the raw material that it was their fortune to encounter and turns it into a performance that simultaneously signifies and distances itself from its site of origination. The [Black] originators provide the performers with a veneer of authenticity, which in turn is reified by the appropriating artist and transformed into a commodity.[510]

In many of the film examples described by Stanfield, the White appropriation of an originally Black culture leads to "faceless homogenization – middle-brow conformity".[511] Arguably, such conformity is present through many of the adult performers in Universal's teen films (especially the Andrews Sisters and other adult vocalists), thus evidencing Hollywood's strategy of simultaneously addressing several audience segments. But at the narrative level and in the dance numbers performed by the Jivin' Jacks and Jills, the process of inspiration, authentication, appropriation, and distancing is largely missing. Instead, swing remains "a vital and energizing American culture" that hasn't lost its authentic quality.[512] Especially in Peggy Ryan's appropriation of Black dance, there is no "refining" or "elevating". Rather, the Black vernacular dance aesthetic has been adopted wholesale – without any negative implications of vulgarity. More an embodiment than an adaptation, Ryan appropriates Black dance so fully that the Black vernacular aesthetic is undeniable in its presence but invisible *as* appropriation. At least implicitly, Ryan's dancing thus exposes essentialist ideas of the naturally rhythmic Black body as a cultural construct while presenting dance as a cultural asset available to anyone. Paradoxically, Ryan's dancing body is therefore racially marked and unmarked at the same time. Her dancing appears as a universalized expression of swing culture's pluralist and democratic spirit, not so much essentialized as a racial Other but presented as the essence of an all-American popular culture – truly vernacular but not vulgar.

Whenever more "refined" – that is, White-coded – dance styles are incorporated into Peggy Ryan's numbers, their status is quickly undermined by her mocking treatment of them. Parodic mockery merges with coolness and ease of execution. Ryan's dancing body and screen persona are unruly and uncontrollable in the sense of defying all norms of White feminine glamour and rules of propriety. At the same time, she is very much in control of herself, with her unruliness the result of a willful act, not of reckless, primitive abandon.

Peggy Ryan's duets with Donald O'Connor further destabilize normative identities, as they pick up conventions of highly gendered roles in dance, only to mock and subvert them by means of parody and slapstick. Donald O'Connor's success

---

510 Stanfield, *Body and Soul*, 30.

511 Stanfield, 40.

512 Stanfield, 40.

exceeded Ryan's, and his fame far outlasted hers.[513] While his renown has endured mostly due to his later roles, especially in *Singin' in the Rain* (1952), it was not originally based on his dance skills. Like Ryan, O'Connor was already a seasoned stage performer by the time he first went to Hollywood as a thirteen-year-old. Yet by all accounts – including his own – he was not a very sophisticated dancer when he was selected for the Jivin' Jacks and Jills at age seventeen. Born into a vaudeville family, he had tap danced onstage from his earliest childhood, picking up steps from others. But having relied on a relatively small number of simple set routines that he would repeat endlessly, he could neither keep up with the repertoire of the other dancers at Universal nor with the pace of learning new routines required by a tight shooting schedule. Choreographic choices, editing, and the common practice of postsynchronizing the tap sounds did enough to conceal his shortcomings as a dancer in the first few films.[514]

While he improved with help from tap dancers Johnny Boyle and Louis DaPron, the studio pushed O'Connor because of his comic talent and charisma, and he would become one of Universal's main moneymakers during World War II.[515] His boyish charm – provocative to adults but unthreatening to peers – made him an idol with teenage girls. Teaming him up with Peggy Ryan in scenes of comic repartee proved a winning formula, even before they were given their own song and dance numbers.[516] The fourth film in the Universal cycle, *Get Hep to Love*, was devised as a star vehicle for O'Connor, yet he had no musical numbers in it. Only with the fifth film, *Top Man*, did he start to get substantial solo turns within the Jivin' Jacks and Jills' dance numbers as well as duets with Peggy Ryan.

"All the Things I Want to Say" from *Mister Big*, for example, is a parody of a conventional romantic duet, in which O'Connor and Ryan alternate exaggerated ballroom-style lifts with slapstick, as they fall over furniture, bump into each other, and pretend to fight. They pick up the mock fighting once more in the film's later "Rude, Crude, and Unattractive" number, where the Jivin' Jacks and

513 For a short biography, see also Cullen, Hackman, and McNeilly, *Vaudeville*, 840–843.
514 Note, for instance, O'Connor's back-row positioning in the Jivin' Jacks and Jills' number in *Private Buckaroo*.
515 Johnny Boyle was an Irish American vaudevillian, employed as a teacher at Universal. O'Connor recounts how, after two weeks, Boyle sent a letter to the studio saying O'Connor was unteachable; see O'Connor, quoted in Frank, *Tap!*, 151. White tap dancer Louis DaPron was the dance director on all but the first three films of the Jivin' Jacks and Jills, and he would often dub O'Connor's tap sounds. O'Connor himself repeatedly stated that he only became a "total dancer" – that is, someone who danced with his whole body – in the 1950s, when working with Gene Kelly and Bob Alton, and he would often downplay his skill: "I guess I was never impressed with myself as a performer. That's just something that I learned when I was a child. Like breathing and eating"; O'Connor, quoted in Frank, *Tap!*, 152.
516 Ryan stated that she would have preferred to dance with Roland Dupree, who "could do it all", and that she wasn't too excited to be "stuck with Donald"; Ryan, quoted in Frank, *Tap!*, 207. O'Connor later acknowledged Ryan as his "one partner that stands out"; O'Connor, "Remembering a Hoofer".

Figure 44. Peggy Ryan and Donald O'Connor in a dance number from *Mister Big* (1943). Credit: Everett Collection.

Jills join them for a full swinging tap routine, again with a series of individual spotlights. *Mister Big* is the film to most prominently showcase Ryan and O'Connor as a dance team, both within group routines and in their own numbers (fig. 44).

"One of Us Has Gotta Go" from *When Johnny Comes Marching Home* illustrates the narrative's love triangle, with Peggy Ryan pining for O'Connor, while he is only interested in Gloria Jean (who joins the dance for a few steps before making way for the professional hoofers).[517] But the number's main function is pure performance, and it is narratively framed as such, with the kids performing it as a rehearsed act for a diegetic audience, not as a spontaneous outburst of feeling. The film's stage finale brings the trio back for "Say It with Dancing", in which Peggy employs plenty of parodic hip-wiggling and grimacing to ridicule the traditionally elegant social dance styles that Donald unsuccessfully tries to demonstrate with Gloria, who eventually again yields the stage to Donald and Peggy's tap dancing.

517 Gloria Jean recalled O'Connor teaching her some dance steps on the set; see MacGillivray and MacGillivray, *Gloria Jean*, 90–91, 132.

In "You're a Lollapalooza" from *This Is the Life*, Ryan comes at O'Connor singing "I'm not the scholarly kind of a character … I only talk vernacular", before they go into their usual slapstick-laden feigned fighting. Ryan's truly vernacular body language underlines the lyrics, which spell out the screen persona implied in most of her other numbers. A similar comic duet from *Top Man* revolves around the jazz/classical dichotomy, with Ryan referring to "the Duke" (Ellington) and "the Count" (Basie) as her heroes, whereas O'Connor parodies a classical music aficionado. Ryan calls him a square, and as the number proceeds with increasingly violent slapstick-dancing and exaggerated, cartoonish jitterbugging, the vernacular jazz aesthetic emerges as the clear winner over the uptight classics.

Of all of O'Connor and Ryan's musical numbers, only "When You Bump into Someone You Know" from *Patrick the Great* is a fairly conventional and cute boy-and-girl routine that is devoid of parody. But even here, the narrative context of repeated exhausting rehearsals eventually leads to moments of slapstick. Their next number in this film, "Don't Move", has them at a fancy reception in glittery evening gown and white tuxedo – a setting and costumes that are rather incongruous with the song's jivey lyrics and their unrestrained jazzy tap dancing.

The roles of Peggy Ryan and Donald O'Connor in these youth musicals combine the era's popular trope of capable kids solving (adult) problems with the theme of mild rebellion against that same adult world. Their characters are generally too harmless to pose a serious threat to the adult social order. Yet their strong physical presence, capability, and vitality invariably outshine their delimiting narrative roles. Through their offbeat and high-energy comedy and dance performances, they challenge codes of proper behavior, enact alternative styles of masculinity and femininity, and demonstrate physical competence (fig. 45).

Neither of the pair matched prevailing ideals of physical attractiveness. Nevertheless, Donald O'Connor originated a new type of male screen idol that was neither as glamorous nor as hypermasculine as the era's adult stars; nor was he the kind of young rebel that would come to prominence with 1950s teen film. Instead, his boyish charm and wit made him a favorite with teenage girls. By contrast, Ryan's gangly figure, expressive body language, and comic persona must have seemed incompatible with ideas of successful heterosexual romance. Her characters are usually pushed to the margins of the romantic plots – she is often a goofy loser who never gets the boy she wants. And the occasional publicity photos attempting to glamorize her are strangely at odds with her actual screen performances, which are comic rather than romantic and glamorous. Ryan and O'Connor don't replace Hollywood's conventional romantic couples as much as they complement them. Many of their films additionally feature a romance

Figure 45. A publicity photo for *Mister Big* (1943) that captures some of the energy of Peggy Ryan and Donald O'Connor's dance numbers. Credit: Mary Evans/Ronald Grant/Everett Collection.

between adults, but these storylines often appear secondary and bland in the face of the exuberant adolescent shenanigans. The one exception is *Patrick the Great*, but this first film to cast O'Connor and Ryan as the main romantic couple would also turn out to be their last as a team. In sum, O'Connor and Ryan appear as simultaneously comic and competent in Universal's teen musicals, and their dancing evokes the African American vernacular as well as the comic vaudeville tradition, which is modernized by way of the swing idiom.[518]

After Donald O'Connor was drafted into the army in 1944, Universal featured Peggy Ryan in another handful of musical comedies, including *Babes on Swing Street* (1944), *That's the Spirit* (1945), and *On Stage Everybody* (1945). These

---

518 Though maybe not a direct or conscious influence, the Black tradition of derision dances provides additional background against which to read many of these performances. The cakewalk is the most famous – and probably the earliest – example in the long tradition of subversive Black performance, which hides powerful critiques of Whites in seemingly harmless clowning. See, for instance, Malone, *Steppin' on the Blues*, 18; and Stearns and Stearns, *Jazz Dance*, 22–23.

movies reuse the narrative formula of "showbiz success through youthful innovation", though only *Babes on Swing Street* actually focuses on youth culture. At the same time, these films appear to be attempts to "normalize" Ryan's screen image somewhat by giving a little more weight to her romantic endeavors and by partly removing the comic subversiveness from her dance numbers. Ryan left Universal in 1945 but would sporadically return to films, and later also television, throughout the 1950s and 1960s.[519]

World War II and Traces of Racial Integration

At a time when swing was already established as a mainstream phenomenon and the most successful White bands, such as Glenn Miller's, had more or less erased the Black roots from their streamlined version of swing, the Jivin' Jacks and Jills incorporated authentic Black vernacular dance into their portrayals of swing's youth culture. This is not to be naïve and claim any sort of intentionally progressive stance for Universal's low-budget musicals. The marginalization of African Americans is no less a fact in these films than in any other Hollywood production of the period. Despite the centrality of Black-based cultural forms, many of the teen musicals have an all-White cast, while only a handful feature Black performers in a specialty act. Unacknowledged White appropriations of Black music and dance alternate with more explicit references, as in the "Amen" number from *What's Cookin'*. Led by the Andrews Sisters, the ensemble sings the song sitting in a circle before everybody gets up and starts dancing. The dance is full of elements taken from Black vernacular culture: hand clapping, fish tails (a move that involves bending sideways and back into an asymmetrical crouching pose) and other jazz steps that emphasize hip movement and low, grounded posture, and the circle formation moving counterclockwise that is reminiscent of the big apple (which in turn probably goes back to the Black Southern tradition of the ring shout).[520] In many ways a typical instance of "love and theft", this number highlights its African American roots as much as it obliterates them by excluding actual Black performers. The song, written for the film by Vic Schoen, evokes clichés of a rural and religious Southern Black musicality through the spiritual-like lyrics about "way down South" where people "feel the spirit". At the same time, the number incorporates the dance fads of a modern, urban, and increasingly interracial swing culture.

---

519 In later years, she taught tap dance and led a group of female dancers in Las Vegas; see Cullen, Hackman, and McNeilly, *Vaudeville*, 985.

520 For the history of the big apple, see Manning and Millman, *Frankie Manning*, 142–152; and the documentary *Dancing the Big Apple 1937: African Americans Inspire a National Craze*, directed by Judy Pritchett, 2010.

Yet only occasionally would the interracial cosmopolitanism of the urban jazz scene find more direct expression in mainstream feature films, and it is no coincidence that the most progressive representations of Black people and Black culture in Universal's teen musicals appear in the films with a war-related story. In *When Johnny Comes Marching Home*, two numbers feature the Four Step Brothers, a Black tap group, dancing to Phil Spitalny's all-female orchestra.[521] While one of the male characters expresses surprise at the presence of the White female musicians, nobody comments on the fact that they accompany a group of Black male dancers. The Step Brothers' dynamic tap routine, with its combination of acrobatics and strong rhythmic components, is a true class act. Performing in top hats, tailcoats, and with canes, the dancers are hardly in need of the "refinement" provided by the excessive mise-en-scène, which has about two dozen female musicians positioned on an oversized stage, many of them playing shiny white instruments, including numerous violins and harps. During the film's finale, the Four Step Brothers return in a similarly opulent setting, again with the girl orchestra, but this time they dance in uniforms, signaling their integration into the unifying patriotic project of World War II.

Top Man, which also uses the war as a backdrop to a formulaic story centering on young love and mild generational conflict, employs a similar strategy of racial integration for Count Basie. The Black pianist-bandleader is first introduced only by his name as one of the selections in a jukebox before appearing in person in a later scene. Significantly, the jukebox lists his "Swinging the Blues" between songs by the Andrews Sisters and Glenn Miller, two of the nation's most successful wartime musical acts, which came to be seen as virtually synonymous with American popular music. When Basie later performs at the teenagers' war benefit show, he is the main attraction: the kids say that they want something "extra special", and label him a "professional", someone who will upgrade their own putatively "amateur" performances. During the band's "Basie Boogie", the White youngsters in the audience can barely contain themselves and finally jump off their seats to start dancing. While young White people did dance to Black bands in real life, especially in the big cities, Hollywood films were reluctant to show this type of interaction between the races. In this scene of Black and White copresence, Black music no longer needs to be "lifted" from its primitive origins and "refined" by Whites. On the contrary, it is the presence of the Black band that upgrades the performance in terms of professionalism and sophistication – as well as in terms of market value. Basie represents the pinnacle of swing culture here, and his music functions as a direct source of energy for America's dancing

---

521 On Phil Spitalny's Hour of Charm Orchestra, one of the most popular all-female bands of the 1930s and 1940s, see McGee, *Some Liked It Hot*, 67–85, 171–179.

Chapter 6 "A Savage Exhibition"? Swing and White Youth Culture in B Movies

youth, who – no longer passive consumers of an exoticized commodity – actively participate in creating an all-American popular culture.

Pluralistic and homogenizing tendencies compete in these kinds of depictions of American culture, in which diversity is acknowledged but also assimilated into the melting pot.[522] Comparatively untainted by racism, the portrayal of African Americans in these films needs to be seen in the context of World War II: the war against fascism in Europe called attention to America's own racial inequalities, and civil rights groups increasingly focused on racial integration and demanded equal rights. The wartime economy gave minority groups access to jobs previously denied to them, and with the government's efforts to promote Black enlistment in the armed forces came a growing pressure to acknowledge the contributions of Black servicemen.[523] These historical events had consequences in the film industry, most notably the agreement between the NAACP and some studio heads about presenting more respectable images of African Americans.[524] During the war years, the narratively nonintegrated musical in particular became a privileged arena for moves towards racial integration, however tentative. Performances like those of Count Basie or the Four Step Brothers thus mark significant moments in this period of transition regarding the cinematic representation of African Americans.

Overall, of course, the representation and White appropriation of Black culture in the films of the Jivin' Jacks and Jills remains in line with the film industry's general tendencies. With Black performers largely absent or marginalized as specialty acts, White dominance is hardly questioned. Nevertheless, unlike in Hollywood's many "White man makes Black jazz respectable" stories, the films' wholehearted embrace of a youthful vernacular swing culture ridicules high culture as well as normative ideas of White respectability. Many performances are coded as subversive and irreverent, youthful and dynamic. Their aesthetics are simultaneously individualistic, collaborative, and participatory. In sum, the Jivin' Jacks and Jills in general – and Peggy Ryan in particular – are perhaps the closest that White dancers in studio-era Hollywood ever came to embodying a Black vernacular aesthetic, and they did it with an emphasis on physical expression that is largely nonsexual and removed from associations with the primitive.

---

522 On similarly contradictory representations in Soundies, see also Kelley, *Soundies Jukebox Films*, 90–92.
523 See, for instance, Griffin, "The Gang's All Here", 27. 20th Century-Fox's all-Black musical *Stormy Weather* (1943), the first Hollywood feature film to explicitly celebrate the achievements of African Americans, has often been interpreted in this way, as a propagandistic effort to promote African American enlistment. See, for instance, Massood, *Black City Cinema*, 42; Knapp, *The American Musical*, 82; and Knight, *Disintegrating the Musical*, 157–158.
524 See Bogle, *Bright Boulevards*, 211–212; and Cripps, *Slow Fade to Black*, 3, 373–389.

Youth Culture, the Vaudeville Aesthetic, and the Adolescent Audience

Building upon genre theorist Rick Altman's well-known "semantic/syntactic/pragmatic approach to genre",[525] Amanda Ann Klein argues that

> while film genres are primarily defined by the repetition of key images (their semantics) and themes (their syntax), film cycles are primarily defined by how they are used (their pragmatics). ...
>
> Cycle studies's focus on cinema's use value – the way that filmmakers, audiences, film reviewers, advertisements, and cultural discourses interact with and affect the film text – offers a more pragmatic, localized approached to genre history.[526]

Presenting images of youth culture in flimsy backstage narratives, the teen swing musicals' repetitive semantics and syntax certainly make them recognizable as a group of similar films. But it is indeed their use – the way they targeted and appealed to a young audience – that defines them as a cycle. Thus, it is instructive to look at how the films' key images and performance styles, on the one hand, and the reduced importance of a coherent narrative ideology, on the other, interact with the contemporaneous public discourses surrounding the films. Notably, discourses of promotion and reception evidence a much stronger focus on swing-era performance practices, and especially on the jitterbugs portrayed in and addressed by the films, than on story content.

In a study of film representations of female adolescence, Georganne Scheiner identifies the musical as the key genre for portraying teenagers in the late 1930s and early 1940s. Young girls were idealized as highly competent beings capable of solving everybody's problems. These ambitious and successful teenagers became personified in Deanna Durbin and Judy Garland, the era's major female adolescent screen presences, while *Babes in Arms* (1939), starring Mickey Rooney and Judy Garland, is credited with establishing the new formula of the youth musical. Scheiner observes a trend towards a "kind of role reversal between parents and children", as in *Babes in Arms*, where "Patsy's and Mickey's youthful optimism is in sharp contrast to their parents' pessimism and discouragement".[527]

Universal's teen musicals with the Jivin' Jacks and Jills have repeatedly been regarded as the smaller studio's answer to MGM's Rooney-Garland vehicles.[528] However, Universal's take on the "kids putting on a show" formula should not

---

525 Altman, *Film/Genre*, 207–215.
526 Klein, *American Film Cycles*, 4–5.
527 Scheiner, *Signifying Female Adolescence*, 78–79.
528 See Hirschhorn, *The Universal Story*, 98; and Scheerer, "Hollywood to Broadway", 22.

Chapter 6 "A Savage Exhibition"? Swing and White Youth Culture in B Movies

be reduced to a mere low-budget imitation of MGM's more polished productions. Rather, it is instructive to look at the differences between these groups of films. First, the focus in Universal's cycle is less on kids solving adult problems (though there are elements of that theme) and more on asserting their own cultural identity, as the films portray an increasingly independent youth culture, albeit one that sometimes needs to be acknowledged by the adult world. Narrative conflicts between generations do reflect real-life debates and actual concerns of parents, educators, and social critics, who feared the negative influences that the mass media in general and jazz/swing culture in particular might have on the young. Yet in their screen versions, these confrontations remain extremely mild, thus both attenuating and legitimizing the swing kids' rebellious behavior. Despite their youthful disobedience, the adolescents are invariably depicted as harmless boys and girls next door.[529]

Another difference concerns the relative importance of narrative in comparison with other elements. Not only do narrative conflicts remain very moderate, more importantly, narrative *overall* is secondary to musical, physical, and comic performance. In many ways, the heterogeneous entertainment offerings in these only partly coherent musicals follow in the footsteps of the vaudeville aesthetic, to which many films, from the early sound era well into the 1940s, are indebted. Henry Jenkins sees the vaudeville tradition and the narrative cinema of classical Hollywood as two competing aesthetic systems, with the former emphasizing "fragmentation and intensification over more classical concerns of character consistency, thematic ambitiousness, or narrative coherence".[530] According to Jenkins, early 1930s anarchistic comedy testifies to the negotiation between these two systems, and Hollywood comedy in general was assimilated into the classical mode of storytelling by the end of the 1930s. Musicals, however, often retained a good deal of vaudeville's focus on "performance, affective immediacy, and atomistic spectacle" over concerns of "character consistency, causal logic, and narrative coherence".[531] Genre criticism's frequent emphasis on the integrated film musical should not obscure the fact that less coherent "aggregate" manifestations of the genre were equally common, at least until the end of World War II.[532] The subgenre of the revue musical was popular throughout the 1930s and

---

529 With respect to the 1950s cycle of juvenile delinquent/rock 'n' roll teen films, Klein notes various strategies to narratively contain the delinquent teenagers. One common pattern is to show their deviant behavior to be innocent and harmless after all; see *American Film Cycles*, 129.
530 Jenkins, "Anarchistic Comedy", 94.
531 Jenkins, 92.
532 See, for instance, Griffin, "The Gang's All Here", 29.

1940s, spawning numerous productions in which the subordination of narrative to performance is easily recognized as an intentional strategy.[533]

With shorter and cheaper (B) films like Universal's teen musicals, the intentions are usually less clear. In general, these films seem to testify to the same kind of wavering negotiation between narrative and performance that Jenkins attributes to early sound comedy. Heterosexual romance – often considered the musical's narrative mainstay[534] – is usually secondary to the showbiz plots. It either appears as a perfunctory subplot or as a mere pretext for highly energetic and often comic – but mostly desexualized – numbers, which do little to develop the characters' relationships or resolve conflict. Overall, the threadbare stories provide flimsy excuses for music and dance performances. The films could thus easily be seen as failed attempts at integrating narrative and numbers, and one could argue that the failure is attributable to the comparatively cheap and quick production processes. For the most part, the teen musicals also lack the lavish spectacles and glamorized star images of the major studios' A-level productions. Opulent settings and extravagant costumes are rare, and with a few exceptions, the mise-en-scène and cinematography remain relatively simple, with many static shots and low cutting rates. Even such comparatively elaborate production numbers as the finale of *What's Cookin'* don't compare with the excessive mise-en-scène and overly polished quality of, for instance, the patriotic finale in MGM's Rooney-Garland vehicle *Strike Up the Band* (1940).[535]

However, neither the reduced narratives nor the comparatively low production values should be considered exclusively in terms of a deficiency (even if they were largely due to budget constraints). Rather, the relative simplicity allows for an emphasis on the expressivity and virtuosity of musical and physical performance itself.[536] Heterogeneous concoctions of music, dance, and (often physical)

---

533 Examples of this include the loose series of Republic's *Hit Parade* musicals (1937, 1941, 1943, and 1947) and Paramount's *Big Broadcast* films (1932, 1936, 1937, and 1938). Even MGM, frequently associated with the integrated musical, produced some notable revue musicals, among them *Ziegfeld Follies* (1945) and *Till the Clouds Roll By* (1946). For an analysis of race, ethnicity, and class in a number of wartime revue musicals, see Cohan, "Star Spangled Shows".

534 See Altman, *The American Film Musical*, 16–27. It is probably no coincidence that the Jivin' Jacks and Jills' only film that centers on a classic dual-focus romance is *Moonlight in Havana*, the only one in the series that accords no significance to either swing or youth culture. It is also the only film with a reduced constellation of only six dancers (without Peggy Ryan and Donald O'Connor), who perform two specialty numbers. None of the dancers has a role in the story, which instead centers on the careers of singers of sweet music, played by Allan Jones and Jane Frazee. The central narrative conflict concerns Jones's career choice between sports and show business. *Moonlight in Vermont* (1943) also features a version of the Jivin' Jacks and Jills without Peggy Ryan and Donald O'Connor. Despite its college setting, this movie also largely bypasses swing culture.

535 Several of MGM's most elaborate youth musicals with Mickey Rooney and Judy Garland were directed and choreographed by Busby Berkeley.

536 Jenkins also points out that the simplicity of the mise-en-scène in vaudeville was as much the result of economic conditions as of purely aesthetic considerations; see "Anarchistic Comedy", 103n21.

Chapter 6 "A Savage Exhibition"? Swing and White Youth Culture in B Movies

comedy, the films pay much less attention to delivering a message than to showcasing the charisma and technical skill of their performers. Sean Griffin sums up the often expressed view that "as a result of the alternative space created by the numbers, musicals have the potential to resist the ideological imperatives of traditional Hollywood narrative".[537] If, as Griffin argues, this applies especially to nonintegrated musicals, then it is even truer in cases where the traditional narrative is itself reduced to a minimum. In the teen musicals, the feeble attempts to integrate musical performances and narrative inconsistencies fail to contain the numbers' questioning of generational, cultural, gender, and class hierarchies. With their reduced, aggregate, and sometimes barely coherent form, these films' relationship to the Hollywood musical's oft assumed conservative ideology is one of allusion more than of strict adherence. Many of these movies appear as if their romantic plots and their messages about traditional family values or national unity were pasted over the variety entertainment as an afterthought. Their loose structures make the films especially susceptible to divergent readings and appropriations, and discourses surrounding the films indicate that neither the industry nor the audience focused on conservative narrative ideologies.

Kelly Schrum observes a discrepancy between how teenagers were represented onscreen in the 1930s and 1940s versus what types of characters and stars actual teenagers wanted to see. She finds that girls mostly strove to emulate romantic beauties, whereas high school characters like Judy Garland and Deanna Durbin were admired for their singing talents but didn't inspire imitation.[538] It is easy to see why this would hold true for such idealized and family-oriented depictions of teenage life as, for instance, in MGM's *Love Finds Andy Hardy* (1938) and its sequels, or the Rooney-Garland youth musicals directed by Busby Berkeley. These were polished productions, steeped in conservative family ideology and offering highly idealized visions of (White) small-town American life in classically structured narratives. The nostalgia, patriotism, and life lessons were carefully scripted and integrated with the musical numbers and showbiz plots rather than pasted on as an afterthought, as appeared to be the case with Universal's teen films. For all their undeniable talent and charisma, Mickey Rooney and Judy Garland didn't appear hip like the Jivin' Jacks and Jills did. Thus, for teen audiences, the elaborate Busby Berkeley numbers or Judy's torch songs might not have compensated for the absence of real swing bands and dancers. In the Universal movies, by contrast, the strong presence of a trendy youth culture, embodied by swing music and dance, provided adolescents with images of youth

---

537 Griffin, "The Gang's All Here", 31.
538 See Schrum, *Some Wore Bobby Sox*, 137, 146, 163.

231

that they could identify with. What's more, the lower status of the films and their stars might, in some sense, even have contributed to their appeal to youngsters. Peggy Ryan, Donald O'Connor, and singer Gloria Jean have all pointed out that they did not make a lot of money during their teen years at Universal but that they were simply excited to have work.[539] Although their films were popular and their names familiar to many moviegoers, they were not superstars in the league of a Mickey Rooney or Judy Garland. Neither MGM's nor Universal's teen movies were rags-to-riches narratives, and the showbiz success of the youthful characters always remained tied to a middle-class community. But in the Rooney-Garland vehicles, the discrepancy between the idealized normalcy onscreen and the actors' superstardom was quite obvious. Perhaps O'Connor and Ryan's boy-and-girl-next-door image appeared to have more of a basis in reality and thus seemed to more credibly mirror the lives and concerns of real-life teens.

Beyond representational and aesthetic concerns, the films' promotion and reception shed light on the connections between cinema, swing culture, and their respective youthful audiences. Producers, exhibitors, and the press clearly expected young audiences to respond favorably to these films, and evidence suggests that these expectations were often met. Film titles, taglines, and publicity materials offer insight into how the studio addressed young moviegoers and their predilection for all things swing – for instance, by referring to teenagers or by emulating the slang of jazz culture. Titles like *What's Cookin'* and *Get Hep to Love* suggest a specific target audience by pointing to the relevance of slang to swing and youth culture, more than they tell us anything about narrative content. Similarly, dialogue containing slang and jokes about adults misunderstanding the juvenile language are clearly geared to those who know "what's cookin'" (for instance in *Patrick the Great*, where the father of O'Connor's character is very confused by the youngsters' jive talk).

What's Cookin' was originally titled *Wake Up and Dream* and received its new title toward the end of production "to appeal to high-school hepcats".[540] The tagline for the film left little doubt about the kinds of attractions offered, promising "It's A Swingeroo... Rootin', zootin' swing-stars... 'teen-stars... hot licks and hep-cats!"[541] Similarly, taglines for *Private Buckaroo* proclaimed: "It Jumps! It Jives! It rocks with red hot rhythm!" and "Yeah Man! ... Even the Jeeps

---

539 According to MacGillivray and MacGillivray (*Gloria Jean*, 129), Donald O'Connor was paid $250 a week around 1943. Peggy Ryan estimated that by the time O'Connor was drafted, he worked for around $600 a week, whereas she received $325 per week; see Ryan, quoted in Frank, *Tap!*, 210.
540 MacGillivray and MacGillivray, *Gloria Jean*, 78.
541 "What's Cookin' (1942)", IMDb, https://www.imdb.com/title/tt0035548/.

are Jivin'!"[542] *Get Hep to Love* was announced as a "Spontaneous Combustion of Juvenile Jive!"[543] – even though the musical numbers are relatively sparse here, and the movie has a more substantial (though highly implausible) plot than most of the other teen films. But as much as the narrative's focus on family values and romance implies a generalized family audience, the publicity targeted a young audience of swing fans, emphasizing the qualities embodied by Donald O'Connor's youthful personality and the swinging dance number featuring Peggy Ryan and the Jivin' Jacks and Jills. Posters for the teen films were often populated with several jitterbugging couples. A poster for *Get Hep to Love*, for example, shows four dancing couples, including O'Connor and Gloria Jean, three of them in jitterbug poses. Adult actors Jane Frazee and Robert Paige are also depicted in a (somewhat awkward) dance pose, even though they never actually dance in the film.[544] According to Gloria Jean's biographers, the film's trailer suggested that one "Get Hep to Love … The Jitterbug Way!"[545]

Allegedly filmed in only eight days, *Mister Big* went into production as *Oh, Say, Can You Swing?* It was finished as *You Can't Ration Love* and then retitled *School for Jive* while awaiting release.[546] Initially stressing swing culture as well as patriotism as the film's main selling points, the studio eventually renamed it *Mister Big* after enthusiastic reactions to Donald O'Connor's performance at previews.[547] He received star billing on posters, but visually he shared the top spot with Peggy Ryan, who was depicted as his equal and dance partner, whereas singing costar Gloria Jean was set apart from the two and figured less prominently in the bottom right corner. The original emphasis on the jive theme was additionally illustrated with two more dancing couples (fig. 46).

Both verbally and visually, the publicity for Universal's teen musicals stressed rhythm and jive, youth and hepness, and the performers who embodied these qualities. Dance featured prominently on the movie posters, in some cases disproportionately to its actual presence in the films. By comparison, little to no attention was devoted to the films' story content. These advertising strategies are quite similar to those that Amanda Ann Klein observes with respect to the 1950s

542 "Private Buckaroo (1942) – Taglines", IMDb, https://www.imdb.com/title/tt0035218/taglines.
543 "Get Hep to Love (1942)", IMDb, https://www.imdb.com/title/tt0034784/.
544 See "Get Hep to Love (1942) – Photo Gallery", IMDb, https://www.imdb.com/title/tt0034784/mediaviewer/rm3327403520.
545 Trailer for *Get Hep to Love*, quoted in MacGillivray and MacGillivray, *Gloria Jean*, 86.
546 On the film's production history, see also MacGillivray and MacGillivray, 129–136.
547 See "Of Local Origin", News of the Screen, *New York Times*, April 20, 1943, TimesMachine; "Mr. Big Himself: Being a Brief Biographical Note about Young Donald O'Connor", *New York Times*, June 13, 1943, TimesMachine; and L. B. F., "At the Globe", review of *Mister Big*, The Screen in Review, *New York Times*, June 14, 1943, TimesMachine.

Figure 46. A poster for *Mister Big* (1943) showing Peggy Ryan and Donald O'Connor in a dance pose, with two additional jitterbugging couples at the bottom. Singing costar Gloria Jean is in the bottom right corner. Credit: Everett Collection.

cycle of rock 'n' roll teen pics, which emphasize the films' musical acts rather than the story or director, aiming to appeal to teenage subcultural tastes.

Film historian Stephen Lowry's approach to historical reception studies offers a useful framework for considering the issue of audience reactions. In an essay on popular film culture during Germany's Third Reich, Lowry contests one-dimensional interpretations of Nazi cinema that attend only to its propagandistic aspects, instead arguing for a more popular culture-oriented approach:

> It remains difficult to judge which elements the audience responded to and how. Narrative structures like closure show the work of ideology in the text and pre-structure the pragmatics of how the audience should understand them. But did they follow such paths? How did various moviegoers interpret movies, and which criteria and values were involved? What if it was not the "message" that interested them at all, but the look, the fashions, the way the star moves and talks? …
>
> Nonverbal communication … can embody lifestyles and represent collective identity, thus forming patterns of sentiment invoked by movies below the level of plot and theme.[548]

548 Lowry, "Movie Reception", 216, 219.

Chapter 6 "A Savage Exhibition"? Swing and White Youth Culture in B Movies

It's not hard to see how the same claim can be made for the American teen musicals of the 1940s. Here too, it remains hard to judge exactly how audiences reacted to particular elements of the films. But an examination of public discourses circulating around the films helps to "reconstruct the interpretive strategies available to the films' original viewers"[549] as well as revealing at least some of the possible reactions. The promotional materials cited above indicate that Universal Studios' strategy was indeed to address lifestyle desires and sensibilities more than to convey a coherent narrative ideology or message. And what is known about the films' reception by the press and the audience suggests that young audiences did respond to these elements, showing more interest in the films' popular culture styles than in their narrative messages.

Attention from the general press was relatively scant, and not even the *New York Times*, which generally attempted to cover every title currently in release, reviewed all of Universal's low-budget musicals. When it did, the reviews were relatively brief and often negative, as illustrated by this colorful assessment of *What's Cookin'*, which is worth quoting in full:

> "What's Cookin'", at Loew's Criterion, is a highly incidental dish of nonsense knocked together by Universal out of a little bit of this (the Andrews Sisters) and a little bit of that (Gloria Jean), all oozing with jam provided by Woody Herman's orchestra and a gang of rug-cutting kids. Cinematically speaking, it's as dull as a plate of stale hash and has no more form or consistency than a bowl of jelly dropped upon the floor. But for youths and their more supple elders who have acquired a taste for jive, it contains (if one may judge by the audience) a few rather juicy plums. One is a musical mélange entitled, appropriately, "Amen!" and another is an unidentified gentleman who beats the drums in Mr. Herman's band. Folks who watch their motion-picture diet are cautioned to beware, however. "What's Cookin'" will sit best on young stomachs – young alligators' stomachs, preferably.[550]

Critic Bosley Crowther's reputation for crushing reviews notwithstanding, this example is fairly representative of the whole cycle's reception in the so-called quality press. The lack of narrative substance and coherence is usually criticized. Sometimes, musical performances are mentioned favorably, but as a review of *When Johnny Comes Marching Home* puts it, "there's a limit to this sort of thing".[551] At least as significant as the value judgment above, however, is Crowther's awareness of the film's appeal to a specific audience segment. Adolescent swing fans may or may not have danced in the aisles during movie screenings, as they reportedly did during Benny Goodman's Paramount concert. But such

---

549 Klein, *American Film Cycles*, 74. See also Staiger, *Perverse Spectators*.
550 Bosley Crowther, "Musical Hash", review of *What's Cookin'*, The Screen, *New York Times*, February 26, 1942, TimesMachine.
551 T. M. P., "At the Palace", review of *When Johnny Comes Marching Home*, *New York Times*, March 5, 1943, TimesMachine.

reports hinting at enthusiastic reactions suggest that for "youths" and those with "a taste for jive", the "juicy" swing performances outweigh whatever the films' other (perceived) shortcomings might be.[552]

As Henry Jenkins points out with regard to early Hollywood sound comedy, the vocabulary used in reviews reflects the fragmentation, heterogeneity, and disunity of the vaudeville aesthetic by characterizing the narratives in terms such as "flimsy", "incidental", "shapeless", or "just thrown together".[553] It is hardly surprising, then, that the criticism leveled at Universal's teen musicals echoes the language of those earlier reviews of comedies. *Chip Off the Old Block*, for instance, was described as "hackneyed, disjointed and thin",[554] and *Patrick the Great* as "another tattered Universal story of showfolks".[555] As with the comedies examined by Jenkins, the Universal films' reception in the established press reflects a bourgeois bias against a heterogeneous vaudevillian aesthetic that is based on performance rather than on conveying a coherent message. That small-town local papers were generally more lenient further points to a discrepancy between popular and elite reception (although this might also have to do with economic imperatives to support local movie theaters). But even in the *New York Times*, there are exceptions of reviews that focus more on the charisma of the performers and their appeal to a young audience than on story content. A review of *Mister Big* forgives the film for its "somewhat frayed" book, conceding that it serves its purpose as "a vehicle that permits the widest latitude for an abundance of jive and rug-cutting, plus sundry other adolescent shenanigans".[556]

Reviews in the trade magazine *Variety* go back and forth between narrative-focused and performance-focused appraisals. Often, disappointed expectations of coherent and convincing narratives inform the negative verdicts, but critics nevertheless acknowledge the performers' skills and the films' appeal to an adolescent audience. A rather devastating review of *Always a Bridesmaid,* for example, expects the film to "appeal to 'teen-age jitterbugs as a supporting feature" while also deploring that the far-fetched story "is lost in the desire to go on with

---

552 Given the custom of segregated film exhibition and the mainstream film industry's general lack of interest in Black audiences, it seems safe to assume that references to audience reactions in the White press concern White audiences, who must have made up the overwhelming majority in mainstream theaters. Whether or not Universal's B musicals made it into Black neighborhood theaters, the Black press only took note of them insofar as they featured Black specialty performers, as was the case with *Mister Big* and *When Johnny Comes Marching Home*.

553 See Jenkins, "Anarchistic Comedy", 99.

554 Bosley Crowther, "Chop, Chop, Chop", review of *Chip Off the Old Block*, The Screen, *New York Times*, March 17, 1944, TimesMachine.

555 T. M. P., "At Loew's State", review of *Patrick the Great*, The Screen, *New York Times*, April 13, 1945, TimesMachine.

556 L. B. F., "At the Globe", review of *Mister Big*, The Screen in Review, *New York Times*, June 14, 1943, TimesMachine.

Chapter 6 "A Savage Exhibition"? Swing and White Youth Culture in B Movies

the singing and jitterbug dancing of the Jivin' Jacks and Jills" whose presence, according to the reviewer, "still remains a mystery although admittedly a capable jitterbug dancing combo".[557] In *Private Buckaroo*, by contrast, "despite total lack of plot structure, 12 musical numbers are spotted along the route of sufficient merit in both rendition and setup to make this one a strong filmmusical programmer".[558] *When Johnny Comes Marching Home* is similarly found to contain "all ingredients necessary for wide audience entertainment".[559] *What's Cookin'* is assumed to be "a strong supporter for the duals and is slated for special attention from youthful swingsters", with the Jivin' Jacks and Jills as a "special attraction for the rug-cutters" – yet another assessment that shows awareness of teenage tastes.[560] A review of *Mister Big* praises the talents and "juvenile spontaneity" of Donald O'Connor and Peggy Ryan, but the author also complains about "too much ensemble dancing by the jitterbug background", thus partly missing the film's point.[561] O'Connor and Ryan are commended repeatedly for their personalities and performances: they "team for wow comedy song-and-dance delivery … while the girl also smacks over a solo appearance for song and knockabout dance" in *Top Man*.[562] Ryan "scores with a neat eccentric dance and a comedy delivery of a tune" in *Get Hep to Love*[563] and "effectively handles novelty 'Gremlin Walk' alone" in *This Is the Life*.[564] O'Connor is called a "fast-rising juvenile film personality" in reference to *Chip Off the Old Block*.[565]

Overall, promotional materials and reviews show that producers, exhibitors, and critics had certain expectations about how young people would respond to specific aspects of these films. In accordance with *Variety*'s predictions, theaters around the country reported favorable reactions of high-school-age audiences.[566] The *New York Times* noted O'Connor's popularity with hip youngsters in its review of *Mister Big*: "as for the junior hepcats of this town, to judge by the reception they accorded him, he is 'solid'".[567]

---

557 Review of *Always a Bridesmaid*, *Variety*, September 29, 1943, 8, Media History Digital Library.
558 Review of *Private Buckaroo*, *Variety*, June 3, 1942, 8, Media History Digital Library.
559 Review of *When Johnny Comes Marching Home*, *Variety*, December 23, 1942, 8, Media History Digital Library.
560 Review of *What's Cookin'*, *Variety*, February 25, 1942, 8, Media History Digital Library.
561 Review of *Mister Big*, *Variety*, May 26, 1943, 8, Media History Digital Library.
562 Review of *Top Man*, *Variety*, September 15, 1943, 10, Media History Digital Library.
563 Review of *Get Hep to Love*, *Variety*, September 30, 1942, 8, Media History Digital Library.
564 Review of *This Is the Life*, *Variety*, May 3, 1944, 23, Media History Digital Library.
565 Review of *Chip Off the Old Block*, *Variety*, February 16, 1944, 10, Media History Digital Library.
566 See, for instance, MacGillivray and MacGillivray, *Gloria Jean*, 86, 135.
567 L. B. F., "At the Globe", review of *Mister Big*, The Screen in Review, *New York Times*, June 14, 1943, TimesMachine.

Jumping the Color Line: Vernacular Jazz Dance in American Film, 1929–1945

In the 1930s and 1940s, Hollywood became increasingly interested in the composition and tastes of its audience. Yet overall, the industry still produced for a broad, intergenerational audience. The general strategy was to reach various segments of the population by catering to diverse tastes simultaneously, whether by way of a double bill marketed as a "balanced program", or by implying that one film offered "everything".[568] Universal's musicals were no exception in this respect. Just like vaudeville or certain forms of comedy, they featured a plethora of heterogeneous material – a little bit of this and a little bit of that, as deplored by Bosley Crowther in the *Times* review quoted earlier – in order to attract a heterogeneous audience. But for all the variety of performance idioms found in these films, modern swing repeatedly emerged triumphant as the most dynamic and quintessentially American cultural form.

Despite the film industry's general "reluctance to abandon the concept of the universal, undifferentiated audience",[569] the discourses in and around these musicals reveal a growing awareness of the youth market's importance, with swing culture's drawing power for its adolescent fans causing Hollywood to tentatively target teens. The films' content, publicity, and reception thus foreshadow the film industry's later exploitation of a separate teen market – a trend often said to have originated in the 1950s.[570] While it is true that teen films were not produced, marketed, and received as their own category until after World War II, Universal's teen musicals of the early 1940s evidence the earlier beginnings of this trend. Just as Amanda Ann Klein claims for the rock 'n' roll teen pics of the 1950s, the teen swing musicals' "use of supposedly up-to-date lingo, music, and dance steps" functions to provide "hip teens with a mirror of their contemporary activities".[571]

Swing had become a mainstream phenomenon by the 1940s and was put in the service of defending American values during World War II. Nevertheless, both music and dance continued to engender lively debates around swing's allegedly detrimental influence on youth as well as much controversy regarding racial integration/segregation. Swing's subversive powers certainly waned in the course of its increasing mainstreaming by White superstars like Glenn Miller or the Andrews Sisters and as it was used for patriotic propaganda. Hollywood's

---

568 Rick Altman shows how studio-era publicity rarely employed generic terms directly. Instead, multiple genres would be evoked indirectly, implying that a film offered everything – that is, a variety of attractions for diverse demographic groups. See *Film/Genre*, 54–58.

569 Stanfield, *Body and Soul*, 180.

570 On the newly emerging concept of the teenager after World War II, see, for instance, Klein, *American Film Cycles*, 102–109. Klein gives a concise overview of how Hollywood (among other industries) discovered teens as an important market demographic and began to target them with specific films in the 1950s. For a historical overview of B/low-budget/exploitation filmmaking, see also McCarthy and Flynn, *Kings of the Bs*.

571 Klein, *American Film Cycles*, 123.

Chapter 6 "A Savage Exhibition"? Swing and White Youth Culture in B Movies

idealized, watered-down representation of the multiple tensions swing culture entailed – class, racial, gender, and generational – is hardly a reflection of reality. There was and is actually very little that is controversial or provocative about these teen films, especially at the narrative level. Their plots are mostly innocuous, and the swing kids' rebellion is alleviated through the caricatures of their opponents, who appear in the shape of stuffy old aunts. Whatever appeared "savage" or "primitive" to skeptical observers of the nation's juvenile jitterbug craze was more than sufficiently moderated here to make the teen musicals fit for family entertainment. And what negative reactions there were to these films were characterized by disdain for their shallowness and imperfection more than by the moral outrage that teenage behavior at live concerts and dance events sometimes provoked. Once again, what is true of the 1950s rock 'n' roll teen pics also applies to the teen swing movies of the 1940s: "dominant culture, represented in this case by film studios, must defuse or deradicalize certain aspects of a subculture in order to ensure that its product is marketable to a more general audience".[572]

Nevertheless, these cinematic representations of swing and its youth culture are significant for at least two reasons: One, the aesthetics and identities embodied in the music and dance numbers often lie outside of the era's dominant Hollywood representations, especially with regard to race and gender. Two, the discourses of promotion and reception reveal connections between the film industry and its predominantly young (White) audience that prefigure the later tendency towards product differentiation in the course of American cinema's increasing juvenilization.[573]

Hollywood Swing as Marginal Mainstream

Swing's enormous popularity could not have gone unnoticed by the film industry. Yet paradoxically, swing in Hollywood became as ubiquitous as it remained marginal. This is especially true with regard to swing dancing, which was mostly relegated to the ghetto of the Black specialty act or the B film's relatively low cultural status. That this strangely marginal but frequent presence in Hollywood films had something to do with the larger swing culture's desegregationist tendencies and the (perceived) rebelliousness of the "savage" young swing fans is at least a compelling hypothesis.

Feature films of various genres occasionally employed swing dancing as a signifier of mass culture and the lower classes. In the romantic comedy *Bachelor Mother* (1939), unemployed Polly (Ginger Rogers) wins a dance contest – much to her

---

572 Klein, *American Film Cycles*, 106.
573 See Stanfield, *Body and Soul*, 180.

dismay, as she ends up with a useless trophy instead of the much-needed fifty-dollar cash prize for second place. Referencing the popularity of cash-prize amateur dance contests and marathons, the comedy frames dance as a survival technique for the Depression-plagued working classes. In another romantic comedy, *Rings on Her Fingers* (1942), a short jitterbug scene is set in a disreputable gambling club, again with the attendant implications of low class. A group of young White dancers (among them Dean Collins and Jewel McGowan in an uncredited appearance) make fun of the uptight dancing of the film's protagonists, played by Henry Fonda and Gene Tierney. And in *City for Conquest* (1940), a melodrama about succeeding in tough New York, the jitterbug functions as a working-class pastime, while ballroom dancing stands for upward social mobility.

In these and numerous other examples, social swing dancing functions mostly as a setting or background to the narrative, adding atmosphere, authenticity, and some entertainment value to a scene. But as a featured cinematic attraction, swing dancing remained marginal. Further, a remarkable number of largely forgotten musicals from the period refer to swing in their titles without actually containing much of it. Apart from the prestigious Astaire-Rogers feature *Swing Time* (1936), this is true mainly of wartime B pictures – for example, *Swing It Soldier* (1941), *Swingtime Johnny* (1943), *Swing Fever* (1943), or *Babes on Swing Street* (1944). That such titles often turned out to be an unfulfilled promise suggests that Hollywood was aware of swing's popularity and capitalized on it yet was reluctant to actually represent it.[574] But even in truly swing-themed musicals, the dancing was often less prominent than one might expect. Hollywood exploited the vogue for big band swing with a number of musicals starring famous White bandleaders.[575] While many of these big band musicals – for instance, *Orchestra Wives* with Glenn Miller (1942) and *Sweet and Low-Down* with Benny Goodman (1944) – contain dance scenes, they are often short. The dancing functions more as a realistic everyday activity than as a screen spectacle that would provide a utopian break from the narrative. Elaborate White swing dance numbers were relatively rare, and when they did occur, they seldom had the same status that was typically accorded a tap, ballroom, or ballet number. Accordingly, swing dancers often remained uncredited.

---

574 According to jazz film collector and historian Ernie Smith, Hollywood produced over fifty films with the word "swing" in the title; see Smith, "Portrait of the Swing Era", xxv.

575 As James Chapman points out in his brief history of the big band musical, the most successful of these films were nostalgic biopics produced long after the end of the swing era, notably *The Glenn Miller Story* (1954) and *The Benny Goodman Story* (1956). Films from the period itself, such as *Hollywood Hotel* (1937) with Benny Goodman or *Sun Valley Serenade* (1941) with Glenn Miller, though fairly successful, never became part of the canon of musicals. See Chapman, "Big Band Musical".

Chapter 6 "A Savage Exhibition"? Swing and White Youth Culture in B Movies

In this context, Universal Studios' cycle of swing teen musicals with the Jivin' Jacks and Jills is all the more noteworthy – both for depicting swing and its youth culture and for the status granted to the dancers. While only *Mister Big* lists all the dancers individually in the end credits, they are usually mentioned as a group towards the end of the opening credits. As seen above, studio publicity took advantage of the visual potential of dance (sometimes even in excess of its actual presence in the films themselves). A strong focus on dance is also apparent in the films' reception in the press, which is full of references to jitterbug dancing – but interestingly not to tap. While the young dancers were originally selected for the Jivin' Jacks and Jills due to their *tap dance* skills, journalists and moviegoers apparently associated them more with teenage rug-cutters dancing the Lindy/jitterbug than with the tap stars of countless other musicals.

Like many other low-budget films, Universal Studios' cycle of teen musicals have been largely ignored by the canonizing discourses of film history and genre criticism. Recent studies of the classical Hollywood musical have critiqued the lopsided focus on the narratively integrated musical. Instead, they present a more nuanced view, which accounts for the differences between studios' styles, individual films, and their varying levels of integration of narrative and numbers.[576] Nevertheless, the focus has been on the Big Five, while the smaller studios' more modest productions remain overlooked. In turn, the relatively scant literature on the B film production of studio-era Hollywood has largely ignored the musical genre – partly perhaps because these films often occupied the upper end of the B segment, also known as "programmers". Thus, while low- to medium-budget musicals didn't have the cultural prestige of A films, they were also spared the stigma of the truly trashy B movies that were less likely to cross over into the A brackets of a double bill.[577] Scholars of the B film have tended to associate the category with the more disreputable "low" genres, such as crime or horror, even though B film production was by no means limited to specific genres.

It is not hard to see why the numerous musical "quickies" produced by Universal (and other studios) would be deemed negligible contributions to the generic corpus of the Hollywood musical. Measured by the standards of so-called quality cinema, these films inevitably fail. With their fragmented, formulaic narratives, relative lack of glamour, and comparatively low production values, they are easy to dismiss as trivial and clumsy. But judging them in terms of a normative aesthetic is largely missing the point. When considered through the lens of

---

576 Significant examples of this are Cohan, "Star Spangled Shows"; and Griffin, "The Gang's All Here", quoted above. For the development of the integrated musical at MGM, see especially Griffin, 22–28.

577 See Jacobs, "The B Film", 158.

historical discourse analysis, the sheer quantity and ubiquity of so-called second-rate musicals make them relevant and worthy of study. As Klein argues:

> The film cycle is a commodity to be assembled, packaged, and sold as quickly as possible, not a timeless piece of art. Thus, the contemporaneity of the cycle has also contributed to its marginalized status in the field of film studies. ...
>
> These kinds of films are significant not so much because of what they are, but because of why they were made, why studios believed that they were a smart investment, why audiences went to see them, and why they eventually stopped being produced.[578]

Universal's cycle of teen swing films was made and succeeded because the films fulfilled certain audience desires, not so much for spectacular and glamorous escapism but for cinematic reflections of an everyday popular culture and its participatory aspects. The films' appeal to a young audience confirms that they offered young White Americans a mirror of their activities in terms of lifestyles and tastes. When swing dance and music were included in more expensive features, they often appeared either more Whitened, refined, and respectable than in the teen musicals, or they were more decidedly marked as racially Other. It was in the marginal form of these low-budget teen films that a nonprimitivist White appropriation of swing's Black music and dance culture was most prevalent. The film industry's more conservative tendencies certainly moderated swing culture's complex tensions of race, class, gender, and generation. But through their youthful vitality and playful physical performance, the dancers in particular embody swing culture's emphasis on individual expression, and their disruptive and unruly dance performances challenge normative White identities and behaviors.

---

[578] Klein, *American Film Cycles*, 8, 20.

CONCLUSION Dance History, the Swing Dance Revival, and Vintage Movies in the Digital Age

In the film *King of Jazz* (1930), a pompous early Technicolor revue musical centering on White bandleader Paul Whiteman and his symphonic jazz, a nearly naked Black male dancer (Jacques Cartier) on a giant drum is supposed to illustrate how "jazz was born in the African jungle to the beating of the voodoo drum", as explained in the movie itself. The dancer's face is never recognizable, and his shiny Black body throws a large shadow on the wall, as if to illustrate the simultaneous absence/presence of Black culture in the film (fig. 47). Strangely enough, this dance scene introduces an excessively staged, all-White performance of George Gershwin's *Rhapsody in Blue*. Despite this brief appearance by a Black dancer, the film is not only a "thorough denial of the African American role in jazz", as Krin Gabbard puts it,[579] it is also conspicuously lacking in actual jazz, even if broadly defined.

Thirteen years later, the all-Black-cast backstage musical *Stormy Weather* (1943) had a bare-chested Bill "Bojangles" Robinson tap dance on large drums in an exoticist production number of the type that might have been seen at the Cotton Club a few years earlier. At the end of the same film, the Nicholas Brothers appear in elegant tailcoats, dancing on small pedestals that are reminiscent of drums, set up between members of Cab Calloway's big band. *Stormy Weather* has appropriately been called a "dictionary of black dance".[580] The film also marks both the culmination and the end of Hollywood's "Black entertainment syndrome", and various scholars have discussed its significance for Black film history at length.[581] As I have suggested in another essay, the shifts in Black screen images that occurred between the late 1920s and the mid-1940s are perfectly epitomized by

---

579 Gabbard, *Jammin' at the Margins*, 10.

580 Clark, "Katherine Dunham's Choreography", 328.

581 See, for instance, Knapp, *The American Musical*, 79–94; Knight, *Disintegrating the Musical*, 147–158; and Massood, *Black City Cinema*, 38–42.

Figure 47. Black dancer Jacques Cartier performs a "voodoo" dance on a giant drum in the otherwise all-White *King of Jazz* (1930).

Stormy Weather's dance performances featuring Bill Robinson and the Nicholas Brothers, respectively.[582] Robinson's jungle number is presented somewhat ambiguously: On the one hand, it is performed without a trace of irony, as a spectacle of exoticized Black entertainment. On the other hand, it is narratively framed as a humiliating experience for the dancer, which he nevertheless transcends by way of his dance skills. But while the film's utopian all-Black world offers Robinson's character a level of narrative emancipation, he still appears as "someone who has learned how to behave, as an actor and dancer for white audiences and within predominantly white contexts", as Raymond Knapp observes.[583] The first Black dancer to have attained and sustained a certain status in Hollywood, Robinson did so in part by conforming to White expectations about submissive Blacks.

By contrast, the younger Nicholas Brothers demonstrate exceptional talent and perfectionism in their elegant performance without bowing to servant stereotypes or essentialist ideas about naturally rhythmic Black bodies. While Robinson is the star of *Stormy Weather*, with the flimsy narrative centered on his character's

---

[582] See Trenka, "Appreciation, Appropriation, Assimilation".

[583] Knapp, *The American Musical*, 86.

Conclusion Dance History, the Swing Dance Revival, and Vintage Movies in the Digital Age

Figure 48. The Nicholas Brothers in the finale of the all-Black-cast musical *Stormy Weather* (1943). Credit: Everett Collection.

career (and an improbable romance with costar Lena Horne), the Nicholases' number is the film's undeniable climax. Surpassing anything done by the aging protagonist, it becomes an implicit farewell to Robinson's performance style and – by extension – Hollywood's narrative control over the Black entertainer as servant. As the brothers, wearing tailcoats and white ties, jump between their drum-like pedestals, the primitivist associations of the "African jungle" are definitely gone (fig. 48). At the same time, there is no more denying the African American role in jazz, as was the case in *King of Jazz* (and many other Hollywood films). Versatile, energetic, and highly expressive as well as elegant, cool, and controlled, the Nicholas Brothers have generally been seen as transgressing, at least symbolically, the limits imposed on Black performers by the White-dominated film industry.[584] With their climactic dance in *Stormy Weather,* the Black class act in the Hollywood film reached a level of aesthetic and narrative independence that was unprecedented and would remain unmatched.[585]

---

584 See, for instance, Hill, *Brotherhood in Rhythm*, chapter 6.

585 As I have argued elsewhere, with *Stormy Weather*'s extended finale dedicated to celebrating the present rather than the past, Hollywood seems to reluctantly admit that Black entertainment has come into its own and is no longer in need of White control; see Trenka, "Appreciation, Appropriation, Assimilation".

Jumping the Color Line: Vernacular Jazz Dance in American Film, 1929–1945

When Lindy hopper Frankie Manning, in his autobiography, spoke of the "power" of dance performance in film with respect to the Nicholas Brothers, he likely didn't mean to suggest that there was any kind of concrete *political* power to be gained from dancing in films.[586] But for Black entertainers of the 1930s and 1940s, the chance to appear in a mainstream movie certainly meant more than just a job and income. It meant an opportunity to present large White audiences with images of Black people that were only partially White-controlled. More than most other performers, it was the dancers who transcended the limits of their time in their non-narrative, physical performances. During their best moments, dancers like the Nicholas Brothers, Jeni LeGon, or Whitey's Lindy Hoppers succeeded in using their cultural capital – their highly skilled dancing bodies – to speak for themselves, as it were, rather than for White-imposed narratives or stereotypes.

Few scholars – whether of dance or film history – would deny this. What I hope to have exemplified throughout this book is the usefulness of looking at performers and films that have all too often been overlooked or relegated to footnote status. The dance performances in forgotten star vehicles, B movies, short films, and Soundies offer a treasure trove of material that evidences the significance of vernacular jazz dance in film as a focal point of American race relations. They help to draw a picture that is not only more complete but also more diverse than an exclusive focus on the already canonized. Many of the productions I have discussed were not intended for posterity but merely as ephemeral entertainment, made to cash in on novelties and passing fads rather than to create lasting works of art. Yet this makes them no less revealing and historically relevant. In the case of feature-length films, it is certainly a historical irony that the very same performances that were ghettoized by the industry at the time are now sometimes treated as the only redeeming element of otherwise forgettable productions. And in the case of theatrical short films and Soundies, these performances are not only the films' raison d'être historically but also the cause for their valuation as historical documents today.

Digital technology has facilitated access to old films and led to a sort of rediscovery of previously marginalized material. The recent reception of and research into some of the films discussed here continues some of the older trends in the history of discovering, documenting, and preserving African American vernacular dance (both on- and offscreen). This research was and is characterized by two general tendencies: one is the overlap and exchange between academia and dance practice; the other is a continued White dominance in the sense that much – though by no means all – of the historical research has been initiated by White scholars

---

586 See Manning and Millman, *Frankie Manning*, 152.

and/or dancers. I would thus like to conclude with a brief look at the past and present of the field.

Mura Dehn's documentary film project *The Spirit Moves* (1950–1986) might well have been the first "academic" attempt at telling the story of African American vernacular jazz dance, and it remains a canonical cinematic document. Dehn, a Russian dancer trained in ballet and modern dance, became fascinated with jazz dance when she saw Josephine Baker perform in Paris in the 1920s. After immigrating to the United States in 1930, she founded her own dance company and dedicated herself to the study of vernacular jazz dance, which she observed and learned in venues such as Harlem's Savoy Ballroom. However, she didn't begin filming *The Spirit Moves* until the 1950s, enlisting some of the best Black dancers of the era to give demonstrations of styles going back as far as the early 1900s, in addition to more recent dances. Dehn was concerned about the loss of jazz dance's rich heritage, considering the history to have gone unrecorded. An obituary for Dehn quoted her as saying that "she turned to film because 'a film would be the first real book we had about these dances'".[587] However, as Karen Backstein points out,

> Dehn's insistence on the need to record jazz dance belies the fact that this art has a long history on film: from the moment cameras started cranking, they captured African Americans tapping, strutting, and high-kicking. Many of the older dances that Dehn restaged for the camera – such as the cakewalk – already existed on film, caught near the height of their popularity, performed by dancers who specialized in those styles. …
>
> But the Hollywood musical's dependence on jazz had perhaps the strongest effect of all.[588]

Backstein's analysis provides a poignant critique of the Russian dancer and filmmaker's problematic role as a historian reporting on a culture she didn't fully understand.[589] Dehn's documentary project is exemplary of the paternalistic attitude of White intellectuals who "unnoticingly asserted their supremacy over the cultures they heralded".[590] *The Spirit Moves* includes footage shot at the Savoy, and the film remains a uniquely valuable document with remarkable dance demonstrations. But Dehn's aesthetic strategies – namely, the restaging of dances in a bare studio and the dry voice-over narration – "sever the dance from the

---

587 "Mura Dehn, a Choreographer and Specialist in Black Dance", *New York Times*, February 14, 1987, TimesMachine. See also the documentary *In a Jazz Way: A Portrait of Mura Dehn*, directed by Louise Ghertler and Pamela Katz, 1987.
588 Backstein, "Keeping the Spirit Alive", 237–238.
589 See Backstein, 233–237.
590 Backstein, 233.

cultural context in which it flourished".[591] Further, by aiming to create a historical document of jazz dance rather than to provide entertainment, Dehn neglected the fact that entertainment is a crucial and constitutive part of the history of vernacular jazz dance.

Perhaps the first person to take the filmed entertainment itself seriously as a historical source was Ernie Smith, son of Hungarian immigrants who were in show business. Smith became fascinated with jazz and swing during his teens in Pittsburgh and began frequenting Black dance halls, where he learned to dance the Lindy hop. After moving to New York, he started collecting jazz films in the 1950s, inspired by Marshall Stearns's jazz history lectures. In 1957, Stearns invited Smith to teach at the Institute of Jazz Studies (founded by Stearns in 1952). Smith included numerous film clips in his lectures, and he insisted on emphasizing the social context and the connections between jazz history, film history, and African American history. He later recalled that, apart from Stearns, very few of the jazz enthusiasts he met in New York in the 1950s and 1960s were interested in films. Many of the films in Smith's collection feature dancers, and Smith explained that one of his key motivations was to set the record straight about tap dancing, so that Black dancers would get the attention they deserved, instead of all the recognition being reserved for the top White stars, such as Fred Astaire and Gene Kelly.[592]

Unlike Mura Dehn, who allied herself with an intellectual, artistic community and unwittingly betrayed a degree of condescension toward her subjects, Ernie Smith had more of an insider's perspective. His enthusiasm for jazz originated from direct exposure to Black vernacular music and dance in his youth. Interviews with him confirm swing culture's appeal for second-generation European immigrants in search of a modern American culture they could identify with. As a teenager during the swing era, he actively participated in the culture, although he was well aware that it was a culture not quite his own. He recalled that very few White people went to the Black Hill City neighborhood in Pittsburgh, where he was first exposed to swing music and the Lindy. Similarly, Marshall and Jean Stearns display a keen sense of their own perspective as observing outsiders in their book, where they aim to give a voice to the dancers themselves, letting them tell their own stories. In the 1980s, White Californian tap and swing dancer Rusty Frank realized the pressing need to record the stories of a generation of dancers that was in the process of disappearing. Tracking down living tap dancers who

---

591 Backstein, 241.

592 See Jennifer Dunning, "Ernie Smith, 79, Jazz Dance Authority", *New York Times*, April 14, 2004, https://www.nytimes.com/2004/04/14/arts/ernie-smith-79-jazz-and-dance-authority.html; LeGon and Smith, interview, Gray; and Smith, interview, Murray. Smith contributed the film list appended to the Stearnses' dance history book; see Stearns and Stearns, *Jazz Dance*, 403–427.

Conclusion Dance History, the Swing Dance Revival, and Vintage Movies in the Digital Age

had been active in the first half of the twentieth century, she interviewed anyone who was willing to share their story, compiling and contextualizing these (auto)biographical sketches in her book *Tap!* Smith, Stearns, and Frank are not only less exoticist in their approach but also more inclusive than Dehn in that they take into account both Black and White contributions to jazz dance history. At the same time, they demonstrate an acute awareness of and respect toward the dance's Black roots and the complexities and injustices of the history of appropriations and adaptations.

At least since the 1980s, African Americans operating at the intersection of scholarship and dance practice have been (re)claiming the discursive agency and made substantial contributions to the field. Brenda Dixon Gottschild, Jacqui Malone, and Thomas F. DeFrantz are some of the key scholar-practitioners, and their important work is not confined to the classic vernacular jazz of the early twentieth century. However, with regard to that period, many important impulses in the field have continued to come from informal, nonacademic contexts, often from White practitioners of the Black-originated vernacular dance styles, who thus perpetuate the old pattern of appropriation while also trying to give credit and show respect to the originators. The swing dance revival of recent decades has played a crucial role here.

In the early 1980s, dancers in the United States, the United Kingdom, and in Sweden more or less simultaneously "rediscovered" the Lindy hop and other swing-era dances.[593] A New York dance studio started to revive the dance with the help of Whitey's veteran Lindy dancer Al Minns, and the fashion slowly caught on. Meanwhile, some dancers overseas also became driving forces in unearthing jazz dance history. Terry Monaghan, a cofounder of London's performance group the Jiving Lindy Hoppers, spent years researching the history of the Savoy Ballroom, which he intended to publish in book form, a project sadly uncompleted by the time of his death in 2011.[594] And Swedish dancer Lennart Westerlund, after seeing Whitey's Lindy Hoppers in *Hellzapoppin'* (1941) at a Stockholm cinema, set out to find surviving dancers in the United States and to locate more films that showed the old-timers during their prime.[595] 1985 was the first year that Frankie Manning was invited to teach at Herräng Dance Camp, an annual event (first held in 1982) in a tiny town on Sweden's east coast, organized

---

593 See Crease, "Future of the Lindy"; Manning and Millman, *Frankie Manning*, 225–242; and Miller with Jensen, *Swingin' at the Savoy*, 233–250.

594 See Mo Dodson, "Terry Monaghan Obituary", *Guardian*, July 20, 2011, https://www.theguardian.com/stage/2011/jul/20/terry-monaghan-obituary. Monaghan's website has been deactivated but remains archived online; see Savoy Ballroom, Wayback Machine, Internet Archive, https://web.archive.org/web/20110716012742/http://www.savoyballroom.com/.

595 Lennart Westerlund, informal presentation, Lindy Focus dance festival, Asheville, NC, December 2011.

by Westerlund's performance group the Rhythm Hot Shots. For Manning, who had retired from dancing in the 1950s and taken a job as a postal worker, this was the beginning of a second career. His rediscovery led to countless engagements at dance events around the world, and he kept teaching and lecturing until his death in 2009. The Rhythm Hot Shots (now the Harlem Hot Shots) invited many other surviving jazz and tap dancers from the swing era, among them Norma Miller of Whiteys' Lindy Hoppers, who also remained active in the scene until shortly before her death in 2019. In the 1990s, young White dancer Peter Loggins from Los Angeles also started collecting films and tracking down original dancers, whom he learned from and interviewed extensively. He may now well be the foremost authority on American social dancing of the first half of the twentieth century; I and many others owe much to his vast knowledge, which he has enthusiastically shared in the informal setting of swing dance events over the years.

At some point, Herräng Dance Camp began selling VHS compilations of film scenes that they considered to be important moments in jazz dance history. Screenings of these clips were a regular part of the nightly entertainment when I first visited Herräng in 1998. At the time, there were already several hundred participants from dozens of countries attending the camp, and there were a growing number of similar events in the US and in Europe. Thus, before YouTube, film performances like those of Whitey's Lindy Hoppers in *Hellzapoppin'* or of the Nicholas Brothers in *Stormy Weather* were probably much better known in this predominantly White swing dance community than among scholars of dance or film history.

In recent years, digital technology has substantially expanded access to these vintage movies. It is hard to overstate the role of the internet and the home video market in making obscure old films accessible again, to a potentially larger audience than ever before. Collectors have digitized many of their treasures – excerpts as well as full-length films – for online viewing on YouTube. Online retailers like Loving the Classics sell DVDs of public domain Hollywood productions that haven't been released officially by the studios.[596] These long-forgotten B movies and vehicles for stars who have faded from public consciousness are not typically discussed in histories of Hollywood cinema, whether academic or popular. Most of these films don't conform to common notions of what constitutes a classic; yet the very existence of these digital editions suggests a certain demand for them. The same can be said of surviving race films, which are increasingly issued on DVD and available from Amazon.

---

596 See Loving the Classics, Jarrett Enterprises, https://www.lovingtheclassics.com.

Important film restoration initiatives have also come from informal contexts, as illustrated by the Vitaphone Project, a nonprofit founded in 1991 by "a group of film buffs and record collectors", according to their website.[597] The organization has been a driving force in locating and researching Vitaphone (and other early sound) films, has collaborated on restoration projects with major studios and archives, and made information available on its website and in regular newsletters. Partly thanks to such restoration efforts, theatrical short films have also experienced a bit of a revival through the home video market, in addition to their growing dissemination on YouTube. The same is true of the Soundies of the 1940s.

It is worth noting the racial aspects in the recent commodification and reception of these old films. Warner Home Video, for instance, has been releasing DVD box sets with dozens of shorts. In the first of these collections, one of the six DVDs is dedicated entirely to Black-cast Vitaphone shorts. Like the Black specialty act in the White-cast Hollywood film back in the day, these African American performances are thus simultaneously segregated and privileged in the DVD box set. At the same time, a few additional Black shorts are included on some of the other DVDs in the same set, which follows a chronological order overall.[598] Similarly, home video editions of Soundies have been partly segregated, partly integrated.[599] Notably, popular as well as academic discourses about musical shorts and Soundies often privilege Black-cast films by highlighting their role in documenting the performances of artists who were marginalized in Hollywood because of their race. Hardly a blurb or a booklet fails to point out that these early "music videos" provide glimpses of Black artists who were otherwise rarely seen onscreen.

The comment sections of online platforms also offer insight into the meanings of these old films for today's audiences. User reviews and discussions on the

---

597 Ron Hutchinson's Vitaphone Project, Patrick Picking, http://www.vitaphoneproject.com.

598 *Warner Bros. Big Band, Jazz & Swing: Short Subject Collection* (Burbank, CA: Warner Home Video, 2010), DVD set. The films on the all-Black disc 2 are *Yamekraw* (1930), *Smash Your Baggage* (1932), *That's the Spirit* (1933), *Pie, Pie, Blackbird* (1932), *Rufus Jones for President* (1933), *An All-Colored Vaudeville Show* (1935), *King for a Day* (1934), and *The Black Network* (1936). Disc 3 contains *Mills Blue Rhythm Band* (1934), disc 4 includes *Jimmie Lunceford and His Dance Orchestra* (1936) and *Hi De Ho* (1937), whereas *Jammin' the Blues* (1944) is included on disc 6.

599 In a series of Soundies compilations issued on DVD by Storyville Films (now defunct), for instance, each disc is dedicated exclusively either to Black or to White bands: for example, *Harlem Roots, Volume 1: The Big Bands* (Havnsø, Denmark: Storyville Films, 2004) features the Soundies of Duke Ellington, Cab Calloway, Count Basie, and Lucky Millinder, whereas *The Big Bands, Volume 1* (Havnsø, Denmark: Storyville Films, 2007) is dedicated to Soundies featuring Stan Kenton, Glen Gray, and several other White bandleaders. These selections – among the first to appear on DVD – represent the high end of Soundies production, featuring mostly famous performers in films of above-average quality. Other compilations, however, present a racially and ethnically diverse mix of relatively obscure material; see, for instance, *Soundies Film Collection* (The Historical Archive, 2006), DVD.

Internet Movie Database (IMDb), for instance, show both the continuities and the shifts in valuation and reception. Black entertainers are still often praised for their supposedly natural talents and frequently valued as the most memorable part of otherwise forgettable movies. At the same time, contemporary viewers overall are more critical of the old films' racism. Scenes with Black artists – whether they appear as musical specialty performers or as servants – are often denounced for their racism as well as praised for showcasing underacknowledged Black talent, and it is not uncommon to find both opinions within the same comment. As scholars of Black film history have pointed out, historically, Black audiences have always engaged in a kind of resistant spectatorship, a "privileging of performance over textuality".[600] That is to say, they were perfectly able to separate the performers from the material they performed and to value a performance despite the limitations of White-imposed narratives and stereotypes. Today, this simultaneous condemnation and appreciation is no longer confined to African American spectatorship. Whoever the viewers of these films are today, many of them seem aware both of the offensiveness of the racial stereotypes and of the skill and charisma displayed by many of the performers within and despite these limitations. Unsurprisingly, however, some modern-day viewers fail to recognize the complexities of racial representations in studio-era Hollywood. To pick just one typical example: a fairly long IMDb user review of *Hooray for Love* (1935) is titled "Waller, Robinson, LeGon transcend weak material", declaring that the "best assets of this so-so show are its three African-American performers". This is very much in line with the original press reviews of this and other "so-so" films, in which Black specialty numbers were perceived as the highlight, while the rest was deemed of mediocre quality. But then, the IMDb reviewer goes on to wonder why LeGon didn't receive more attention during her prime years, speculating that this "can't be entirely down to racism, as other black performers were working steadily during that period".[601] The idea that gender might intersect with racial discrimination does not seem to occur to this particular viewer. Further, despite evidencing a general awareness of the industry's racist casting practices, the reviewer fails to note the questionable content of the number – namely, the stereotypical depiction of Black people as happy-go-lucky entertainers and the subliminal message that they need nothing *but* music and dancing to be happy.

If IMDb is anything to go by, the predominantly White-cast B musicals from the late swing era don't have a large following nowadays. For most of the films with

---

600 Everett, *Returning the Gaze*, 191. See also Knight, *Disintegrating the Musical*.

601 F Gwynplaine MacIntyre, "Waller, Robinson, LeGon transcend weak material", review of *Hooray for Love*, April 14, 2007, IMDb, https://www.imdb.com/review/rw1636933/.

the Jivin' Jacks and Jills, there are only a few user reviews and even fewer discussions. Where comments exist, they indicate that the films' original emphasis on the "hep" youth culture of their day isn't lost on today's audience. Modern-day viewers easily forgive the flimsy story content and general mediocrity of the productions in light of the charisma of the performers, whose youthful charm, energy, comic talent, and dance skills are praised. The films are appropriately perceived as "only" entertainment but also valued *as* such. Overall, comments evidence both nostalgia and an awareness of the films' historical function in providing young audiences with a mirror of their lifestyle and culture.

The question of how historical perspective has (or hasn't) changed the evaluation of the films and performances explored in this book would be a good point of departure for further research. In any case, many of the films I have discussed are in circulation again today, in part thanks to digital technology, and their history is being researched, documented, and disseminated. However, as noted above, much of this research started long before the internet and often outside of institutionalized academic contexts. Beginning with the work of Marshall and Jean Stearns, the field has always to a large extent relied on oral testimony, whether within or outside of academia. As for more recent examples, Jacqui Malone's work on and with tap dancer Charles "Cholly" Atkins or Constance Valis Hill's book on the Nicholas Brothers come to mind as first-rate scholarly work created in collaboration with the dance practitioners themselves.[602] But there has been other important work that did not originate in academic environments. The autobiographies of Lindy hoppers Norma Miller and Frankie Manning, for example,[603] offer invaluable and highly engaging testimonies to an aspect of cultural history that might easily have been lost if it hadn't been for the enthusiasm of early swing dance "revivalists" like Lennart Westerlund or Terry Monaghan. Along with the tap dance world, the contemporary swing dance community thus deserves some recognition for its contributions to preserving the history of vernacular jazz dance in its manifold varieties.[604] In sum, the field has profited enormously from the

---

602 See Atkins and Malone, *Class Act*; and Hill, *Brotherhood in Rhythm*.

603 See Manning and Millman, *Frankie Manning*; and Miller with Jensen, *Swingin' at the Savoy*.

604 On a side note, there are certainly good reasons to be critical of the swing dance revival, which has taken on global proportions since its beginnings in the 1980s. One such reason is that in North America and Europe, where the biggest scenes are, the swing dance community remains overwhelmingly White, despite recent efforts to be more inclusive. By and large, the scene is firmly rooted in a White middle class, which conceives of swing dancing as an innocently wholesome, fun activity. (For African Americans, of course, the prime site of struggle in popular culture moved to hip-hop a long time ago.) Another problematic aspect lies in the preservationist efforts by some (usually White) professional dancers who copy dance routines from old films, restaging them with the greatest possible accuracy – sometimes to the point of lifelessness. These meticulous recreations seem to largely miss the point of a living Black vernacular culture, which feeds on continuity through creative appropriation and remodeling of the past rather than nostalgic conservation.

exchange between dancers, scholars, and dedicated fans. Like Ernie Smith, who had a job in advertising and dedicated his spare time and money to his jazz film collection, a (frequently nerdy) fan culture of private collectors, history buffs, and dancers – both amateur and professional – has been enriching scholarship from the margins, so to speak. The history of vernacular jazz dance studies thus makes an excellent case for the value of historical research coming from informal, unofficial contexts.

The 1920s, 1930s, and 1940s were the golden age of vernacular jazz dance. Of the people who actively shaped the jazz dance culture of that period, many were already gone by the time the Stearnses began work on their book in the 1960s. And most of those who did survive into the twenty-first century passed away in recent years: Lindy legend Frankie Manning in 2009 at the age of ninety-five; tap dancer Jeni LeGon in 2012, at ninety-six; "Queen of the Soundies" Mabel Lee and Norma Miller of Whitey's Lindy Hoppers both in 2019, aged ninety-seven and ninety-nine, respectively.[605] It is not least thanks to the research and preservation efforts described above that we know more about their stories. Now that the original performers are gone, these stories remain – along with the many films that captured the dancers at the peak of their powers.

---

605 See Terry Monaghan, "Frankie Manning, the Ambassador and Master of Lindy Hop, Dies at 94", *New York Times*, April 28, 2008, https://www.nytimes.com/2009/04/28/arts/dance/28manning.html; Bruce Weber, "Jeni LeGon, Singer and Solo Tap-Dancer, Dies at 96", *New York Times*, December 16, 2012, https://nyti.ms/V2ipua; Brian Seibert, "Mable Lee, Tap-Dancing 'Queen of the Soundies', Dies at 97", *New York Times*, February 14, 2019, https://nyti.ms/2UY2Mqs; and Robert D. McFadden, "Norma Miller, Lindy-Hopping 'Queen of Swing', Is Dead at 99", *New York Times*, May 6, 2019, https://nyti.ms/2J5lgmP.

FILMOGRAPHY

Unless otherwise noted, all films listed are US productions.

[1939 New York World's Fair: Savoy Ballroom Exhibit], silent amateur footage, creator unknown, 1939.
42nd Street, dir. Lloyd Bacon, 1933.
After Seben, dir. S. Jay Kaufman, 1929.
Air Force, dir. Howard Hawks, 1943.
Air Mail Special, dir. unknown, 1941.
Ali Baba Goes to Town, dir. David Butler, 1937.
An All-Colored Vaudeville Show, dir. Roy Mack, 1935.
Always a Bridesmaid, dir. Erle C. Kenton, 1943.
The Amos 'n' Andy Show, creators Charles J. Correll, Freeman F. Gosden, 1951–1953.
Artie Shaw and His Orchestra, dir. Roy Mack, 1939.
Babes in Arms, dir. Busby Berkeley, 1939.
Babes on Swing Street, dir. Edward C. Lilley, 1944.
Bachelor Mother, dir. Garson Kanin, 1939.
Backstage Blues, [dir. William Forest Crouch?], 1943.
Ballet mécanique, dirs. Fernand Léger, Dudley Murphy (uncredited), France, 1924.
Barber Shop Blues, dir. Joseph Henabery, 1933.
Basin Street Boogie, dir. Arthur Leonard, 1942.
Belle of the Nineties, dir. Leo McCarey, 1934.
The Benny Goodman Story, dir. Valentine Davies, 1956.
The Big Broadcast, dir. Frank Tuttle, 1932.
The Big Broadcast of 1936, dir. Norman Taurog, 1935.
The Big Broadcast of 1937, dir. Mitchell Leisen, 1936.
The Big Broadcast of 1938, dir. Mitchell Leisen, 1938.
Birth of the Blues, dir. Victor Schertzinger, 1941.
Black and Tan, dir. Dudley Murphy, 1929.
Blackbird Fantasy, dir. Herbert Moulton, 1942.
The Black Network, dir. Roy Mack, 1936.
Bli-Blip, dir. Josef Berne, 1942.
Block Party Revels, dir. William Forest Crouch, 1943.
Bones, dir. Ernest R. Dickerson, 2001.
Born to Dance, dir. Roy Del Ruth, 1936.
Bowery to Broadway, dir. Charles Lamont, 1944.

Bright Road, dir. Gerald Mayer, 1953.
Broadway Highlights No. 4, Paramount Headliner series, dir. unknown, 1935.
The Broadway Melody, dir. Harry Beaumont, 1929.
Broadway Melody of 1936, dir. Roy Del Ruth, 1935.
A Bundle of Blues, dir. Fred Waller, 1933.
By an Old Southern River, dir. unknown, 1942.
By Request, dir. Roy Mack, 1935.
Cab Calloway's Hi-De-Ho, dir. Fred Waller, 1934.
Cab Calloway's Jitterbug Party, dir. Fred Waller, 1935.
Cab Calloway: Sketches, American Masters series, dir. Gail Levin, 2012.
Cabin in the Sky, dir. Vincente Minnelli, 1943.
Café Metropole, dir. Edward H. Griffith, 1937.
Carmen Jones, dir. Otto Preminger, 1954.
Carolina Blues, dir. Leigh Jason, 1944.
Car Wash, dir. Michael Schultz, 1976.
Cats Can't Dance, dir. William Forest Crouch, 1945.
Check and Double Check, dir. Melville W. Brown, 1930.
Chicken Shack Shuffle, dir. William Forest Crouch, 1943.
Chip Off the Old Block, dir. Charles Lamont, 1944.
City for Conquest, dir. Anatole Litvak, 1940.
College Swing, dir. Raoul Walsh, 1938.
Congo Clambake, dir. unknown, 1942.
Cow-Cow Boogie, dir. Josef Berne, 1942.
Crazy House, dir. Jack Cummings (uncredited), 1930.
A Damsel in Distress, dir. George Stevens, 1937.
"Dance Contest at Savoy Ballroom", New York City Paramount News, dir. unknown, 1938.
"Dancing: Broadway Stages Big Orgy of Ball-Room Eccentricities", British Movietone News, dir. unknown, 1937.
Dancing Darkies, dir. William K. L. Dickson, 1896.
Dancing Lady, dir. Robert Z. Leonard, 1933.
Dancing the Big Apple 1937: African Americans Inspire a National Craze, dir. Judy Pritchett, 2010.
A Day at the Races, dir. Sam Wood, 1937.
Deep South, dir. Leslie Goodwins, 1930.
Dishonour Bright, dir. Tom Walls, United Kingdom, 1936.
Dispossessed Blues, dir. William Forest Crouch, 1943.
Double Deal, dir. Arthur Dreifuss, 1939.
Down Argentine Way, dir. Irving Cummings, 1940.
Easter Parade, dir. Charles Walters, 1948.
Easy Street, dir. Dudley Murphy, 1941.
The Emperor Jones, dirs. Dudley Murphy, William C. de Mille (uncredited), 1933.
Everybody Sing, dir. Edwin L. Marin, 1938.
Fools for Scandal, dir. Mervyn LeRoy, 1938.
From the Minuet to the Big Apple, Paramount Headliner series, dir. Leslie Roush, 1937.

Filmography

Get Hep to Love, dir. Charles Lamont, 1942.
Give Out, Sisters, dir. Edward F. Cline, 1942.
The Glenn Miller Story, dir. Anthony Mann, 1954.
Gold Diggers of 1933, dir. Mervyn LeRoy, 1933.
The Green Pastures, dir. Marc Connelly, 1936.
Groovie Movie, dir. Will Jason, 1944.
Hallelujah, dir. King Vidor, 1929.
Harlem-Mania, dir. Murray Roth, 1929.
Hearts in Dixie, dir. Paul Sloane, 1929.
Hellzapoppin', dir. Henry C. Potter, 1941.
He Was Her Man, dir. Dudley Murphy, 1931.
Hi De Ho, dir. Roy Mack, 1937.
Hi De Ho, dir. Josh Binney, 1947.
The Hit Parade, dir. Gus Meins, 1937.
Hit Parade of 1941, dir. John H. Auer, 1940.
Hit Parade of 1943, dir. Albert S. Rogell, 1943.
Hit Parade of 1947, dir. Frank McDonald, 1947.
Hollywood Canteen, dir. Delmer Daves, 1944.
Hollywood Hotel, dir. Busby Berkeley, 1937.
Hooray for Love, dir. Walter Lang, 1935.
Hot Chocolate (a.k.a. *Cottontail*), dir. Josef Berne, 1941.
How to Dance the Shag, dir. Al Christie, 1937.
Imitation of Life, dir. John M. Stahl, 1934.
In a Jazz Way: A Portrait of Mura Dehn, dir. Louise Ghertler, 1987.
International House, dir. A. Edward Sutherland, 1933.
In the Shadow of Hollywood: Race Movies & the Birth of Black Cinema, dir. Brad Osborne, 2007.
It Comes Up Love, dir. Charles Lamont, 1943.
It Happened in Harlem, dir. Bud Pollard, 1945.
"It Takes 'Hot Dogs' to Win the Lindy Hop", Pathé News, dir. unknown, 1931.
I Walked with a Zombie, dir. Jacques Tourneur, 1943.
Jammin' the Blues, dir. Gjon Mili, 1944.
The Jazz Singer, dir. Alan Crosland, 1927.
Jeni LeGon: Living in a Great Big Way, dir. Grant Greschuk, Canada, 1999.
Jimmie Lunceford and His Dance Orchestra, dir. Joseph Henabery, 1936.
Juke Box Joe's, dir. unknown, 1944.
Juke Box Saturday Night, dir. B. K. Blake, 1944.
Jungle Jig, dir. unknown, 1941.
Just Around the Corner, dir. Irving Cummings, 1938.
Keep Punching, dir. John Clein, 1939.
Killer Diller, dir. Josh Binney, 1948.
King for a Day, dir. Roy Mack, 1934.
King of Burlesque, dir. Sidney Lanfield, 1936.
King of Jazz, dir. John Murray Anderson, 1930.

King Solomon's Mines, dirs. Robert Stevenson, Geoffrey Barkas, United Kingdom, 1937.
Lazybones, dir. Dudley Murphy, 1941.
Let's Scuffle, dir. unknown, 1942.
Life in Harlem: A Documentary Film of America's Negro Metropolis, Colored America on Parade series, dir. unknown, 1940.
The Little Colonel, dir. David Butler, 1935.
The Littlest Rebel, dir. David Butler, 1935.
Love Finds Andy Hardy, dir. George B. Seitz, 1938.
Love in the Rough, dir. Charles Reisner, 1930.
Manhattan Medley, dir. Bonney Powell, 1931.
Manhattan Merry-Go-Round, dir. Charles Reisner, 1937.
The Merry Monahans, dir. Charles Lamont, 1944.
Mills Blue Rhythm Band, dir. Roy Mack, 1934.
Minnie the Moocher, dir. unknown, 1942.
Mister Big, dir. Charles Lamont, 1943.
Moonlight in Havana, dir. Anthony Mann, 1942.
Moonlight in Vermont, dir. Edward C. Lilley, 1943.
Murder at the Vanities, dir. Mitchell Leisen, 1934.
Noble Sissle and Eubie Blake Sing Snappy Songs, dir. Lee DeForest, 1923.
Ol' King Cotton, dir. Ray Cozine, 1930.
On Stage Everybody, dir. Jean Yarbrough, 1945.
On with the Show!, dir. Alan Crosland, 1929.
Orchestra Wives, dir. Archie Mayo, 1942.
The Outline of Jitterbug History, dir. Josef Berne, 1942.
Panama Hattie, dirs. Norman Z. McLeod, Roy Del Ruth (uncredited), Vincente Minnelli (uncredited), 1942.
Paper Doll, dir. Josef Berne, 1942.
Patrick the Great, dir. Frank Ryan, 1945.
The Pickaninny Dance, dir. William K. L. Dickson, 1894.
Pie, Pie, Blackbird, dir. Roy Mack, 1932.
Porgy and Bess, dir. Otto Preminger, 1959.
Private Buckaroo, dir. Edward F. Cline, 1942.
Radio City Revels, dir. Benjamin Stoloff, 1938.
Rebecca of Sunnybrook Farm, dir. Allan Dwan, 1938.
A Rhapsody in Black and Blue, dir. Aubrey Scotto, 1932.
Rhythmania, dir. unknown, 1943.
Rings on Her Fingers, dir. Rouben Mamoulian, 1942.
Rufus Jones for President, dir. Roy Mack, 1933.
Rug Cutter's Holiday, dir. unknown, 1943.
Sanders of the River, dirs. Zoltán Korda, Alfred Hitchcock (uncredited), United Kingdom, 1935.
Show Boat, dir. Harry A. Pollard, 1929.
Show Boat, dir. James Whale, 1936.
Show Boat, dir. George Sidney, 1951.
Singin' in the Rain, dirs. Stanley Donen, Gene Kelly, 1952.

Smash Your Baggage, dir. Roy Mack, 1932.
Somebody Loves Me, dir. Irving Brecher, 1952.
Soundies: A Musical History, dir. Chris Lamson, 2007.
The Spirit Moves, dir. Mura Dehn, 1950–1986.
Stage Door Canteen, dir. Frank Borzage, 1943.
Start Cheering, dir. Albert S. Rogell, 1938.
Step Up, dir. Anne Fletcher, 2006.
St. Louis Blues, dir. Dudley Murphy, 1929.
St. Louis Blues, dir. Allen Reisner, 1958.
Stormy Weather, dir. Andrew L. Stone, 1943.
Strike Up the Band, dir. Busby Berkeley, 1940.
Sugar Hill Masquerade, dir. unknown, 1942.
Sun Valley Serenade, dir. H. Bruce Humberstone, 1941.
Sweet and Low-Down, dir. Archie Mayo, 1944.
Swing Cat's Jamboree, dir. Roy Mack, 1938.
Swing Fever, dir. Tim Whelan, 1943.
Swing for Your Supper, dir. unknown, 1941.
Swing It Soldier, dir. Harold Young, 1941.
Swing Time, dir. George Stevens, 1936.
Swingtime Johnny, dir. Edward F. Cline, 1943.
Symphony in Black: A Rhapsody of Negro Life, dir. Fred Waller, 1934.
Take My Life, dir. Harry M. Popkin, 1942.
That's the Spirit, dir. Roy Mack, 1933.
That's the Spirit, dir. Charles Lamont, 1945.
This Is the Life, dir. Felix E. Reist, 1944.
This'll Make You Whistle, dir. Herbert Wilcox, United Kingdom, 1936.
This Was Paris, dir. John Harlow, United Kingdom, 1942.
Till the Clouds Roll By, dir. Richard Whorf, 1946.
Top Man, dir. Charles Lamont, 1943.
Top of the Town, dir. Ralph Murphy, 1937.
Vogues of 1938, dir. Irving Cummings, 1937.
The Wedding of Jack and Jill, dir. Roy Mack, 1930.
What's Cookin', dir. Edward F. Cline, 1942.
When Johnny Comes Marching Home, dir. Charles Lamont, 1942.
While Thousands Cheer (a.k.a. *Crooked Money*), dir. Leo C. Popkin, 1940.
Yamekraw, dir. Murray Roth, 1930.
Yes, Indeed!, dir. Josef Berne, 1941.
Ziegfeld Follies, dir. Lemuel Ayers, 1945.
A Zoot Suit with a Reet Pleat, dir. Josef Berne, 1942.

Bibliography

Almonte, Jerry S. "Know Your Jazz Dancer: Marie Bryant". *Wandering & Pondering* (blog). February 23, 2010. http://jsalmonteproductions.com/wanderingandpondering.

Aloff, Mindy. "Remembering a Hoofer: An Interview with Donald O'Connor". *DanceView Times* 1, no. 3 (October 2003). http://archives.danceviewtimes.com/dvny/features/2003/o%27connor.html.

Altman, Rick. *The American Film Musical.* Bloomington: Indiana University Press, 1987.

Altman, Rick. *Film/Genre.* London: BFI / Palgrave Macmillan, 1999.

Association of Motion Picture Producers and Motion Picture Producers and Distributors of America. "The Production Code". In *Movies and Mass Culture*, edited by John Belton, 135–149. London: Athlone, 1996.

Atkins, Cholly, and Jacqui Malone. *Class Act: The Jazz Life of Choreographer Cholly Atkins.* New York: Columbia University Press, 2001.

Backstein, Karen. "Keeping the Spirit Alive: The Jazz Dance Testament of Mura Dehn". In *Representing Jazz*, edited by Krin Gabbard, 229–243. Durham, NC: Duke University Press, 1995.

Banes, Sally. "TV-Dancing Women: Music Videos, Camera-Choreography, and Feminist Theory". In *Television: Aesthetic Reflections*, edited by Ruth Lorand, 213–234. New York: Peter Lang, 2002.

Baudry, Jean-Louis. "Ideological Effects of the Basic Cinematographic Apparatus". Translated by Alan Williams. In *Narrative, Apparatus, Ideology: A Film Theory Reader*, edited by Philip Rosen, 286–298. New York: Columbia University Press, 1986.

Belton, John. Introduction to "The Production Code". In *Movies and Mass Culture*, edited by John Belton, 135–149. London: Athlone, 1996.

Billman, Larry. *Film Choreographers and Dance Directors: An Illustrated Biographical Encyclopedia with a History and Filmographies, 1893 through 1995.* Jefferson, NC: McFarland, 1997.

Bogle, Donald. *Blacks in American Films and Television: An Encyclopedia.* New York: Garland, 1988.

Bogle, Donald. *Bright Boulevards, Bold Dreams: The Story of Black Hollywood.* New York: One World Ballantine Books, 2005.

Bogle, Donald. *Brown Sugar: Over One Hundred Years of America's Black Female Superstars.* New expanded and updated ed. New York: Continuum, 2007.

Bogle, Donald. *Dorothy Dandridge: A Biography.* New York: Amistad, 1997.

Bogle, Donald. *Toms, Coons, Mulattoes, Mammies, and Bucks: An Interpretive History of Blacks in American Films.* 4th ed. New York: Continuum, 2006.

Bourne, Stephen. *Nina Mae McKinney: The Black Garbo.* Duncan, OK: BearManor Media, 2011. Kindle.

Bradley, Edwin M. *The First Hollywood Sound Shorts, 1926–1931*. Jefferson, NC: McFarland, 2005.

Brannigan, Erin. *Dancefilm: Choreography and the Moving Image*. Oxford: Oxford University Press, 2011.

Brooks, Jodi. "Ghosting the Machine: The Sounds of Tap and the Sounds of Film". *Screen* 44, no. 4 (Winter 2003): 355–378.

Carroll, Noël. *Engaging the Moving Image*. Yale Series in the Philosophy and Theory of Art. New Haven, CT: Yale University Press, 2003.

Chapman, James. "A Short History of the Big Band Musical". In *Film's Musical Moments*, edited by Ian Conrich and Estella Tincknell, 28–41. Edinburgh: Edinburgh University Press, 2006.

Clark, VèVè A. "Performing the Memory of Difference in Afro-Caribbean Dance: Katherine Dunham's Choreography, 1938–1987". In *Kaiso! Writings by and about Katherine Dunham*, edited by VèVè A. Clark and Sara E. Johnson, 320–340. Madison: University of Wisconsin Press, 2005.

Clark, VèVè A., and Sara E. Johnson, eds. *Kaiso! Writings by and about Katherine Dunham*. Madison: University of Wisconsin Press, 2005.

Cohan, Steven. "Star Spangled Shows: Utopia and History in the Wartime Canteen Musical". In *The Sound of Musicals*, edited by Steven Cohan, 82–92. Basingstoke, UK: Palgrave Macmillan, 2010.

Cosgrove, Stuart. "The Zoot-Suit and Style Warfare". *History Workshop Journal* 18, no. 1 (Autumn 1984): 77–91. https://doi.org/10.1093/hwj/18.1.77.

Crease, Robert P. "Divine Frivolity: Hollywood Representations of the Lindy Hop, 1937–1942". In *Representing Jazz*, edited by Krin Gabbard, 207–228. Durham, NC: Duke University Press, 1995.

Crease, Robert P. "The Future of the Lindy and the New York Swing Dance Society". Epilogue to *Swingin' at the Savoy: The Memoir of a Jazz Dancer*, by Norma Miller, with Evette Jensen, 255–261. Philadelphia: Temple University Press, 1996.

Cripps, Thomas. *Black Film as Genre*. Bloomington: Indiana University Press, 1979.

Cripps, Thomas. *Making Movies Black: The Hollywood Message Movie from World War II to the Civil Rights Era*. New York: Oxford University Press, 1993.

Cripps, Thomas. *Slow Fade to Black: The Negro in American Film, 1900–1942*. London: Oxford University Press, 1977.

Cullen, Frank, Florence Hackman, and Donald McNeilly. *Vaudeville Old & New: An Encyclopedia of Variety Performers in America*. 2 vols. New York: Routledge, 2007.

DaPron, Louis. Oral history interview by Danny Daniels. May 19, 1978. Danny Daniels' History of American Tap series. Video recording. Performing Arts Research Collections, Jerome Robbins Dance Division, New York Public Library for the Performing Arts.

DeFrantz, Thomas F., ed. *Dancing Many Drums: Excavations in African American Dance*. Studies in Dance History. Madison: University of Wisconsin Press, 2002.

Dinerstein, Joel. *Swinging the Machine: Modernity, Technology, and African American Culture between the World Wars*. Amherst: University of Massachusetts Press, 2003.

Dismond, Geraldyn. "The Negro Actor and the American Movies". In *Close Up 1927–1933: Cinema and Modernism*, edited by James Donald, Anne Friedberg, and Laura Marcus, 73–76. Princeton, NJ: Princeton University Press, 1998.

Driscoll, Catherine. *Teen Film: A Critical Introduction*. Film Genres. Oxford: Berg, 2011.

Dyer, Richard. *Heavenly Bodies: Film Stars and Society*. 2nd ed. London: Routledge, 2004.

Dyer, Richard. *In the Space of a Song: The Uses of Song in Film.* London: Routledge, 2012. Kindle.

Dyer, Richard. "Is *Car Wash* a Musical?" In *Black American Cinema*, edited by Manthia Diawara, 93–106. New York: Routledge, 1993.

Dyer, Richard. *Only Entertainment.* 2nd ed. London: Routledge, 2002.

Dyer, Richard. *Stars.* New ed. With a supplementary chapter and bibliography by Paul McDonald. London: BFI Publishing, 1998.

Dyer, Richard. *White.* London: Routledge, 1997.

Ellis, John. *Visible Fictions: Cinema – Television – Video.* London: Routledge, 1982.

Emery, Lynne Fauley. *Black Dance from 1619 to Today.* 2nd, rev. ed. With a foreword by Katherine Dunham. Hightstown, NJ: Princeton Book Company, 1988.

Engelbrecht, Barbara. "Swinging at the Savoy". *Dance Research Journal* 15, no. 2 (Spring 1983): 3–10.

Erenberg, Lewis A. *Swingin' the Dream: Big Band Jazz and the Rebirth of American Culture.* Chicago: University of Chicago Press, 1998.

Everett, Anna. *Returning the Gaze: A Genealogy of Black Film Criticism, 1909–1949.* Durham, NC: Duke University Press, 2001.

Feuer, Jane. *The Hollywood Musical.* 2nd ed. Bloomington: Indiana University Press, 1993.

Feuer, Jane. "The Self-Reflective Musical and the Myth of Entertainment". In *Hollywood Musicals: The Film Reader*, edited by Steven Cohan, 31–40. In Focus: Routledge Film Readers. London: Routledge, 2002.

Frank, Rusty E. *Tap! The Greatest Tap Dance Stars and Their Stories, 1900–1955.* Rev. ed. New York: Da Capo Press, 1994.

Friedman, Ryan Jay. *Hollywood's African American Films: The Transition to Sound.* New Brunswick, NJ: Rutgers University Press, 2011.

Gabbard, Krin. *Jammin' at the Margins: Jazz and the American Cinema.* Chicago: University of Chicago Press, 1996.

George-Graves, Nadine. *The Royalty of Negro Vaudeville: The Whitman Sisters and the Negotiation of Race, Gender, and Class in African American Theater, 1900–1940.* New York: St. Martin's Press, 2000.

Giordano, Ralph G. *Social Dancing in America: A History and Reference.* 2 vols. Westport, CT: Greenwood Press, 2006–2007.

Gomery, Douglas. *Shared Pleasures: A History of Movie Presentation in the United States.* London: BFI Publishing, 1992.

Gottschild, Brenda Dixon. *The Black Dancing Body: A Geography from Coon to Cool.* New York: Palgrave Macmillan, 2003.

Gottschild, Brenda Dixon. *Digging the Africanist Presence in American Performance: Dance and Other Contexts.* Westport, CT: Praeger, 1996.

Gottschild, Brenda Dixon. *Waltzing in the Dark: African American Vaudeville and Race Politics in the Swing Era.* New York: Palgrave, 2000.

Govenar, Alan. *Untold Glory: African Americans in Pursuit of Freedom, Opportunity, and Achievement.* New York: Broadway Books, 2007. Kindle.

Grant, Barry Keith. "Jazz, Ideology and the Animated Cartoon". In *Film's Musical Moments*, edited by Ian Conrich and Estella Tincknell, 17–27. Edinburgh: Edinburgh University Press, 2006.

Griffin, Sean. "The Gang's All Here: Generic versus Racial Integration in the 1940s Musical". *Cinema Journal* 42, no. 1 (2002): 21–45.

Guarino, Lindsay, and Wendy Oliver, eds. *Jazz Dance: A History of the Roots and Branches*. Gainesville: University Press of Florida, 2014.

Gubar, Susan. *Racechanges: White Skin, Black Face in American Culture*. Race and American Culture. New York: Oxford University Press, 2000.

Guerrero, Ed. *Framing Blackness: The African American Image in Film*. Culture and the Moving Image. Philadelphia: Temple University Press, 1993.

Hall, Stuart. "What Is This 'Black' in Black Popular Culture?" In *Representing Blackness: Issues in Film and Video*, edited by Valerie Smith, 123–133. London: Athlone, 1997.

Hansen, Miriam Bratu. "The Mass Production of the Senses: Classical Cinema as Vernacular Modernism". In *Reinventing Film Studies*, edited by Christine Gledhill and Linda Williams, 332–350. London: Arnold, 2000.

Haskins, Jim. *The Cotton Club*. New York: Hippocrene Books, 1994.

Hazzard-Gordon, Katrina. *Jookin': The Rise of Social Dance Formations in African-American Culture*. Philadelphia: Temple University Press, 1990.

Herzog, Amy. "Discordant Visions: The Peculiar Musical Images of the Soundies Jukebox Film". *American Music* 22, no. 1 (Spring 2004): 27–39.

Hill, Constance Valis. *Brotherhood in Rhythm: The Jazz Tap Dancing of the Nicholas Brothers*. New York: Cooper Square Press, 2012. Kindle.

Hill, Constance Valis. *Tap Dancing America: A Cultural History*. Oxford: Oxford University Press, 2010.

Hirschhorn, Clive. *The Universal Story*. London: Octopus Books, 1983.

Hoffmann, Bernd. "Alltag im Jazz-Himmel: Die Musical Shorts der 1930er Jahre". In *Musikpädagogik und Musikkulturen: Festschrift für Reinhard Schneider*, edited by Andreas Eichhorn and Helmke Jan Keden, 103–125. Musik – Kontexte – Perspektiven 4. München: Allitera Verlag, 2013.

Hoffmann, Bernd. "Lindy Hop und Cotton Club – Tanz im frühen US-amerikanischen Film". In *Bewegungen zwischen Hören und Sehen: Denkbewegungen über Bewegungskünste*, edited by Stephanie Schroedter, 501–517. Würzburg: Königshausen & Neumann, 2012.

Hoffmann, Bernd. "Ruß im Gesicht: Zur Inszenierung US-amerikanischer Musical Shorts". *Jazzforschung / Jazz Research* 44 (2012): 159–184.

Hoffmann, Bernd. "'Und der Duke weinte'. Afro-amerikanische Musik im Film: Zu Arbeiten des Regisseurs Dudley Murphy aus dem Jahre 1929". *Jazzforschung / Jazz Research* 39 (2007): 119–152.

Hoffmann, Bernd. "Way down upon the Suwannee River: 'Jazz'-Adaptationen im frühen experimentellen Tonfilm der USA". In *Musik – Pädagogik – Dialoge: Festschrift für Thomas Ott*, edited by Andreas Eichhorn and Reinhard Schneider, 86–103. Musik – Kontexte – Perspektiven 1. München: Allitera Verlag, 2011.

Hose, Wally. *Soundies*. St. Louis, MO: Wally's Multimedia, 2007.

Hubbard, Karen, and Terry Monaghan. "Negotiating Compromise on a Burnished Wood Floor: Social Dancing at the Savoy". In *Ballroom, Boogie, Shimmy Sham, Shake: A Social and Popular Dance Reader*, edited by Julie Malnig, 126–145. Urbana: University of Illinois Press, 2009.

Jacobs, Lea. "The B Film and the Problem of Cultural Distinction". In *Hollywood: Critical Concepts in Media and Cultural Studies*. Vol. 1, *Historical Dimensions: The Development of the American Film Industry*, edited by Thomas Schatz, 147–160. London: Routledge, 2004.

Jenkins, Henry III. "Anarchistic Comedy and the Vaudeville Aesthetic". In *Hollywood Comedians: The Film Reader*, edited by Frank Krutnik, 91–104. In Focus: Routledge Film Readers. London: Routledge, 2003.

Jenkins, Henry. *What Made Pistachio Nuts? Early Sound Comedy and the Vaudeville Aesthetic*. Film and Culture. New York: Columbia University Press, 1992.

Kalinak, Kathryn. "Disciplining Josephine Baker: Gender, Race, and the Limits of Disciplinarity". In *Music and Cinema*, edited by James Buhler, Caryl Flinn, and David Neumeyer, 316–335. Music / Culture. Hanover: Wesleyan University Press / University Press of New England, 2000.

Kelley, Andrea. "From Attraction to Distraction: The Panoram Machine and Emerging Modes of Multi-Sited Screen Consumption". *Continuum: Journal of Media & Cultural Studies* 28, no. 3 (2014): 330–341. https://doi.org/10.1080/10304312.2014.900881.

Kelley, Andrea. "'A Revolution in the Atmosphere': The Dynamics of Site and Screen in 1940s Soundies". *Cinema Journal* 54, no. 2 (Winter 2015): 72–93. https://doi.org/10.1353/cj.2015.0012.

Kelley, Andrea J. *Soundies Jukebox Films and the Shift to Small-Screen Culture*. Techniques of the Moving Image. New Brunswick, NJ: Rutgers University Press, 2018.

Kelley, Robin D. G. "The Riddle of the Zoot: Malcolm Little and Black Cultural Politics During World War II". In *American Studies: An Anthology*, edited by Janice A. Radway, Kevin K. Gaines, Barry Shank, and Penny von Eschen, 280–289. Chichester, UK: Wiley-Blackwell, 2009.

Klein, Amanda Ann. *American Film Cycles: Reframing Genres, Screening Social Problems, & Defining Subcultures*. Austin: University of Texas Press, 2011.

Knapp, Raymond. *The American Musical and the Performance of Personal Identity*. Princeton, NJ: Princeton University Press, 2006.

Knight, Arthur. *Disintegrating the Musical: Black Performance and American Musical Film*. Durham, NC: Duke University Press, 2002.

Knight, Arthur. "Star Dances: African-American Constructions of Stardom, 1925–1960". In *Classic Hollywood, Classic Whiteness*, edited by Daniel Bernardi, 386–414. Minneapolis: University of Minnesota Press, 2001.

Landay, Lori. "The Flapper Film: Comedy, Dance, and Jazz Age Kinaesthetics". In *A Feminist Reader in Early Cinema*, edited by Jennifer M. Bean and Diane Negra, 221–248. Durham, NC: Duke University Press, 2002.

LeGon, Jeni. The HistoryMakers® Video Oral History Interview with Jeni LeGon. By Larry Crowe. July 28, 2004. The HistoryMakers® African American Video Oral History Collection, Chicago, IL.

LeGon, Jeni. Papers. 1930s–2002. Archives Center, National Museum of American History, Smithsonian Institution, Washington, DC.

LeGon, Jeni, and Ernie Smith. Telephone interview by Acia Gray. January 7, 2001. Closing the Gap project, International Tap Association. Transcript. Performing Arts Research Collections, Jerome Robbins Dance Division, New York Public Library for the Performing Arts.

Lehman, Christopher P. *The Colored Cartoon: Black Representation in American Animated Short Films, 1907–1954*. Amherst: University of Massachusetts Press, 2007.

Lewis, David Levering. *When Harlem Was in Vogue*. New York: Penguin Books, 1997.

Liebman, Roy. *Vitaphone Films: A Catalogue of the Features and Shorts*. Reprint ed. Jefferson, NC: McFarland, 2010.

Loggins, Peter. "The History of Collegiate Shag". CollegiateShag.com. http://collegiateshag.com/history.html.

Lott, Eric. *Love and Theft: Blackface Minstrelsy and the American Working Class*. Race and American Culture. New York: Oxford University Press, 1993.

Lowry, Stephen. "Movie Reception and Popular Culture in the Third Reich: Contextualization of Cinematic Meanings in Everyday Life". In *Film – Kino – Zuschauer: Filmrezeption / Film – Cinema – Spectator: Film Reception*, edited by Irmbert Schenk, Margrit Tröhler, and Yvonne Zimmermann, 213–227. Zürcher Filmstudien 24. Marburg: Schüren Verlag, 2010.

MacGillivray, Scott, and Jan MacGillivray. *Gloria Jean: A Little Bit of Heaven; Her Authorized Biography*. New York: iUniverse, 2005.

MacGillivray, Scott, and Ted Okuda. *The Soundies Book: A Revised and Expanded Guide*. New York: iUniverse, 2007.

Malone, Jacqui. *Steppin' on the Blues: The Visible Rhythms of African American Dance*. Urbana: University of Illinois Press, 1996.

Maltby, Richard. "Sticks, Hicks and Flaps: Classical Hollywood's Generic Conception of Its Audiences". In *Identifying Hollywood's Audiences: Cultural Identity and the Movies*, edited by Melvyn Stokes and Richard Maltby, 23–41. London: BFI Publishing, 1999.

Maltin, Leonard. *The Great Movie Shorts*. New York: Crown Publishers, 1972.

Manning, Frankie, and Cynthia R. Millman. *Frankie Manning: Ambassador of Lindy Hop*. Philadelphia: Temple University Press, 2007.

Mask, Mia. *Divas on Screen: Black Women in American Film*. Urbana: University of Illinois Press, 2009.

Massood, Paula J. "African American Stardom Inside and Outside of Hollywood: Ernest Morrison, Noble Johnson, Evelyn Preer, and Lincoln Perry". In *Idols of Modernity: Movie Stars of the 1920s*, edited by Patrice Petro, 227–249. Star Decades: American Culture / American Cinema. New Brunswick, NJ: Rutgers University Press, 2010.

Massood, Paula J. *Black City Cinema: African American Urban Experiences in Film*. Culture and the Moving Image. Philadelphia: Temple University Press, 2003.

Massood, Paula J. *Making a Promised Land: Harlem in 20th-Century Photography and Film*. New Brunswick, NJ: Rutgers University Press, 2013.

Maurice, Alice. "'Cinema at Its Source': Synchronizing Race and Sound in the Early Talkies". *Camera Obscura* 17, no. 1 (49), (2002): 30–71. https://doi.org/10.1215/02705346-17-1_49-31.

McCarthy, Todd, and Charles Flynn, eds. *Kings of the Bs: Working within the Hollywood System; An Anthology of Film History and Criticism*. New York: E. P. Dutton, 1975.

McGee, Kristin A. *Some Liked It Hot: Jazz Women in Film and Television, 1928–1959*. Middletown, CT: Wesleyan University Press, 2009.

McLean, Adrienne L. *Being Rita Hayworth: Labor, Identity, and Hollywood Stardom*. New Brunswick, NJ: Rutgers University Press, 2004.

McLean, Adrienne L. "Flirting with Terpsichore: Dance, Class and Entertainment in 1930s Film Musicals". In *The Sound of Musicals*, edited by Steven Cohan, 67–81. Basingstoke, UK: Palgrave Macmillan, 2010.

McLean, Adrienne L. "Putting 'Em Down Like a Man: Eleanor Powell and the Spectacle of Competence". In *Hetero: Queering Representations of Straightness*, edited by Sean Griffin, 89–110. SUNY series, Horizons of Cinema. Albany: State University of New York Press, 2009.

McNally, Karen. "'My, My, Ain't That Somethin'": The Nicholas Brothers and Definitions of Class, Race and American Identity". Paper presented at the Annual Conference of the European Association of Dance Historians, London, October 2011.

Meeker, David. *Jazz on the Screen: A Jazz and Blues Filmography*. Library of Congress, Washington, DC, 2019. PDF. https://tile.loc.gov/storage-services/master/music/jots/200028017/0001.pdf.

Miller, Frank. "Fools for Scandal (1938)". TCM. Turner Classic Movies. https://www.tcm.com/tcmdb/title/2896/fools-for-scandal#articles-reviews?articleId=139710.

Miller, Norma, with Evette Jensen. *Swingin' at the Savoy: The Memoir of a Jazz Dancer*. Philadelphia: Temple University Press, 1996.

Mizejewski, Linda. *Ziegfeld Girl: Image and Icon in Culture and Cinema*. Durham, NC: Duke University Press, 1999.

Mulvey, Laura. "Visual Pleasure and Narrative Cinema". In *Feminism and Film Theory*, edited by Constance Penley, 57–68. New York: Routledge, 1988.

Mundy, John. *Popular Music on Screen: From the Hollywood Musical to Music Video*. Music and Society. Manchester: Manchester University Press, 1999.

Outman, Forrest. "Why 'Jitterbug' and 'Swing' Are Not Dances". *Dance History Blog*. DanceHistorian.com. December 14, 2013.

Peiss, Kathy. *Zoot Suit: The Enigmatic Career of an Extreme Style*. Philadelphia: University of Pennsylvania Press, 2011.

Pilgrim, David. "The Tragic Mulatto Myth". Jim Crow Museum of Racist Memorabilia, Ferris State University (Big Rapids, MI). November 2000, edited 2012. https://ferris.edu/htmls/news/jimcrow/mulatto/.

Pitet, Jean-François. "Dotty Saulters: The Petite Singer Larger Than Life (Part 1)". *The Hi De Ho Blog*. July 5, 2014. http://www.thehidehoblog.com/blog.

Pitet, Jean-François. "Dotty Saulters: The Petite Singer Larger Than Life (Part 2)". *The Hi De Ho Blog*. July 12, 2014. http://www.thehidehoblog.com/blog.

Potamkin, Harry A. "The Aframerican Cinema". In *Close Up 1927–1933: Cinema and Modernism*, edited by James Donald, Anne Friedberg, and Laura Marcus, 65–73. Princeton, NJ: Princeton University Press, 1998.

Regester, Charlene. *African American Actresses: The Struggle for Visibility, 1900–1960*. Bloomington: Indiana University Press, 2010.

Ries, Frank W. D. "Sammy Lee: The Broadway Career". *Dance Chronicle* 9, no. 1 (1986): 1–95. http://www.jstor.org/stable/1567595.

Ries, Frank W. D. "Sammy Lee: The Hollywood Career". *Dance Chronicle* 11, no. 2 (1988): 141–218. https://www.jstor.org/stable/1567697.

Rogin, Michael. *Blackface, White Noise: Jewish Immigrants in the Hollywood Melting Pot*. Berkeley: University of California Press, 1998.

Ross, Sara. "'Good Little Bad Girls': Controversy and the Flapper Comedienne". *Film History* 13, no. 4 (2001): 409–423. http://www.jstor.org/stable/3815458.

Schatz, Thomas. *The Genius of the System: Hollywood Filmmaking in the Studio Era*. New York: Pantheon Books, 1988.

Scheerer, Robert. "From Hollywood to Broadway". Interview by Steve Zee. *On Tap* (International Tap Association), Spring 2005, 20–23.

Scheiner, Georganne. *Signifying Female Adolescence: Film Representations and Fans, 1920–1950*. Westport, CT: Praeger, 2000.

Schrum, Kelly. *Some Wore Bobby Sox: The Emergence of Teenage Girls' Culture, 1920–1945*. Girls' History & Culture. New York: Palgrave Macmillan, 2004.

Scott, Joan W. "Gender: A Useful Category of Historical Analysis". *The American Historical Review* 91, no. 5 (December 1986): 1053–1075. http://www.jstor.org/stable/1864376.

Shary, Timothy. *Teen Movies: American Youth on Screen*. Short Cuts. London: Wallflower Press, 2005.

Shohat, Ella, and Robert Stam. *Unthinking Eurocentrism: Multiculturalism and the Media*. London: Routledge, 1994.

Smith, Ernie. Oral history interview by James Briggs Murray. September 27, 1986. Video recording. Moving Image and Recorded Sound Division, Schomburg Center for Research in Black Culture, New York.

Smith, Ernie. "Portrait of the Swing Era". Preface to *Swingin' at the Savoy: The Memoir of a Jazz Dancer*, by Norma Miller, with Evette Jensen, xi–xxxvii. Philadelphia: Temple University Press, 1996.

Smith, Susan. *The Musical: Race, Gender and Performance*. Short Cuts. London: Wallflower Press, 2005.

Staiger, Janet. *Perverse Spectators: The Practices of Film Reception*. New York: New York University Press, 2000.

Stanfield, Peter. *Body and Soul: Jazz and Blues in American Film, 1927–63*. Urbana: University of Illinois Press, 2005.

Stearns, Marshall, and Jean Stearns. *Jazz Dance: The Story of American Vernacular Dance*. Cambridge, MA: Da Capo Press, 1994. First published 1968 by Macmillan (New York).

Stowe, David W. *Swing Changes: Big-Band Jazz in New Deal America*. Cambridge, MA: Harvard University Press, 1994.

Trenka, Susie. "Appreciation, Appropriation, Assimilation: *Stormy Weather* and the Hollywood History of Black Dance". In *The Oxford Handbook of Dance and the Popular Screen*, edited by Melissa Blanco Borelli, 98–112. Oxford: Oxford University Press, 2014.

Tucker, Sherrie. *Swing Shift: "All-Girl" Bands of the 1940s*. Durham, NC: Duke University Press, 2000.

Watkins, Mel. *Stepin Fetchit: The Life and Times of Lincoln Perry*. New York: Vintage Books, 2006.

Watts, Jill. *Hattie McDaniel: Black Ambition, White Hollywood*. New York: Amistad, 2005.

White, Bobby. "9 Clips of Classic Black Lindy Hoppers Who Aren't Whitey's (Geek Version)". *Swungover* (blog). June 24, 2014. https://swungover.wordpress.com/2014/06/24/9-clips-of-classic-black-lindy-hoppers-who-arent-whiteys-geek-version/.

White, Bobby. "Swing History 101: The Birth of Lindy Hop (Early 1900s–1929)". *Swungover* (blog). October 2, 2013. https://swungover.wordpress.com/2013/10/02/swing-history-101-the-birth-of-lindy-hop-early-1900s-1929/.

Willis, Corin. "Blackface Minstrelsy and Jazz Signification in Hollywood's Early Sound Era". In *Thriving on a Riff: Jazz and Blues Influences in African American Literature and Film*, edited by Graham Lock and David Murray, 40–61. Oxford: Oxford University Press, 2009.

INDEX OF NAMES AND TITLES

42nd Street	29

A

Ace and Eddie	fn135
Adams, Carol	139
After Seben	162–163
Air Force	212
Air Mail Special	136–137, 142, 187, fn450
Albritton, Lynn	142–143, fn343, 145, 147, 153
Alexander, Danny	71
Ali Baba Goes to Town	104–108, fn231, 110, 112, 113, fn249, 116, 120, fn411
All-Colored Vaudeville Show, An	67–69, fn598
Allen, Gracie	fn411
Allen, Henry "Red"	146
Alton, Bob	fn515
Always a Bridesmaid	214, 217, 236
Amos 'n' Andy Show, The	122
Anderson, Ivie	81, 166, 167, fn402, 172, 173, 174
Andrews, Patty	210
Andrews Sisters	207, fn490, 208, 210, 211, 212, 220, 225, 226, 235, 238
Armstrong, Louis	56
Artie Shaw and His Orchestra	77
Astaire, Fred	18, 28, 53, 69, fn134, 102, 116, 119–120, 124, fn411, 204, fn482, 207, 240, 248
At Home Abroad (stage show)	103
Atkins, Charles "Cholly"	fn4, fn287, 253

Autry, Gene	176

B

Babb, Dorothy "Dottie"	fn489
Babes in Arms	228
Babes on Swing Street	224–225, 240
Bachelor Mother	239
Backstage Blues	fn343, 145
Baker, Josephine	18, fn38, 25, fn107, 247
Ballet mécanique	fn154
Barber Shop Blues	76, 90, 91
Barton, James	162, fn386
Basie, Count	95, 136–137, 187, 207, 223, 226–227, fn599
Basin Street Boogie	137–138
Baxter, Warner	1
Beasley, Snookie	167
Beavers, Louise	45, 117, 126, fn295
Belle of the Nineties	fn147
Bennett, Joan	1
Benny Goodman Story, The	fn575
Berkeley, Busby	216, fn535, 231
Berlin, Irving	fn63
Bernardi	104
Berry, Halle	12
Berry Brothers	fn250, 118, fn265
Beyoncé	12
Big Broadcast, The (1932)	fn147, fn533
Big Broadcast of 1936, The	fn533
Big Broadcast of 1937, The	fn533
Big Broadcast of 1938, The	fn533
Billy and Ann	144, 147
Birth of the Blues	119

269

Black and Tan	41–43, 50, 79–81, fn151, 89	Carmen Jones	fn49, fn81, 148
		Carmichael, Hoagy	fn356
Blackbird Fantasy	fn356	Carolina Blues	fn296
Black Network, The	67, 69–70, fn598	Cartier, Jacques	243, 244
Blake, Eubie	25, 65	Car Wash	fn341
Bli-Blip	fn296, 152	Castle, Nick	183
Block Party Revels	fn343, 143–145, 147	Catron, Stanley	197
Bones	123	Cats Can't Dance	150, 151
Born to Dance	fn502	Check and Double Check	fn147
Bow, Clara	31, 32	Chicken Shack Shuffle	149–150, 151
Bowery to Broadway	fn489	Chip Off the Old Block	212, 236, 237
Boyle, Johnny	221, fn515	City for Conquest	240
Bradley, Will	137, 138	Clavin, Frank	123
Briggs, Bunny	48, fn287	College Swing	205
Bright, Lois	121	Collins, Dean	240
Bright Road	122	Congaroos	165, 197
Broadway Highlights No. 4	fn99	Congo Clambake	fn356
Broadway Melody, The (1929)	26	Connolly, Bobby	fn239
Broadway Melody of 1936	103	Cook, Louise	40
Brodie, Buster	192	Cottontail see Hot Chocolate	
Brooks, Louise	31	Covan, Willie	fn95, fn509
Brown, Dewey	fn137	Cow-Cow Boogie	fn356
Brown, James "Buster"	fn287	Crawford, Joan	31
Brown, Stanley	58–60	Crazy House	fn158
Bryant, Marie	127, fn296, 152, fn362	Crinoline Choir	fn402, 174
Bunch, John "Tiny"	177, fn422	Crooked Money see While Thousands Cheer	
Bundle of Blues, A	46–47, 50, 81, 89	Crosby, Bing	119
Burns, George	fn411	Crouch, William Forest	fn315, fn343
By an Old Southern River	fn322	Crump, Freddy	60
By Request	75, 90		

C

D

Cab Calloway's Hi-De-Ho (1934)	44, 84, 85, 86	Dahl, Mitzi	fn146
		Damsel in Distress, A	fn411
Cab Calloway's Jitterbug Party	84, 87	Dancer, Earl	96, 99, 103, 114
Cabin in the Sky	fn49, fn264, fn460	Dancing Darkies	fn9
Café Metropole	fn269	Dancing Lady	29
Calloway, Cab	fn4, fn6, 21, 77, 78, fn147, 84–89, fn166, 90, fn194, 110, 112, 113, 121, fn275, 130, 148, 154, 175–176, 243, fn599	Dandridge, Dorothy	fn81, 98, 117, fn294, fn295, 148–149, fn355, fn356, 153
		DaPron, Louis	206, fn488, 221, fn515
		Davis, Eddie	fn422
Cantor, Eddie	104–107, 108, fn234, 112	Davis, Sammy, Jr.	62–64, 65, 66

Day at the Races, A	1, 164, 165–174, fn401, 175, 177, 179, 184, 190	Four Blackbirds	117, fn261, fn485
Deep South	56	Four Congaroos *see* Congaroos	
DeForest, Lee	25	Four Covans	45, fn95
DeFrantz, Thomas F.	249	Four Hot Shots	1, 3
Dehn, Mura	247–249	Four Knobs	147
DiMaggio, Joe	176	Four Step Brothers	76, 90, 207, 226, 227
Dishonour Bright	104, 116	Frank, Rusty	124, 248–249
Dispossessed Blues	142–143, fn343, 144, 147	Frazee, Jane	179, 210, fn534, 233
Dorsey, Jimmy	fn452	Frazier, Raymond	75
Double Deal	116, 117, 120–121	*From the Minuet to the Big Apple*	188
Down Argentine Way	14, fn30		
Downes, William	182, fn428	**G**	
Dudley, Bessie	46, 47, 81, 84	Gaillard, Slim	181
Dunham, Katherine	18, fn38, 123	Gambarelli, Maria	101, fn215
Dupree, Roland	fn489, fn516	Ganaway, "Twistmouth" George	fn389
Durbin, Deanna	228, 231	Garland, Judy	119, fn289, 164, 177, 207, fn501, 228, 230, fn535, 231–232
E		Gary, Ted	fn146
Early to Bed (stage show)	122	Geil, Joe "Corky"	fn489
Easter Parade	119–120, 124	Gershwin, George	243
Easy Street	fn356	*Get Hep to Love*	211, 218, 221, 232, 233, 237
Ebsen, Buddy	103	Gibson, Ella	167
Ebsen, Vilma	103	Gibson and Thompson	fn135
Ellington, Duke	1, 11, 21, 41, 43, 46, 78–84, fn147, 87–89, fn166, fn194, 127, 152, fn402, 174, 187, fn460, 223, fn599	*Give Out, Sisters*	206, 211, 217
		Glenn Miller Modernaires	138
		Glenn Miller Story, The	fn575
		Gloria Jean	207, 208, 210, 211, 212, 222, fn517, 232, 233, 234, 235
Emperor Jones, The	fn49		
Everybody Sing	1, 164, fn411, 177, 178	*Gold Diggers of 1933*	29, 35
		Gooding, Sally	74
F		Goodman, Benny	fn6, 202–204, 205, 212, 235, 240, fn575
Fay, Vivien	170	Gordon, Mack	fn248
Fields, Dorothy	fn248	Gottschild, Brenda Dixon	249
Five Hot Shots	79–81	Gould, Dave	173, fn411
Five Racketeers	67	Grable, Betty	196, 205
Fletcher, Dusty	fn137	Gray, Gilda	fn77
Follow the Sun (stage show)	103	Gray, Glen	fn599
Fonda, Henry	240	Green, Sammy	75
Fools for Scandal	108–113, fn244, 117, fn261	Greenidge, George	167, fn422
Foran, Dick	212	*Green Pastures, The*	fn49, 28

271

Greschuk, Grant	124, 125
Groovie Movie	fn333, 158, 191–196, 198

H

Hall, Adelaide	67
Hallelujah	20, 26, fn49, 28, 29–39, fn62, fn63, 40, 41, 43, 44, 45, 60–61, 65, 100
Hammond, John	203
Harlem Cuties	144–145, 147
Harlem Honeys	129, 149
Harlem Hot Shots *see* Rhythm Hot Shots	
Harlem-Mania	58–61, 90
Harris and Hunt	129, 149
Hart, Lorenz	108, fn244, 112
Haynes, Daniel L.	30, 34
Hayworth, Rita	94, fn189, 218
Hearts in Dixie	26, fn49, 28, fn61
Hellzapoppin' (stage show)	179
Hellzapoppin'	158, 164, 165, 179–186, fn443, fn446, 190, 249, 250
Henabery, Joseph	62, 76, 90
Henderson, Fletcher	fn6, fn194, 204
Herbert, Tom	188
Herman, Woody	208, 209, 210, 212, 216, 235
He Was Her Man	fn77
Hi De Ho (1937)	84, 87, 90, fn598
Hi De Ho (1947)	fn164, 121, fn275
Hill, Florence	46, 47, 81
Hite, Les	108, 109, 110
Hit Parade, The (1937)	fn533
Hit Parade of 1941	fn533
Hit Parade of 1943	fn533
Hit Parade of 1947	fn533
Holiday, Billie	82, 84
Hollywood Canteen	fn490
Hollywood Hotel	fn575
Holt, David	fn489
Hooray for Love	9, 93, 96–103, 106, 108, 110, 112, 113, fn249, 114, fn269, 120, 126, 142, fn406, 252
Hopkins, Claude	75, 76, 90
Horne, Lena	11, 92, fn186, 98, 117–119, fn264, 126, fn295, 245
Hot Chocolate (a.k.a. *Cottontail*)	187, fn443, fn450
Hot Mikado, The (stage show)	178
Hour of Charm Orchestra *see* Spitalny, Phil	
Howard, Bob	122
How to Dance the Shag	187
Hutton, Betty	120
Hutton, Ina Rae	29, fn60

I

Imitation of Life	fn54, 44
International House	fn147
It Comes Up Love	212
It Happened in Harlem	127
I Walked with a Zombie	119

J

James, Harry	212
James, Leon	167, 169, 197
Jammin' the Blues	fn296, fn598
Jazz Caribe	123
Jazz Cinq Band	123
Jazz Singer, The	4
Jazz Tap! (stage show)	123, 124
Jeni LeGon: Living in a Great Big Way	124
Jimmie Lunceford and His Orchestra	73, 76, 89, fn598
Jiving Lindy Hoppers	249
Jivin' Jacks and Jills	22–23, 198, 201, 206–217, fn488, fn489, fn493, 219–222, fn514, fn515, 225, 227, 228, fn534, 231, 233, 237, 241, 253
Johnson, Ann	fn428, 186, 197
Johnson, Dorothy "Dot"	177, fn422
Johnson, Harold "Chic" *see* Olsen and Johnson	
Johnson, Winnie	137, fn327
Jolson, Al	fn274
Jones, Allan	165, fn534

Jones, Frances "Mickey" 182, fn428
Juke Box Joe's 139, fn333
Juke Box Saturday Night 138–139
Jungle Jig fn356
Just Around the Corner fn113
Keeler, Ruby 28, fn274

K

Keep Punching 165, 177, 178–179
Kelly, Gene fn515, 248
Kennedy, Alphonse 58–60
Kenton, Stan 191, fn449, fn599
Kern, Jerome 204
Killer Diller 197
King for a Day 71–73, fn598
King of Burlesque fn230
King of Jazz 54, 243, 244, 245
King Solomon's Mines 104
Krupa, Gene 187

L

Lane, Willa Mae 96
LaRedd, Cora 47–50, fn99, fn127
Lazybones fn356
Lee, Gypsy Rose fn231
Lee, Mabel 129, 149–152, fn360, 254
Lee, Sammy 106, fn230, fn231, fn411
Léger, Fernand fn154
LeGon, Jeni 9, 21, 92, 93–128, fn188, fn214, fn231, fn232, fn234, fn235, fn249, fn261, fn269, fn274, fn275, fn278, fn291, fn406, fn411, fn485, 219, 246, 252, 254
LeTang, Henry fn287
Let's Scuffle fn322
Life in Harlem – A Documentary Film of America's Negro Metropolis fn389
Lindbergh, Charles fn370
Little Colonel, The fn113, 100
Littlest Rebel, The fn113
Loggins, Peter vii, 250
Lombard, Carole 111

Love Finds Andy Hardy 231
Love in the Rough fn158
Lunceford, Jimmie 89, fn276

M

Mack, Roy 47, 62, fn127, 65, 67, 73, 75, fn146, 84, 87, 90, 217
Madame Sul-Te-Wan fn295
Malls, Johnny 167
Malone, Jacqui 249
Manhattan Medley 163
Manhattan Merry-Go-Round 1, 164, 175–176, fn417, 177, fn422, fn431, 190
Manning, Frankie vii, 1, fn376, fn391, fn392, fn394, 165, 169, 173, 175, 177, fn422, 178, fn423, fn428, 183, 184, 186, fn443, fn446, 196, 197, 246, 249–250, 253, 254
Manone, Wingy fn332
Marin, Edwin L. 177
Marrier, Carrie fn135
Marx Brothers 165, fn395, 171
Marx, Harpo 166, 172, 173, 174
Mason, Melissa 177
Matthews, Babe 72
Mattison, Johnny 206
McDaniel, Hattie 45, 117, 126, 127, fn295
McDonald, Grace fn489, 211, 213, 217
McGee, Jack fn489
McGowan, Jewel 240
McHugh, Jimmy fn248
McKinney, Nina Mae 20, 29–39, fn62, 40, 41, 43–44, fn94, 45, 50, 65, 69, 90, 91, 98, 100, 119, 127, fn295, 152
McLeod, Norman Z. 118
McNab, Jane fn489
McNab, Jean fn489
Merry Monahans, The fn489
Middleton, Lucille fn422
Miller, Ann 119, 218, fn509

273

Miller, Danny	121	Niesen, Gertrude	117
Miller, Dorothy	167	*Noble Sissle and Eubie Blake*	
Miller, George	121	*Sing Snappy Songs*	25
Miller, Glenn	fn356, 225, 226, 238, 240, fn575	Noel, Hattie	fn137
Miller, Norma	vii, fn391, fn392, 167, 169, 178, fn428, 185, 250, 253, 254	**O**	
		O'Connor, Donald	201, fn488, 207, fn489, 211, 212, 214, 217, 220–224, fn514, fn515, fn516, fn517, fn534, 232, fn539, 233, 234, 237
Millinder, Lucky	fn599		
Mills, Florence	99, fn286		
Mills Blue Rhythm Band	44, 73–74, 91, fn598	*Ol' King Cotton*	56
		Olsen and Johnson (John "Ole" Olsen and Harold "Chic" Johnson)	179, 181
Mills Brothers	fn356		
Minnelli, Vincente	118		
Minnie the Moocher	154	*On Stage Everybody*	224
Minns, Al	182, fn428, 184, 249	*On with the Show!*	35, 45
Miranda, Carmen	219	*Orchestra Wives*	240
Mister Big	211, 214, 221–222, 224, 233, 234, 236, fn552, 237, 241	O'Sullivan, Maureen	165
		Outline of Jitterbug History, The	158, 187–192, fn446, 194–196
Mitchell, Dolores	fn489		
Monaghan, Terry	249, 253	**P**	
Monroe, Marilyn	fn189, fn289	Paige, Robert	179, 210, 233
Moonlight in Havana	206, fn534	Pan, Hermes	fn411
Moonlight in Vermont	fn534	*Panama Hattie*	118
Moore, Phil	117, fn262, 118	*Paper Doll*	fn356
Mordecai, Jimmy	40	Parsons, Louella	100, fn214
Morris, Earl J.	108–110, fn234	Parton, Jackie Lewis	148
Morton, Jelly Roll	146	*Patrick the Great*	211, 216, 223, 224, 232, 236
Murder at the Vanities	fn147		
Murphy, Dudley	fn49, fn77, 41, 62, 79, fn151, 81, fn154	Payton, Lew	fn135
		Pelican Players	123
		Perry, Lincoln *see* Stepin Fetchit	
Murray, Arthur	187–188	Peters Sisters	105, fn234, fn249
Muse, Clarence	56	*Pickaninny Dance, The*	fn9
		Pie, Pie, Blackbird	65, 68, 69, 90, fn598
N		Pitts, Juanita	127
Nicholas, Fayard	65–67, 70, 114, fn250, fn287	Pollard, Fritz	fn315
		Pollard, Mildred	fn422
Nicholas, Harold	65–67, 70, fn250, fn296	Popp, Kaye	197
Nicholas Brothers	1, 11, 14, fn30, 54, 65–70, fn132, fn134, 92, fn234, 110, fn250, 126, fn296, fn356, 183, 243–246, 250, 253	*Porgy and Bess*	fn49, 148
		Powell, Eleanor	28, fn95, 93, 94, fn189, 102, fn216, 103, 111, 115, 119, 217–218, fn502, fn509

Index of Names and Titles

Prima, Louis fn146, 205
Private Buckaroo 206, 212, 214, 215, fn514, 232, 237
Purnell, Mattie 163

R

Radio City Revels 164, 177
Rahn, Muriel fn137
Rall, Tommy 214
Raymond, Gene 96, 101
Rebecca of Sunnybrook Farm fn113
Reed, Leonard fn287
Revel, Harry fn248
Rhapsody in Black and Blue, A 56
Rhythmania 129, 146, 149–150
Rhythm Hot Shots 250
Richmond, June 153
Ricker, Billy fn428
Ricker, Willamae 167, 182, fn428, 184, 197
Rings on Her Fingers 240
Roberson, Orlando 75
Robeson, Paul 25, fn49, 44, 104, fn289
Robinson, Bill "Bojangles" 9, 54, 71–72, 92, 93, 95–102, fn196, 108, fn232, 112, 113, 114, 118, fn269, 120, 126, fn322, fn406, 204, 219, 243–245, 252
Rocco, Maurice 3, fn4, 7
Rodgers, Richard 108, fn244, 112
Rogers, Ginger 28, 53, fn189, 120, 204, 207, 239, 240
Rooney, Mickey 207, 228, 230–232, fn535
Roosevelt, Franklin Delano 105
Roth, Murray fn124
Rubbottom, Doris fn135
Rufus Jones for President 62–65, 73, 90, 91, fn389, fn598
Rug Cutter's Holiday 146
Rushing, Jimmy 136–137
Ryan, Peggy 23, 201, fn488, 207, fn489, 211, 213, 214, 215, 216, 217–225, fn502, fn516, 227, fn534, 232, fn539, 233, 234, 237

S

Saggau, Charles "Chuck" fn453
Sampson, Deryck 150
Sanders of the River 44
Saulters, Dorothy 1, fn4, 9
Savage, Archie 123
Sawyer, Geneva fn269
Scheerer, Robert "Bobby" 207, fn489
Schoen, Vic 225
Scott, Hazel 92, fn186, fn295
Scott, Raymond fn249
Seeley, Blossom 120
Show Boat fn81
Shuffle Along (stage show) 25, fn47
Singin' in the Rain 221
Sissle, Noble 25, 48
Six Knobs 147
Sloane, Paul 26
Slyde, Jimmy fn287
Smash Your Baggage 70–71, 73, fn598
Smith, Bessie 43, fn151
Smith, Ernie 202, 248–249, fn592, 254
Smith, Lennie fn453
Smith, Pete 191, 192, fn451, 194, 195
Smythe, Vanita 153
Snoop Dogg 123
Snow, Valaida 153
Snowden, "Shorty" George 159, 162, fn385, 163
Somebody Loves Me 120
Sothern, Ann 96
Spencer, Prince fn287
Spirit Moves, The 247
Spitalny, Phil 226, fn521
Spivey, Victoria 30, fn85
Stage Door Canteen 212
Start Cheering fn243, 117, fn261, 205
Stearns, Jean 248
Stearns, Marshall 248–249
Stepin Fetchit (Lincoln Perry) fn59
Step Up fn9
Stewart, Slam 181

275

St. Louis Blues (1929)	43, fn151	**V**	
St. Louis Blues (1958)	fn49	Vaughn, Kay	fn453
Stormy Weather	20, fn49, 110, 118, fn264, fn523, 243–245, fn585, 250	Veloz, Jean Phelps	fn333, 192, 193, fn453
		Vidor, King	26, 29
		Vogues of 1938	1–3, fn4, 4, 7–8, 9
Strike Up the Band	230		
Sugar Hill Masquerade	187, fn450	**W**	
Sun Valley Serenade	fn30, fn356, fn575	Wallace, Babe	fn135
Sweet and Low-Down	240	Waller, Fats	96, 100, 101, 122, 126, 130, 148, 154, fn406, 252
Swing Cat's Jamboree	fn146		
Swing Fever	240	Waller, Fred	62, 81–82, 84–85, 87
Swing for Your Supper	fn356	Walsh, Arthur	fn333, 192, 193, fn453, 195
Swingin' the Dream (stage show)	178	Washboard Serenaders	70
Swing It Soldier	240	Washington, Fredi	41–44, 48, 74, 79, 81, fn295, 152
Swing Time	204, 240		
Swingtime Johnny	240	Waters, Ethel	45, 62–63, fn128, 96, 103, fn295, 169, fn401
Symphony in Black: A Rhapsody of Negro Life	82–84		
		Watson, Eleanor "Stumpy"	fn422
		Webb, Chick	fn6
T		*Wedding of Jack and Jill, The*	217, fn501
Take My Life	fn277	West, Buster	177
Temple, Shirley	fn95, 54, 72, 100	Westerlund, Lennart	vii, 249–250, 253
Tharpe, Sister Rosetta	153	*What's Cookin'*	206, 208–211, 212, 216, 217, 225, 230, 232, 235, 237
That's the Spirit (1933)	47–50, fn127, fn598		
That's the Spirit (1945)	224	*When Johnny Comes Marching Home*	207, fn489, 222, 226, 235, fn552, 237
This Is the Life	fn489, 218, 223, 237		
This'll Make You Whistle	104	*While Thousands Cheer* (a.k.a. *Crooked Money*)	fn277
This Was Paris	fn235		
Thomas, Irene	fn333, fn453	White, Herbert "Whitey"	164, fn392, fn393, fn394, 177, 178, 186
Thomas, Norman	58		
Three Brown Girls	109, 110	White, Paul	fn356, 152
Three Brown Jacks	76	Whiteman, Paul	243
Three Dukes	73–74	Whitey's Lindy Hoppes	1, 22, 136–137, fn327, 142, 157, 158, fn376, 164–191, fn392, fn393, fn401, fn411, fn450, 195, 197, fn460, 200, 246, 249, 250, 254
Three Whippets	67		
Tierney, Gene	240		
Till the Clouds Roll By	fn533		
Tip, Tap, and Toe	75, 90	Whitman, Ernest	fn137
Top Man	207, fn489, 216, 219, 221, 223, 226, 237	Whitman Sisters	95, fn195
		Williams, Bert	fn286
Top of the Town	217, fn502	Williams, Henry "Rubberlegs"	71, fn135
Troupe One	123	Williams, Joe	fn328
Tucker, Earl "Snakehips"	82–84, fn158, fn162	Williams, Russell	197
		Wilson, Eunice	67

Winfield, Raymond 75, fn140

Y

Yamekraw 39–41, 56, fn124, fn598
Yes, Indeed! fn356

Z

Ziegfeld, Florenz 35–36
Ziegfeld Follies (stage show) 7, 35–36, fn77
Ziegfeld Follies fn533
Zoot Suit with a Reet Pleat, A fn356